Contents

CHARTERED ACCOUNTANTS IRELAND CODE OF ETHICS

PART ONE CAPITAL GAINS TAX

Chartered Accountants Ireland Code of Ethics

The Chartered Accountants Ireland *Code of Ethics* applies to all aspects of a Chartered Accountant's professional life, including dealing with corporation tax issues, capital gains tax issues, capital acquisitions tax issues and stamp duty issues. The *Code of Ethics* outlines the principles that should guide a Chartered Accountant, namely:

- Integrity
- Objectivity
- Professional Competence and Due Care
- Confidentiality
- Professional Behaviour

As a Chartered Accountant, you will have to ensure that your dealings with the tax aspects of your professional life are in compliance with these fundamental principles. Set out in **Appendix B** is further information regarding these principles and their importance in guiding you on how to deal with issues which may arise throughout your professional life, including giving tax advice and preparing tax computations.

Part One

Capital Gains Tax

Capital Gains Tax: Introduction, General Principles and Administration

This text contains section references in relation to the different taxes that are examinable. Students do not need to know the section numbers.

Learning Objectives

After studying this chapter you will have developed a competency in the following:

- That CGT applies to disposals of capital assets.
- Who is chargeable and understanding that death does not trigger a disposal for CGT and assets transfer at market value.
- The rate of tax is 30%, which is payable by 15 December 2012 for disposals by 30 November 2012 and 31 January 2013 for disposals in December 2012.
- How to calculate a gain, including using market value in disposals between connected parties and gifts; allowing enhancement expenditure; allowing indexation for expenditure incurred before 2003, based on when expenditure was incurred; allowing only part of the cost, where there is a part disposal.
- Treating spouses and civil partners, including taxing a husband on gains of a wife who lives with him and the nominated civil partner on the gains of the other civil partner, unless there is separate assessment; disposals typically being at no gain/no loss; each having an annual exemption if each has sufficient gains; only allowed to have one principal private residence; allowed to use each other's losses.
- Dealing with losses, including offsetting capital losses and capital losses forward against gains in year; only allowed to carry back losses from year of death; restriction on offset of losses on chattels, losses between connected persons, losses on development land and assets qualifying for capital allowances.

1.1   The Basic Charge to Capital Gains Tax (CGT)

Legislation introduced taxation on capital gains arising from the disposal of chargeable assets on or after 6 April 1974. The legislation has been modified by amendments contained in subsequent Finance Acts.

The charge to CGT is now contained in the Taxes Consolidation Act 1997 (TCA 1997). There are four basic elements which must apply before the provisions relating to the taxation of capital gains come into operation. These are as follows:

- There must be a **disposal**
- of an **asset**
- by a **chargeable person**
- after **5 April 1974**

1.2   Disposal

In order for a liability to tax to arise, a disposal of an asset must take place or must be deemed to take place. A disposal for these purposes will occur in each of the following situations:

1. on the sale of an asset;
2. on the sale of part of an asset (part disposal);
3. on the gift of the whole or part of an asset;
4. on the receipt of a capital sum resulting from the ownership of an asset, e.g. receipt of compensation for damage or injury to assets or the receipt of a capital sum in return for forfeiture or surrender of rights;
5. capital sum received as consideration for use or exploitation of assets;
6. transfer of an asset to a trust or a corporate body;
7. an exchange of assets in a barter transaction;
8. on the occasion of the entire loss or destruction of an asset (e.g. if a painting is destroyed in a fire) there is a disposal of the painting whether or not any insurance proceeds are received; and
9. where an asset becomes negligible in value and Revenue allow a claim for loss relief, there is a deemed disposal of the asset (see **Section 1.13.8**).

1.3   Assets

Assets for the purpose of the taxation of capital gains include all forms of property including options and property created by the person disposing of it, e.g. copyrights, patents and goodwill. Debts and foreign currency are also taxable assets. The basic rule is that any capital asset of an individual or company is a chargeable asset unless it is specifically exempt from CGT or corporation tax on chargeable gains. Specifically included is an interest in property, e.g. a lease.

1.4   Chargeable Persons

CGT is charged on gains realised by individuals, partnerships and trusts. Capital gains realised by companies are also chargeable but are assessed to corporation tax and not CGT (except in the case of development land).

1.5   Computation of Gain or Loss

1.5.1   General

The capital gain is the difference between:

1. the **consideration for the disposal** of the asset or the deemed consideration (e.g. **market value** in the case of a gift or disposal between connected persons); and
2. the **cost of acquisition** of the asset or its **market value** if not acquired at arm's length (e.g. property acquired by way of inheritance or gift).

If any part of the sales consideration is taken into account in computing income tax profits or losses, it is excluded from the amount under 1 above.

Any expenditure which is allowable as a deduction from income tax profits, or which would be so allowable if the asset had been employed as a fixed asset of a trade, is excluded from 2 above.

Allowable expenditure for CGT purposes is confined to expenditure included on capital account, i.e. it excludes expenditure deductible in calculating income. It includes the following:

1. **Incidental costs of acquisition or disposal**, e.g. agent's commission, stamp duty, valuation cost, cost of transfer or conveyance, auctioneers', accountants' or solicitors' fees and advertising costs.
2. Any cost associated with the **creation of an asset** which was not acquired, e.g. copyright, goodwill of a business.
3. Expenditure incurred for the purposes of **enhancing the value** of the asset which is reflected in the state of the asset at the time of disposal, e.g. improvements to property. To be allowable, the expenditure must neither have been abortive nor must its value have wasted away before the disposal of the asset. Expenditure incurred in establishing, preserving or defending an owner's title or interest in an asset is allowable within this definition.

Example

A typical CGT computation for an asset sold during 2012 might be outlined as follows:

J. Jones – Capital Gains Tax Computation for 2012

		€	€
Sales Proceeds (or market value)			X
Deduct:	Allowable Costs		
	– Original Cost of Asset or Market Value @ 6/4/74 (if bought prior to 6/4/74)	X	
	– Incidental Costs of Acquisition	X̲	
		X indexed @	(X)
	– Enhancement Expenditure	X̲ indexed @	(X̲)

continued overleaf

GAIN		X
Deduct:	Loss Relief (if any)	(X)
		X
Deduct:	Annual Exemption (max €1,270)	(X)
TAXABLE GAIN		X
CGT payable: Taxable gain at 30%		

If there is a contingent liability, it is ignored and the gain or loss is calculated as if this liability did not exist. If the contingency happens and the liability is paid, then at that stage the gain or loss is re-calculated allowing this liability which has now crystallised and has been paid. This will typically lead to a repayment of CGT overpaid.

1.5.2 Indexation Relief

The legislation introduced indexation relief to permit the effects of inflation to be taken into account in computing chargeable gains on disposals of assets. However, it is only available for assets acquired before 2003.

The relief operates by permitting the cost of any asset (including enhancement expenditure) to be adjusted for inflation by reference to the increases in the Consumer Price Index over the period of ownership of the asset.

The provisions introducing indexation relief also introduced another fundamental change in the law relating to the taxation of capital gains. **All assets owned at 6 April 1974 are deemed to have been disposed of and immediately re-acquired at their market value at that date**.

The deemed disposal and re-acquisition at 6 April 1974 of assets held on that date means that, for the purposes of applying the indexation multiplier, such assets are regarded as acquired in 1974/75 and their base cost is their 6 April 1974 market value. The multiplier effectively measures the change in the level of the Consumer Price Index from the mid-February preceding the year of assessment in which the asset is disposed of. The table of indexation factors for CGT will be provided in your examination and is included in the tax reference material included at Appendix A at the end of the book.

When using the tables, you should note that the tax years up to 2001 ran from 6 April to 5 April. The 2001 tax year was 6 April 2001 to 31 December 2001. All years since then are January to December.

The Finance Act 2003 provided that **indexation relief will only be available in respect of the period of ownership of an asset up to 1 January 2003**. Accordingly, assets acquired in 2003 or subsequent years will not qualify for any indexation relief. Where assets acquired in 2002 or prior tax years are sold in 2003 or subsequent years, the cost of such assets is indexed using the multipliers applicable for disposals in 2003.

The following important points should be noted about inflation relief:

1. Inflation relief applies to **all** assets without exception but is restricted to a significant degree in the case of development land.
2. Inflation relief cannot increase an allowable loss to an amount greater than the actual monetary loss. The allowable loss is restricted to the actual loss.

> **Example**
> Mary bought shares for €1,000 in June 2000. She sold them for €800 in August 2012. What is the allowable loss?
>
> | | | € |
> |---|---|---|
> | Proceeds | | 800 |
> | Cost | 1,000 × 1.144 | (1,144) |
> | "Loss" | | (344) |
>
> As Mary made an actual loss of €200, the allowable loss is €200.

3. Inflation relief cannot convert a monetary gain into an allowable loss. In these circumstances, the disposal is at "no gain/no loss", i.e. effectively the disposal is ignored for tax purposes.

> **Example**
> Joe bought shares for €1,000 in June 2000. He sold them for €1,100 in May 2012. What is the taxable gain?
>
> | | | € |
> |---|---|---|
> | Proceeds | | 1,100 |
> | Cost | 1,000 × 1.144 | (1,144) |
> | "Loss" | | (44) |
>
> As Joe made an actual gain, the disposal is at "no gain/no loss".

4. The interaction of inflation relief and the use of a 6 April 1974 valuation instead of cost can result in an actual monetary gain or loss being increased. In such circumstances, as at 2 above, the taxable gain or allowable loss is restricted to the actual gain or loss.

   The interaction of inflation relief and the use of a 6 April valuation instead of cost can result in the conversion of an actual monetary gain into a loss or an actual monetary loss into a gain. In such a scenario, as at 3. above, the disposal is deemed to be at no gain/no loss.

1.5.3 Enhancement Expenditure

Where enhancement expenditure has been incurred on an asset and is **reflected in the asset at the date of disposal**, the cost and the cost of each subsequent item of **enhancement expenditure** is deductible. The chargeable gain is calculated as the difference between the various items of expenditure, (i.e. both original cost and enhancement expenditure as adjusted for indexation) and the sale proceeds. Enhancement expenditure is **indexed** from the date **when it was incurred**.

> **Example**
> A public house was acquired in November 1998 at a cost of €450,000. Enhancement expenditure was incurred as follows:
>
> | | | € |
> |---|---|---|
> | (1) | November 1999 | 100,000 |
> | (2) | November 2001 | 15,000 |
> | (3) | November 2003 | 10,000 |
>
> *continued overleaf*

The public house was sold in September 2012 for €1,850,000.

Computation of Taxable Gain		€	€
Sale proceeds			1,850,000
Deduct:			
Allowable cost:			
1998/99 expenditure:	€450,000 × 1.212	545,400	
1999/00 expenditure:	€100,000 × 1.193	119,300	
2001 expenditure:	€15,000 × 1.087	16,305	
2003 expenditure:	€10,000	10,000	(691,005)
			1,158,995
Annual exemption			(1,270)
Net gain			1,157,725
CGT @ 30%	= €347,317		

1.5.4 Special Rules Relating to Allowable Deductions

1. Treatment of Interest

Interest payments in general are not allowable deductions in the computation of capital gains. There is one specific exception to this rule. The exception is made in the case of a **company** which incurs **interest on money borrowed to finance the construction of any building, structure or works**. Such interest will be allowed as a deduction to the extent that the company has charged to capital the interest on the borrowed funds and no deduction was, or could have been, availed of by the company for the interest in computing its profits for the purposes of corporation tax.

2. Insurance Premiums

Insurance premiums paid to protect against damage to an asset are specifically **not an allowable deduction**.

3. Foreign Tax

Where the person making a disposal of a foreign asset incurs a charge to foreign tax and the foreign tax is incurred in a country with which Ireland has a **double taxation treaty** which provides for relief in respect of tax on capital gains, relief is given by deducting the foreign tax paid from the Irish CGT, i.e. **credit relief**.

> **Example**
> Jones realised a gain of €500,000 on the disposal of a property in Paris, after annual exemption in March 2012. The French CGT payable was €80,000. The computation is as follows:
>
> | | € |
> |---|---|
> | Chargeable gain | 500,000 |
> | Irish CGT payable @ 30% | 150,000 |
> | Less: Credit for French CGT paid | (80,000) |
> | Balance of Irish CGT payable | 70,000 |

Where the person making a disposal of a foreign asset incurs a charge to foreign CGT on the gain arising and **no double taxation relief** is available for the foreign CGT suffered, then the **foreign CGT may be deducted** in computing the amount of the gain which is chargeable to Irish CGT.

Example

Smith sold a capital asset located in Libya, a country with which Ireland does not have a double taxation treaty, for €900,000. The indexed cost of the asset was €398,730. The Libyan tax paid on the capital gain was €80,000. The computation is as follows:

	€
Total sale proceeds	900,000
Less: foreign CGT	(80,000)
Net proceeds	820,000
Less: indexed cost	(398,730)
Less: annual exemption	(1,270)
Taxable	420,000
Irish CGT @ 30%	126,000

---

4. Grants

No deduction is allowed in computing chargeable gains for any expenditure which has been met by the provision of government, Public or Local Authority grants (whether Irish or foreign).

1.5.5 Part-disposal

We have seen earlier that the partial disposal of an asset is a chargeable event for CGT purposes. Where a portion of an asset is sold, the sale proceeds are known but the issue arises as to **how much of the original cost of the asset is allowable as a deduction in computing the chargeable gain or allowable loss arising on the part disposal**.

TCA 1997 provides that the **portion of the original cost** of the total asset which is allowed against the consideration received on the part disposal is to be confined to the proportion of the original cost of the asset which the value of the part being disposed of bears, at the time of disposal, to the market value of the whole asset. The formula is, therefore:

$$\text{Original Cost} \times A/(A + B)$$

where A is the amount of the proceeds of the part disposal (or market value if appropriate), and B is the market value of the portion of the asset which is retained.

Example

Assume an asset cost €1,000 on 1 September 2011 and that nine months later part of the asset was sold for €600. The market value of the remainder of the asset is €700. The chargeable gain in respect of the disposal would be computed as follows:

	€
Sales proceeds	600
Less: Allowable cost €1,000 × €600/(€600 + €700)	(462)
Chargeable Gain	138

Note: The balance of the cost of €538 (€1,000 − €462) will be carried forward against any future disposal of the remainder of the asset.

> **Example**
> Asset cost €10,000 on 10 April 1982. Part of the asset was sold on 10 November 2006 for €27,000. At that time, the market value of the remainder of the asset at that date was €50,000. The remainder was sold on 1 November 2012 for €30,000.
>
> The individual is married. Calculate the CGT liability for 2012.
>
> | | | € |
> |---|---|---:|
> | Proceeds | | 30,000 |
> | Cost | €10,000 − [€10,000 × €27,000/(€27,000 + €50,000)] × 2.253 = | (14,630) |
> | | | 15,370 |
> | | Annual exemption | (1,270) |
> | | | 14,100 |
> | | × 30% | |
> | | CGT due | 4,230 |

1.5.6 Application of Market Value

Normally where a disposal is at arm's length and the consideration is known in money terms the consideration is accepted for CGT purposes. Where, however, the transaction is:

1. between connected persons:

    There is a definition of connected persons in the law. The *main* people are:
    - **Spouse** (husband or wife, **civil partner** and **relatives** (brother, sister, uncle, aunt, niece, nephew, ancestor or lineal descendant (including step-child or adopted child). It should be noted that the definition of "relative" does not include cousins.
    - **In-laws**, i.e. husband, wife or civil partner of a relative or husband, wife or civil partner of a relative of the person's spouse or civil partner.
    - **Partners**, i.e. a person is connected with any person with whom s/he is in partnership and with the spouse or relative of his/her partners.
    - **A company** is connected with another person if that person has control of the company or if that person and the persons connected with him together have control of the company, with companies under common control being connected persons.

2. not at arm's length (e.g. gift),
3. for a consideration that is not valued in money terms or is a barter transaction,
4. the acquisition or disposal of an asset wholly or partly for a consideration that cannot be valued,
5. the acquisition of an asset by way of a distribution of property in specie from a company e.g. in a winding-up situation,
6. the acquisition of an asset in connection with an office or employment or in recognition of past services from an office or employment,

market value is then deemed to be the consideration for the purpose of determining the chargeable gain or allowable loss.

1.6   Time of Disposal

The time of disposal for CGT purposes is determined by reference to special rules contained in TCA 1997. The date of disposal determines the rate of CGT that applies, e.g. gains arising on the disposal of assets on or after 7 December 2011 are subject to CGT at 30% (see **Section 1.9.1**). The date when a gain accrues determines when the CGT must be paid, e.g. CGT arising on gains accruing in October 2012 must be paid by 15 December 2012. Normally the date of disposal and the date a gain accrues is the same date. An exception to this rule is in the case of disposals, which are subject to a compulsory purchase order (see below). Briefly, the rules for the time of disposal are as follows:

1.   In the case of an **UNCONDITIONAL CONTRACT**, the date of the contract is the relevant date irrespective of the date of the conveyance or transfer of the asset (i.e. "the closing date" is not relevant).

2.   In the case of a **CONDITIONAL CONTRACT**, the general rule is that the time of the disposal for the purposes of CGT is the date on which the condition is satisfied. A conditional contract is a contract which is subject to a condition which must be satisfied before there is a binding contract between the parties, e.g. a contract for the sale of land which is subject to planning permission being granted in respect of the land.

3.   In the case of **GIFTS**, the date of disposal is the date on which the property effectively passes, e.g. in the case of the gift of a chattel, the date that the chattel is delivered is the date of disposal for CGT purposes. This rule also applies to gifts into settlements.

4.   In the case of **COMPULSORY PURCHASE ORDERS**, the date of disposal is the earlier of the date upon which the amount of compensation is agreed or the date when the acquiring authorities enter the land. The date the gain accrues in the case of a compulsory purchase is however the date on which the compensation is received unless the recipient dies before compensation is received, in which case the gain is deemed to accrue immediately before death.

5.   In **COMPENSATION CASES**, the effective date is usually the date of receipt of the compensation, e.g. the date of receipt of insurance proceeds on the destruction of an asset.

1.7   Assets Situated Abroad

1.7.1   Location of Assets

The legislation contains rules for determining the location of assets. These rules are particularly relevant to **an individual who is not Irish domiciled but who is resident or ordinarily resident** in the State. Such an individual is chargeable to CGT on chargeable gains accruing on the disposal of assets situated outside the State (outside the State and the UK before 20 November 2008) only to the extent that he remits the gains to this country. Accordingly, it will be important for such an individual to establish that the gains were realised from the disposal of assets which were in fact situated outside the State (and outside the UK before 20 November 2008). The following are the main rules which apply:

1. Rights or interests in **IMMOVABLE** or **TANGIBLE MOVABLE PROPERTY** are situated where the property is situated.
2. In general, **DEBTS** are situated in Ireland if the creditor is resident in Ireland. **A JUDGEMENT DEBT** is situated where the judgement is recorded.
3. **SHARES OR SECURITIES** issued by a government, governmental authority or municipal authority are situated in the country where that Authority is established.
4. **SHARES IN, OR SECURITIES OF, A COMPANY INCORPORATED IN THE STATE** are situated in the State.
5. **OTHER REGISTERED SHARES AND SECURITIES** are situated where they are registered and, if registered in more than one register, where the principal register is situated.
6. **GOODWILL** of a business is situated at the place where the trade, business or profession is carried on.

1.8 Annual Exemption

Individuals are entitled to an annual exemption of **€1,270**. If the **chargeable gains** do not exceed €1,270 for 2012, no tax is due. If the gains exceed €1,270, only the excess is chargeable.

If an individual is married or in a civil partnership, **each spouse** or civil partner **is entitled to the €1,270 allowance**. If one spouse or civil partner does not avail of the allowance, it *cannot* be transferred to the other spouse or civil partner.

Example

Single individual sold the following in March 2012:

(a) A building for €100,000. It had cost €75,000 on 1 October 1997.
(b) Shares in an unquoted trading company for €20,000. These cost €1,000 on 1 March 1990.

		€
Building:	Proceeds	100,000
	Cost €75,000 × 1.232	(92,400)
		7,600
Shares:	Proceeds	20,000
	Cost €1,000 × 1.503	(1,503)
		18,497

Summary	€
Total gains	26,097
Less: exemption	(1,270)
	24,827
CGT due @ 30%	7,448

> **Example**
> Holly and Robin are married. During 2012, they had the following disposals:
> - On 5 July, Holly sold shares for €12,000. The shares cost her €11,500 on 5 March 2010.
> - On 8 August, Robin sold a building for €350,000. It had cost him €290,000 on 7 January 2006.
>
> As both assets were acquired 2003 onwards, there is no indexation.
> Holly had a capital gain of €500 (€12,000 – €11,500).
> Robin had a capital gain of €60,000 (€350,000 – €290,000).
> Holly can claim an annual exemption of €1,270. As her gains are less than €1,270, she has no CGT liability.
> Robin can claim an annual exemption of €1,270. However he cannot claim for the part of her exemption that Holly could not use. Therefore, his CGT liability is 30% × (€60,000 – €1,270), i.e. €17,619.

1.9 Rate of Tax, Date of Payment and Returns

1.9.1 Rate of CGT

CGT is charged by reference to **years of assessment for individuals**. A CGT year is the same as an income tax year (i.e. up to 6 April 2001 it ran from 6 April to following 5 April each year, the tax year 2001 covers the period 6 April 2001 to 31 December 2001; and the tax year 2002 and subsequent tax years is the **calendar year**).

The rate of CGT for 2012 is 30%

The rate of CGT was 25% from April 2009 to 6 December 2011 and 22% from 15 October 2008 to 7 April 2009. It was generally 20% for the previous 10 years. (There is a higher rate for development land whose value has increased due to certain planning decisions and for life assurance products, but these are not examinable at CAP 2 level.)

1.9.2 Date of Payment

Self assessment applies to CGT.

There is no requirement for preliminary tax to be paid in respect of CGT.

For 2012, a person's CGT liability is payable in two amounts. The first amount, known as "**tax payable for the initial period**" is payable on or before **15 December in the tax year**. "Tax payable for the initial period" means the **tax which would be payable for the tax year if it ended on 30 November in that year instead of 31 December**. By deeming the tax year to end on 30 November, this means that all reliefs, e.g. losses carried forward from previous years or the annual exemption amount, are taken into account in calculating the person's chargeable gains and, thus, his CGT liability for the period.

The second amount, known as "**tax payable for the later period**" is payable on or before **31 January after the end of the tax year**. "Tax payable for the later period" means the **tax payable for the tax year less tax payable for the initial period**.

Example

An individual disposes of an asset in June 2012 giving rise to a chargeable gain of €10,000 and disposes of a second asset in December 2012 giving rise to a chargeable gain of €8,000. The individual had a loss forward of €3,000 from the disposal of shares in 2011. CGT is payable by the individual as follows:

Tax Payable for Initial Period

	€
Chargeable gains 1/1/2012 – 30/11/2012	10,000
Less losses from 2011	(3,000)
Less annual exemption	(1,270)
Taxable gain	5,730
CGT @ 30%	1,719

Tax Payable for Later Period

	€
Total chargeable gains in 2012	18,000
Less losses from 2011	(3,000)
Less annual exemption	(1,270)
Taxable gains	13,730
CGT @ 30%	4,119
Less tax payable for initial period	(1,719)
Tax payable for later period	2,400

CGT for 2012 is payable as follows:

	€
On or before 15 December 2012	1,719
On or before 31 January 2013	2,400

It should be noted that tax due for the initial period is calculated **ignoring any losses that might arise in the tax year after 30 November**. Accordingly, where capital losses arising in the period 1 December to 31 December exceed chargeable gains arising in the same period, a refund of CGT will be due. Assuming in the above example the asset disposed of by the individual in December 2012 instead of a gain, gave rise to an allowable loss of €4,000, the individual would still be required to pay CGT of €1,719 on 15 December 2012. However, after the end of the tax year he would be entitled to claim a refund as follows:

	€
Total chargeable gains in 2012	10,000
Less allowable losses in 2012	(4,000)
Less losses from 2011	(3,000)
Less annual exemption	(1,270)
Taxable gains	1,730
CGT @ 30%	519
Less tax payable for initial period	(1,719)
Refund due	(1,200)

1.9.3 Returns

A return of chargeable gains must be made on or before 31 October in the year following the year of assessment, i.e. for 2012 the return must be made by 31 October 2013. This return will normally be made on a **Form 11**, (the self-assessment annual income tax return) where the individual pays income tax under the self-assessment system or on **Form CG1** where the individual is not within the self-assessment system for income tax purposes.

Failure to submit this return on time will result in the application of a **surcharge** of 5% of the CGT liability or €12,695, whichever is lower, if filed within two months of the due date. The surcharge is 10% or €63,485, whichever is lower, if the return is filed more than two months after the due date.

With effect from 1 July 2009, interest on overdue tax is charged at the rate of 0.0219% per day or part of a day (approx 8% pa). Prior to this date, the daily rate was higher.

1.10 Spouses, Civil Partners and Cohabitants

1.10.1 General

Each spouse or civil partner is a separate "person" for CGT purposes and their gains or losses should be computed separately. The residence and domicile status of each spouse or civil partner must be considered individually to decide whether or not that person is chargeable to CGT.

1.10.2 Charge to Tax

The chargeable gains accruing to a married woman in any year of assessment during which she is **"living with her husband"** will be assessed on the husband unless an application for separate assessment for CGT purposes has been made or the couple elect for any assessments to be raised on the wife. The net gains which accrue in a year of assessment to civil partners **living together** are charged on the nominated civil partner unless either civil partner has applied to be charged separately.

1.10.3 Annual Exemption

Each spouse or civil partner is entitled to an annual exemption of €1,270. This is NOT transferrable if unused.

1.10.4 Disposal by One Spouse ~~~ther

**A disposal of an asset from one spo
a CGT liability**, provided that the co
separated (see **Section 1.10.8**). The
value which gives rise to no gain o
party, there is a **chargeable gain
ownership by both husband and
is determined accordingly. The**

- where the asset concerne
  partner; or
- where the spouse or civil
  for the year of assessme
  subsequent disposal in t

In these two situations, ther
market value, regardless o

1.10.5 Principal Priva

Only one residence can
and wife or two civil p
their principal privat

or civil partner to another (by sale, gift or on death), the period of ownership should be treated for the purposes of the principal private residence relief as beginning at the date of acquisition by the spouse or civil partner who first acquired the residence.

1.10.6   Separate Assessment

If either spouse or civil partner makes an election for separate assessment before 1 April in the year following the year of assessment, then separate assessment will apply for the earlier year of assessment and for all subsequent years of assessment until it is withdrawn. A notice withdrawing an election for separate assessment must be made before 1 April in the year following the year of assessment to which the notice relates.

1.10.7   Losses

The general rule, where a married woman is living with her husband in the year of assessment, is that the net chargeable gains accruing to one spouse for that year of assessment should be reduced as far as possible by any unutilised allowable losses accruing to the other spouse (taking into account losses brought forward) for the same year of assessment. The same rule applies to civil partners.

Example: Year of Marriage

Date of marriage 1 October 2012

Gains and losses accruing	Husband	Wife	
	€	€	
1 January 2012 to 30 September 2012			
Net chargeable gains	4,800	100	
Net allowable losses		(200)	disposal prior to marriage
1 October 2012 to 31 December 2012			
Net chargeable gains	0	25	
Net Gains	4,800	(75)	Net Losses

The wife's net losses for 2012 are set off against the husband's gains, the husband being assessed for the year on net gains of €3,455 (i.e. €4,725 less the €1,270 exemption).

By making an application before 1 April following the year of assessment, a husband or wife or civil partner may decide that their net loss accruing in that particular year of assessment shall be carried forward for set off against his or her future gains instead of being set off against the other's net gains accruing in the year. A fresh application is needed in respect of losses of each year.

Separated and Divorced Couples

tion **1.10.4**, for a married couple or civil partners to benefit from the of a capital asset between spouses or civil partners, they must be

be living together for the exemption to apply, Revenue the year of separation are transferred at no gain/no loss (subject to the exceptions for trading stocks and spouse or civil partner not within the charge to Irish CGT outlined at **Section 1.10.4**). If there is a loss in the year of separation, the loss of one spouse or civil partner may be used by the other.

Years following separation

A charge to CGT does not arise where a person disposes of an asset **to a spouse or civil partner** as a consequence of a **legal obligation** under a **Deed of Separation** or an **Order of a Court**, including on a divorce or dissolution (subject to the exceptions for trading stocks and spouse or civil partner not within the charge to Irish CGT outlined at **Section 1.10.4**).

This means that each asset is treated as being disposed of for an amount that gives rise to neither a gain nor a loss in the hands of the spouse or civil partner disposing of the asset. The spouse or civil partner acquiring the asset is deemed to acquire the asset on the same day and at the same cost as the spouse or civil partner who originally acquired it.

A husband and wife or two civil partners continue to be connected persons following a separation. All disposals between spouses following a separation which take place after the year of separation or outside of a legal deed of separation/court order will be deemed to be at market value regardless of the actual consideration (see **Section 1.5.6**) and CGT calculated in the normal way. Following a divorce or dissolution, a couple cease to be connected persons as they are no longer a husband and wife or civil partners.

Example

Joe and Anne separate. As part of a deed of separation, Joe transfers the following assets to Anne:

- Shares worth €100,000 (which he had purchased ten years previously for €20,000)
- His interest in the family home (cost €30,000 twenty years previously)

Joe will not be liable for any CGT on either of these disposals to Anne, regardless of whether the transfers take place in the year of separation or subsequently.

If Anne subsequently sells any of the shares, she will be liable for any CGT which arises. The gain will be calculated as if she had purchased the shares herself, ten years previously at the original cost of €20,000.

Example

Jack and Jill, who were married for years, separated permanently on 7 January 2007.

On 5 April 2007 Jack transferred to Jill shares in ABC plc valued at €20,000 which he had acquired in 2003 for €5,000. In 2008 Jack transferred to Jill shares in XYZ plc valued at €25,000 which he had acquired in 2003 for €2,500. On 5 March 2012 Jack and Jill were granted a decree of divorce. The Order giving effect to the divorce provided that Jill's interest in an investment property which the couple had jointly acquired in 2004 should be transferred to Jack. Jill's interest in the investment property was transferred to Jack on 1 May 2012. Jack sold the property in November 2012.

Jack would not have been liable to CGT on the transfer of shares in ABC plc to Jill in 2007 as this was the year of separation. Jill is deemed to have acquired these shares for €5,000 in 2003. Jack would have been liable to CGT on the transfer of shares in XYZ plc valued at €25,000 to Jill in 2008. The inter-spousal exemption did not apply as they were not living together. Jill is treated as acquiring these shares in 2008 for €25,000.

Jill will not be liable to CGT on the disposal of her interest in the investment property to Jack as it is made under an Order of a Court. The gain on the disposal of the property by Jack in November 2012 will be calculated as if Jack had purchased the entire interest in the property in 2004.

1.10.9 Cohabitants

A charge to CGT does not arise where a person disposes of an asset to a cohabitant as a consequence of a property adjustment order made under section 174 of the Civil Partnership and Certain Rights and Obligations of Cohabitants Act (CPCROCA) 2010 on, or following, the ending of a relationship between cohabitants. Under CPCROCA 2010 a cohabitant is one of two adults (whether of the same or the opposite sex) who have lived together in an intimate and committed relationship for a period of at least two years if they have dependent children, or five years if not.

A disposal of an asset by an individual to his/her cohabitant as a result of such an order is treated as being disposed of for such an amount that gives rise to neither a gain nor a loss in the hands of the transferor. The transferee is deemed to acquire the asset on the same day and at the same cost as the transferor.

These rules do not apply to the transfer of trading stock or where the transferee could not be taxed in the State for the year of assessment in respect of a gain on a subsequent disposal in that year.

Apart from in the above circumstances, cohabitants are treated as unconnected persons and are assessed as single persons for CGT purposes. Disposals between cohabitants, other than under an order as set out above on the ending of the relationship, give rise to chargeable gains/allowable losses and, if they are made at less than market value, are deemed to be made at market value for CGT purposes in the same manner as any other non-arm's length transaction.

> **Example**
> Derek and Paul have lived together for 10 years and are now separating. As Paul is financially dependent on him, Derek agrees to give Paul an investment property. This investment property has a market value of €300,000 and cost Derek €250,000 in 2003. This is a gift from Derek to Paul and therefore transfers at the market value of €300,000. Derek is taxable on the gain of €50,000. Paul's cost of the property for a future disposal is €300,000.
>
> If instead the transfer of the investment property was as a result of an Order made under section 174 of CPCROCA 2010, the property would transfer at no gain/no loss. Therefore, Derek would have no taxable gain and Paul's cost of the property for a future disposal would be €250,000.

1.11 Partnerships

Dealings in partnership assets are treated as dealings by the individual partners and not by the firm. Chargeable gains or allowable losses, therefore, accruing on the disposal of partnership assets are apportioned among the partners in accordance with their profit sharing ratio. An individual's share of a partnership allowable loss may, therefore, be set off against private gains and vice versa.

Partnership goodwill is a chargeable asset and consequently a gain on the disposal by a partner of his share of a firm's goodwill is chargeable.

The special rules relating to disposals between connected persons will apply on disposals and acquisitions between partners as partners are deemed to be connected persons. In addition to a person being connected with all his/her business partners, that person is also connected with the husband/wife/relatives of any of his/her partners.

"Relative" is defined as brother, sister, uncle, aunt, niece, nephew, ancestor, lineal descendant, step child or an adopted child.

> **Example**
>
> A and B are in partnership sharing profits and losses as to 60% and 40% respectively. In November 2012 the partnership disposed of a building which it had originally acquired for €30,000 in June 1983. It realised €100,000 on disposal.
>
> | Computation of Gain | € |
> |---|---|
> | Sale proceeds | 100,000 |
> | Deduct: Cost €30,000 Indexed at 2.003 | (60,090) |
> | | 39,910 |
> | Apportioned as to A 60% × €39,910 = | 23,946 |
> | Apportioned as to B 40% × €39,910 = | 15,964 |
> | | 39,910 |
>
> Each partner would be entitled to claim any personal capital losses against the above gains and, of course, would be entitled to claim his annual personal exemption.

1.12 Connected Persons

1.12.1 Meaning of Connected Person

Where there is a transaction between "connected persons", the consideration is **deemed to be the open market value**. Any consideration agreed between the connected persons is ignored for the purposes of computing chargeable gains or allowable losses. The definition of connected persons in section 10 TCA 1997 is very broad. The following are the *main* persons:

1. **Spouse, Civil Partner, Relatives and In-Laws:** Relative includes brother, sister, uncle, aunt, niece, nephew, ancestor, lineal descendant, (including step child or an adopted child), but it does not include a cousin. In-laws include spouse or civil partner of a relative, or spouse or civil partner of a relative of the person's spouse or civil partner. In the two instances where an inter-spouse or inter-civil partner transaction is regarded as a disposal (i.e. where the asset concerned forms part of the trading stock or where the spouse or civil partner who acquired the asset could not be taxed in the State) the spouses or civil partners are regarded as connected persons and the trading stock or other asset is deemed to be transferred at open market value, no matter what consideration is agreed between the spouses or civil partners.

2. **Partners:** a person is connected with any person with whom s/he is in partnership and with the spouse or relatives of his/her partners.

3. **Company:** a company is connected with another person if that person has control of the company or if that person and the persons connected with him together have control of the company. Companies under common control are also connected persons.

1.12.2 Losses

Where a disposal to a connected person results in an allowable loss, that loss may only be set **off against chargeable gains on disposals to the same connected person**.

1.12.3 Treatment of a Series of Transactions between Connected Persons

If an individual owns a number of assets and the value of the assets taken together is greater than the sum of the individual assets then, if one of those assets is disposed of to a connected person, the value of the asset sold is the higher proportionate value of the total assets, and not the lower value of that individual asset. This is an anti-avoidance rule that does not arise frequently.

1.13 Losses

1.13.1 General

Losses are computed in the same manner as gains. If the asset is sold for less than the allowable cost of acquiring and enhancing the asset, then it is disposed of at a loss and that loss is an allowable loss. However if the asset disposed of is an exempt asset, then the loss is not allowable. At **Section 4.5.1** it states that Irish Government securities are exempt assets, so a loss on such a security is not an allowable loss. An allowable loss may arise in certain circumstances even where the asset is not disposed of, e.g. a loss arising from the value of an asset becoming negligible. Subject to certain specific exceptions, allowable losses may not be carried back prior to the year of assessment in which they are incurred. They may not be set off against taxable income.

In general, a loss is an allowable loss if, had there been a gain on the disposal of the asset, the gain would have been a chargeable gain.

Allowable losses arising must be set off against chargeable gains accruing in the same year of assessment against gains chargeable at the highest rate of tax first insofar as this is possible and, to the extent that there is an unutilised balance, the losses must be carried forward and set off against chargeable gains arising in the earliest **subsequent** year.

All available loss relief must be utilised before relief for the €1,270 annual exemption may be taken.

Example

An individual has the following gains/losses for 2012

			€
15 January	Asset 1	Gain	4,000
23 May	Asset 2	Gain	2,000
17 August	Asset 3	Loss	4,000
29 November	Asset 4	Gain	€3,000

The individual has allowable losses forward of €2,000 from 2011. Loss relief will be claimed as follows:

	Total
	€
Chargeable gains	9,000
Deduct: 2012 allowable losses	(4,000)
Deduct: allowable losses forward	(2,000)
	3,000
Deduct: Annual exemption	(1,270)
Net taxable gains after loss/annual exemption	1,730
CGT due @ 30%	519

1.13.2 Carry-back of Losses Terminal Relief

The general rule is that capital losses cannot be carried back to earlier years. An exception to this rule is made in the case of **losses which accrue to an individual in the year in which he dies**. These losses may be carried back and set against gains of the three years of assessment preceding the year of assessment in which the individual died.

Example

Mr X dies on 31 August 2012. In the period 1 January 2012 to 31 August 2012, Mr X made disposals of assets and realised allowable losses of €5,000.

The losses of €5,000 will first be available for set off against any chargeable gains assessed on Mr X in 2011, then against any chargeable gains in 2010 and, finally, against any chargeable gains in the tax year 2009. Any overpaid tax will be repaid by the Revenue.

1.13.3 Losses on Chattels

We will see later that where a chargeable chattel is disposed of for less than €2,540, any loss on the disposal should be computed as if the consideration for the disposal had been €2,540.

1.13.4 Losses between Connected Persons

Losses realised by a person on a disposal of an asset to another person with whom he is connected may not be set off against any other chargeable gains realised by him except on a chargeable gain realised on the disposal by him of an asset to the same connected person.

1.13.5 General Restrictions on Loss Relief

The following general rules apply in relation to relief for capital losses:

1. Losses may not be set off against gains of an earlier year of assessment except in the case of losses accruing to an individual in the year of death.
2. Relief may not be given more than once in respect of any loss.
3. If the loss is realised and relief could be given for that loss against income profits (e.g. by way of a balancing allowance), then no relief is available for that loss against chargeable gains (see example in **Section 1.13.6**).
4. A loss accruing to a person who is not resident or ordinarily resident in the year of assessment is not an allowable loss for CGT purposes unless, if a gain had accrued instead of a loss on the disposal, the person would have been chargeable on the gain. Thus, in general, relief for capital losses arising to non-resident persons is limited to losses incurred on the disposal of:

    (a) land in the State;
    (b) mineral assets in the State;
    (c) rights in the Irish Continental Shelf;
    (d) shares of an unquoted company deriving their value from assets at (a) to (c) above; and
    (e) assets of a business carried on in the State through a branch or agency.

5. There is no loss relief available in respect of assets situated outside the State (outside the State and UK up to 20 November 2008) for non-domiciled individuals who are assessed on the remittance basis.
6. Indexation cannot increase a loss (see **Section 1.5.2**).
7. The substitution of market value at 6 April 1974 for cost cannot increase a loss (see **Section 1.5.2**).

1.13.6   Losses on Assets Qualifying for Tax Capital Allowances

Expenditure which qualifies for capital allowances represents an allowable cost for CGT purposes. However, to the extent that a loss on an asset has been covered by capital allowances no further relief is allowed for CGT purposes.

> **Example**
>
> | Cost of factory (qualifying for industrial | € |
> |---|---|
> | buildings allowance) | 150,000 |
> | Sale proceeds | 120,000 |
> | Capital losses | 30,000 |
>
> Assuming the tax written down value of the building is €100,000, a balancing charge of €20,000 will arise. The capital loss allowable is restricted as follows:
>
> | | € | € |
> |---|---|---|
> | Capital loss | | 30,000 |
> | Allowances claimed | 50,000 | |
> | Balancing charge | (20,000) | |
> | Net allowances granted | | (30,000) |
> | Allowable capital loss | | Nil |
>
> If the written down value of the building was nil the allowable capital loss would still be nil, i.e.
>
> | | € | € |
> |---|---|---|
> | Capital loss | | 30,000 |
> | Allowances claimed | 150,000 | |
> | Balancing charge | (120,000) | |
> | Net allowances granted | | (30,000) |
> | Allowable capital loss | | Nil |

In general, **capital losses arising on the sale of assets qualifying for tax capital allowances will only be allowable for CGT purposes to the extent, if any, by which they exceed the capital allowances granted for income tax purposes** (including any balancing allowance). Such an unlikely situation might arise, e.g. in the case of a sole trader who used an asset partly for business and partly for private use. In such a case a capital loss arising on disposal would not be fully relieved by way of a balancing allowance (due to restriction for private element) and some measure of CGT loss relief might then be available.

1.13.7   Losses and Development Land

The legislation contains certain restrictions on the utilisation of loss relief. The position may be summarised as follows:

1.   Realised capital losses arising in respect of **disposals of non-development land** assets **may not be deducted from gains arising on the disposal of development land**.
2.   Realised losses in respect of disposals of **development land** may be set against realised capital gains in respect of **disposals of any asset** (including development land).

The net effect is to ensure that gains arising on the disposal of development land may only be reduced by realised losses in respect of development land disposals. Development land is covered in more detail in **Chapter 4**.

1.13.8 Negligible Value Claims

Where a person owns a capital asset, whose value is now negligible, the person may make a claim to the Inspector of Taxes for relief for the unrealised loss. Even though there is no disposal of an asset, if the Inspector is satisfied that the value of an asset has become negligible, the Inspector may allow relief for the loss. The loss relief is allowed when the claim is made. On a strict interpretation of the law, a loss under this law is allowable only in the year of claim. However, in practice, a claim made within 12 months of the end of the year of assessment (or accounting period for a company) for which relief is sought will be allowed by Revenue, provided that the asset was of negligible value in the year of assessment or accounting period concerned. The word 'negligible' is not defined and has its normal meaning, i.e. not worth considering; insignificant.

Example

Joe owns two assets. The first is 1,000 shares in a bank, which he bought for €15 per share, and which are now worth 50c per share. The second asset is 1,500 shares in Defunct Ltd, which he bought for €10 per share. A liquidator has been appointed to Defunct Ltd and it is insolvent.

Joe is entitled to make a claim for the loss of €15,000 (1,500 × €10), and this will be allowed by the Inspector as the shares have negligible value. While he has suffered a very significant unrealised loss on the shares in the bank, the shares have more than negligible value and, therefore, he cannot get relief for the unrealised loss. He can only get relief if he sells the bank shares.

1.14 Death and Personal Representatives

1.14.1 General

The assets which a deceased person was competent to dispose of are deemed to be acquired on his death by the personal representatives or by the beneficiary at the **market value at the date of death**. The deemed transfer at market value at date of death does not give rise to a chargeable disposal for CGT purposes and, accordingly, no liability will attach to the estate of the deceased in respect of any gains realised on the asset over his lifetime. The converse is also true in that no allowable losses are crystallized on a death. The **base cost** for the purposes of a subsequent disposal, by the personal representatives or by the beneficiaries, of an asset acquired on death will be the market value at the date of death, irrespective of when the death occurred, and indexation relief is applied from the date of death to this base cost. This is subject only to the exception that if the death occurred prior to 6 April 1974, then the market value at 6 April 1974 will form the base cost.

1.14.2 Personal Representatives

Personal representatives of the deceased are treated as a single and continuing body of persons, regardless of the fact that the individuals who are the personal representatives may change from time to time. They are deemed to have the same status as regards residence, ordinary residence and domicile as the deceased had at the time of his death.

CGT assessable on the deceased in respect of disposals prior to his death may be assessed and charged on the personal representatives. Though the assessment is made on the personal representatives, the pre-death disposals and gains are deemed to be the disposals and gains of the deceased for the purpose of the €1,270 annual exemption applicable to individuals and, therefore, the €1,270 exemption is available.

Personal representatives are chargeable to CGT on any gains which arise during the course of the administration of the estate and are entitled to relief in respect of any losses on disposals made by them. However, no carry back of losses incurred on disposal of the deceased's assets by the personal representatives is available, nor is there any entitlement to annual exemption.

If the personal representatives transfer assets to a legatee under the terms of the will of the deceased, a disposal is not deemed to take place for CGT and, accordingly, no chargeable gain or allowable loss will arise on the transfer. The legatee is deemed to acquire the assets at the same time and at the same value as did the personal representatives (i.e. at the market value at the date of death of the deceased) for the purposes of any subsequent disposal by him.

Example

Patrick died on 1 February 2012 leaving his entire estate to his sister Janet. Patrick's assets consisted of his house valued at €650,000 on 1 February 2012 which he had acquired in 1996 for €75,000 and shares valued at €20,000 on 1 February 2012 which he had acquired in 1998 for €40,000. Patrick's personal representatives sold the shares in July 2012 for €23,000. Patrick's house was transferred to his sister in December 2012 at which date it was valued at €600,000. Patrick had incurred a loss of €5,000 on the disposal of other shares in January 2012.

The personal representatives are deemed to take over Patrick's assets on the date of his death at their valuation on that date. No CGT arises as a result of the transfer to the personal representatives. On the sale of the shares by the personal representatives, a CGT liability of €900 arises, calculated as follows:

	€
Proceeds	23,000
Market value at date of Patrick's death	(20,000)
Gain	3,000
CGT @ 30%	900

The personal representatives are not entitled to an annual exemption or to use the capital loss incurred by Patrick prior to his death.

The transfer of the house to Janet in December 2012 is not a chargeable event for CGT purposes; no allowable loss arises to the personal representatives. Janet is deemed to have acquired the house on 1 February 2012, the date of Patrick's death, for its valuation of €650,000 on that date.

(Please note that while the house had increased in value and the shares had reduced in value during Patrick's lifetime, this gain and loss are never realised and are ignored, i.e. these assets transfer at market value at the date of death.)

1.15   Deed of Family Arrangement

If, within **two years of death**, the disposition of a property under a will or on intestacy is varied by a deed of family arrangement, then the deed is deemed to have retrospective effect from the date of death. The arrangement does not, therefore, constitute a disposal for CGT purposes and is not, therefore, an occasion of charge to CGT.

The two-year time limit may be extended at the discretion of the Revenue Commissioners. In practice this relief is available in any case where property, transferred by will or intestacy, is by some form of deed redistributed within the family. The persons receiving the redistributed assets are in effect put in the same position as legatees would have been for the purposes of any subsequent sale by them of the asset, i.e. they will be deemed to have acquired the assets at the market value at the date of death of the deceased for the purposes of calculating any future gain or allowable loss and for the purposes of indexation.

A similar relief is available for CAT.

Questions (to Chapter 1)

Review Questions

(See Suggested Solutions to Review Questions at the end of this textbook.)

Question 1.1

Inflated Gains

1. Maurice purchased a holiday home for €20,000 on 2 February 1985 and subsequently sold it on 30 November 2012 for €80,000. Incidental legal costs on purchase amounted to €600 and €750 on sale.
2. Vincent bought shares in a plc in December 1991 for €1,200. He sold the shares for €9,300 on 1 April 2012.

3.

		Cost	Date of Purchase	M.V.@ 6/4/74	Sale Proceeds
		€		€	€
(a)	John sold a capital asset on 31/12/2012	7,600	June '01	N/A	7,800
(b)	Philip sold a capital asset on 31/12/2012	3,000	July '80	N/A	2,700
(c)	Paul sold a capital asset on 31/12/2012	5,700	June '73	5,800	5,500
(d)	Oliver sold a capital asset on 31/12/2012	15,000	July '80	N/A	18,000

Requirement
Compute the CGT due or allowable losses in each case.

Note: You are to assume that the individuals had no other realised gains or losses during the year.

Question 1.2

Enhancement Examples

1. James constructed a hotel in July 1992 for €260,000. He received a Bord Fáilte capital grant of €10,000. Additional expenditure was incurred as follows:

		€
August 2001	Repair roof	3,000
May 2004	Three new bedrooms added	90,000

James sold the hotel on 31 May 2012 for €650,000.
James had no other capital gains during 2012.

Requirement
Compute the CGT payable by James.

2.   Declan purchased a public house on 6 April 1998 for €85,000. Additional expenditure was incurred as follows:

	€
Additional games room 6 August 2001	20,000
Additional lounge bar 1 February 2003	39,250

Declan sold the public house for €400,000 on 1 July 2012. Declan had no other capital gains during 2012.

Requirement
Compute the CGT payable by Declan on the sale.

Question 1.3

Joe Loss died on 27 July 2012. In the period 1 January 2012 to 27 July 2012 he made disposals of three assets as follows:

		€
Asset 1:	Chargeable gain	1,500
Asset 2:	Chargeable gain	200
Asset 3:	Allowable loss	(7,500)

In the four previous years of assessment, Joe had been assessed on net chargeable gains (after the annual exemption).

	€
2011	100
2010	150
2009	250
2008	1,000

Requirement
Compute the relief available to Joe in respect of the net loss incurred by him in the year of death. Take the annual exemption at €1,270 for all years.

Question 1.4

Michael Gain made the following disposals of plc shares on 6 October 2012.

	Cost	Date Purchased	Proceeds
	€		€
1,000 Courtaulds plc	888	6/11/1974	1,162
1,550 Box plc	1,732	7/5/1981	1,662
500 Cox plc	1,693	7/12/1993	16,000
400 Nox plc	623	1/3/2005	1,305

Michael is not married and had no other chargeable gains during 2012.

Requirement

Compute chargeable gains (if any) made by Michael and the CGT payable (if any) for 2012.

Question 1.5

Morry Bund died on 6 August 2012.

His history of gains and losses up to the date of death was as follows:

	2008	2009	2010	2011	Period 1/1/2012 – 6/8/2012
Gains	9,000	5,000	7,000	–	–
Rate of tax	22%	25%	25%	–	–
Losses	–	–	–	–	(16,000)

Mr Bund's estate on death included the following assets:

1. A holiday cottage bought in June 1999 for €20,000. The valuation at the date of death was €82,000. It was sold by the personal representatives in December 2012 for €88,000 in order to raise funds to pay off estate creditors.
2. Shares in a plc bought in May 2000 for €5,000 and valued at €30,000 at the date of death. They were transferred to Mrs Bund by the personal representatives in November 2012, when their value had fallen to €22,000. Mrs Bund sold them in December 2012 for €27,000.

Requirement

Calculate the CGT consequences arising on the above events for 2012.

Question 1.6

Derek Cotter is 35 years old and has completed the following capital transactions for the year ended 31 December 2012. He has lived in Ireland all his life.

1. On 12 January 2012, he sold a 5% holding, with a market value of €50,000, in the family tanning business to his sister for €40,000. Derek had inherited the shares from his father in January 2000 when they had a market value of €8,000.
2. On 5 February 2012, he sold his holiday home in Florida for €320,000. Derek had acquired the property for €110,000 on 30 October 1999.

3.   On 5 May 2012, he sold shares in a plc for €30,000. Derek had purchased the shares for €50,000 in April 2002.

4.   On 10 December 2012, he sold a house (not his principal private residence) in Foxrock, Dublin for €2,000,000. Derek had acquired the house and garden in December 1992 for €300,000. Derek sold the garden of one acre for €500,000 on 30 April 2001. The remainder of the house and garden was valued at €1,000,000 on 30 April 2001. The house did not have any development value at 10 December 2012.

5.   On 21 December 2012, he gifted an antique chair to his nephew Tom. The chair had been purchased for €2,600 on 3 December 2001. On 21 December 2012, the chair was valued at €3,500.

Requirement

Compute Derek's CGT liability for the tax year 2012 and state the due dates for the payment of this liability.

Territoriality Rules

Learning Objectives

After studying this chapter you will have developed a competency in the following:

- Individuals who are resident or ordinarily resident and also domiciled are liable to CGT on worldwide gains
- Individuals who are resident or ordinarily resident, but not domiciled, are liable to CGT on Irish gains and other gains only if remitted to the State
- Individuals who are neither resident nor ordinarily resident are only liable to CGT on gains on disposals of specified assets
- There is anti-avoidance legislation under which people temporarily non-resident are liable to CGT on disposal of certain assets while non-resident

2.1 Recap of Rules on Resident, Ordinarily Resident and Domiciled

At CAP 1, students studied income tax and the rules as to when an individual is:

- Resident
- Ordinarily resident
- Domiciled

The charge to CGT also depends on whether an individual is Irish resident, ordinarily resident and/or domiciled. To recap, the meaning of these terms is set out below.

"Resident"

An individual is resident in the State in any year of assessment in which he:

- is present a total of 183 days or more in the State; or
- is present more than 30 days in the State in that year and, in that year and the previous year taken together, spends 280 days or more in the State; or
- elects to be so resident, being in the State in that year with the intention, and in such circumstances that make it likely, that he will be resident in the following year of assessment.

"Ordinarily Resident"

An individual is ordinarily resident in the State in any year of assessment in which he has been resident in the State in the three previous years of assessment. Once he becomes ordinarily resident, he remains so until a year of assessment in which he has been non-resident in each of the three previous years of assessment.

"Domicile"

"Domicile" is a legal term. Briefly put, a person's domicile is the country where he is deemed to have his permanent home in law. This is normally the country in which he resides with the intention of remaining permanently. It should be stressed, however, that an individual may be domiciled in a country without actually residing in it.

2.2 Individual is Resident or Ordinarily Resident

Liability to CGT depends on whether an individual is resident or ordinarily resident and the type of asset.

An Irish domiciled individual who is resident or ordinarily resident in the State for 2012 (1 January to 31 December 2012) is chargeable to CGT on worldwide chargeable gains made on the disposal of assets.

A foreign domiciled individual, who is resident or ordinarily resident in the State for 2008 and future years, is only liable on Irish gains (Irish and UK gains up to 20 November 2008) and on other gains to the extent that they are remitted to the State, i.e. the remittance basis applies. There is **no loss relief available in respect of assets situated outside Ireland (and UK on or after 20 November 2008) for non-domiciled individuals who are assessed on the remittance basis**.

Where an individual is taxed on a remittance basis, the rate of CGT which applies to remitted gains is the rate of CGT which applied when the disposal was made.

Example
Hans Vervoort is a Belgian domiciled individual who has been resident in Ireland for many years. On 22 October 2008, when the Irish rate of CGT was 22%, Hans disposed of a property in Belgium. Hans did not remit the proceeds from this disposal to Ireland until 2012. Hans will be liable in 2012 to Irish CGT at 22% of the gain which arose on the disposal of the property.

While an Irish domiciled person who is non-resident, but is still ordinarily resident, is liable to Irish CGT, Irish domiciled individuals had been able to avoid Irish CGT by being resident in certain tax treaty countries. However, there is an anti-avoidance rule that charges to tax certain disposals by temporary non-residents – see **Section 2.4**.

2.3 Individual is not Resident and not Ordinarily Resident

An individual who is neither resident nor ordinarily resident is not liable to Irish CGT on the disposal of an asset unless it is a disposal of a specified Irish asset, i.e. disposals of foreign assets or Irish non-specified assets are outside the charge to CGT for an individual who is neither resident nor ordinarily resident. However, the disposal may be caught under the temporary non-resident anti-avoidance rules dealt with at **Section 2.4**.

2.3.1   Specified Irish Assets

Gains arising on the disposal of certain **specified Irish assets** are chargeable to CGT irrespective of the residence or ordinary residence of the owner. The specified assets are:

(a)   LAND and BUILDINGS in the State.

(b)   MINERALS in the State or any rights, interests or other assets in relation to mining or minerals or the searching for minerals, including exploration or exploitation rights within the limits of the Irish Continental Shelf.

(c)   UNQUOTED SHARES deriving their value, or the greater part of their value from (a) or (b) above.

(d)   Assets situated in the State which at or about the time when the gains accrued were used for the purposes of a trade carried on in the State through a BRANCH or AGENCY, or used, or held, or acquired by, or for the purposes of the branch or agency.

You will recall that an individual is ordinarily resident in the State if resident in the State for the preceding three tax years. To become non-ordinarily resident, the individual must not be resident for at least three tax years. Therefore, if an individual wishes to avoid Irish tax on the disposal of a foreign asset or on an Irish asset which is not a specified asset, the individual must become both non-resident and non-ordinarily resident. This would mean that the individual would have to be non-resident for three tax years before the Irish CGT could be avoided under this general rule.

Remember that there is also the temporary non-residents rules dealt with at **Section 2.4** which apply to disposals of certain shares, even if the individual is not caught under the normal residence and ordinary residence rules. Therefore a person who is neither resident nor ordinarily resident can be liable to Irish CGT either because the person disposes of a **specified asset** or because the person disposes of **shares** and is caught under the temporary non-resident anti-avoidance rules.

Example

During 2012, Mary made the following disposals:

1.   Gain of €10,000 on sale of shares in Irish plc, a company quoted on the Irish Stock Exchange
2.   Gain of €100,000 on sale of land in Galway
3.   Gain of €50,000 on sale of shares in UK plc, a company quoted on the London Stock Exchange
4.   Loss of €5,000 on sale of shares in Completely Irish plc, a company quoted on the Irish Stock Exchange
5.   Loss of €8,000 on sale of shares in Lyons plc, a company quoted on the Paris Stock Exchange

If Mary is Irish domiciled and resident or ordinarily resident, she is liable to Irish CGT on all the gains and is allowed loss relief for all the losses.

If Mary is not Irish domiciled, but is resident or ordinarily resident, she is liable to Irish CGT on Irish gains only (i.e. 1 and 2) and allowed loss relief for Irish losses only (i.e. 4).

If Mary is not resident or ordinarily resident, she is liable on specified assets only and therefore is taxable only on 2 and is not entitled to relief for either of the losses.

2.3.2   Administration, including Withholding Tax

Because of the difficulty in collecting CGT due by non-residents, the Inspector of Taxes can issue a notice of assessment at any time including before the end of the tax year, and in this instance the CGT is due two months after the making of an assessment or three months from the date of disposal, whichever is later.

The law provides for a withholding tax of **15%** to be deducted from the purchase price of certain specified assets by the purchaser, where a tax clearance certificate is not provided. The purchaser is required to pay the amount deducted to the Collector-General within 30 days and is also required to forward information relating to the acquisition of the asset to the Revenue Commissioners. The vendor of the asset is entitled to set off the amount deducted against any CGT due on the disposal.

The assets which are potentially liable to the withholding tax are:

- land in the State;
- minerals in the State or any mineral or mining rights;
- exploration or exploitation rights in a designated area;
- unquoted shares deriving their value from any of the above assets; and
- goodwill of a trade carried on in the State.

The law does not apply where the value of the asset disposed of **does not exceed €500,000**. If an asset exceeding this value is sold in parts to the same person or connected persons, then those disposals are to be treated as one disposal. Where a deduction cannot be made from the purchase price because the consideration is in non-monetary form, the purchaser is still required to pay the 15% withholding tax to the Revenue Commissioners, but this is recoverable by the purchaser from the vendor. This provision, in relation to consideration in a non-monetary form, does not however apply in the case of gifts as the Revenue may assess the tax on the donee, i.e. the recipient of the gift.

A vendor may complete a form CG50 and apply for a clearance certificate to receive the proceeds without any withholding tax. The Inspector will issue a clearance certificate (CG50A) if he is satisfied that:

- the vendor is resident in the State;
- no CGT is due on the disposal; or
- the vendor has already paid the CGT due on the disposal of the asset and there is no CGT outstanding from a previous disposal of the asset.

While an Irish resident can get the clearance certificate, non-residents must pay any CGT due if they want to receive the clearance certificate and avoid the 15% withholding tax.

2.4 Temporary Non-residents

2.4.1 Background

There is an anti-avoidance rule to tax Irish domiciled individuals who are temporarily non-resident and who would otherwise not pay Irish CGT due to tax treaty protection. This law seeks to stop individuals, who expect to make a gain on disposal of shares, avoiding Irish CGT by becoming non-resident or becoming tax resident in a treaty country, disposing of the shares so that no Irish CGT is payable, and then returning to Ireland within a few years. If the person is, for more than five tax years, not tax resident in Ireland, then a tax charge cannot arise under this section.

2.4.2 Liability to Irish Tax

The law imposes a CGT charge in respect of a *deemed* disposal of "relevant assets" owned by an individual on the last day of the tax year for which the individual is taxable in the State prior to becoming taxable elsewhere.

"Relevant assets" are a holding in a company which, when the person ceases to be chargeable to CGT in the State (i.e. the last day of the tax year in which the person departs):

- is **5% or more by value** of the **issued share capital** of the company; or
- has a **value in excess of €500,000**.

If a person disposes of all, or part, of such relevant assets during a period of five tax years or less during which he or she is outside the charge to CGT under normal rules, the person will be liable to CGT on this disposal as if the person had disposed of those assets, or that part of those assets, on the last day of the tax year in which he/she was resident before departing, for a consideration equal to their market value on that date, i.e. 31 December. For example, if a person leaves in December 2012 and returns in 2018, there could be a charge under this legislation if the disposal of the relevant assets takes place in the years 2013 to 2018 inclusive. If the individual waited until 2019, there would be no charge.

Whereas the gain on the deemed disposal arises before the individual ceases to be resident in the State, for self assessment purposes, the gain is required to be included in the individual's tax return and the CGT in respect of it accounted for, in the year in which the individual again becomes taxable in the State. Credit will be given in respect of any foreign tax payable on an actual disposal of the assets where such tax is payable in a territory with which Ireland has a double taxation treaty.

Therefore, this CGT charge will only arise if the individual:

- is Irish domiciled and has been Irish tax resident prior to departing temporarily from the State;
- disposes of relevant assets (i.e. certain shares) in the intervening years and only to the extent of the disposal; and
- is not taxable in the State in respect of any gains on the disposal of relevant assets for a period of five years or less before again becoming so taxable.

> *Example*
>
> Richie Rich owns 40% of the shares in Teleireland Ltd. These shares cost him €200,000 in 1999/2000. On 30 June 2012, he is offered €50 million for his shares. A friend has told him that if he goes to live in Portugal in 2012 and disposes of the shares in 2013, then he will not have any CGT liability on the gain on his shares, even if he returns to the State in a couple of years time. He has heard that this is not correct, as there is some anti-avoidance rule. However, he understands that he can avoid this rule, if he is non-resident for a sufficiently long period.
>
> He wants you to advise him. You are to assume that the shares are worth €52 million on 31 December 2012. Ignore the annual exemption.
>
> If Richie Rich does, as his friend suggests, and is non-resident for five years or less between the year of departure and the year of return and he disposes of the shares in this intervening period, then he will be liable to CGT in the year in which he returns and the gain will be calculated as follows:
>
> | | | € |
> |---|---|---|
> | Deemed proceeds | Market value at 31 December 2012 | 52,000,000 |
> | Cost of shares | €200,000 × 1.193 | (238,600) |
> | Gain | | 51,761,400 |
> | CGT @ 30% | | 15,528,420 |
>
> If, alternatively, he waited and is non-resident for more than five years between the year of departure and the year of return, then this anti-avoidance rule would not apply and he would not have to pay this CGT.

Questions (to Chapter 2)

Review Questions

(See Suggested Solutions at the end of this textbook.)

Question 2.1

Jacques, a French domiciled individual, has been resident in Ireland since September 2003. During 2012 he made the following disposals:

(a) Disposed of 8,000 shares in a French family trading company for €65,000 on 15 May 2012. Jacques had acquired 16,000 of these shares in August 1994 for €60,000. Jacques used €10,000 of the proceeds received to improve his Dublin home. The remaining €55,000 he put on deposit in a bank in Paris.

(b) Disposed of a UK rental property for €200,000 on 1 October 2012. Jacques acquired this property in November 1996 for €180,000. He carried out extensive renovations on the property in the period January / February 1997 which cost €30,000 in total. He lodged the proceeds in his bank account in Dublin.

(c) Disposed of H plc shares for €24,000 on 3 December 2012. Jacques had acquired these shares in June 1998 for €8,025. H plc is an Irish company.

Jacques did not have any chargeable gains in 2011. He did, however, incur a loss of €15,000 on the sale of shares in a German trading company. Jacques remitted the proceeds from this sale to an Irish bank account.

Requirement
Calculate Jacques's CGT liability for 2012.

Shares

3.1   Introduction

Shares present special problems when attempting to compute gains or losses on disposal.

> *Example*
> Joe bought the following shares in X Ltd:
>
> | | € |
> |---|---|
> | 1,000 in January 2004 for | 2,000 |
> | 1,000 in January 2005 for | 8,000 |
>
> If he sells say 1,000 shares today – how would his base cost be determined?

The general rule is that disposals of shares are to be identified with purchases on a first in/first out (FIFO) basis. This gives the taxpayer the maximum advantage as inflation relief on such disposals is treated as being in respect of assets owned for the longest period, i.e. the longest held shares are deemed to be disposed of first (see example below).

Example

Ordinary shares in Abbott Limited, a trading company		Number	Cost
			€
May 1981	Bought	100	100
July 1982	Bought	300	300
May 1986	(Sold) (FIFO)	(100)	
7 April 1989	Bought	400	425
May 1991	Bought	500	600 (i.e. €1.20 each)
May 2008	(Sold)	(300)	
June 2012	(Sold)	(525)	(Sale proceeds €21,000)

The disposals are dealt with on the following basis:

1. **May 1986 Disposal:** The FIFO rule applies and the 100 shares sold are deemed to be those purchased in May 1981.
2. **May 2008 Disposal:** The sale of 300 shares in May 2008 is deemed to be a disposal of the 300 shares acquired for €300 in July 1982.
3. **June 2012 Disposal:** The sale of 525 shares in June 2012 for €21,000 would give rise to the following gains. Two separate disposals are deemed to have taken place:

		€
a.	Disposal of 400 shares acquired on 7 April 1989	
	Proceeds 400 @ €40 (i.e. sale price per share)	16,000
	Deduct: €425 indexed at 1.503	(639)
		15,361
b.	Disposal of 125 shares out of the 500 originally acquired in May 1991 at a total cost of €600.	€
	Proceeds 125 @ €40 (i.e. sale price per share)	5,000
	Deduct: Cost $\frac{125}{500} \times 600 = €150$	
	(original cost of 125 shares) indexed @ 1.406	(211)
		4,789

The above example illustrates the method of computation though the gains would, of course, be subject to the individual's annual exemption. The rate of CGT applicable to both disposals would be 30%.

3.2   Calls on Shares

Where the shares or debentures are issued and paid for by calls, then if **any call is paid more than 12 months after the allotment of the shares** or debentures, the expenditure is treated as **enhancement expenditure** for purposes of inflation relief. Inflation relief will, therefore, be applied to the call payment on the basis of the actual date of payment of the call amount. This is an anti-avoidance provision designed to prevent the taxpayer from claiming that the expenditure was actually incurred on the original date of issue of the shares and applying indexation relief to the call amount from that date.

Consider the CGT position if €1 shares were issued at par and only 5c was paid up at the date of issue of the shares, the balance of 95c per share not being called until immediately prior to the disposal of the shares. Unless this anti-avoidance provision existed, indexation might be claimed from the date of acquisition of the shares on the full par value, irrespective of the length of the period during which the share had been fully paid up.

Example

Mr Sing applied for 10,000 €1 ordinary shares of Globtrots Ltd., a trading company.

Mr Sing paid 20c on application on 1 June 1991 and a further 30c on allotment on 1 November 1991.

In November 1997 Mr Sing paid a call of 50c per share, the 10,000 shares allotted to him then being fully paid.

Mr Sing sells the shares on 2 May 2012 for €50,000

Computation

	€	€
Sale proceeds		50,000
Deduct allowable costs:		
€5,000 paid y/e 5 April 1992 indexed @ 1.406	7,030	
€5,000 paid y/e 5 April 1998 indexed @ 1.232	6,160	(13,190)
Chargeable gain		36,810
Less: Exemption		(1,270)
Taxable gain		35,540
CGT @ 30%		10,662

3.3 Rights Issues

New cash paid in by a shareholder on the taking up of his rights under a rights issue is treated as enhancement expenditure at the date on which the cash is paid. Inflation relief, referable to the enhancement expenditure is, therefore, based upon the actual date the enhancement expenditure is made. However, for other purposes, such as identification of assets, this rule does not apply so that the rights taken up are deemed to be part of the original asset to which the rights refer, e.g. for the purposes of applying the FIFO rule. In other words, the rights are effectively deemed to be part of the original holding acquired on the same date as the original holding was acquired.

Example

Jim acquired 1,000 €1 ordinary shares in Axel plc on 1 May 1989 for €1,000.

On 1 June 1993 he acquired a further 2,000 shares for €5,000.

On 1 January 1997 Axel plc made a rights issue of 1 for 5 at a price of €3 per share issued.

On 1 May 2012 he sold 1,600 shares at €50 each.

Step 1: Identify the make-up of Jim's holding, prior to the sale on 1 May 2012

HOLDING ACQUIRED 1 MAY 1989

				€
1,000	Shares	Cost		1,000
200	Shares (rights issue appropriate to the 1,000 original shares are deemed to have been acquired on the same day for application of FIFO rule)	Cost		600
1,200	Total shares			

continued overleaf

HOLDING ACQUIRED 1 JUNE 1993

			€
2,000	Shares	Cost	5,000
400	Shares (rights issue)	Cost	1,200
2,400	Total shares		

Step 2: Apply the FIFO rule to the holdings acquired at 1 May 1989 and 1 June 1993 to determine which shares are deemed to be disposed of in the sale on 1 May 2012.

The 1,600 shares sold are comprised of:

1,200	Shares from holding at 1 May 1989
400	Shares from holding at 1 June 1993 (i.e. 1/6th of total June 1993 holding)
1,600	Total shares

Computation N.B. the disposal is treated as the separate disposal of two distinct holdings, acquired in May 1989 and June 1993

(a) Disposal of 1,200 May 1989 Holding

	€	€
Sale proceeds 1,200 @ €50		60,000
Deduct:		
Original 1,000 shares cost €1,000 May 1989 indexed @ 1.503	1,503	
Rights issue 200 shares cost €600 January 1997 indexed @ 1.251	751	(2,254)
Gain		57,746

(b) Disposal of 400 shares of June 1993 Holding

	€	€
Sale proceeds 400 @ €50		20,000
Deduct:		
Original June 1993 2,000 shares × 1/6 = 333 shares. Cost of 333 shares @ €2.50 each = €832 indexed @ 1.331	1,107	
Rights issue 400 shares × 1/6 = 67 shares. Cost of 67 shares @ €3 each = 200 indexed @ 1.251 January 1997)	250	(1,357)
Gain		18,643

Summary

	€
Gain applicable to May 1989 holding	57,746
Gain applicable to June 1993 holding	18,643
	76,389
Deduct: annual exemption	(1,270)
	75,119
CGT @ 30%	22,536

3.4   Bonus Issues

For the purposes of the FIFO rule, shares acquired as a result of bonus issues are deemed to have been acquired at the same time as the original holdings to which they relate. As no consideration is paid by the shareholders on receipt of the bonus shares, the complex calculations necessary in the case of rights issues are not required.

Example

Joe originally acquired 1,000 shares on 1 June 1990 for €2,000.

- On 1 June 1994, he bought 500 more at a cost of €1,500.
- On 1 January 1996, a bonus issue of 2 for 5 was made.
- On 1 June 2012, Joe sold 2,000 shares for €20 each.

Prior to the sale on 1 June 2012, Joe's total holding of 2,100 shares was made up as follows:

Holding 1 June 1990

			€
Original	1,000 shares	Cost	2,000
Bonus issue	400 shares	Cost	Nil
	1,400		2,000

Holding 1 June 1994

			€
Original	500 shares	Cost	1,500
Bonus issue	200 shares	Cost	Nil
	700		1,500

Computation

The 2,000 shares sold are deemed to have been comprised of:

(a)   the holding of 1,400 acquired 1 June 1990 for €2,000
(b)   600 of the holding of 700 shares acquired 1 June 1994 for a total of €1,500.

	€
Sale proceeds 1,400 shares @ €20 each	28,000
Allowable cost: €2,000 × 1.442	(2,884)
Gain	25,116

	€
Sale proceeds 600 shares @ €20 each	12,000
Allowable cost: 600/700 × €1,500 = €1,286 @ 1.309	(1,683)
Gain	10,317

Note: Above gains subject to the annual exemption.

3.5   Acquisition within Four Weeks of Disposal and Disposal within Four Weeks of Acquisition

This is an anti-avoidance provision designed to prevent taxpayers benefiting by the creation of artificial losses. The transactions involved are commonly referred to as "Bed & Breakfast" transactions.

3.5.1   *Acquisition within Four Weeks of Disposal*

In this situation a loss accrues to a person on the disposal of shares and such person reacquires shares of the same class within four weeks after the disposal.

The effects of the provision are best explained with an example:

> **Example**
> Harry owns 1,000 shares in X Ltd which he originally purchased at €5 each. On 30 December 2012, the shares are quoted at €1 each. Harry does not wish to sell his 1,000 shares, as he believes they will rise in price in the future but, at the same time, wishes to claim loss relief for the paper loss which he has suffered. He cannot do this unless he has a realisation, i.e. a disposal. Accordingly, he arranges to sell his 1,000 shares at €1 each on 30 December 2012 on the understanding that his stockbroker will re-purchase a further 1,000 shares on the market two to three days later. Accordingly, Harry will realise a loss of €4,000 on the disposal which, in the absence of anti-avoidance provisions, would be available to set off against any gains he has realised in 2012. In addition, he will also still own 1,000 shares in X Ltd.

The legislation prevents this arrangement by providing that as the disposal and re-acquisition of the same class of shares took place within four weeks, then the loss arising can only be set against the subsequent gain arising on the disposal of the shares which have been re-acquired, i.e. the loss cannot be set against other gains.

3.5.2   *Disposal within Four Weeks of Acquisition*

In this situation a person acquires shares and within four weeks after the acquisition disposes of shares of the same class. Again the effects of the provision are best explained with an example:

> **Example**
> An individual owns 3,000 shares in a company which have fallen in value since they were purchased. He has other realised gains in the tax year and wishes to offset the losses accrued on his holding of 3,000 shares but also wishes to retain the investment. He, therefore, purchases a further 3,000 shares in the company which he sells within four weeks. If FIFO applied, the disposal of the 3,000 shares would be deemed to come out of the original holding of 3,000 shares which were purchased at the higher price, thereby realising a loss to set against his other realised gains.

To avoid this effect, the FIFO rule is set aside in relation to the disposal within four weeks, and the 3,000 shares sold are treated as being those which were acquired within the four week period. In other words, the "last in/first out" (LIFO) rule replaces the FIFO rule. It should be noted that LIFO replaces FIFO in all situations where there is an acquisition of shares followed by a disposal of the same class of shares within four weeks of the acquisition even where the FIFO rule would not result in a loss.

The anti-avoidance provision also applies to married persons and civil partners living together, preventing one spouse or civil partner selling the shares on the open market and having the other spouse or civil partner reacquire the shares.

3.6   CGT Treatment of Employee Share Options

A share option is a common feature in the remuneration package of a company executive. It usually consists of the right to subscribe at a specified price for a specified number of shares in his employer company during a specified period of time. The income tax treatment of share options has been covered in your CAP 1 course. You will recall that different tax treatment applies depending on whether the share option scheme is approved or unapproved.

3.6.1 Share Option Schemes

With effect from 24 November 2010, Approved Share Option schemes have been abolished. Therefore, no further approved options may be granted, so all options are liable to income tax. Also, options granted before then under an Approved Share Option scheme, but exercised on or after 24 November 2010, are liable to income tax and not CGT.

An **employee is subject to income tax on the exercise** of a share option and, **possibly, on the grant of the option,** depending on the exercise period.

For CGT purposes, **any gain which is chargeable to income tax is treated as being additional consideration given by the employee for the shares acquired on the exercise of the option**.

Example

Patrick is granted an option by his employer, XYZ plc, to subscribe for 1,000 €1 ordinary shares at a price of €1 each at any time in the following eight years. He is granted this right by reason of his employment at a time when the shares are valued at €3 each. Some time later Patrick exercises the option, at a time when each €1 ordinary share in XYZ plc is worth €10 and takes up the 1,000 shares in XYZ plc.

At the **date of grant** of the option, Patrick is chargeable to income tax on the difference between the option price (€1 per share) and the market value (€3 per share) – total €2,000 taxable at his marginal rate (as the option is longer than seven years).

At the date of exercise of the option he is chargeable to income tax on the full gain, with credit for the tax paid at the date of grant of the option, i.e. **he is charged to income tax on the difference between the amount paid for the shares (€1 per share) and the market value at the date of exercise of the option (€10 per share) – €9,000, with a credit for the tax paid on the gain of €2,000**. He has effectively been charged to income tax on €9,000; €2,000 at the date of grant, and €7,000 at the date of exercise.

What is Patrick's base cost for his shares should he now choose to dispose of them?

	€
Actual sum subscribed	1,000
Gain chargeable to income tax to be treated as consideration	9,000
TOTAL	10,000

If Patrick disposed of his shares immediately for €10,000 on exercising his option (which is a frequent occurrence in practice, since employees often cannot finance the holding of the shares they acquire under option schemes), **he would have no gain and no loss for CGT**.

3.6.2 Approved Share Option Schemes – Pre 24 November 2010

The position in relation to approved share option schemes granted and exercised before 24 November 2010 where the **employee holds the shares for at least three years** (from the date of acquiring the option) can be summarised as follows:

- there was no tax charge on the receipt of the option;
- there was no tax charge on the exercise of the option; and
- the shares obtained on foot of the option are **within the CGT regime** and not the income tax regime, and have a base cost equal to the sum paid for them.

Example

John works for ABC plc. At 1 January 2007 he received options over 1,000 shares in the company exercisable at any time within the following six years at the market price of the shares at 31 December 2006. The option scheme was approved by Revenue.

On 31 March 2008 John exercised his option and acquired the 1,000 shares for the sum of €10,000 (the shares having been worth €10 each on 31 December 2006).

On 1 January 2012, John sold the shares for €30,000.

Because the share option scheme was approved as such by the Revenue Commissioners, neither income tax nor CGT was chargeable at that time of grant or exercise.

Joe held the shares for a period of three years from the date upon which he acquired the option. Accordingly, on 1 January 2012, John is treated as having a CGT disposal in respect of his shares. His base cost in that computation is €10,000. The sale proceeds are €30,000, so John has made a gain of €20,000 which would lead to a tax cost of €6,000. It is assumed that John's annual CGT exemption is otherwise utilised.

Questions (to Chapter 3)

Review Questions

(See Suggested Solutions to Review Questions at the end of this textbook.)

Question 3.1

Louise, a single person, disposed of 5,000 shares in Tedu Ltd, a trading company, for €15,000 in June 2012. She acquired 4,000 shares in July 2003 for €1.50 per share. In October 2003, the company declared a 1:2 bonus issue.

Requirement
Calculate Louise's CGT liability for 2012.

Question 3.2

On 2 May 2012, Lorraine McCarthy, a single person, gifted the following shares in Arco Ltd, a trading company:

- 5,000 to her sister Mary
- 5,000 to her brother Kevin

She had acquired her shares in Arco Ltd as follows:

1 July 1972	6,000 shares @ 19c each
1 November 1983	Rights issue 2 for 1 @ 34c each

She took up her rights issue fully.

At 6 April 1974, the shares were worth 22c each and, at 2 May 2012, they were worth €1.68 each.

Requirement
Compute her CGT liability for 2012.

Question 3.3

Martin Doyle, a married man, acquired 4,000 ordinary shares in Dublin Ltd, a trading company, in May 1967 for €1,000. The market value of each share at 6 April 1974 was 75c. On 6 January 1988, Dublin Ltd made a rights issue to existing shareholders. The offer was 1 share for every 2 held at a rights price of €3 per share. Martin took his full entitlement under the rights issue. The market value per share after the rights issue was €4.

On 6 July 2012, Martin sold 1,500 shares in Dublin Ltd to his wife Orla, and 900 shares to his only son Gerry for €1,500 and €900 respectively. The market value of each share on that date was €10.

On 6 October 2012, Martin sold the balance of his shares on the market for €12 each.

Requirement
Compute CGT payable by Martin Doyle.

4

Development Land and Exemptions and Reliefs

Learning Objectives

After studying this chapter, you will have developed a competency in the following:

- Development land is land the market value of which at the date of disposal exceeds its current use value.
- All costs reflected in the value of the development land when disposed of are deductible, but only the current use value at date of acquisition may be indexed.
- Losses on non-development land may not be offset against gains on development land, but losses on development land may be offset against both gains on development land and other gains.
- Disposals of certain capital assets are exempt, which means gains are not taxable and losses are not allowable.
  - Gains on non-wasting chattels are exempt where the proceeds are €2,540 or less.
  - Gains on wasting chattels are exempt. However, if the asset qualified for capital allowances it is taxable.
  - Subject to certain conditions, a site disposed of to a child is exempt if worth €500,000 or less, does not exceed an acre and child is to construct their PPR on it.
  - A gain on the disposal of a principal private residence (PPR) is exempt to the extent that it was occupied as a PPR. If not occupied for the full period, partial exemption applies based on the period of occupancy. There are deemed occupancy rules for working elsewhere (subject to conditions), and the final 12 months is always exempt. If the PPR is development land, only the increase in current use value qualifies for PPR relief.
  - Gains on properties in the EEA, purchased between 7 December 2011 and 31 December 2013, where the property is held for at least seven years are exempt. Where such property is held for more than seven years, the gains attributed to that seven-year period are exempt from CGT.

4.1   Development Land – Introduction

There is a special CGT treatment for disposals of development land made on or after 28 January 1982.

"Development Land" is defined as: "Land in the State, the consideration for the disposal of which, or the market value of which at the time at which the disposal is made, exceeds the current use value of that land at the time at which the disposal is made, and includes shares deriving their value or the greater part of their value directly, or indirectly, from such land, other than shares quoted on a Stock Exchange".

The **"Current Use Value"** of land at any particular time means: "The market value at that time, if the market value were calculated on the assumption that it was, at that time, and would remain unlawful to carry out any development in relation to the land other than development of a minor nature."

A similar definition is also provided in relation to shares in an unquoted company which derive their value, or the greater part of their value, directly or indirectly from land.

The rate of CGT applicable to development land is the normal rate, i.e. 30%. (Please note that in the case of certain disposals of development land, there is a "windfall gain" tax rate of 80%, which applies on the amount by which the land increased in value as a result of certain planning decisions. This tax is not examinable.)

4.2   Development Land – Restriction of Indexation Relief

In the case of development land acquired prior to 6 April 1974, indexation may only be applied to such part of the market value of the asset at 6 April 1974 as is equal to the "current use value" of the asset on that date.

In the case of development land acquired after 6 April 1974, **indexation relief may only be applied to the part of the consideration paid on purchase which relates to the "current use value"** of the asset together with the appropriate portion of total incidental costs of acquisition at that date.

In relation to the application of indexation relief under the above rules, it should be particularly noted that **enhancement expenditure after acquisition of the asset may not be indexed**.

Example 1

		€
Sale proceeds development land 1 August 2012		150,000
Original cost of acquisition 1 January 1973		10,000
Total market value 6 April 1974		30,000
"Current use value" at 6 April 1974		14,000
Enhancement expenditure May 1986		5,000

Capital Gains Tax Computation 2012	€	€
Sale proceeds		150,000
Deduct: current use value @ 6 April 1974		
€14,000 indexed @ 7.528	105,392	

continued overleaf

Add: balance of market value @ 6 April 1974	16,000	
Add: enhancement expenditure May 1986	5,000	
Total allowable costs		(126,392)
		23,608
Deduct: annual exemption		(1,270)
Taxable		22,338
CGT @ 30%		6,701

Example 2

		€
Sale proceeds development land 1 August 2012		200,000
Original cost of acquisition 1 July 1982		40,000
"Current use value" 1 July 1982		21,000
Incidental costs of acquisition		1,000
Enhancement expenditure June 1986		3,000

Capital Gains Tax Computation 2012	€	€
Sale proceeds		200,000
Deduct: current use value on purchase €21,000		
Indexed @ 2.253	47,313	
Incidental costs referable to current use value		
$€1,000 \times \dfrac{21,000}{40,000} = €525$ indexed @ 2.253	1,183	
Balance of original cost	19,000	
Balance of incidental costs	475	
Enhancement expenditure	3,000	(70,971)
Taxable gain		129,029
Deduct: annual exemption		(1,270)
Taxable		127,759
CGT @ 30%		38,328

4.3 Development Land – Restriction of Loss Relief

Normally allowable losses for CGT may be set off against other chargeable gains realised in the same year of assessment or, alternatively, carried forward against chargeable gains in future years. The legislation relating to development land provides that allowable **losses on assets other than development land may not be set off against gains arising on the sale of development land**. However, allowable **losses arising on the disposal of development land may be set against the gains arising on any type of chargeable asset**.

4.4 Disposals of Development Land for €19,050 or Less

The special CGT rules relating to restriction of indexation and loss reliefs, which normally apply to sales of development land, are specifically excluded from operation where **the total sales consideration** (not the amount of the gain) for disposals of development land by an individual **does not exceed €19,050 in any year of assessment**. It should be noted that this special relief is restricted to an individual and is not available to a company.

4.5   Exemptions and Reliefs

4.5.1   Securities of the Government, Local Authorities and Semi-State Bodies

This exemption includes all Government securities, land bonds, stock of Local Authorities and securities issued by Semi-State bodies such as the ESB, Bord na Mona, Housing Finance Agency, Bord Gais Eireann, and An Post.

4.5.2   Non-wasting Chattels (Tangible Movable Property) Sold for €2,540 or Less

A non-wasting chattel is defined as "tangible movable property" which has a predictable useful life of **more than 50 years**.

A gain arising to an **individual** on the disposal of non wasting chattels is exempt if the consideration does not exceed €2,540.

Though the term "tangible movable property" is not defined, it covers, for example, paintings, antiques, postage stamps.

Where the consideration exceeds €2,540, there is a marginal relief which restricts the "tax payable" to one half of the excess of the proceeds over €2,540. It is the consideration **after deduction of expenses of sale** which is compared with €2,540 for the purposes of this exemption. The annual exemption is only taken into account to the extent that it cannot be utilised against other chargeable gains when computing a tax liability figure on disposal of the non-wasting chattel for the purpose of comparison with the tax liability arrived at under the marginal relief formula. It should be noted that a company or a trust cannot benefit from this exemption.

Example
A work of art bought for €100 and sold for €1,900 in August 2012. There is no chargeable gain.

Example
Note: Assume no indexation relief applies, i.e. asset acquired after 31 December 2002, and that there are no other gains.

	Situation A	Situation B
	€	€
Cost	(1,400)	(2,550)
Sales proceeds	2,550	2,590
Overall gain	1,150	40
Less: exemption (assume used on other gains)	(Nil)	(Nil)
Gain	1,150	40
Tax @ 30%	345	12
Half the excess of sale proceeds over €2,540	5	25
Therefore, CGT payable	5	12

Where a loss is incurred on the disposal of a chattel for less than €2,540, the allowable loss is restricted by deeming the **CONSIDERATION** to be exactly €2,540.

Think about this carefully, as it is **NOT QUITE** the opposite of relief for gains. There the **TAX PAYABLE** must not exceed half the excess over €2,540; the **ALLOWABLE LOSS** is limited to the excess of cost over €2,540.

Compare these examples with those relating to gains above:

Example			
		€	€
2 works of art	Cost	(2,600)	(2,600)
	Sale proceeds	1,400	1,900
Actual loss		(1,200)	(700)
Allowable loss – in each case cost less €2,540		(60)	(60)
Note: Expenses of sale in these circumstances are added to the allowable loss, and not deducted from the consideration for the purpose of the €2,540 limit. If the expenses on each sale were €30, the allowable loss would be increased to €90.			

Note: The €2,540 exemption rule does not apply to currency and commodity futures in addition to **not** applying to wasting assets.

4.5.3 Wasting Chattels

A gain arising on the disposal of tangible movable property which is a wasting asset does not give rise to a charge to tax.

A "wasting chattel" is defined as a chattel with a **predictable life not exceeding 50 years,** for example, livestock, bloodstock, private motor car, yachts, aeroplanes and caravans. These assets include durable consumer goods which waste away over their lifetime and whose residual value is negligible so that gains will not normally arise on their ultimate disposal. Plant and machinery is always to be regarded as having a predictable life of less than 50 years and is always a wasting asset. Accordingly, antique plant or machinery, e.g. an antique clock or a vintage car, is deemed for tax purposes to have a predictable life of less than 50 years even though in reality such an asset may be older than 50 years.

The exemption is **not** given, however, where the chattels are business assets used in a trade or profession **and** which qualify for capital allowances. The reason for this is that capital allowances up to the full cost of those assets are given for income tax purposes. If capital allowances were not claimed, then the exemption will still not operate if the allowances **could** have been claimed.

No loss claim is available in respect of assets qualifying for capital allowances. If the asset is sold for less than its cost, its capital allowances (including a balancing allowance where necessary) could be claimed and double relief cannot be given.

Treatment of Wasting Chattels which have Qualified for Capital Allowances
As outlined above, the exemption from CGT on gains realised from the disposal of wasting chattels does not apply to the extent that the chattels have qualified for capital allowances.

If the entire asset has qualified for capital allowances and the allowances have not been restricted due to private usage, then any loss arising on disposal of the asset will not be allowable for CGT purposes as it will have been effectively relieved for income tax or corporation tax purposes.

Example 1

	€
Business equipment cost	10,000
Tax WDV at date of sale	2,000
Sale proceeds	4,500

Computation

Sale proceeds	4,500
Cost	(10,000)
"Loss"	(5,500)
Loss allowed for CGT purposes	Nil

The "loss" of €5,500 has been fully relieved for income tax purposes as follows:

	€
Original cost	10,000
Less: tax WDV at date of sale	(2,000)
Capital allowances granted during period of ownership	8,000 (A)
Sale proceeds	4,500
Less: tax WDV at date of sale	(2,000)
Balancing charge on disposal	2,500 (B)

Capital allowances granted A − B = €5,500

If a wasting asset is sold and the asset has qualified without restriction for capital allowances purposes, then any gain arising after indexation relief has been taken into account is fully chargeable to CGT.

Example 2

	€
Business equipment cost	1,000
Tax WDV at date of sale	Nil
Sale proceeds	4,500

Asset owned by single individual for four years.
Assume indexation factor to be applied is 1.8 and that the annual exemption applies.

Computation

	€
Sale proceeds	4,500
Cost €1,000 indexed at 1.8	(1,800)
Gain	2,700
Less: exemption	(1,270)
Chargeable gain	1,430 @ 30% = €429

Note: The total capital allowances granted during the period of ownership will be recaptured on sale by means of a balancing charge.

4.5.4 Disposal of a Site to a Child

There is a CGT exemption under section 603A TCA 1997, where a parent or the civil partner of a parent **disposes of a site to a child** (or certain foster children) of the parent on or after 6 December 2000 for the purpose of enabling the child to **construct a dwelling** house on the land which is to be occupied by the child **as his or her only or main residence**. Such a disposal is **exempt** from CGT provided the market value of the site at the date of the disposal does not exceed €500,000 (the limit was previously €254,000 but this was increased to €500,000 in respect of disposals made on or after 5 December 2007). The site area is limited to one acre (0.4047 hectare) (excluding the area of the house to be built) for disposals on or after 1 February 2007.

Where the child subsequently disposes of a site which qualified for exemption as outlined above to any person other than a spouse or civil partner and the land does not contain a dwelling house which:

1. was constructed by the child since the time of the acquisition of the land; **and**
2. has been occupied by the child as his or her only or main residence for a period of three years,

the chargeable gain which would have accrued to the parent is treated as accruing to the child.

Where the transfer of a site to a child has qualified for exemption, a further transfer of a site to that child will not qualify for exemption unless the chargeable gain which would have accrued on the transfer of the first site to the child is treated as accruing to the child.

4.5.5 Disposals of Works of Art Loaned for Public Display

Gains on disposals of fine art objects with a market value of at least €31,740 which were on loan and displayed in an approved gallery or museum for not less than 10 years (for items first loaned on or after 2 February 2006; prior to this date the period was six years) are exempt from CGT.

4.5.6 Miscellaneous Property

The law provides that certain gains are **exempt** from CGT. The *main* exempt gains are:

1. Bonuses payable under Post Office instalment savings schemes.
2. Winnings from betting, lotteries, sweepstakes or games with prizes.
3. Sums obtained as compensation or damages for any wrong or injury suffered by an individual in his person or in his profession or in his vocation. This exemption extends to damages for personal or professional wrong, or injuries such as libel and slander.

4.6 Principal Private Residence (PPR) Exemption

4.6.1 Introduction

The general rule is that gains accruing on the disposal of the main residence of an individual are exempt from CGT. Grounds up to one acre (0.4047 hectares) (exclusive of the site of the house) around the house are exempt. If there is more than one acre of land, then the acre to be taken is that which would be most suitable for occupation and enjoyment with the residence.

Only one house per person qualifies for exemption, and spouses or civil partners count as one person for this purpose. A person with two or more residences will nominate which one will qualify for relief by giving notice to the Inspector of Taxes within two years of the beginning of the period of ownership of the two or more residences. Unless such notice is given, the Inspector may decide the matter, subject to the taxpayer's rights of appeal within 21 days to the Appeal Commissioners.

There is full exemption only where the owner has occupied the house throughout his period of ownership. Where occupation has been only for part of the period of ownership the exempt part of the gain is the proportion given by the formula:

$$\frac{\text{Period of occupation post 6 April 1974} \times \text{chargeable gain}}{\text{Total period of ownership post 6 April 1974}}$$

Any period before 6 April 1974 is ignored. The period of occupation is deemed to include certain periods of absence provided:

1. that the individual has **no other exempt residence** at the time; and
2. the period of absence was both preceded by, and followed by, a period of occupation.

It is not necessary for the periods of occupation to immediately precede and follow the periods of absence. It is enough that there was occupation at some time before and after absence. The periods of absence which are deemed to be periods of occupation subject to the above condition are:

1. **any periods** in which the owner was required by his employment to **work wholly outside Ireland**; and
2. any period **not exceeding four years,** or any periods which together do not exceed four years, throughout which, because of the individual's place of work or a condition of employment, the individual had to reside away from his/her home, most likely elsewhere in Ireland and, therefore, he could not occupy his private residence. Where such periods exceed four years, only four years are deemed to be periods of occupation.

There is also a general rule whereby **the last 12 months of ownership are included in the period of occupation** as long as the owner was in occupation at some time during the period of ownership.

In addition to the deemed periods of occupation set out in the legislation, by concession Revenue also provide for two further periods of deemed occupation as follows:

1. Any period of absence during which:
    (a) the individual (who normally lives alone) was receiving care in a hospital, nursing home, or convalescent home, or was resident in a retirement home on a fee-paying basis, and
    (b) the private residence remained unoccupied (or only occupied by a relative rent-free for the purpose of security or maintaining the house in a habitable condition), should be treated as a period of occupation.
2. Where an individual has a house constructed on land they already own, provided the house is completed within a year of the acquisition of the land and occupied as the individual's PPR by the individual, the period from the date the land was acquired and the house was first occupied shall be treated as a period of occupation of the house as a main residence.

If part of the house is used for the purpose of a trade or profession, the gain may be apportioned, and the part used for the trade is not exempt.

It should be noted in the case where full exemption is not available then partial relief will apply to reduce the liability of any chargeable gain arising.

Example
Owen Gough bought a freehold house for €6,000 on 1 April 1985. He lived in it until 30 September 1995 when he moved into a rented flat. He let the house until he sold it on 1 October 2012 for €220,000.

In the period 30 September 1995 to October 2012, there is one year's deemed occupation, i.e. the last 12 months of ownership.

Therefore, the CGT liability is:	€
Proceeds	220,000
Cost €6,000 indexed at 1.819	(10,914)
Chargeable gain	209,086
Less: exempt portion:	
$\dfrac{10.5 \text{ years} + 1 \text{ year}}{27.5 \text{ years}} \times €209{,}086$	(87,436)
Chargeable gain	121,650
Chargeable @ 30%	36,495

It is assumed that the annual exemption has been utilised against other gains.

If, alternatively, there is a loss, then the loss on the PPR is not allowable. However, if there would only be a partial exemption if the house were sold at a gain, e.g. the house had only been a PPR for part of the period of ownership, then a similar part of the loss is disallowed, but the balance is allowable.

Example
Una bought a house for €250,000 on 1 May 2004. She lived in it until 1 May 2006 when she let it. On 1 May 2012 she sold the house.

If she sold it for €300,000, her capital gain would be:

	€
Proceeds	300,000
Cost	(250,000)
Gain	50,000
Exempt portion	
$\dfrac{2 \text{ years} + 1 \text{ year}}{8 \text{ years}} \times €50{,}000$, i.e. 3/8 × €50,000	(18,750)
Chargeable gain	31,250

This would be added to any other gains, and her CGT for 2012 would be calculated, net of any capital losses and annual exemption.

If she sold it for €210,000, she would have a loss of €40,000.

As it was her PPR for part of the time she owned it, the fraction of the loss which is not allowed is the same fraction of any gain which would be taxed, i.e. 3/8ths of the loss (€15,000) is not allowed. The balance (€25,000) is an allowable loss.

4.6.2 House Occupied by Dependent Relative

The legislation extends the PPR exemption to a gain arising on the disposal of a private residence owned by an individual and occupied by a dependent relative as his/her PPR.

To qualify for the relief, the following conditions must be satisfied:

1. The house must have been provided to the dependent relative free of any charge of whatsoever nature.
2. For complete exemption, the house must have been occupied by the dependent relative as his sole private residence throughout the full period of ownership.
3. The house must be occupied by a dependent relative of the individual claiming the relief.

A 'dependent relative', in relation to an individual, means

a) a relative of the individual, or of the wife or husband of the individual, who is incapacitated by old age or infirmity from maintaining himself or herself, or
b) a person, whether or not he or she is so incapacitated, and—
   (i) who is the widowed father or widowed mother of the individual or of the wife or husband of the individual, or
   (ii) who is the father or mother of the individual or of the wife or husband of the individual and is a surviving civil partner who has not subsequently married or entered into another civil partnership.

Relief is also given where the residence is occupied by a dependent relative of a civil partner of the individual claiming the relief, provided that all the other conditions are satisfied.

For any particular individual only one house can qualify for the relief at a particular time. However, in the case of married couples or civil partners, relief can be claimed by each spouse or civil partner in respect of a disposal of a PPR owned by the spouse or civil partner and occupied in accordance with the conditions of the relief by a dependent relative **of that spouse or civil partner**.

Relief is also available on the disposal of a house by the trustee of a trust where the house was settled property and it was occupied by a beneficiary of the trust under the term of the trust deed.

4.6.3 Restriction of PPR Exemption

The exemption available from CGT on the disposal of one's PPR is restricted to the extent that the gain is derived from the development value of the property. Only the portion of any gain arising which refers to the **increase in the current use value of the residential property is exempted from tax**, the balance of the gain arising is effectively treated as a gain on disposal of development land. However, the provisions do not apply if the sale proceeds do not exceed €19,050.

Example

A private individual sells their residence with grounds on 1 June 2012 for €350,000. The individual owned the residence since June 1997 when it cost €20,000. The sale proceeds of €350,000 are deemed to be split as to €200,000 current use value and €150,000 "hope value". The June 1997 cost of €20,000 is to be split as to €12,000 current use value and €8,000 "hope value".

The gain in terms of current use value of €188,000 is exempt as it relates to the PPR. The gain in terms of "hope value" of €142,000 is fully taxable as no indexation relief is available. If there are incidental costs of acquisition or disposal, they are to be apportioned between the current use value element and the "hope value" element.

4.6.4 House used Partly for Trade

PPR relief is available on the portion of the house which is used as a residence.

Calculate PPR:

$$\frac{\text{Period of occupation}}{\text{Period of ownership}} \times \text{Gain} \times \% \text{ which is used as residence}$$

Example

Gerry Skelly purchased a house on 1 July 1973 for €10,000 exclusive of €1,000 costs. From 1 July 1973 to 1 February 1988 Skelly occupied approximately 75% of the house as his PPR. The remaining portion of the house was used solely for his veterinary surgeon's practice.

Skelly took rented accommodation for both his private residence and veterinary practice with effect from 1 February 1988. On 30 June 2012 Skelly sold the house for €350,000 (gross). Costs amounted to €15,000.

Skelly is married. The market value of the house at 6 April 1974 was €15,000.

Compute Skelly's liability to CGT for the tax year 2012

Computation of CGT for 2012

	€	€
Sale proceeds	350,000	
Less: costs of sale	(15,000)	335,000
Allowable cost		
Market value @ 6/4/74	15,000	
Indexed @ 7.528		(112,920)
Total gain		222,080
As 75% of the house was occupied by Skelly as his PPR, this portion of the gain is subject to the PPR exemption		
222,080*75% *178mths/459mths		(64,592)
Chargeable gain		157,488
Deduct: annual exemption		(1,270)
		156,218
CGT payable @ 30%		46,865

Note:

Period of ownership

6/4/74 to 1/2/88	13 years 10 mths occupied	166 mths
1/2/88 to 30/6/11	23 years 5 mths	281 mths
1/7/11 to 30/6/12	1 year deemed occupied	12 mths
Total		459 mths

If, alternatively, Gerry Skelly advised your manager that he occupied the house from 1 July 1973 to
1 February 1992 and you knew from the tax file that he ceased to occupy the house on
1 February 1988, what should you do?

As you know that the information is not correct and your client must have made a mistake, you should advise your manager of the correct date based on the file and the calculation on that basis, so that he can raise it with Gerry Skelly and give him the correct tax computation.

4.7 Relief for Disposals of Certain Property bought 7 December 2011 to 31 December 2013

The Finance Act 2012 introduced the new section 604A TCA 1997. Under this legislation, a portion or all of the gain on the disposal of property (land and buildings) acquired in the European Economic Area (EEA) in the period 7 December 2011 to 31 December 2013 is relieved from CGT if the property is held for seven years. The conditions for the relief to apply are as follows:

1. the land and buildings must be acquired for a consideration equal to their market value (but see **Section 4.7.1** re acquisitions from relatives) in the period commencing on 7 December 2011 and ending on 31 December 2013;
2. the land and buildings must be situated in the EEA, i.e. EU countries (including Ireland), Iceland, Liechtenstein and Norway;
3. any income from the land and buildings must be liable to Irish tax, i.e. income tax or corporation tax;
4. the land and buildings must continue to be owned by that same person for at least seven years; and
5. there must be no tax arrangements in place which give additional tax relief beyond that intended by the section.

If these conditions are satisfied, then a proportion of any gain is not taxable and a proportion of any loss is not allowable. The proportion is the proportion that seven years bears to the period of ownership of the property.

Example 1

Freya, an Irish resident individual, bought a commercial building in Dublin on 15 March 2012 for €500,000. She is liable to Irish tax on the rent she receives from letting the building.

If she sells the building in say 2017 for €800,000, she will be taxable on the gain of €300,000.

If she sells the building on 15 March 2019 for €900,000, she will have a gain of €400,000. She will have owned it for 7 years, so the proportion is 7/7, i.e. she will be exempt from CGT on the gain.

If she sells the building on 15 March 2021 for €1,400,000, she will have a gain of €900,000. She will have owned it for 9 years, so the proportion is 7/9, i.e. she will be exempt from CGT on €700,000 of the gain and taxable on €200,000.

Example 2

Bizz Limited, an Irish resident company, bought a block of apartments in London on 14 June 2012 for €20,000,000. The rent from these apartments is liable to Irish corporation tax.

On 14 December 2019 it sold the apartment block for €19,000,000, generating a loss of €1,000,000.

As the property has been owned for at least 7 years – 7.5 years, 7/7.5 of the loss is not allowable.

The allowable loss is restricted to 0.5/7.5 x €1,000,000 = €66,667.

If Bizz Limited sold the apartments any time before 14 June 2019, the full loss would be allowable as the property would not have been owned for at least 7 years.

4.7.1 Acquisition of Property from a Relative

This relief applies to property acquired in the period commencing on 7 December 2011 and ending on 31 December 2013, if the consideration is equal to market value. However, where the property is acquired from a relative, it can be acquired at under-value, provided that the consideration paid is at least 75% of the market value.

Example

Stuart owns a commercial property in Cork. He acquired it for €800,000 in May 2010. It is still worth €800,000. If Stuart disposes of the property to his son Andrew, irrespective of consideration paid, as outlined in **Section 1.5.6**, it will be deemed to be transferred at market value.

As the property is only worth what he paid for it, Stuart will have no gain and no CGT. Provided that Andrew pays at least €600,000 (75% of €800,000) for the property then this property can qualify for section 604A relief, provided that the conditions are satisfied, including owning it for at least 7 years.

Questions (to Chapter 4)

Review Questions

(See Suggested Solutions at the end of this textbook.)

Question 4.1

Philip Even is married and, during the tax year 2012, he completed the following transactions:

1.   He gave a gift on 1 July 2012 of a painting to his wife. He bought the painting in June 1988 for €8,000 and its current market value is €17,000.
2.   On 1 September 2012 he sold two acres of development land to his son John for €10,000. The land has planning permission for residential development. The market value of the land on 1 September 2012 was €200,000. He originally bought it on 1 June 1982 for €5,000. At that date the current use value of the land was €3,000.
3.   He sold a small farm for €260,000 on 1 June 2012. He originally acquired the farm by gift from his wife on 25 December 1992. The market value of the farm at that date was €50,000. The farm is not development land. His wife originally acquired it for €32,000 on 1 July 1990.
4.   He sold his entire holding of Irish Government National Loan Stock on 1 July 2012 for €8,000. He had originally acquired it for €6,100 on 1 February 2004.
5.   He sold an antique necklace for €1,500 on 7 August 2012. He had bought the necklace nine months earlier for €1,100.
6.   He sold a painting on 8 August 2012 for €900. He had bought the painting in January 2004 for €1,200.
7.   He gifted one of his licensed premises to his mother on 1 August 2012. The market value of the premises at that date was €875,000. He originally bought the premises on 1 January 1983 for €50,000. In June 1989 he extended the original premises at a cost of €60,000. In March 2006 he further extended the premises at a cost of €50,000.
8.   He sold a second piece of development land on 1 October 2012 for €18,000. He had acquired this land four months earlier for €10,000.
9.   On 1 June 2012 he sold an antique vase for €1,800. He had bought the vase for €700 in June 1992.

Philip had agreed unutilised loses forward at 1 January 2012 of:

(i)   Losses unrelated to development land of €6,000.
(ii)   Losses in respect of disposals of development land of €1,500.

Requirement
Compute Philip Even's CGT liability for 2012.

Question 4.2

(a)   Mrs. O'Sullivan sold a large freehold commercial property on 6 October 2012. She had owned it for many years and it had been continuously let to tenants at a commercial rent. The details given to you are:

	€
Disposal proceeds	1,585,000
Legal costs of disposal	12,500
Agent's commission	7,000

The property had been extended on 6 June 1994 at a cost of €162,000. The agreed value at 6 April 1974 was €60,000.

Requirement (a)
Calculate the chargeable gain in respect of the above disposal.

(b)   Mrs. O'Sullivan had 10 acres of development land adjoining a housing estate. She acquired the land in June 1970 for €5,000. She has received an offer for the land of €1.8 million. The market value of the land at April 1974 was €25,000 and its current use value at that date was €12,500.

Requirement (b)
You are required to calculate the CGT payable on the assumption the land is sold for €1.8 million on 31 May 2012. (Ignore the annual exemption).

Question 4.3

Bill O'Rourke bought a substantial residence on one acre in Rathgar, Dublin on 6 April 1986 for €75,000. His incidental costs on purchase were €4,251.

Mr. O'Rourke accepted an offer from a developer and signed a contract for sale on 10 June 2012 for the residence and one acre at a selling price of €1.68 million. Incidental costs of disposal were €18,000. The value of the place as a residence at the date of disposal was €800,000.

Throughout the period of ownership, Mr. O'Rourke had used the property as his PPR.

Requirement
You are required to compute the chargeable gain in respect of his disposal.

Question 4.4

On 1 January 2012, Mr. Smart, a single man, sold a shop premises which he had owned as an investment. The sale price was €695,000 and costs of disposal amounted to €7,000. He had never occupied the premises himself and had never carried on a trade in the property.

He purchased the premises in 1973. The property was professionally valued as at 6 April 1974, when it was valued at €10,000. Enhancement expenditure of €12,000 was incurred on 6 December 1991.

On 1 October 2012, Mr. Smart reinvested €580,000 in an investment property let in four units.

On 1 June 2012, Mr. Smart sold a holiday cottage to his nephew for €16,000. Mr. Smart had purchased the cottage on 6 July 1987 for €25,000. The market value of the cottage on 1 June 2012 was €20,000.

Requirement

You are required to advise Mr. Smart of his CGT liability, if any, for the tax year 2012, giving reasons for your conclusions.

Question 4.5

Christine Martin, a single woman, entered into the following transactions during 2012.

1. On 1 August 2012, Christine disposed of a derelict shop for €224,000. The derelict shop was adjacent to a shopping centre which wished to expand. The current use value of the property at the date of disposal was €80,000. Auctioneer's fees amounted to €3,100. Christine had purchased the property in March 1992 for €63,000, its then current use value, and it has been vacant since then. Christine used €40,000 of the sale proceeds to repay the outstanding mortgage on the property.

2. On 20 October 2012, Christine sold 2,000 shares in MAX plc for €4.50 each. She had acquired 1,500 shares in March 1995 for €6,800. In July 1997, MAX plc had a rights issue of 1 for 5 at €3.50 which Christine took up. In January 1998, MAX plc had a 1 for 2 bonus issue of shares immediately after which the shares were valued at €2.50 each.

3. On 5 May 2012, Christine disposed of a painting for €2,600. She had inherited the painting on the death of her mother on 20 December 2003, at which date it had a value of €1,900. The painting was a family heirloom which was considered to have a value of €100 on 6 April 1974.

Requirement

Compute the CGT payable by Christine Martin for 2012.

Transfer of a Business to a Company

Learning Objectives

After studying this chapter, you will have developed competency in the following:

- The transfer of capital assets by a sole trader into a company owned by the individual is a disposal and, therefore, a CGT liability may arise on, for example, goodwill, buildings, and machinery.
- CGT on these gains may be deferred to the extent that the value of the assets transferred is taken in shares. If any value is taken in cash or cash equivalents (e.g. liabilities taken over, director's loan account) then that proportion of the gain is taxable currently, i.e.:

$$\frac{\text{Cash/cash equivalents}}{\text{Total value of assets}} \times \text{gains} = \text{currently taxable}$$

- The balance of the gain is deferred, i.e. it is deducted from the base cost of the shares.

5.1 Sole Trader transfers Trade to Company

Where a sole trader carries on a trade, he/she owns all the assets of the trade including the capital assets. If the capital assets are disposed of, the individual sole trader has to calculate a gain or loss on the disposal and pay any CGT due. If the individual sole trader decides to incorporate the business, i.e. transfer the trade, including some or all of its assets and liabilities to a company, then the individual will typically have a disposal of capital assets (e.g. goodwill, building, machinery, etc.) to the company and therefore will have to consider the CGT implications and any reliefs – see **Section 5.2** below. When transferring the assets, it is critical to remember that this a disposal between connected parties and therefore all assets must transfer at market value. Therefore all assets transferred, including goodwill, must be at market value. This chapter deals with the taxation of these gains and the relief that is available, provided the conditions are satisfied.

When the assets are transferred to the company, they now belong to the company. If the capital assets are subsequently sold by the company, it is liable to corporation tax (capital gains tax in the case of development land) on any gain that it makes when you compare the market value at the date of transfer compared to the consideration on disposal by the company. **Chapter 26** deals with companies and capital gains.

5.2 Relief Available

As an individual and a limited company are separate legal entities, the transfer of business assets to a company by an individual will be a chargeable event for CGT purposes. For example, the disposal of capital assets such as goodwill, buildings, machinery by the individual to the company triggers a CGT liability for the individual. However, under section 600 TCA 1997, CGT on the disposal of business assets to a company may be deferred, provided the business and all its assets (or all its assets other than cash) are transferred in consideration for the issue of shares in the company. To avail of this relief, the business must be transferred as a going concern to the company. The deferral continues until the shares are disposed of by the individual who transferred the assets to the company.

Please note that, similar to many CGT reliefs, the relief will not apply unless it is shown that the transfer has been effected for bona fide commercial reasons and does not form part of any arrangement or scheme of which the main purpose or one of the main purposes is avoidance of liability to tax.

The net gain on the transfer of the chargeable assets to the company is calculated in the usual way, and the proportion appropriate to any cash or deemed cash consideration is assessed immediately. The balance of the total net gain, i.e. the deferred gain, is apportioned rateably over the shares received thereby reducing the base cost of the shares for the purposes of any subsequent disposal. The allowable cost of future disposals of the shares for the purposes of indexation is the original cost of the shares (at the time they are first issued) less the amount of the deferred gain.

If any liabilities of the trade such as trade creditors are taken over by the company, then this is treated as a cash payment to the former proprietor and the deferred gain is reduced accordingly. Similar treatment applies if part of the consideration is satisfied by the creation in the company of a loan account in favour of the individual. (**Note:** There is a Revenue concession such that, where an individual transfers a business to a company, in exchange for shares only, and assets exceed liabilities, bona fide trade creditors taken over will not be treated as consideration. See **Example 2** below.)

When the normal gain arising on the transfer of the chargeable assets to the company has been calculated the amount to be deferred is calculated by applying the formula:

$$\frac{\text{Consideration in form of shares}}{\text{Total value of assets taken over}} \times \text{Chargeable gain (after indexation relief)}$$

If more than one class of shares is issued, the deferred gain is deducted from the cost of the shares on the basis of the relative market values of each class of shares at the time of acquisition.

5.3   Limitations on the Relief

1. The fact that liabilities of the trade taken over by the company are treated as cash consideration for the purposes of calculating the deferral relief seriously reduces the benefit to be gained from claiming the relief.
2. Capital gains that arise in a company in effect suffer CGT twice, once in the company on disposal of the asset by the company, and again on the shareholder on disposal (by sale or liquidation) of the shares. Thus appreciating assets such as land and buildings are open to an effective double charge to CGT if placed in a company.
3. The relief is not available unless all the assets of the trade including land and buildings are transferred to the company. An exception for cash was noted above.
4. The deferred gain reduces the base cost of the shares in the event of a subsequent disposal. However, if it is the individual's intention to benefit from retirement relief (see **Chapter 6**) or to never sell the shares, then this is not a concern.

The following example will illustrate how the relief is calculated.

(**Note:** The greatest problem many students have with this topic is an accounting/shares issue and not a tax issue, i.e. how to value the shares. Once you remember that the value of the shares is the difference between the market value of the assets and the amount received in cash and deemed cash (e.g. liabilities taken over), then the computation is significantly easier.)

Example 1

Mr. X transferred his business with all its assets, other than cash, to a company on 30 November 2012. In consideration for the transfer, the company, X Ltd, issued 10,000 ordinary shares at par fully paid and paid Mr. X €600,000 in cash.

At the date of transfer the balance sheet of the business was as follows:

		€
Assets	Goodwill at cost	29,000
	Trading stock	250,000
	Buildings	250,000
	Cash	50,000
		579,000
Liabilities	Trade creditors	100,000
	Capital account	479,000
		579,000

continued overleaf

At the date of transfer the market value of the assets was as follows:

	€
Goodwill	250,000
Trading stock	300,000
Buildings	1,300,000
	1,850,000
Trade creditors	(100,000)
Net value of assets transferred	1,750,000

The market value of the assets was €1,850,000. The cash (€600,000) and deemed cash (Creditors €100,000) totalled €700,000. Therefore, the shares are worth €1,150,000.

The cost of the chargeable assets at acquisition on 5 December 1999 were as follows:

	€
Goodwill	29,000
Buildings	250,000

The chargeable gains are computed as follows:

	Dec 1999	Index	Adjusted Base Cost	Current M.V.	Chargeable Gain
Trading stock	€		€	€	€
(not chargeable – gain liable to income tax)					
Goodwill	29,000	1.193	34,597	250,000	215,403
Buildings	250,000	1.193	298,250	1,300,000	1,001,750
					1,217,153

Deferred Gain:

$$\frac{\text{Value of shares issued}}{\text{Total consideration}} \times €1,217,153$$

$$\frac{€1,150,000}{€1,850,000} \times €1,217,153 = €756,609 \text{ deferred gain}$$

Chargeable gain		€
€1,217,153 – €756,609	=	460,544
Less exemption	=	(1,270)
		459,274 @ 30% = €137,782

Allowable Cost of Shares for Future Disposal:

Cost of shares	1,150,000
Less: Deferred gains	(756,609)
Cost for subsequent disposals of the shares issued to Mr. X	393,391

Example 2

Ms. Y transferred her business with all its assets (other than cash) and liabilities to a company on 30 June 2012. In consideration for the transfer, the company, Y Ltd, issued 10,000 ordinary shares at par fully paid.

At the date of transfer the balance sheet of the business was as follows:

		€
Assets	Trading stock	250,000
	Buildings (at cost)	250,000
	Cash	50,000
		550,000
Liabilities	Trade creditors	100,000
	Capital account	450,000
		550,000

At the date of transfer the market value of the assets was as follows:

	€
Goodwill (Note 1)	250,000
Trading stock	300,000
Buildings (Note 1)	1,300,000
Total value of assets transferred	1,850,000
Trade creditors	(100,000)
Net value of assets transferred	1,750,000

Note 1

The business was set up in June 1990. The building was bought at that time. The goodwill has no base cost as it was not acquired.

The chargeable gains are computed as follows:

Chargeable Gains

	Cost June 1990	Index	Indexed Cost	M.V.	Gain
	€		€	€	€
Trading stock (not chargeable – gainliable to income tax)					
Goodwill	Nil			250,000	250,000
Buildings	250,000	1.442	360,500	1,300,000	939,500
					1,189,500

Under the Revenue concession, where an individual transfers a business to a company, in exchange for **shares only,** and assets exceed liabilities, **bona fide trade creditors taken over will not be treated as consideration**. As this transfer satisfies these conditions, all of the gain may be deferred.

Allowable Cost of Shares for Future Disposal:	€
Cost of shares	1,750,000
Less: deferred gains	(1,189,500)
Cost for subsequent disposals of the shares issued to Ms Y	560,500

Example 3
Bill transferred all his business assets and liabilities to FCS Ltd in exchange for 15,000 ordinary shares of €1 each in FCS Ltd and €25,000 cash on 31 March 1999

Bill's balance sheet at 31 March 1999 read as follows:

		Cost	Market Value @ 6 April 1974
	€	€	€
Premises (at cost – 19 August 1970)		10,000	18,000
Goodwill		15,000	8,000
Debtors		13,000	N/A
Stock		12,000	N/A
Cash		4,000	
		54,000	

Less:	Creditors	5,000	
	Tax due	1,000	(6,000)
			48,000

Market values at 31 March 1999 were agreed as follows:

	€
Premises	200,000
Goodwill	100,000
Debtors	13,000
Stock	18,000
	331,000

FCS Ltd had agreed to pay creditors €5,000 and taxation €1,000 on behalf of Bill.

On 31 July 2012, Bill sold the 15,000 ordinary shares in FCD Ltd to FCD for €300,000.

Requirement Calculate the chargeable gains arising from these transactions in 2012.

Solution
Disposal 31 March 1999 (Disposal of Business):

	€	€
Value of assets transferred at 31 March 1999:		331,000
Taken in cash	25,000	
Debts paid by FCS Ltd.	6,000	31,000
Value of shares (balance)		300,000
Proportion of consideration taken in Shares:	300	
	331	
Premises: 6/4/74 value: €18,000 × 6.215 =	111,870	
Proceeds	200,000	
Gain		88,130
Goodwill: 6/4/74 value: €8,000 × 6.215 =	49,720	
Proceeds	100,000	
Gain		50,280
Debtors		
Stock	No chargeable gain	
Cash		
Total gain		138,410

continued overleaf

Bill would have claimed relief to the extent that the sale proceeds were taken by way of shares in the company. In effect this relief consisted of a deferral of the CGT payable on the amount of the consideration taken in the form of shares in the company.

Chargeable part of gain: $\dfrac{31}{331} \times €138,410 = €12,963$

This gain was taxed in the normal way at the appropriate rate.

Gain deferred €138,410 − €12,963 = €125,447

	€
Cost of shares	300,000
Less: deferred gain	(125,447)
Net cost	174,553

Disposal 31 July 2012 (shares)

	€
Sale proceeds:	300,000
Cost €174,553 × 1.212	(211,558)
Chargeable gain:	88,442

Example 4

Mr Harris carried on a wholesale distribution business from 8 May 1990 to 5 May 2012.

With effect from 6 May 2012, Mr Harris agreed to merge his business with a similar one carried on by Mr. Hoyle. A new company H&H Ltd will take over their businesses as going concerns.

Proceeds for disposal of Mr Harris's assets will be as follows:

(1) Goodwill valued at €60,000 is to be satisfied by issue of 50,000 €1 ordinary shares in H&H Ltd valued at €50,000 and €10,000 cash. The market value of goodwill at 8 May 1990 acquired on set up of business was €5,000.

(2) Debtors and stock as per the balance sheet at 5 May 2012 are €8,000 and €10,000 respectively. Stock per balance sheet was valued at historical cost. Having regard to current cost prices, it was agreed that stock would be taken over at a value of €12,000. Mr Harris agreed to take 10,000 ordinary shares and €10,000 cash for these two items. There were no other business assets.

Requirement Calculate the CGT liability for 2012 on the basis that this was his only disposal for that year and indicate the cost of shares in H&H Ltd for CGT purposes.

Solution

	€	€
Consideration – goodwill		60,000
Market value May 1990 – 5,000 × 1.442		(7,210)
Gain		52,790
Value of assets transferred (60,000 + 8,000 + 12,000)	80,000	
Amount taken other than in shares (i.e. cash)	(20,000)	
Amount taken in shares	60,000	

continued overleaf

Gain chargeable in 2012

$\frac{20}{80} \times €52,790 =$ 13,198

Less: annual exemption   (1,270)
                                                                  11,928
                                              CGT @ 30% =   3,578
Cost of shares   60,000
Less: deferred gains (€52,790 – €13,198)   (39,592)
Cost for CGT purposes   20,408

Questions (to Chapter 5)

Review Questions

(See Suggested Solutions to Review Questions at the end of the textbook)

Question 5.1

Jack O'Dowd has run a successful retail business for a number of years. To facilitate expansion of the business and to access the lower corporation tax rate, he decided to form a limited company, O'Dowd Ltd. The business (i.e. all assets and liabilities) was transferred to O'Dowd Ltd on 30 June 2012 in exchange for 200,000 €1 ordinary shares and cash of €50,000. The cash was left outstanding on a loan account.

The balance sheet of the business immediately prior to the transfer was as follows:

	Notes	€	€
Warehouse at cost	(1)	120,000	
Depreciation to date		(12,000)	108,000
Plant and machinery at cost		46,000	
Depreciation to date		(14,000)	32,000
Debtors		117,000	
Stock		48,000	
Creditors		(55,000)	
Net current assets			110,000
			250,000
Jack O'Dowd's capital account			250,000

Notes:
(1) The warehouse was purchased on commencement of the business in May 1981.
(2) Market values as at 30 June 2012 were as follows:

	Notes	€
Warehouse		400,000
Plant and machinery	(2a)	40,000
Goodwill	(2b)	130,000
Net current assets		110,000

(2a) The market value of no individual item exceeded its original cost.

(2b) The value of goodwill was built up over the years by Jack.

Jack sold an antique vase on 5 December 2012 for €88,000. The vase had cost €7,000 in 1972 and had a market value on 6 April 1974 of €10,000. He sold shares in ABC plc for €5,000 on 7 December 2012 which cost him €10,000 on 9 July 1998. Jack, who is single, has no other disposals in the year ended 31 December 2012. He had a capital loss forward of €10,000.

Requirement
(a)   Calculate the CGT liability of Jack O'Dowd for the tax year 2012.
(b)   State when this CGT liability is payable by Jack O'Dowd.
(c)   Calculate the base cost of the shares in O'Dowd Ltd for CGT purposes.

Retirement Relief

6

Learning Objectives

After studying this chapter, you will have developed competency in determining and applying retirement relief rules to disposals of shares and other business assets. You will know that:

- The individual must be at least 55 years of age to qualify for the relief, but does not have to retire from participating in the business.
- Retirement relief is a very important relief, particularly where **a parent wants to transfer the business to a child during the parent's lifetime**. (If the individual leaves the business on a death, there is no CGT).
- The relief covers two situations, namely disposals
  - **to a "child"** – A "child" includes a child of a civil partner, certain foster children, favourite niece/nephew and a child of a deceased child (section 599 TCA 1997).
  - all **other cases** (section 598 TCA 1997).

"Child" – Section 599 Relief

- Disposals of trade assets to a 'child' may be fully **relieved from tax** provided that the relevant sole trader business, share of partnership, share in family company or qualifying asset owned by the individual and used by the company has been owned for at least **10 years**, ending on the date of the disposal.
- The sole trader/partnership situation (or qualifying asset owned by the individual and used by the company) is very simple as it is the **gains on capital trade assets or the asset used by the company, which are relieved**.
- In the case of disposals of **shares**, there are three additional issues to bear in mind, namely:
  - the **individual disposing** of the shares must have been a **working director for 10 years**, during which 10-year period he must have been a **"full-time" working director for at least five years,**

- the company must have been **a family company**, i.e. minimum shareholding requirements, **for at least 10 years** ending with the date of the disposal; and
- the **value of the shares** is assumed to derive only from the chargeable capital assets of the company. Therefore if there are any **non-qualifying capital assets** (e.g. investment assets), only a **proportion of the gain is relieved**.

- If the shareholder owns **land and buildings**, plant or machinery for at least **10 years**, which is **used** throughout by the **company** and this is disposed of at the **same time** and to the **same person** as the shares, then full retirement relief applies.
- As the relief is to facilitate the passing on of businesses between generations, **the "child" must not dispose of the trade/shares/assets for six years**. If the "child" does, there is a full clawback of the relief, i.e. the gain not taxed on the "parent" is taxed on the "child".

All Other Cases – Section 598 Relief

- In this case, relief from CGT is only given to the extent that the proceeds from the sale of qualifying assets do not exceed **€750,000**. If proceeds exceed €750,000, marginal relief may be available.
- As before, the sole trader business, share of partnership, shares in the family company or qualifying asset leased to the company must have been held for **10 years**.
- Because the relief arises in respect of a disposal outside the close family, **there is no question of a clawback** if the purchaser subsequently sells the trade/shares.

Sole trader

- The relief only applies if proceeds for chargeable business assets are €750,000 or less. In the sole trader or partnership situation, you just need to check the proceeds on disposal of capital trade assets – typically goodwill, land, buildings and plant and machinery. If proceeds are less than €750,000, all the gains on those assets are relieved. Gains on non-qualifying assets – typically investments – are fully liable.
- If **proceeds exceed €750,000**, then there is **marginal relief** that limits the amount of tax on qualifying assets to half the excess of the proceeds over €750,000. **Again gains on non-qualifying assets are fully liable**.
- If marginal relief does not apply, then all gains are fully taxable.

Shares

- Where a *company* is involved, the situation is somewhat more complicated. As for disposals to "children", the individual disposing of the shares must have been a **working director for 10 years**, during which 10-year period he must have been a **"full-time" working director for at least five years**, and it must be a family company
- Regarding the valuation of shares, there is the need to firstly **establish what amount of the proceeds on sale of shares relates to trading capital assets only**, out of total capital assets liable to CGT. If this amount is less than €750,000, **then the same proportion of the gain is relieved**. As for a child, the proportion of the proceeds and the gain is determined by looking only at the chargeable capital assets of the company.

- If the proceeds related to qualifying assets are in excess of €750,000, then marginal relief may apply, i.e. **to limit tax on qualifying assets to half the excess proceeds**. Gains attributable to non-qualifying assets are fully taxable.
- **If marginal relief does not apply, the gain on disposal of the shares is fully taxable**.
- If the shareholder owns **land and buildings**, plant or machinery for at least **10 years** which is used by the **company** and this is disposed of at the **same time** and to the **same person** as the **shares**, then full retirement relief applies provided the market value of the shares and assets disposed of is not in excess of €750,000. Marginal relief may apply.

Other Issues

- The **annual exemption is not available** in a tax year that retirement relief is claimed.
- In determining whether the 10-year tests have been satisfied in relation to period of ownership of an asset or period of directorship, there are special rules that allow a spouse or civil partner to benefit from the other spouse's or civil partner's ownership in certain situations. Similarly **where a business is transferred to a company** (and the relief from CGT provided for in section 600 TCA 1997 is claimed – see **Chapter 5**), **the period as sole trader can be taken into account.**
- The rules for individuals aged 66 or more are changing from 1 Janauary 2014.

6.1 Introduction

Certain gains arising on the disposal of "qualifying assets" by an *individual* who has attained the age of *55 years* may be exempt from CGT if certain conditions are satisfied.

There is no requirement that the individual in question actually retires. The amount of relief that will be available depends upon whether the assets are disposed of to the taxpayer's children as defined or, alternatively, to third parties.

If retirement relief is claimed, the annual exemption of €1,270 is not due for other disposals in the year of assessment.

The relief will not apply where the sole or main purpose of the disposal of qualifying assets is the avoidance of tax and not for genuine commercial reasons.

6.2 Assets Qualifying for Relief

Relief is available in respect of disposals of **qualifying assets**. The main qualifying assets are as follows:

1. **Chargeable business assets** of the individual which had been owned by him for at least 10 years ending with the date of disposal and which have been his chargeable business assets throughout this 10-year period.

Chargeable business assets are **assets used for the purposes of a trade, profession, farming or employment carried on by the individual, or by the individual's family company**.

While stocks (inventories) and debtors (receivables) are assets used for the purposes of the trade, any gain on disposal of these assets is not subject to CGT. Therefore, these will not be chargeable assets for this purpose.

There are two requirements in the above definition:

- first, the assets in question must have been owned for 10 years; and
- secondly, the assets must have been actually used for the trade, profession, etc. for the 10-year period.

The requirement for **10-year ownership does not apply to assets which are tangible, moveable property**, e.g. moveable plant and equipment. The definition of **chargeable business assets** does not include assets which are not employed for the purposes of a trade, e.g. assets held as investments, such as shareholdings or rented property, **but does include goodwill**.

2. **Shares owned by the individual for at least 10 years, ending on the date of the disposal, in a trading or farming company which is the individual's family company** (see definition in (i) below). The individual must have been a **working director of the company for at least 10 years**, during which period he has been a **full-time working director for at least five years**. In addition the company must have been the individual's **"family" company for at least a 10-year period** ending with the date of the disposal.

Note: *the 10-year period for which the individual must have been a working director of the company does not have to be the 10-year period ending with the date of the disposal.*

3. Shares owned by the individual for at least 10 years, ending on the date of the disposal, in a company which is a **member of a trading group the holding company** of which has been the individual's family company for a period of **10 years** ending with the date of the disposal. The individual must have been a **working director of the company for at least 10 years**, during which period he has been a **full-time working director for at least five years**.

A company is a member of a "trading group" if the business of the group taken together consists wholly or mainly of the carrying on of one or more trades or professions.

As the relief applies to the disposal of shares by an individual, it generally covers the sale of shares in a holding company.

4. **Land and buildings, machinery or plant** which the individual has owned for a period of not less than **10 years** ending with the disposal and which:

    - was **used throughout that period** for the purposes of the relevant company (i.e. the family company referred to in 2 and 3 above); and
    - is **disposed of at the same time and to the same person as the shares** in the family company.

This is similar to the rule that applies in CAT business relief, i.e. assets owned personally can qualify for retirement relief provided that they were used for the business of the company and are disposed of at the same time and to the same person as the shares in the company.

The definition of qualifying assets also includes certain farming and fishing payments and assets.

The following points are relevant in relation to the above and subsequent definitions regarding "qualifying assets":

(i) Family Company:

A **family company** is one in which the individual claiming relief controls:

(a) at least 25% of the voting rights; or

(b) at least 10% of the voting rights and at least 75% of the total voting rights (including his own 10%) are controlled by members of his **family** or a member of the family of the individual's civil partner.

A family is defined as meaning the individual's spouse or civil partner, or a brother, sister, ancestor, or lineal descendant of the individual or of his/her spouse or civil partner.

(ii) Full-Time Working Director:

This means a director who is required to devote substantially the whole of his time to the service of the company in a managerial or technical capacity. However, it is only necessary for the individual to have been a full-time working director in the company concerned for five years out of the required 10 years, i.e. the individual must have been a working director for the whole 10 years, and on a full-time basis only for at least five of the 10 years.

(iii) Trading Company:

This is defined as a company whose business consists wholly or mainly in the carrying on of a trade or trades. It also applies to professions.

(iv) Holding Company

This is defined as a company whose business (disregarding any trade carried on by it) consists wholly or mainly of the holding of shares or securities in one or more companies which are 75% subsidiaries.

(v) 75 per cent subsidiary

A company is a 75% subsidiary of another company if not less than 75% of its ordinary share capital is owned directly or indirectly by that other company.

(vi) Trading or Farming Group

This is defined as a group of companies consisting of the holding company and its 75% subsidiaries, the business of whose members consists wholly or mainly of carrying on a trade(s).

In applying the 10-year test, the following points should be noted:

1. The period of ownership of qualifying assets of a spouse or civil partner is taken into account in determining the period of ownership of the individual. Also, where the

spouse or civil partner of an individual has died, the individual takes the period of use of an asset by the deceased spouse or civil partner into account as if it were a period of use of the asset by the individual.

2. Continuity of the period of directorship between a deceased spouse or civil partner and a surviving spouse or civil partner is provided for, i.e. if a spouse or civil partner has been a full-time working director and dies, then the surviving spouse or civil partner is treated as having been a full-time working director for that period. However, there is no such continuity where the spouse or civil partner is alive, i.e. if a spouse or civil partner has shares in a family company, but has not been a full-time working director, then he/she cannot qualify for retirement relief by taking into account the period for which a spouse/civil partner, who is still alive, was a full-time director.

3. Continuity of ownership is available where new business assets replace older business assets so that the period of ownership of the old assets counts when a disposal of the new assets take place, i.e. the period of ownership of both old and new assets are aggregated in determining the qualifying period of 10 years.

4. The period that an individual was a director of a company will be deemed to include the period during which the individual was a director of another company where, under the scheme of reconstruction or amalgamation, shares in that other company were exchanged for shares in the first-mentioned company.

5. As indicated above, it is not necessary to satisfy the 10-year test in the case of "tangible moveable property".

6.3 Disposal of Sole Trader Business

If the sole trader, who is aged 55 or more, only owns chargeable assets which are used for the purposes of the trade and the assets (other than tangible moveable property) have been owned for at least 10 years, then full relief may be available. However, if the proceeds on these chargeable business assets exceed €750,000 and the disposal is to someone other than a child, then either marginal relief or no relief is available.

Example

Anna, aged 56, disposes of her sole trader business for €800,000. The value is derived from the following assets and liabilities:

	€
Premises	600,000
Goodwill	90,000
Equipment	50,000
Debtors	100,000
Stock	70,000
Liabilities	(110,000)
	800,000

Anna set up the business in 2000, when she bought the premises.

As Anna is at least 55, has owned the chargeable business assets (other than equipment) for at least 10 years, the value of the chargeable business assets is not greater than €750,000 (it is €740,000, i.e. €600,000 + €90,000 + €50,000) and the only chargeable assets are chargeable business assets, Anna is exempt from CGT on disposal of the business.

Example

Tom, aged 58, disposes of his sole trader business for €900,000. The value is derived from the following assets and liabilities:

	€
Premises	600,000
Goodwill	90,000
Equipment	50,000
Investment (cost €50,000 in 2004)	80,000
Debtors	100,000
Stock	90,000
Liabilities	(110,000)
	900,000

Tom set up the business in 1999, when he bought the premises.

As Tom is at least 55, has owned the chargeable business assets (other than equipment) for at least 10 years and the value of the chargeable business assets is not greater than €750,000 (it is €740,000, i.e. €600,000 + €90,000 + €50,000), Tom is exempt from CGT on disposal of the trade assets. However the disposal of the investment is liable to CGT. On the basis that this is his only chargeable disposal in 2012, his CGT is:

	€
Proceeds	80,000
Cost	(50,000)
Gain	30,000
CGT @ 30% (no annual exemption)	9,000

6.4   Disposal of Shares

If the assets which are subject to disposal are shares in a family company or a holding company which is a family company, then the following points are relevant:

1. Provided that the transfer of the business from the sole trader/partnership to the company qualified for the **transfer of a business to a company** relief outlined in **Chapter 5**, the period of ownership of qualifying assets is computed by aggregating the period of ownership both prior to and after incorporation of the family company, and the period of ownership of the business prior to incorporation by the individual will qualify as a period throughout which he was a full-time working director of the family company for the purposes of satisfying the qualifying assets test, and

2. Where shares are sold and the company owns assets which are non-chargeable business assets only a portion of the gain qualifies for retirement relief. The amount of the gain which qualifies for relief is the proportion of the gain which the value of the company's **chargeable business assets** bears to the value of the company's **total chargeable assets**, i.e.:

$$\text{Gain on Disposal of Shares} \times \frac{\text{Value of Chargeable Business Assets}}{\text{Value of Total Chargeable Assets}}$$

Where the shares are disposed of to someone other than a "child" (see **Section 6.5**) in determining whether the consideration limit of €750,000 has been exceeded, sale proceeds are apportioned between the value of the company's **chargeable business assets and other chargeable assets which are not chargeable business assets**, i.e.:

$$\text{Proceeds for Sale of Shares} \times \frac{\text{Value of Chargeable Business Assets}}{\text{Value of Total Chargeable Assets}}$$

Chargeable Business Assets includes goodwill, land and buildings used for trade purposes and plant and machinery used for trade purposes. *It excludes stocks and debtors (as they are not capital assets) and assets held as investments (as they are not trade assets).*

Total Chargeable Assets includes chargeable business assets and assets held as investments. *It excludes stocks and debtors.*

Example – Family Trading Company

A limited company's assets had the following market value:

	€
Land and buildings	700,000
Equipment	10,000
Goodwill	30,000
Trading stock	30,000
Trade debtors	40,000
Quoted investments	50,000
	860,000
Deduct: liabilities	(60,000)
	800,000

In this example the sale proceeds to be taken into account for the purposes of the relief would be computed as follows:

$$\text{Sale Proceeds of Shares} \times \frac{\text{Chargeable Business Assets (€700,000 + €10,000 + €30,000) = €740,000}}{\text{Total Chargeable Assets (€700,000 + €10,000 + €30,000 + €50,000)}}$$
$$= €790,000$$

€800,000 × €740,000 / €790,000 = €749,367. As this is not greater than €750,000, the proceeds limit has been satisfied. Accordingly retirement relief may be claimed.

The portion of the gain arising on the sale of the shares which will qualify for retirement relief is the amount of the gain × €740,000/€790,000.

In the case of a holding company, this formula would take into account the asset position of the whole trading group, i.e.:

$$\text{Sales Price of Shares in holding Company} \times \frac{\text{Value of Chargeable Business Assets of Trading Group}}{\text{Value of total Chargeable Assets of Trading Group}}$$
(Excluding shares in other group members)

6.5 Disposal to Person Other than a "Child"

Retirement relief applies where the sale proceeds on the disposal of qualifying assets do not exceed €750,000. The assets may be sold piecemeal over a number of years, but if the aggregate consideration for all the qualifying assets sold since 6 April 1974 exceeds €750,000, then the relief will be withdrawn. (**Note: Qualifying assets** only include assets in respect of the disposal of which retirement relief could have been claimed. Accordingly, disposals of business assets by the individual before he reached age 55 are ignored in determining whether the €750,000 limit has been breached).

Marginal relief applies where the proceeds of disposal are in **excess of €750,000**. In such cases, the CGT payable cannot exceed half the excess of the aggregate proceeds over €750,000.

For the purposes of calculating the €750,000 proceeds threshold, qualifying assets transferred to a spouse or civil partner are included at market value. Thus, while the transfer of an asset to a spouse or civil partner will not give rise to a chargeable disposal for CGT purposes, it does, however, form part of the €750,000 threshold exemption limit and may, therefore, restrict the amount of relief available where a disposal is made to someone other than a "child".

A further important point in relation to the €750,000 threshold is that the proceeds (or market value as applicable) on disposals to qualifying "children" as defined do not affect the €750,000 threshold limit.

If the disposal arises due to the receipt by an individual of a payment made by **a company on the acquisition of its own shares,** which is not treated as a distribution, but as a capital disposal (see **Section 7.3** for conditions to be satisfied), this capital receipt will be treated as coming within the scope of retirement relief and will, therefore, be taken into account for the purpose of the €750,000 threshold.

Example – Disposal of Sole Trader Business
Sam, **a sole trader** aged 60 sold his 30-year old business for €250,000 in October 2012

		Market Value 6 April 1974
	€	€
Freehold	150,000	2,000
Goodwill	19,000	3,000
Investments	20,000	1,000
Debtors	71,000	
Creditors	(10,000)	
	250,000	

Freehold + goodwill: exempt as under €750,000

Investments	20,000
€1,000 × 7.528	(7,528)
	12,472
× 30% = CGT due	3,742

Example – Disposal of Sole Trader Business 2
A newsagent, who qualifies for the €750,000 proceeds exemption relief, gives one of his two shops to his wife (market value €700,000) and sells the other shop to an unconnected third party for €90,000 (allowable indexed cost say €30,000). Both shops were owned for 11 years and disposed of on 1 May 2012

		€
Total aggregate consideration:	M.V. of transfer to wife	700,000
	Sale to third party	90,000
		790,000
Excess of aggregate consideration over €750,000		40,000
Maximum CGT liability (€790,000 − €750,000) × 1/2		20,000
CGT liability on disposal to wife (transfers between husband and wife not chargeable)		Nil

continued overleaf

CGT payable on disposal to third party: €
Sale proceeds   90,000
Less: Indexed cost   (30,000)
Gain   60,000
Less: Annual exemption   (1,270)
Taxable   58,730
CGT at 30%   17,619

As the CGT liability computed in the normal way is well below €20,000 there is no benefit in claiming the €750,000 proceeds exemption relief.

Note: If he had claimed retirement relief, no annual exemption of €1,270 would be due.

Example – Disposal of Shares

Joe is married and aged 65. He bought shares in a family trading company in 1975/76 for €1,000. He has been a full-time working director since then. He sold the shares in October 2012 for €780,000.

		€
	Factory	425,000
	Goodwill	125,000
	Debtors	60,000
	Liabilities	(50,000)
		560,000
Proceeds		780,000
Cost	€1,000 × 6.080	(6,080)
		773,920
	Less exemption	(1,270)
		772,650

Taxed at 30% = €231,795 CGT due in normal manner.

If he were to claim retirement relief, the maximum CGT is: €780,000 − €750,000 = €30,000 × 50%
= €15,000

CGT due. Therefore, he should claim retirement relief.

Example – Family Trading Group Da-Jo Holdings Ltd

David and Joe Sheahan (brothers), both aged at least 55, own a successful Irish trading group. The trade has grown from humble beginnings when Joe and David set it up for almost nothing – assume nil cost. The group is now valued at circa €10 million (on the basis of the trade/goodwill and asset portfolio within the group). The group structure is as follows:

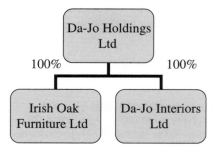

continued overleaf

Da-Jo Holdings Ltd is a 100% parent of both companies in the group. **David owns 90% of Da-Jo Holdings Ltd and Joe owns 10%.** They have owned the company shares for over 20 years. Both men devote all their working time to the group's business and have been directors of Da-Jo Holdings Ltd since the 80s. Joe wishes to sell his 10% holding for €1 million (March 2012).

Compute the retirement relief available if the chargeable business assets of the group are €6.5 million and the chargeable assets of the group which are not chargeable business assets, are €1.5 million.

Assets available in the group

	€
Chargeable business assets of the group	6.5m
Chargeable assets which are not chargeable business assets	1.5m
Non-chargeable assets (net)	2.0m
Market value of the group	10.0m

Retirement relief available to Joe on his 10% holding

€1m × €6.5m/€8m = €812,500

Retirement relief not available on €1m − €812,500 = €187,500

	CBA	Investment Assets
	€	€
Proceeds of disposal	812,500	187,500
Less base cost (assumed)	0	0
Chargeable gain	812,500	187,500
Taxed at 30%	243,750*	56,250*
Marginal relief restricts CGT payable to	31,250	no relief

*Joe's CGT liability in respect of the chargeable business assets is limited to the lower of 50% of the excess consideration above €750,000 and the computed tax liability of €243,750. As 50% of the excess is €31,250 (i.e. €812,500 less €750,000 at 50%), retirement relief will limit the CGT payable on qualifying assets to €31,250. CGT of €56,250 arising in respect of the value attributable to investment assets will be payable as normal. Joe's total CGT liability will therefore be €87,500.

6.6 Disposal to a "Child"

1. This relief applies to chargeable business assets (same assets as qualify for sales outside the family) which are transferred to the person's **"child"**. In addition to natural children, stepchildren and adopted children, the definition of "child" includes:

    ■ A child of the civil partner of the individual.

    ■ **Nieces** or **nephews** who have **worked substantially on a full-time basis for five years** in the business or company also qualify. The reference to nephew/niece does *not* include nephews/nieces of the spouse or civil partner of the individual disposing of the asset.

    ■ A foster child who resided with and was under the care of and maintained at the expense of the individual making the disposal for a period of five years, or periods which together amounted to five years, up to the time that such foster child reached 18 years of age. A claim cannot be based on the uncorroborated testimony of one witness.

    ■ A child of a deceased child of the individual or the civil partner of the individual, a child of the civil partner of a deceased child of the individual and a child of the civil partner of a deceased child of the civil partner of the individual.

2. Provided the necessary conditions are satisfied, no liability arises on the disposal of qualifying assets by an individual to a "child". **No monetary limit** applies to this relief, e.g. disposal may be €10 million to each of say five children.

3. The "child" is deemed to acquire the assets at **market value** at the **date of disposal** for the purpose of any subsequent sale by him/her.

4. If the "child" **disposes of the assets within six years** of the date he acquires the assets, the "child" will have to pay the CGT which would have been payable by the parent/civil partner of parent/uncle/aunt, if the parent/civil partner of parent/uncle/aunt had not qualified for full relief from CGT on a disposal to the "child". **You should check if they could avail of €750,000 retirement relief to a person other than a "child" or marginal relief**. This CGT is payable in addition to the "child" being taxable on any gain that the "child" realises on the disposal.

5. Where a parent or civil partner of parent disposes of farming land to a child and the consideration for the disposal is other land, then no gain will arise on the disposal by the child. The parent or civil partner of parent is deemed to have acquired the land at the same date and for the same consideration that the child originally acquired it and is deemed to have farmed that land for the same period as the child farmed it.

Example 1 – Transfer of Shares to a Child

Andrew, who is aged 60, transferred his 100% shareholding in his wholesale company to his daughter Louise in 2012. The market value of the shares at the date of transfer was €800,000. He had acquired the shares in January 1982 for €1,000. He was a full-time director of the company and the company held no investment assets.

No CGT is due. If Louise disposes of the shares within six years, she will have a liability to CGT on her disposal and also on the original disposal by her father to her.

Example 2 – Transfer of Shares to a Child

Paddy, who is aged 57, is in a civil partnership with Joe. He transferred his 100% shareholding in Paddy Ltd, a trading company, to Joe's daughter Carol in August 2012. The market value of the shares at the date of transfer was €1 million.

The shares were acquired fifteen years ago for €40,000. Assume an indexation factor of 2.5. He was a full-time director of the company throughout the period of ownership.

The market value of the assets of the company at the date of transfer were:

	€
Premises	450,000
Goodwill	350,000
Stocks and debtors	300,000
Investments	150,000
	1,250,000
Creditors	(250,000)
Net value	1,000,000

As Carol is the daughter of Paddy's civil partner Joe, this is a disposal to a "child" and there is no limit on the proceeds.

	€
Computation: deemed proceeds	1,000,000
Cost €40,000 × 2.5	(100,000)
	900,000
Less exempt: €900,000 × $\dfrac{€450,000 + €350,000}{€450,000 + €350,000 + €150,000}$ =	(757,895)
	142,105

Chargeable gain 142,105 × 30% = €42,631 CGT due.

Example – Where there is incomplete information.

Dan Peterson, now aged 64, set up Peterson Ltd on 30 June 1995 and commenced trading as a wholesale distributor. He subscribed for 217,000 €1 ordinary shares at par (cost €217,000).

Dan has been a full-time working director since 1 July 1995.

On 1 July 2006 Dan gave his wife, Siobhan 50% of the shares in PETERSON Ltd when the market value of these shares was €200,000. The company did not own any investments at that time. Siobhan was appointed a director of the company and was fully engaged from that time. Both Dan and Siobhan are Irish resident and domiciled.

On 31 December 2012 Dan was approached by a multinational company who offered him €800,000 for the sale of his shareholding in PETERSON Ltd. The company was valued at €1.6 million.

PETERSON LIMITED: Balance Sheet at 31 December 2012:

	€
Fixed Assets	
Tangible assets	
Investment property	140,000
Investment in FRUIT Ltd	100,000
Trade premises	210,000
Plant and equipment	57,000
Fixtures and fittings	56,000
Motor vehicles	72,000
	635,000
Financial Assets	
Government stocks	30,000
TOTAL FIXED ASSETS	665,000
Current Assets	
Stock	220,000
Debtors	450,000
Cash	156,000
TOTAL CURRENT ASSETS	826,000
TOTAL CREDITORS	(520,000)
NET CURRENT ASSETS	306,000
NET ASSETS	971,000
CAPITAL AND RESERVES	
Called up share capital	20,000
Profit and loss account	951,000
	971,000

The above values also represent the market value of the company's assets except with regard to the following assets:

Market Value	€
Investment property	250,000
Trade premises	270,000
Government stocks	35,000

Calculate the CGT payable by Dan should he decide to sell his shares

Step 1 Calculate the gain assuming no retirement relief

Market value of shares at 31 December 2012	800,000
Cost 30/06/95 €217,000 × 1.277 × 50%	(138,555)
Chargeable gain	661,445

continued overleaf

Step 2 Apportion market value between the assets in the company to get the value of goodwill, if any

	€
Total value of company at 31/12/12	1,600,000
Attributable to:	
Investment property	(250,000)
Shareholding in Fruit Ltd	(100,000)
Trade premises	(270,000)
Plant, fixtures and vehicles	(185,000)
Government stocks	(35,000)
Current assets	(826,000)
Creditors	520,000
Value of goodwill (missing figure)	454,000

Step 3 Apportion market value between chargeable business assets, non-chargeable business assets and non-chargeable assets

Chargeable business assets:	€
Goodwill	454,000
Trade premises	270,000
Plant, fixtures and vehicles	185,000
	909,000

Chargeable assets:	
Chargeable business assets	909,000
Shareholding in Fruit Ltd	100,000
Investment property	250,000
	1,259,000

Note: Government stocks and current assets are not chargeable assets and are therefore ignored.

Step 4 Sales proceeds relating to chargeable business assets

€800,000 × €909,000/€1,259,000 = €577,601

	€
Sales proceeds relating to chargeable business assets of this sale	577,601
Market value of gift of shares to Siobhan in PETERSON Ltd	200,000
Aggregate proceeds relating to sale of business assets	777,601

As this exceeds the €750,000 lifetime limit, then retirement relief cannot be claimed. However marginal relief may be claimed

(€777,601 − €750,000) × 50% = €13,801

Step 5 Portion of the original gain relating to chargeable business assets
€661,445 × €909,000/€1,259,000 = €477,564 × 30% = €143,269 – this is higher than the marginal relief so pay €13,801 in respect of this portion of the gain.

Step 6 The balance of the gain €661,445 − €477,564 = €183,881 is taxable at @30% = €55,164.

Dan's CGT liability:

	€
Marginal relief claim re chargeable business assets	13,801
CGT on balance	55,164
Total liability	68,965

6.7 Concession Regarding Age where Individual has Medical Problems

Where an individual disposes of 'qualifying assets' before his/her 55th birthday, the Revenue Commissioners will consider claims for relief where all the following conditions are present:

■ The claimant is, due to **severe or chronic ill health**, unable to continue farming, or in his/her trade, profession, office or employment or as a working director in a relevant company.
■ At the time of disposal the conditions for relief, other than the age requirement, are satisfied.
■ At the time of disposal, the claimant is **within 12 months of his/her 55th birthday**.

An individual claiming retirement relief on these grounds must provide medical evidence of the illness and outline the circumstances in which the relief is being claimed.

6.8 Disposals in 2014 or Later by Individuals Aged 66 or Over

With effect from **1 January 2014**, disposals by individuals **aged 66 or over** are subject to different limits to those applying to individuals aged 55 or more but less than 66 years of age.

For disposals other than to children, as defined, the proceeds limit is **€500,000** instead of €750,000.

For disposals to children, as defined, where the market value of the qualifying assets is greater than **€3,000,000**, relief will only be given as if the consideration for the disposal had been €3,000,000. This means that the consideration in excess on €3,000,000 is taxable.

Example

Joanne Phelan is 66 years of age. She has a very successful trading company, Prime Limited, the shares in which she has owned for over 30 years. She has been a full-time working director of the company during that time. The only chargeable assets of the company are chargeable business assets for retirement relief. The company is worth €10 million. The shares cost €5,000 and the indexation factor is, say, 4. She advises you that she is going to retire when she is 68 in 2014 and give her shares to her son Jack. Advise her as to the CGT implications of disposing of the shares to Jack in 2012 (or 2013) versus 2014, assuming no change in value of the company or in tax law.

If Joanne disposes of the shares in 2012 or 2013, she will have no taxable gain as all the conditions for retirement relief have been satisfied. If Jack sells the shares within six years, he will have to pay the CGT Joanne did not pay.

If she disposes of the shares in 2014 when she is at least 66 (she will be 68), there will be relief but it will only be given as if the consideration for the disposal had been €3 million. Therefore, assuming no change in the value of the company, the rate of tax, etc., her CGT would be calculated as follows:

	€
Deemed consideration	10,000,000
Indexed cost €5,000 × 4	(20,000)
Gain	9,980,000
Relief €3,000,000 – €20,000	(2,980,000)
Taxable gain	7,000,000
CGT @ 30%	2,100,000

Therefore by disposing of the shares in 2012 or 2013, Joanne has avoided CGT of €2.1 million. If Jack sells the shares within six years, he will have to pay the CGT that Joanne did not pay.

Please note that there is a flaw in the legislation which means that a disposal to a child in 2014 or later by an individual aged 66 or more, will not qualify for relief if the proceeds are €3,000,000. Revenue has advised that this flaw will be corrected next year.

6.9 Summary of Conditions to be Satisfied

The summary below sets out the key issues only and does not deal with all issues which may arise. Therefore, it is important to read all of the chapter.

6.9.1 Sole Trader

- At least 55 years of age.
- Owned chargeable business assets for at least 10 years (plant and machinery – no minimum period) or owned by spouse or civil partner and individual for 10 years.
- Proceeds limit of €750,000 on qualifying assets if disposed of to other than a child.
- Must be for genuine commercial reasons and not the avoidance of tax.

6.9.2 Shareholder

- At least 55 years of age.
- Shares owned for at least 10 years ending on the date of the disposal (or owned by spouse and individual for 10 years) if qualified for transfer of business to a company, can include period as sole trader.
- Shares in trading company or trading group.
- Shares in family company (at least 25% or, alternatively, 10% with 75% owned by family).
- Working director for at least 10 years, of which at least five years were full-time (or working by spouse or civil partner if spouse or civil partner is deceased; if qualified for transfer of business to a company, can include period as sole trader).
- Proceeds limit of €750,000 on qualifying assets if disposed of to other than a child (remember to count the value of a building if it is transferred separately – see **Section 6.9.3**).
- Must be for genuine commercial reasons and not the avoidance of tax.

6.9.3 Land, Buildings, Plant and Machinery Owned by an Individual and used by his/her Family Company

- At least 55 years of age.
- Owned land, buildings, plant or machinery for at least 10 years ending with the date of the disposal.
- Land/buildings/plant used by family/trading company for at least 10 years ending with the date of disposal.
- Disposed of land, etc. at same time and to same person as shares in family trading company.
- Shares in family/trading company must also qualify for retirement relief.
- Proceeds limit of €750,000 on qualifying assets if disposed of to other than a child (remember to count the value of the shares – see **Section 6.9.2**).
- Must be for genuine commercial reasons and not the avoidance of tax.

Questions (to Chapter 6)

Review Questions

(See Suggested Solutions to Review Questions at the end of this textbook.)

Question 6.1

On 1 August 2012, Jim Hughes who is 60 years of age transferred 20% of the shares in his family trading company to his son Paul (market value of the 20% – €800,000). Jim Hughes had acquired these shares in the family company on 1 December 1974, when the market value of these shares (i.e. shares being gifted) was €40,000.

Requirement
(a) You are required to compute the CGT payable in respect of this transaction, indicating the year for which it will be assessed and by whom it will be payable.
(b) You are required to state what CGT would become payable, and by whom it would be payable, assuming that Paul Hughes, who is single, sells his 20% of the private company for €900,000 on 1 December 2012.

Question 6.2

For the past thirty plus years Sean Humbert, aged 63, has operated TARA FOODS Ltd. as a very successful company in the catering sector. Sean is now considering, in December 2012, the transfer of his business by way of gift to his only son, Michael. Sean has been a full-time working director of the company since it was incorporated in 1977, with himself as the 100% beneficial owner.

The share capital of the company comprises 100 ordinary shares of €1 each. Sean subscribed for his shares at par value in July 1977. Of the 100 shares, 99 are registered in Sean's name and the remaining share is registered in the name of Sean's wife, and is held in trust for Sean.

The shares in TARA FOODS Ltd. carry a current value of €800,000 derived from the following assets and liabilities:

	Market Values
	€
Goodwill	600,000
Equipment	50,000
Stock	40,000
Trade debtors	25,000
Quoted investments	120,000
Trade creditors	(35,000)
	800,000

The property from which the company operates is owned personally by Sean Humbert and it is Sean's intention to transfer the property to Michael by way of gift, in addition to the shares in TARA FOODS Ltd. The property was purchased by Sean for €28,000 in July 1977. The current market value of the property is €300,000.

Requirement

(a)   Set out your views on Sean's eligibility for retirement relief on the proposed transfer of his shares and business premises to Michael. The basis for your views should be outlined together with an indication of the amount of relief available in the circumstances as outlined.

(b)   Compute the CGT liability which will arise if Sean makes the proposed transfers to Michael.

(c)   Under what circumstances would the retirement relief claimed at (**b**) be withdrawn?

(d)   How would the Revenue recover the CGT due should the retirement relief fail to be clawed back?

Question 6.3

On 1 November 2012, on the occasion of his 60th birthday Colin, a widower, made the following gifts:

To his son Sean:	Notes	Market Value At 1 November 2012
100% of the shares in an unquoted trading company, Crawford Sportswear Ltd.	(1)	€500,000
Premises occupied by Crawford Sportswear Ltd	(1)	€250,000
To his daughter Esther:		
A holiday cottage in France	(2)	€120,000
Cash		€50,000
To his wife's sister Jean:		
An antique brooch	(3)	€3,000

Notes

(1)   Crawford Sportswear Ltd is engaged in the sale of sportswear. Colin had carried on this trade as a sole trader since 1980, until he incorporated Crawford Sportswear Ltd on 1 January 2005. On 1 January 2005 Colin transferred the entire assets and liabilities of the trade other than the cash and the shop premises to Crawford Sportswear Ltd in exchange for shares in the company. On 31 December 2004 the market value of the trade's assets and liabilities were as follows:

	Market Value €
Premises (Note)	125,000
Fixtures and fittings (Note)	50,000
Goodwill	80,000
Stocks	120,000

Debtors	25,000
Cash	10,000
Creditors	110,000

Note

Colin acquired the premises on 1 June 1980 for €20,000. Following the transfer of the business to Crawford Sportswear Ltd, the premises were let at full market rent by Colin to the company. The market value of no single item of fixtures and fittings exceeded its original cost at 1 January 2005.

Colin has always been a full-time working director of the company.

At 1 November 2012, all of the company's assets consisted of assets in use, and which have always been in use, for the purpose of the company's trade.

(2)   Colin inherited the holiday cottage in France from a French cousin. Colin's cousin died on 10 October 1983 at which date the cottage was valued at €25,000. A number of complexities arose in the administration of his cousin's estate and the legal ownership of the cottage was not transferred to Colin until 11 January 1985 at which date the cottage was valued at €30,000.

(3)   Colin had inherited the brooch from his wife on her death on 1 December 2003. The brooch was then valued at €2,400. Colin's wife had inherited the brooch from her own mother in May 1987 when the brooch was valued at €1,500.

Requirement
Calculate Colin's CGT liability for 2012 on the assumption that no other assets were disposed of during the year.

Acquisition by a Company of its Own Shares

Learning Objectives

After studying this chapter you will have developed a competency in the following:

- Where a quoted company buys back its own shares, it is typically treated as a disposal of shares by the shareholder and, as such, is liable to CGT.
- Where an unquoted company buys back its own shares, it is treated as a distribution of profits and, therefore, there is potential dividend withholding tax (DWT) to be considered: the individual shareholder is taxable under Schedule F, whereas a company is exempt from corporation tax on the distribution.
- If certain conditions are met, an unquoted company buying back its own shares will be treated as a disposal of shares and, therefore, CGT treatment will apply. The buy-back must satisfy the following conditions:
  - be by a trading company or a holding company of a trading company;
  - benefit the trade;
  - not be part of a scheme;
  - vendor must be resident (or ordinarily resident for an individual);
  - vendor must have owned shares for five years;
  - vendor's shareholding must be substantially reduced by the buy-back; and
  - vendor must not be connected with the company after the buy-back.

7.1   Overview

A company is legally entitled to acquire/buy back its own shares or shares of the parent company. A company, particularly a quoted company, might do this if management were of the view that the shares were good value at present. A company, particularly an unquoted company, might do this **if a shareholder wishes to dispose of shares and another shareholder(s) did not want to buy the shares**.

We will see in **Chapter 27** that any distribution out of assets of the company in respect of shares, except any part of it which represents a repayment of capital, is a distribution for tax purposes, i.e. the difference between what the shareholder subscribed for the shares and what he/she is now receiving is taxable under Schedule F, if the shareholder is an individual. The income tax liability is typically at 41% plus Universal Social Charge of up to 10%. There will be PRSI at 4% also if the individual is liable under class S.

Chapter 9 of Part 6 TCA 1997 sets out the tax treatment of an acquisition by a company of its own, or its holding company's, shares. Where the relevant conditions are satisfied, the sale of the shareholder's shares is subject to CGT treatment at a rate of 30%, rather than income tax treatment. The law deals separately with quoted and unquoted companies.

7.2   Quoted Companies

A buy-back (including the redemption, repayment and purchase) of its own shares by a quoted company (or of its own shares by a subsidiary of a quoted company) is not treated as a distribution. Consequently, the disposal of the shares by the shareholders(s) concerned is within the charge to CGT.

There is a condition which must be satisfied by quoted companies, i.e. a share buy-back must not be part of a scheme or arrangement, the main purpose (or one of the main purposes of which) is to enable the owner of the shares to participate in the profits of the company or of any of its 51% subsidiaries, without receiving a dividend. If this condition is not satisfied, the share buy-back is treated as a distribution. Quoted companies must include in their annual corporation tax return details of any share buy-backs undertaken in an accounting period, indicating whether the buy-back is to be treated as not being a distribution.

7.3   Unquoted Companies

Where an unquoted trading or holding company buys back its own shares (or its holding company's shares) from a shareholder who is not a dealer in those shares, the payment made to the shareholder is, subject to certain conditions being satisfied, not to be treated as a distribution. As the payment is not to be treated as a distribution, **CGT treatment** applies to the shareholder's disposal of the shares.

7.3.1   Conditions to be Satisfied

The conditions that *must* be satisfied if such a purchase is not to be treated as a distribution are:

- The company must be a trading company or a holding company of a trading company.
- The motive test, i.e. the acquisition of the shares by the company must be wholly or mainly for the ***benefit of the trade*** of the company or any of its 51% subsidiaries.

Attached in the Appendix is an extract from Tax Briefing 25 dealing with the Revenue's interpretation of "the benefit of the trade" test.

■ The buy-back must not be part of a scheme or arrangement, the purpose of which is to enable the shareholder to participate in the profits of the company or any of its 51% subsidiaries without receiving a dividend.

■ The vendor of the shares must be **resident** and (except for a company) ordinarily resident for the year of assessment (accounting period for a company), in which the shares are bought back. This ensures that the vendor is within the charge to Irish CGT.

■ The vendor must have **owned the shares throughout a *five-year period*** ending with the date of the buy-back. The period of ownership of a spouse or civil partner living with a vendor at the date of the buy-back is aggregated with that of the vendor. However, where an Approved Profit Sharing Scheme has appropriated the shares to a participant, the period is reduced to three years. If the vendor inherited the shares from the previous owner, the vendor's period of ownership is deemed to include the period of ownership of the previous owner. In addition, where the shares are inherited the required period of ownership is reduced to three years.

■ Where the vendor's shareholding in a company is not fully purchased, redeemed or repaid, then generally his/her ***shareholding*** and entitlement to **share of profits** must be ***substantially reduced***. Both the nominal value of shareholding and the profit entitlement must, after the sale of the shares, be reduced **by at least 25%**.

Example

D Ltd has an issued share capital of 100,000 €1 ordinary shares, of which E holds 20,000 (that is, 2/10ths or 20%). If E sells 5,000 shares to D Ltd, D Ltd's issued share capital is reduced for tax purposes to 95,000 shares, of which E holds 15,000, a fraction of 15/95ths or 15.79%.

Thus, although E has sold 25% of the original holding, E's percentage holding has been reduced by only 21%, and the buy back will not qualify for CGT treatment (i.e. it will be treated as a distribution). To achieve a reduction of 25%, E would need to sell 5,890 shares.

---

and

■ The **vendor is not connected with the company** or group company, after the buy-back, i.e. the vendor and the vendor's associates must not, after the buy-back of the shares, be entitled to more than 30% of the capital, voting rights or assets on a winding up of the company.

There is a very long definition of an associate in the law. The *main* people are:

■ A husband and wife or civil partners living together are associated with one another and a person under the age of 18 is an associate of his or her parents and their spouses or civil partners (no other relatives are treated as associated).

■ A person who has control of a company is associated with that company.

■ Two companies which are controlled by the same person are associated.

7.3.2 Buy-back of Shares to Pay Inheritance Tax

The various conditions necessary for a buy-back not to be treated as a distribution are waived where it can be shown that shares had to be disposed of in order to discharge inheritance tax in respect of an inheritance by that shareholder of the company's shares or to repay borrowings used to pay the inheritance tax. All, or almost all, of the payment made by the company acquiring the shares (apart from any CGT paid by the shareholder on the disposal of the shares) must be applied in paying the inheritance tax, on time, i.e., by 31 October or to repaying borrowings used to pay inheritance tax. For this rule to apply, the shareholder must not otherwise have been able to discharge the inheritance tax due without undue hardship. Where the shareholder has borrowed, it must be the case that there would have been hardship unless the shareholder had both borrowed to pay the inheritance tax and disposed of the shares to the issuing company to repay the money borrowed.

7.3.3 Other Issues

Even though the buy-back is not treated as a distribution for the shareholder, it is a distribution for the purposes of the close company surcharge, i.e. it would reduce the amount liable to the surcharge.

It does not matter whether the buy-back is treated as a distribution or a capital gain; there is no tax deduction for the company.

In respect of treasury shares:

- ◼ treasury shares which are not cancelled by a company are treated as cancelled immediately when they are acquired by the company;
- ◼ no allowable loss arises on cancellation of treasury or other shares by a company, regardless of whether the shares are actually cancelled or are treated as cancelled for tax purposes; and
- ◼ reissues of treasury shares are treated as new issues of shares.

A return is required to be made to the Inspector by companies which buy back their own shares or acquire their holding companies' shares, where such companies consider exemption from the distribution treatment applies to those acquisitions. The time limit for making such a return is nine months from the end of the accounting period in which the acquisition takes place. There is provision for penalties for failure to make returns.

Example

Harry and Peter, two Irish residents, set up Super Friends Ltd to sell electronic equipment in 1992. Harry owns 80% of the shares, while Peter owns 20%. The company has been very profitable and now has revenue reserves of €2 million. Harry believes that the success of the company is due totally to his efforts. He believes that Peter does not really contribute to the success of the company and is more interested in his golf handicap. There have been a number of acrimonious Board meetings and as a result Harry has decided to "buy out" Peter. Peter is happy to dispose of his shares provided that he receives €1 million and pays CGT at 30% and not the higher income tax.

If Harry were to buy the shares, he would need €1 million. As Harry does not have that amount of cash, he would have to either borrow the money (which would have to be repaid) or get money from the company (on which he would be liable to income tax).

If Super Friends Ltd bought back the shares from Peter, then Harry would own all the shares, without having to find the cash to actually buy the shares. Peter will be liable to income tax on the cash received from Super Friends Ltd in excess of the amount he contributed for the shares. However if he satisfies the following conditions, he will be liable to CGT on the gain, and not income tax:

1	Trading or holding company?	Yes
2	Will the acquisition benefit the trade?	Yes, there is disagreement between shareholders.
3	Is Peter resident and ordinarily resident in Ireland in 2012?	Yes resident
4	Has Peter owned the shares for five years?	Yes
5	Is Peter selling all his shares, or at least substantially reducing his shareholding?	Yes, he is selling all his shares
6	Is Peter not connected with Super Friends Ltd after the disposal?	Yes

As all the conditions have been satisfied, Peter will be liable to CGT on the disposal of the shares to Super Friends Ltd.

Appendix 7.1: Extract from Tax Briefing 25 Outlining the Revenue Commissioners' Views as to "The Benefit of the Trade" Test

Revenue will normally regard a buy-back as benefiting the trade where for example:

■ There is a disagreement between the shareholders over the management of the company and that disagreement is having or is expected to have an adverse effect on the company's trade and where the effect of the transaction is to remove the dissenting shareholder.

■ The purpose is to ensure that an unwilling shareholder who wishes to end his/her association with the company does not sell the shares to someone who might not be acceptable to the other shareholders.

Examples of this would include:

– An outside shareholder who has provided equity finance and wishes to withdraw that finance.

– A controlling shareholder who is retiring as a director and wishes to make way for new management.

– Personal representatives of a deceased shareholder where they wish to realise the value of the shares.

– A legatee of a deceased shareholder, who does not wish to hold shares in the company.

The above examples envisage the shareholder selling his/her entire shareholding in the company and making a complete break from the company. If the company is not buying **all** the shares owned by the vendor, or if the vendor is selling all the shares but retaining some connection with the company (e.g. directorship), it would seem unlikely that the transaction would benefit the company's trade.

However, there may be situations where:

■ For sentimental reasons, a retiring director of a company wishes to retain a small shareholding in the company.

■ A controlling shareholder in a family company is selling the shares to allow control to pass to his/her children but remains on as a director for a specified period purely because an immediate departure from the company at that time would otherwise have a negative impact on the company's business.

In such circumstances it may still be possible for the company to show that the main purpose is to benefit its trade.

Questions (to Chapter 7)

Review Questions

(See Suggested Solutions to Review Questions at the end of this textbook.)

Question 7.1

Alan Doyle has been a director of ANNALLY Ltd since the company was incorporated in August 1990. The company is a large importer of toys from the Far East and it distributes these in Ireland and the UK.

Alan is 60 years of age and intends retiring from the business shortly. His original investment in company shares was €10,000 in €1 ordinary shares. There was no share premium account. His brothers, Mark and Colm, also own 10,000 €1 shares between them, and they will continue to run the company as directors after Alan's retirement.

Alan has recently had his shares valued and was pleasantly surprised to discover that they are worth €600,000. He has asked Mark and Colm to purchase these shares, but they have told him that they do not have sufficient funds.

You have been approached for advice on the possibility of the company acquiring its own shares from Alan.

Requirement

(a)   State the conditions that must be in place in order that the proceeds from a company acquiring its own shares can be treated as a share disposal for CGT purposes.

(b)   Compute Alan's liability to CGT if all the conditions are met.

(c)   State the tax consequences for Alan and the company if the conditions are not met.

Part Two

Stamp Duty

General Principles and Conveyance or Transfer on Sale

8

Learning Objectives

After studying this chapter you will have developed a competency in the following:

■ How a charge to stamp duty arises.
■ What rates of stamp duty apply.

The Chartered Accountants Ireland *Code of Ethics* applies to all aspects of a Chartered Accountant's professional life, including dealing with stamp duty issues. As outlined at the beginning of this book, further information regarding the principles in the *Code of Ethics* is set out in **Appendix B**.

8.1 Background

Up to 15 December 1999, the law governing stamp duties was contained in the Stamp Act 1891 and the Stamp Duties Management Act 1891 with subsequent Finance Acts amending and adding to these provisions. The Stamp Duties Consolidation Act (SDCA) 1999 was brought into law with effect from 15 December 1999. The SDCA consolidates into a single Act the legislation on stamp duties previously contained in the Stamp Act 1891, the Stamp Duties Management Act 1891 and subsequent Finance Acts.

8.2 Charge to Stamp Duty

Section 2 SDCA 1999 provides that

■ any instrument (i.e. **written document**) specified in the first schedule to the SDCA which is:

1. **executed in the State**; or
2. relates to any **property situated in the State**; or
3. relates to any matter or thing done or to be done in the State

is chargeable with stamp duty, subject to exemptions provided for in the Act.

As the tax applies to written documents, if a transaction is not in writing, but is executed by conduct (e.g. delivery) or by oral agreement, there is no stamp duty.

Stamp duty is charged on the VAT-exclusive consideration in the case of conveyances, transfers on sale and leases.

The following should be noted in relation to the above:

8.2.1   Instrument

While an instrument is defined as "including every legal document", the important thing to note is that an instrument is a written document of some sort, which acts as a mechanism for doing something. Accordingly, **where no written document is produced, no stamp duty can arise**.

For example, oral agreements which are not then put into writing do not attract stamp duty. Nor do agreements recorded on film, tape, etc.

8.2.2   First Schedule

The First Schedule to the SDCA lists instruments of various types and describes the stamp duties attaching to them.

The stamp duty can be one of two types:

1. Ad valorem – where the amount of stamp duty depends on the value of the consideration or property affected by the instrument concerned.
2. Fixed – where the instrument attracts a set amount of stamp duty regardless of the value of the property affected by the transaction.

Any instrument not falling within the First Schedule is not subject to stamp duty. Certain instruments which do not themselves fall within the First Schedule are deemed to be instruments within it for stamp duty purposes.

8.2.3   Executed in the State

Executing an instrument means doing whatever is necessary to make the instrument operable or effective. For most written agreements, this means signing the agreement. In some cases, e.g. deeds of covenant, instruments are not executed until signed and sealed.

8.2.4   Property Situated in the State

The rules relating to where property is situated have already been covered in previous chapters on CGT.

In summary, the legal status of various types of property is as follows:

Property	Location
Shares in registered form	Where share register is kept
Simple contract debts	Where debtor resides
Land and buildings	Where located
Goodwill	Where business is carried on

8.2.5   Matters/Things Done or to be Done in the State

This is a very wide provision. It covers situations such as the performance of services in Ireland.

Example 1
Pat and Catherine agree that Pat will buy Catherine's collection of antique books for €10,000. No written agreement was drawn up and accordingly no stamp duty arises.

Example 2
An agreement is signed in Killarney to transfer a painting kept in Bermuda from one party to another. The agreement is subject to Irish stamp duty as it is executed in the State.

Example 3
An agreement is signed in Chicago to transfer a building in Dundalk. The document is stampable as it relates to property situated in the State.

Example 4
Mr. X signs an agreement in France whereby he agrees to provide accountancy services in Ireland in return for the transfer of a French property to him. Stamp duty may arise on the agreement as it relates to a thing to be done in the State.

8.3   Conveyance or Transfer on Sale

Conveyance:

A conveyance is an instrument whereby any property, immovable or moveable, tangible or intangible, is transferred from one person to another.

The term "conveyance" is usually thought of as being the document which transfers ownership in land following the signing of contracts for sale. However, as outlined above, it has a much wider meaning. For instance, it includes court orders.

On Sale:

The term "on sale" implies that two considerations have been satisfied.

1.   There has been an agreement to sell the property with all the necessary conditions of contract law satisfied (offer, acceptance, consideration).
2.   The consideration is in the form of money. This rule is extended by legislation deeming certain transactions for non-monetary consideration to be conveyances on sale.

In the First Schedule to the SDCA, there are three heads of charge for conveyances or transfers on sale. The two of importance to us are:

1. Conveyance or transfer on sale of any stocks or marketable securities.
2. Conveyance or transfer on sale of any property other than stocks or marketable securities.

8.3.1 Stocks and Securities

For stamp duty to arise under this head, there must be:

1. a sale;
2. of shares/securities.

Duty is chargeable at 1% of the consideration, rounded down to the nearest euro, subject to a minimum payment of €1. There is an exemption from the 1% stamp duty on share transfers where the duty involved is €10 or less.

> **Example**
> Paul sells shares in Damascus Ltd, an Irish incorporated private company, to Peter for €1,250.
>
> | | | € |
> |---|---|---|
> | The stamp duty liability is | 1% × €1,250 = | 12.50 |
> | | Stamp duty | 12.00 (rounded down) |

The document that is the conveyance for these purposes is the share transfer form.

The transfer or conveyance on sale of shares and marketable securities of **a company not registered in the State** are **not subject to Irish stamp duty**. This is provided that the conveyance covered does not relate to:

1. any Irish immovable property;
2. any Irish registered stocks and marketable securities.

Stocks must be in a company registered in the State or relate to Irish immovable property.

Purchase by a company of its own shares
Technically, when a company purchases its own shares, a liability to stamp duty arises. However, in practice, shares in unquoted companies can be converted into redeemable shares and redeemed. No stamp duty arises on redemption of these shares.

8.3.2 Property Other than Shares

The most common example of stamp duty arising under this head is on sales of lands and buildings. Sales of freehold land and assignments of leasehold interests in land are covered under this head of charge. The creation of a leasehold interest is charged under the "lease" heading. Transfers of business property such as goodwill are also within this heading.

The rates of stamp duty increase as the value of the consideration increases. The rates applicable are outlined in the Appendix to this chapter and depend on whether the property is residential property or non-residential property.

Residential Property
Subject to transitional provisions, with effect from 8 December 2010, the rates of stamp duty on residential property were changed and all the reliefs which were available to first-time buyers and to purchasers of new residential property were repealed. The rates are set out in the Appendix and are **1% on the first €1,000,000 of the consideration and 2% on the balance**, rounded down to the nearest euro.

Example
Mary buys a residential property with a value of €1,250,000. The stamp duty payable is as follows:

		€
–	First €1,000,000 @ 1%	10,000
–	Balance €250,000 @ 2%	5,000
–	Total	15,000

Non-residential Property

In the case of non-residential property such as commercial buildings, farms, land and goodwill, the rate is **2%** of the consideration, rounded down to the nearest euro, for instruments executed on or after 7 December 2011. In the case of a mixed use property, the consideration must be apportioned on a just and reasonable basis between the residential and non-residential parts of the property. (Note: the rates applying before 7 December 2011 were as high as 6%.)

Example
Susan buys a shop and an apartment over the shop for €900,000. The estate agent advises that the value of the shop is €750,000 and the apartment is €150,000. The stamp duty payable is

Shop:	€15,000 (€750,000 @ 2%)
Apartment:	€1,500 (150,000 @ 1%)
Total stamp duty	€16,500

8.4 Deemed Conveyance on Sale

8.4.1 Consideration Consists in All or in Part of Shares

Person transfers property for cash plus shares

The instrument conveying the property is liable to stamp duty as a deemed conveyance on sale. The consideration for stamp duty purposes is the **cash plus the value of the shares**.

The transfer of the shares is also liable as a conveyance on sale of stock or marketable securities at 1% (unless new shares are issued).

Person transfers property for shares only

The conveyance is a deemed conveyance on sale with the consideration being the **market value of the shares**. In such circumstances, the transfer of the shares is not separately stampable.

Example 1
Large plc, an Irish registered company, has offered to purchase an office building from Tiny Tim, who will receive shares in Large plc as consideration.

Tiny Tim is Irish resident and the agreements and conveyances to sell the property are executed here. The share transfer certificates are drawn up. The stamp duty consequences are:

1. The conveyance of the office building is stampable. The consideration is the value of the shares transferred.
2. The share transfer certificates are not liable to stamp duty.

Example 2

The facts are the same as outlined in Example 1 only Tiny Tim is to receive a mixture of shares plus cash.

Both the conveyance of the buildings and the share registration forms are stampable at 2% and 1% respectively.

8.4.2   Conveyance in Consideration of Debts

Eamonn owes Kathleen €80,000. He transfers property worth €100,000 to her for €20,000 in forgiveness of the debt.

Stamp duty is chargeable on the cash consideration of €20,000 plus the value of the debt forgiven – €80,000, i.e. €100,000 in total.

8.4.3   Contracts Treated as Conveyance on Sale

A contract is not necessarily the instrument which conveys a property. Accordingly in the past it was possible to avoid stamp duty by letting a transaction rest at contract stage.

Anti-avoidance provisions were introduced whereby contracts which are not conveyances are deemed to be conveyances for stamp duty purposes. These include:

1.   contracts for the sale of equitable estates or interests in property; and
2.   contracts for sale of any estate or interest in property, except:

- immovable property in the State;
- property locally situated outside the State;
- goods and merchandise;
- stocks and marketable securities; and
- ships, vessels or aircraft.

In practice, this provision means that contracts for sale of intangible assets are deemed conveyances on sale. Contracts for sale of assets such as goodwill, trademarks, copyrights, patents, designs, licenses, book debts, cash on deposit at bank and the benefit of contract are deemed conveyances on sale. However, sales or other dispositions of intellectual property are exempt (see **Chapter 9**).

Example

John sells Irish goodwill of his business to Bob for €100,000. A contract is drawn up to evidence the agreement. The contract will be a deemed conveyance on sale and will be liable to 2% stamp duty.

Bob is a tax client of the firm where you are employed. He rings your manager, who is at a meeting, and asks to be put through to a person working for your manager. Bob explains to you that his friend has suggested that he re-draft the contract and change the consideration to €50,000 and give John cash of €50,000. In this way Bob could pay stamp duty on only €50,000 and at a rate of 4%. What should you do?

What Bob is suggesting is not legal and is not ethical. As Bob is a client of your manager, it is more appropriate that your manager would explain this to him. Therefore, you should advise Bob that you will get your manager to ring him when his meeting ends. You should tell your manager about the call.

> **Example**
> Bill sells an Irish patent to Ann for €100,000. A contract is drawn up to evidence the agreement. The sale is exempt from stamp duty as it is intellectual property.

Resting on Contract

It is important to note that the following provision will not come into operation until the Minister for Finance appoints an operative date by Ministerial Order. This has not happened to date.

Where 25% or more of the consideration has been paid in respect of a contract or agreement for the sale of an estate or interest in land in the State, then stamp duty will arise. This duty is payable where the conveyance has not been stamped within 30 days of receiving the proceeds.

Where stamp duty has been paid in accordance with this section, then no stamp duty is payable on a conveyance or transfer under that contract or agreement. Revenue will either denote the payment of duty to the conveyance or transfer or will transfer the duty to the conveyance or transfer on production of a stamped contract or agreement.

8.4.4 Voluntary Disposition Inter Vivos (Gifts)

A conveyance of property by way of gift is not a conveyance on sale as there is no sale. However it is deemed to be a conveyance on sale for stamp duty purposes. The consideration is the market value of the property conveyed.

This is a point of particular importance in estate planning when assessing whether or not assets should be gifted now or transferred as part of a person's estate by inheritance. Stamp duty is payable in relation to a gift.

> **Example – No stamp duty arises on foot of an inheritance**
> Mr X approaches you for advice in relation to whether or not he should gift a plot of land worth €200,000 to his brother now or provide that his brother will receive the land on his death by way of an inheritance.
>
> Stamp duty implications if he gifts now => €200,000 @ 2% = €4,000. However, consanguinity relief would be available in this situation (see **Section 9.2**) as this is a transfer between relations as defined. This would reduce the stamp duty payable by 50%. Therefore, the final stamp duty payable would amount to €2,000.
>
> This will be a liability of Mr X's brother.
>
> Stamp duty payable by inheritance => no stamp duty payable by Mr X's brother on receipt of the land by inheritance.

8.4.5 Contract for Sale of Leasehold Interest

A contract for sale of leasehold interest will be subject to stamp duty if:

1. the purchaser takes possession of the property; and
2. the leasehold interest is not conveyed within nine months of that time.

This section has been deleted by an Act in 2008, but the deletion is to come into operation by way of Ministerial Order. This has not happened to date.

Appendix 8.1:   Rates of Stamp Duty

Shares
1%

Residential Property
Instruments executed on or after 8 December 2010

Consideration	Rate
First €1,000,000	1%
Balance	2%

Non-Residential Property
Instruments executed on or after 7 December 2011
2%

Exemptions and Reliefs

> **Learning Objectives**
>
> After studying this chapter you will have developed a competency in the following:
>
> ▪ The main exemptions from stamp duty.
> ▪ The reliefs from stamp duty, including consanguinity relief, transfers between associated companies and farm consolidation relief.

9.1   Exemptions

The *main* exemptions are as follows:

1. Transfers of Government stocks.
2. Wills.
3. Under section 96 SDCA 1999, a conveyance or transfer of property between spouses and civil partners is exempt for as long as the spouses are married and the civil partners' relationship has not been dissolved. Therefore, even if a married couple or civil partners separate, transfers between them continue to be exempt as they are still married or in a civil partnership. If a married couple get divorced or a civil partnership is dissolved, any transfers of property between former spouses or civil partners made under an Irish court order (or a foreign court order which is recognised as valid in the State) are also exempt from stamp duty. After divorce or dissolution of a civil partnership, if a former spouse or civil partner voluntarily gives, for example, a house to the former spouse or civil partner, this would be liable to stamp duty.
4. Conveyances, transfer or lease of land made for charitable purposes in the State or Northern Ireland.
5. Under section 81AA SDCA 1999, there is a full relief from stamp duty on a transfer of an interest in land to a "young trained farmer", up to 31 December 2012. As this exemption from stamp duty is to encourage the transfer of farmland (including buildings) to a new generation of farmers with relevant qualifications, the transfer may be by way of gift or sale.

Conditions

The farmer must:

- be less than 35 years of age on the date of execution of the deed of transfer;
- also have attained one of the FETAC, HETAC or university agricultural qualifications or have received a letter from Teagasc (if the young farmer does not have the qualification at the date of transfer, the stamp duty can be paid and a refund sought subsequently, provided the qualification is received and the refund sought within four years); and
- furnish a declaration to the effect that he will, for a period of **five years** from the date of execution of the deed of transfer:
  - spend not less than 50% of his or her normal working time farming the land; and
  - retain ownership of the land.

The exemption granted will be clawed back, by way of a penalty, if the land is disposed of within five years from the date of execution of the deed of transfer and is not replaced by other land within one year of disposal. If part of the land is disposed of then the clawback will relate only to the portion disposed.

6. Any instrument for the sale, transfer or other disposition of intellectual property, as defined. Intellectual property includes patents, trademarks, copyright, registered designs, inventions, domain names etc. The definition of intellectual property is the same as the definition of intangible assets for corporation tax purposes in **Chapter 22.4**.

7. Conveyances of immovable property situated outside the State (subject to some conditions).

8. A cohabitant, as defined under the Civil Partnership and Certain Rights and Obligations of Cohabitants Act 2010, who receives property, under a property adjustment Order issued by the Court under section 174 of that Act, from the individual with whom he/she was cohabiting, is exempt from stamp duty under section 174 of that Act.

9.2 Transfers Between Relations (Consanguinity Relief or Associated Relatives Relief)

Instruments covered are:

1. conveyance or transfer on sale of property other than marketable securities and residential property; and
2. conveyance or transfer of property other than marketable securities and residential property, operating as a voluntary disposition inter vivos (gift).

This relief applies to transfers of the **entire** beneficial interest in **non-residential property** (other than shares) to most relatives, i.e. where the person to whom the property is being transferred (or each of them if there is more than one transferee) is related to the transferor in one of the following ways:

- Lineal descendant (child, grandchild, etc.)
- Parent
- Grandparent

- Step-parent
- Husband, wife or civil partner
- Brother/sister of parent (i.e. aunt, uncle)
- Brother or sister
- Lineal descendant of a parent (e.g. step-brother/sister)
- Lineal descendant of a husband/wife (e.g. step-child)
- Lineal descendant of a brother/sister (e.g. nephew/niece)
- Civil partner of a parent
- Lineal descendant of a civil partner

Duty is charged at **half the normal rate**. This relief applies to instruments executed prior to 1 January 2015. This relief does not apply to leases or transfers of shares or transfers of residential property. Transfers to spouses or civil partners are exempt.

The conveyance must contain a certificate certifying the relationship.

You will recall from earlier chapters that there is a CGT exemption where a parent disposes of a site to a child for the child to build a home. There was a stamp duty exemption also, but it was repealed with effect from 8 December 2010. Such a disposal is a disposal of non-residential land (rate of 2%) and consanguinity relief would apply.

> **Example**
> Ben gives his granddaughter, Jane, Irish land worth €100,000.
> The stamp duty payable on this voluntary disposition inter vivos would be €100,000 @ 2% = €2,000. If associated relatives relief is claimed, it would be reduced to €1,000.

> **Example**
> Margaret gives her grandson, Tarzan, Irish shares worth €50,000 and residential property worth €200,000.
>
> The stamp duty is €50,000 × 1% = €500 on the shares, and €200,000 × 1% = €2,000 on the residential property. No associated relatives relief is due on either property, as the property is shares and residential property.

9.3 Transfers Between Associated Companies

Stamp duty chargeable under the three "conveyances on sale" headings in the First Schedule to the SDCA 1999 (deemed transfers included) can be reduced to 0% where transactions are between "associated companies" as defined in section 79 SDCA 1999.

One company is associated with another if there is a 90% direct or indirect relationship between them in terms of:

(a) ordinary share capital (ordinary shares excluding fixed rate preference shares);
(b) profits available for distribution; and
(c) assets available for distribution on a winding up.

Examples

1.

A Ltd

90%

B Ltd

Conveyances on sale between A Ltd and B Ltd will qualify for the reduced rate of 0%

2.

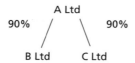

A Ltd

90%   90%

B Ltd   C Ltd

Transfers between A Ltd and B Ltd, and between B Ltd and C Ltd will qualify for the relief.

3.

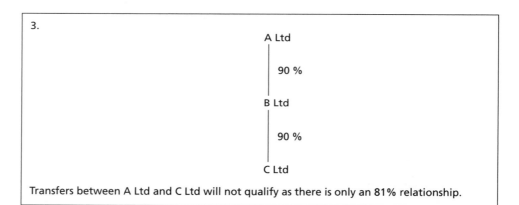

A Ltd

90 %

B Ltd

90 %

C Ltd

Transfers between A Ltd and C Ltd will not qualify as there is only an 81% relationship.

If the companies cease to be associated within two years of the date of the conveyance or transfer, then full stamp duty will be payable.

Example 1

Arklow Ltd transfers freehold land worth €1 million to its 100% subsidiary, Gorey Ltd.

Stamp duty would normally be 2% of €1 million = €20,000.

If associated companies relief is claimed, then stamp duty will be nil.

Example 2

Arklow Ltd grants Gorey Ltd, its 100% subsidiary, a leasehold interest in land. The premium payable is €900,000 with no annual rent.

The transaction is chargeable under the "Lease" heading and accordingly associated companies relief is not available.

Stamp duty liability is 2%, i.e. €18,000.

9.4   Farm Consolidation Relief

Subject to certain conditions, farmers can swap agricultural land and pay no, or a substantially smaller amount of, stamp duty. If both land holdings are of equal value, no stamp duty is payable. If one holding of land is more valuable than the other, then stamp duty is chargeable only on the difference in market values. If the land exchanged is sold within five years then there is a clawback of the relief.

Subject to certain conditions farmers can sell and purchase farm land in order to consolidate their holdings. The sales and purchases must be within 18 months of each other for this relief to apply. Stamp duty will only be payable where the value of the farm land acquired exceeds the value of the farm land sold.

Administration

Learning Objectives

After studying this chapter you will have developed a competency to understand:

- That stamp duty is payable within 30 days of execution of the instrument but, as a matter of practice, Revenue extend this to 44 days.
- Who is liable to pay the stamp duty due.
- The operation of the self-assessment system for stamp duty.

10.1 When is Stamp Duty Payable?

Stamp duty is payable within 30 days of execution of the instrument concerned. However, as a matter of practice, Revenue extends this date so that the duty on the instrument must be paid **within 44 days** of the date of first execution of the instrument.

10.2 Who is Liable to Pay Stamp Duty?

In theory, it is a matter for agreement between the parties to the transaction as to who is responsible for the stamp duty.

The stamp duty legislation does contain provisions to decide who the "accountable person" is, if the Revenue Commissioners have to sue for the stamp duty, as follows:

- the purchaser or transferee in the case of a transfer on sale;
- the lessee in the case of a lease;
- either party in the case of a gift or sale at undervalue (voluntary disposition inter vivos).

10.3 Electronic Stamping via ROS

Before the introduction of electronic filing of stamp duty returns (e-stamping), an instrument had to be physically presented for stamping by the Revenue Commissioners who would heat-seal a foil/hologram stamp to the document to denote that the stamp duty had been paid. Under e-Stamping, a person uses ROS (Revenue On-Line Service) to file the stamp duty return and pay stamp duty on line and receive a stamp certificate as part of that on-line transaction. This stamp certificate is printed and attached to the instrument, to denote the instrument as stamped.

Alternatively, the statutory return may be filed in paper format. However, this is only allowed where Revenue have excluded a person from the requirement to file electronically.

This only happens where the accountable person:

■ does not have sufficient access to the internet to comply with the requirements; or
■ in the case of an individual, is prevented by age or mental or physical infirmity from being able to comply with the requirements.

10.4 Self Assessment

The Finance Act 2012 provides for the introduction of self assessment for stamp duty for instruments executed on or after 7 July 2012. Up to the introduction of self assessment, certain documents had to be sent to Revenue for them to adjudicate (check that a relief or exemption was due or the valuation was correct in the case of a gift) before a stamp duty certificate would issue.

Similar to other taxes, under self assessment for stamp duty, the accountable person (usually the purchaser) files the return, calculates and pays the stamp duty and may be subject to audit at a later stage. As with other taxes, if the accountable person has a doubt about the application of stamp duty law to a particular transaction, the person can lodge an "expression of doubt". If the Revenue do not agree with the position adopted by the accountable person, he/she has a right of appeal against Revenue's decision.

If a return is not filed within 30 days, there is a fine of €3,000 and there is a surcharge of:

■ 5% of the stamp duty liability or €12,695, whichever is lower, if the return is filed within 2 months of the due date; and
■ 10% of the stamp duty liability or €63,485, whichever is lower, if the return is filed more than 2 months after the due date.

As with other taxes, if stamp duty is paid late, interest is payable at 0.0219% per day or part of a day.

Transfer of a Business

Learning Objectives

After studying this chapter you will have developed a competency in the following:

■ The stamp duty on sale of a business and how to minimise the liability.
■ The stamp duty on transfer of a business in return for shares.

11.1 Stamp Duty Consequences on Acquisition of Business Assets

---

Example 1

X Ltd agrees to sell its business to Y Ltd for a cash sum of €300,000. It is agreed that the following assets and liabilities will be transferred to Y Ltd.

	€
Plant and machinery	150,000
Goodwill	30,000
Debtors	250,000
Patents and designs	100,000
	530,000
New creditors	(230,000)
Net worth of business	300,000

A written agreement is drawn up to evidence the sale of the business

---

As there is a contract, Y Limited will have the following stamp duty liability (before claims for exemptions, etc.):

1. The contract for sale is stampable as a deemed conveyance on sale due to the fact that the sale of certain intangibles has been dealt with by it, i.e. goodwill, debts, patents and designs.

2. As the entire transaction has been dealt with in one agreement, the total consideration for stamp duty purposes is:

	€
Cash consideration for net assets	300,000
Creditors	230,000
Stampable consideration	530,000
Stamp duty @ 2%	10,600

11.2 Minimising Stamp Duty on Acquisition of Business Assets

Y Limited can minimise its stamp duty liability as follows:

1. Transfer plant and machinery by physically delivering it to Y Ltd and by not evidencing the sale/transfer in writing.

   As there is no instrument, no stamp duty can arise.

2. Do not transfer debtors and creditors to Y Ltd. Instead let X Ltd (or Y Ltd as its agent) collect the debts and use them to pay off the creditors.

3. The patents and designs – avail of exemption for intellectual property.

Therefore, only the goodwill is liable.

11.3 Transfer of a Business to a Company in Exchange for Shares

Where a company issues shares in exchange for non-cash consideration, the company, except where it is an unlimited company, is required to file with the Companies Registration Office a copy of any written contract involving the issue of the shares. Where there is no written contract, the company is required to file a Form 52 ('Particulars of a contract relating to shares') instead. Under the Companies Acts, Form 52 is deemed to be an instrument for stamp duty purposes and is subject to stamp duty as if it were a contract. As set out in **Section 8.4.3**, certain contracts are deemed to be liable to stamp duty as conveyances on sale. This would include contracts for the sale of assets such as goodwill, book debts and cash on deposit. Accordingly, the issue of shares in a company in exchange for assets of a business will be liable to stamp duty as if it were a contract for the acquisition of the assets of the business. Stamp duty will, therefore, be payable in respect of assets such as goodwill, debtors and cash in respect of which stamp duty is payable at contract stage.

Example

Brian transferred his business, including all its assets, to a company on 1 September 2012. In consideration of the transfer, the company, B Ltd, issued 1,000 ordinary shares fully paid up. Brian intends to claim incorporation relief (see **Chapter 5**) on the transfer of the business to B Ltd. At the date of the transfer, the market value of the assets transferred by Brian to B Ltd consisted of:

	€
Land and buildings	600,000
Plant and machinery	130,000
Goodwill	150,000
Debtors	80,000
Stocks	120,000
Cash	70,000
	1,150,000

B Ltd will be liable to stamp duty as follows:

	€
Land and buildings	600,000
Goodwill	150,000
Debtors	80,000
Cash	70,000
Total subject to stamp duty	900,000
Stamp duty at 2%	18,000

No stamp duty is payable on plant and machinery and stocks sold by way of contract. Title to these assets may pass by delivery.

Brian could opt not to transfer cash to B Ltd and would then save stamp duty of €1,400 (€70,000 @ 2%). If Brian were to opt to not transfer the debtors to B Ltd in order to save paying stamp duty, he could not claim incorporation relief as he must transfer all of the assets of the business, or all except cash, in exchange for shares in order to get the relief.

Part Three

Capital Acquisitions Tax

Introduction to Capital Acquisitions Tax

> The Chartered Accountants Ireland *Code of Ethics* applies to all aspects of a Chartered Accountant's professional life, including dealing with capital acquisitions tax issues. As outlined at the beginning of this book, further information regarding the principles in the *Code of Ethics* is set out in **Appendix B.**

As its name would indicate, Capital Acquisitions Tax (CAT) is a tax on acquisitions, i.e. the person who receives a benefit pays the tax. The benefit can be either a gift or an inheritance. As with any tax, there are rules for determining:

- whether a benefit is to be treated as a gift or an inheritance;
- whether it is liable to tax in Ireland;
- how the taxable benefit is to be computed, e.g. how it is valued, what deductions are allowed, what special reliefs/exemptions are available, how you deal with special situations;
- how you calculate the tax; and
- the administration of the tax system.

You will find that the rules for dealing with gifts and inheritance are almost completely the same. All benefits (be they gifts or inheritances) are taxed together. However there are some differences between gifts and inheritances which are summarised in the notes at **Section 13.9.** However, the differences are relatively minor. **Chapters 12 to 20** set out the rules governing CAT. They are based on the **Capital Acquisitions Tax Consolidation Act (CATCA) 2003** as amended by the subsequent Finance Acts (prior to its enactment, there was the Capital Acquisitions Tax Act 1976 as amended each year).

The term "capital acquisitions tax" may refer to either gift or inheritance tax. The general scheme of CATCA 2003 is to tax **recipients** on the gratuitous acquisition of property, either by way of gift or inheritance, subject to certain exemptions, reliefs and tax-free thresholds. As would be expected, the primary liability for payment of the tax rests with the recipient of the property, i.e. it is in effect a tax on acquisitions.

Broadly speaking, if an individual becomes entitled to any property or benefit, for less than full consideration, and there is no death involved, then that individual is deemed to have received a **gift**. The amount of the gift is represented by the full market value of the property or benefit taken as reduced by any consideration given, and any debts or encumbrances taken over. Alternatively, if the benefit or property is received as a result of a death, the beneficiary is deemed to have taken an **inheritance**. The amount of the inheritance is calculated in the same manner as for gifts. **Now the main difference between gift tax and inheritance tax is that the first €3,000 of the total taxable value of the total gifts taken from a single disponer in the same year is exempt from CAT**. There is no equivalent exemption for inheritances.

The amount of CAT levied in any situation will depend upon a number of factors including the following:

- The **relationship** between the recipient of the gift/inheritance and the person from whom the gift/inheritance is taken.
- The **taxable value** of the gift/inheritance received.
- The **aggregate** of the taxable value of all previous benefits taken by the beneficiary from persons belonging to the same **group threshold** on or after **5 December 1991**.
- The year in which the gift/inheritance is taken as the group threshold is subject to indexation.

The CAT payable is the excess of the tax on Aggregate A over the tax on Aggregate B. The tax rate is **30%** for gifts and inheritances taken **on or after 7 December 2011**. The rates of tax before 7 December 2011 are set out in **Appendix 16.1**.

Aggregate A equals the taxable value of the current gift or inheritance plus the taxable value of all previous gifts or inheritances taken by the beneficiary from persons with the same group threshold **on or after 5 December 1991**; and

Aggregate B equals the taxable value of all previous gifts or inheritances taken by the beneficiary from persons with the same group threshold on or after 5 December 1991, excluding the current benefit.

The three group thresholds for 2012 are as follows:

Group A €250,000, where the donee or successor is, on the day the gift or inheritance is taken,

- the child, or the minor child of a deceased child, of the disponer, or
- the child of the civil partner of the disponer, or minor child of a deceased child of the civil partner of the disponer, or
- the minor child of the civil partner of a deceased child of the disponer, or
- the minor child of the civil partner of a deceased child of the civil partner of the disponer.

A child includes an adopted child and a step child. For the purposes of the Group A threshold, it is also deemed to include a natural child who has been adopted by someone else and also a foster child, subject to certain conditions.

The Group A threshold also applies to inheritances taken by a parent on the date of death of his/her child, provided that the inheritance is not a limited interest. (Therefore, the Group A threshold does not apply to an inheritance of a limited interest from a child or any gift from a child.)

Group B €33,500 where the donee or successor is, on the day the gift or inheritance is taken, a lineal ancestor (other than the above detailed inheritances taken by parents), a lineal descendant (other than a child or minor child of a deceased child as set out in Group A above), a brother, a sister, a child of a brother or of a sister or a child of a civil partner of a brother or sister, of the disponer.

Group C €16,750 in all other cases.

(These figures are included in the *Tax Reference Material* given to you when you sit the exam.)

The law used to provide for indexation of group thresholds, but this no longer applies. However, recent Finance Acts have reduced the base threshold amount. Gifts or inheritances taken from 7 December 2011 onwards have a lower group threshold than in previous years.

Example 1

On 25 May 2012, Ann Peters received an inheritance with a taxable value of €50,000 from her uncle. She had received no other gifts or inheritances from any source since 5 December 1991.

Requirement

Compute the CAT liability on the inheritance from her uncle.

Computation

As she has no previous benefits, there is nothing to aggregate. Therefore, just tax current benefit.

	€
Taxable value	50,000
Group threshold: €33,500 @ Nil	
Balance: €16,500 @ 30% =	4,950
CAT liability	4,950

Example 2

On 14 February 2012, Jack O'Hara received an inheritance with a taxable value of €300,000 from his father. Jack had previously received the following benefits, net of small gift exemption where relevant:

- gift of €10,000 on 1 December 1990 from his brother
- inheritance of €5,000 on 20 December 1998 from his sister
- gift of €160,000 on 14 June 2002 from his mother

Requirement

Compute the CAT liability, if any, on the February 2012 inheritance from his father.

Computation

1. Calculate CAT on "Aggregate A", i.e. CAT on gifts and inheritances taken since 5 December 1991 from persons in the Group A threshold.

		€
Aggregate A: current inheritance from father		300,000
Gift from mother 14 June 2002		160,000
Total		460,000
CAT on Aggregate A:		
Group threshold:	€250,000 @ Nil	
Balance:	€210,000 @ 30% =	63,000
CAT on Aggregate A		63,000

continued overleaf

2. Calculate CAT on "Aggregate B", i.e. CAT on gifts and inheritances taken since 5 December 1991 from persons in the Group A threshold excluding the current benefit.

   Aggregate B = €160,000, i.e. gift from mother 14 June 2002. As this is less than the group threshold amount of €250,000, CAT on Aggregate B = Nil.

3. CAT on current benefit = CAT on Aggregate A less CAT on Aggregate B, i.e. €63,000 – Nil = €63,000.

Position up to 1 December 1999

The method of calculating CAT for gifts or inheritances taken before 1 December 1999 was different to that outlined above. The rules are briefly outlined in **Chapter 16**.

Gift Tax and Inheritance Tax

Learning Objectives

After studying this chapter you will have developed competency to understand:

- The basic elements needed for a gift or inheritance to arise. The key element is that the beneficiary did not pay fully for the gift or inheritance.
- A gift becomes an inheritance if the person making the gift dies within two years of making the gift.
- Gifts and inheritances between spouses and civil partners are exempt.
- Gifts and inheritances taken by joint tenants are taxed the same as gifts and inheritances taken as tenants in common.
- The treatment of gifts made or received by a company.
- The few, but important, differences between gifts and inheritances.
- The tax treatment of disclaimers.

13.1 Imposition of CAT on Gifts

Gift tax is charged on the taxable value of every taxable gift.

The term 'taxable value' refers to the amount on which gift tax (i.e. CAT) is levied while the term 'taxable gift' refers to the circumstances in which property comprised in a gift is within the scope of the charge to gift tax. Both these matters will be examined in detail later.

13.2 Basic Elements of a Gift

For the purposes of CAT, section 5 CATCA 2003 provides that a **gift is deemed to be taken** when:

- a **disposition** is made;
- by a **disponer**;
- whereby a **donee**;
- becomes **beneficially entitled in possession**;

- otherwise than **on a death**;
- to **any benefit**;
- otherwise than for **full consideration in money or monies worth paid by the donee**.

The above definition of a gift contains many items which need to be examined carefully.

13.2.1 Disposition

The disposition represents the method by which the ownership of the property or benefit involved is transferred. For every gift, there must be a disposition but every disposition is not necessarily a gift, e.g. if one sells a car at market value, this is a disposition but not a gift. The term is specifically defined in CATCA 2003 very widely and includes the following:

1. Any act by a person as a result of which the value of his estate is reduced, e.g. the transfer of property otherwise than for full consideration.
2. An omission or failure to act by an individual, as a result of which the value of his estate is reduced.

Example
The passing of a resolution by a company which results directly or indirectly in one shareholder's property being increased in value at the expense of the property of any other shareholder, if that other shareholder could have prevented the passing of the resolution by voting against it.

---

3. Payment of money.
4. The grant or creation of any benefit.
5. The transfer of any property or benefit by will or on intestacy (intestacy means that a person dies without making a will).

The "disposition" may, therefore, be said to be the legal method of alienating the property in favour of a beneficiary, e.g. the deed of conveyance in respect of the transfer of a farm, the trust deeds in relation to the transfer of property to a trust fund, or the act of delivery in the case of the transfer of moveable property.

13.2.2 Disponer

The disponer is the person who directly or indirectly is the **source of the financial benefit** comprised in the disposition. This is usually very straightforward, e.g. a parent gifts shares to a child. In this case the parent is the disponer. It is important to establish who the disponer is as the amount of benefit which can be taken tax-free depends on the recipient's relationship with the disponer. This is dealt with in **Chapter 16**.

Other examples of the disponer include:

- The deceased in the case of a will or an intestacy.
- The settlor in the case of property transferred to express or discretionary trusts.
- A person who has made a reciprocal arrangement with a third party to provide property comprised in a disposition to a second person, i.e. the disponer would be the first person and not the third party who directly gave the property to the second person.

> **Example**
> Brian owes Alan €10,000. Alan agrees to waive the debt if Brian transfers shares valued at €10,000 to Alan's brother James.
>
> In this case, the financial source of James's benefit (and therefore the disponer) is Alan and not Brian who actually provided the property.

13.2.3 Donee

This is simply the person who receives the gift.

13.2.4 Entitled in Possession

This expression is defined in CATCA 2003 as meaning "**having a present right to the enjoyment of property** as opposed to having a future such right".

A gift is not deemed to be taken until the happening of the event upon which the donee becomes beneficially entitled in possession to the benefit. The date of this event is referred to as the "date of the gift" in CATCA 2003. The **"date of the gift"** is defined as the date upon which the recipient of the gift becomes beneficially entitled in possession to the benefit, i.e. the date the recipient receives an immediate benefit as opposed to a right to receive a benefit in the future.

> **Example**
> If a father gives his son €10,000, the date of the disposition is the actual date of payment of the money and the date of the gift is the same date because the son immediately becomes entitled in possession to the benefit.

However, it should be noted that the "date of the gift" is not necessarily the same date as the "date of the disposition". This is important as the beneficiary is only liable when entitled in possession.

> **Example**
> If a father gives his solicitor €20,000 to give to his son when the son marries, the date of the disposition is the date of payment of the money to the solicitor, but the date of the gift will only arise when the son actually gets married, as it is only at that time that the son will have a present right (as opposed to a future right) to enjoy the funds.

> **Example**
> A father gives (by deed of conveyance) his son the right to use a property for a period of 10 years with absolute ownership of the property passing to his grandson after the 10-year period has expired. The deed of conveyance is the **disposition**. In the son's case, he receives an immediate benefit, i.e. the use of the property (though for a limited period only). In the son's case, the **date of the gift** corresponds to the date of the disposition. We will see later how the father's gift to the son is valued when we deal with limited interests.
>
> The grandson is not treated as having received a gift until he becomes entitled in possession, i.e. until the 10-year period has elapsed. In his case, the date of the **disposition** (i.e. the date of execution of the deed) and the **date of the gift** are completely different. When the 10-year period has elapsed the grandson is treated as having received the gift direct from his grandfather. It is only when the 10-year period elapses that he becomes **entitled in possession**.

13.2.5 On a Death

If a person becomes beneficially entitled in possession to any benefit on a death otherwise than for full consideration, then he is deemed to take an inheritance. A "gift", therefore, arises *otherwise* than on a death.

The expression **on a death** is specifically defined in CATCA 2003 – see **Section 13.8.1**. In addition to covering the situation where property passes directly on the death of a person, it is also **deemed** to include a gift where **the disponer has died within two years of making the gift**.

Such a gift effectively becomes an inheritance. For gifts or inheritances taken before 1 December 1999, this was very relevant as gift tax was payable at 75% of the inheritance tax rates. Since gifts and inheritances are taxable at the same rate, it does not create an additional tax now. The only impact of this rule is that the conditions for the dwelling house exemption are more onerous for gifts than inheritances. Therefore, the gift of a dwelling house may not qualify for exemption but, if the gift becomes an inheritance, the dwelling house exemption may apply – see **Section 16.8**.

13.2.6 Benefit

This is widely defined in CATCA 2003 to include "any estate, interest, income or right". This definition would clearly include the following items:

- an absolute interest/ownership in property;
- a life interest in property; and
- an annuity or other periodic payment.

Where the benefit involved does not comprise the absolute interest then CATCA 2003 provides a statutory method of valuing the "benefit". This will be covered later.

Examples
1. Jim transfers ownership of his farm to Joe – Joe takes an absolute interest in the farm.

2. Jim gives Joe a right to the use of his farm for Joe's life – Joe takes a limited interest in the farm (i.e. a life interest).

3. Jim gives Joe the use of his farm for 16 years – Joe takes a limited interest in the farm (i.e. an interest for a certain period).

In the last two examples it can be seen that the benefit taken may not represent the full value of the property transferred. In the first case where full ownership passed, the benefit taken was equal to the full value of the farm. In the second two instances, the benefit taken represented less than the full value of the farm. It is, of course, only the value of the actual benefit taken which is taxable and not necessarily the full value of property comprised in the gift or inheritance. The calculation of taxable values (annuities) and the valuation of limited interests is dealt with in **Chapter 18**.

13.2.7 Consideration in Money or Money's Worth Paid by the Donee

There can be no gift if full consideration in money or money's worth is paid by the recipient of the benefit. Any consideration, monetary or otherwise, given by the recipient therefore reduces the value of any benefit taken for the purposes of CAT.

> **Examples**
> 1. X transfers his hotel worth €2,000,000 to Y for €2,000,000 - clearly there is no gift here as full consideration has been paid.
> 2. X transfers the hotel to Y for €1,200,000 - here the gift comprises the full value of the hotel, i.e. €2,000,000 less €1,200,000, i.e. €800,000.
> 3. X transfers the hotel to Y subject to Y giving Z €500,000 - this involves two gifts as follows:
>   (i)   the hotel less €500,000 from X to Y; and
>   (ii) €500,000 from X to Z.

It should be noted in the last case that both gifts are derived from X and that the payment of €500,000 from Y to Z does not constitute a gift by Y to Z. This is because X is effectively the source of the benefit to Z, although X provided the gift indirectly via Y.

13.3 Gifts Taken by Joint Tenants

To understand the provisions relating to joint tenants, it is first necessary to be clear on the distinction between ownership of property as joint tenants and ownership of property as tenants in common.

If two or more persons own a particular property as **tenants in common**, each tenant in common is **entitled to dispose of his interest** on death as he wishes, i.e. according to the provisions of his will, or according to the laws applicable to intestacy. This is the most common way of owning property.

In contrast, where a person who owns property as a joint tenant with one or more others dies, his share of the property does not form part of his estate, but immediately is transferred in equal shares to the remaining joint tenants. A **joint tenant** therefore, on his death, **cannot dispose** of his part or interest in the property to whomsoever he wishes.

Where a gift is taken by two or more persons as joint tenants, the liability to CAT in respect of such a gift is to be computed in exactly the same manner as if the joint tenants had taken the gift as tenants in common in equal shares, i.e. the joint tenancy is ignored.

13.4 Exemption of Gifts Between Spouses and Civil Partners

Under section 70 CATCA 2003, a **gift** taken by a donee, who is at the **date of the gift**, the **spouse** or the **civil partner** of the disponer is **exempt from gift tax** and is not taken into account in calculating CAT on later gifts or inheritances (i.e. **no aggregation**). The exemption of civil partners applies since 1 January 2011.

A similar exemption applies to inheritances.

13.5 Gifts by and to Companies

Where a private company makes or receives a gift, the liability to CAT is to be determined by looking through the company, or any series of such companies, to the **ultimate individual shareholders** and by treating the shareholders as having made or received the gift.

13.6   Gift Splitting/Connected Persons

Section 8 CATCA 2003 is an **anti-avoidance** section and is designed to prevent the avoidance of CAT through the medium of **passing property through one or more middlemen** before vesting ownership in the final recipient.

In the absence of anti-avoidance legislation, this practice could save substantial CAT through the utilisation of more advantageous tax-free thresholds than might otherwise be available if the gift were made directly from the original disponer to the final recipient.

Example

A grandfather wished to give his grandson €200,000 in January 2012. If the gift is made directly to the grandson, the tax-free threshold applicable is only €33,500. However, if the grandfather were to first gift the €200,000 to his son, this would be exempt as it is under the tax-free threshold applicable between father and son of €250,000. The son could then subsequently gift the €200,000 to his son (i.e. the grandson) again, without attracting liability.

Section 8 prevents this by providing that where A makes a gift to B and B, within the period commencing **three** years before and ending three years after the date of the gift from A, makes a disposition under which C takes a gift, then C is deemed to have taken the gift from A directly.

C, the final recipient, is deemed to take an inheritance from the original disponer in the above circumstances if A, the original disponer, dies within two years of the date of the original disposition to B.

Clearly, also if A dies within two years, the first recipient of the benefit, i.e. B, would also take an inheritance.

The effect of section 8, therefore, is that where property is gifted on within three years before or after the original disposition, then *two gifts* are deemed to have been made by the original disponer as follows:

1.   a gift by the original disponer to the first recipient, i.e. B in our example above; and
2.   a gift by the original disponer to the final recipient, i.e. C in the above example.

Both gifts are taxable in the normal way.

Section 8 does not apply in the following circumstances:

1.   Where it can be shown that the original disposition was not made with a view to enabling or facilitating the making of the subsequent disposition or with a view to facilitating the recoupment in any manner of the cost of the disposition to the final recipient.

The second part of the above saver would clearly not operate in the following circumstances:

Example

B borrows €100,000 from his bank and subsequently gifts it to C. By previous arrangement, A at a later date, (but within three years of the date of B's gift to C) gifts €100,000 to B. B then subsequently uses A's gift to repay the loan.

In this example there are again two gifts as follows:

(a) the deemed gift from A to C; and
(b) the gift from A to B.

---

2. Section 8 only applies to gifts and therefore will not have effect unless the original and subsequent benefits are gifts rather than inheritances, i.e. if the gift splitting occurs as a result of an **intervening death then the provisions are not invoked**.
3. Revenue will not invoke this legislation where a gift is taken by a **married child** of the disponer of a house or site for a house, and the married child has to **transfer the property into the name of the child and his/her spouse in order to get a mortgage** from a lending institution.

13.7 Imposition of CAT on Inheritances

Inheritance tax is charged and payable on the taxable value of every taxable inheritance taken by a successor.

The term "taxable value" refers to the amount upon which inheritance tax (i.e. CAT) is levied and "taxable inheritance" refers to whether or not a particular inheritance is within the scope of inheritance tax. These terms are dealt with in detail later.

A person who takes an inheritance is referred to as a "successor".

13.8 Basic Elements of an Inheritance

Under section 10 CATCA 2003, the elements which make up an inheritance are as follows:

- there must be a **disposition**;
- made by a **disponer**;
- whereby a **successor**;
- becomes **beneficially entitled in possession**;
- **on a death**;
- to any **benefit**;
- otherwise than for a full consideration in money or money's worth **paid by the successor**.

We see, therefore, that the basic elements constituting an inheritance correspond to those constituting a gift subject to the following exceptions:

1. An inheritance is taken *on a death* while a gift is taken otherwise than on a death.
2. The recipient of the benefit is referred to as the *successor* and not the donee.

> **Example**
>
> Jim dies and by will gives his brother Alex a life interest in his farm with remainder to his cousin Michael absolutely.
>
> The date of Alex's inheritance is Jim's death while the date of Michael's inheritance is Alex's death.

13.8.1 Meaning of "On a Death"

CATCA 2003 defines this term as meaning a benefit taken under any of the following circumstances:

1. Under the terms of a will (whether the benefit is taken immediately or after an interval).
2. Under an intestacy, i.e. individual dies without leaving a will.
3. Under a disposition where the disponer dies within two years of the date of the disposition.
4. An appointment of property from a discretionary trust where the trust was created by the will of a deceased person.
5. On the termination of a life interest by the death (or the deemed death)* of the life tenant or at a definite interval after such a death.
   *Advance termination of limited interest is not on the syllabus.
6. On the death of a person who is a joint tenant.
7. On the happening of any event following the termination of an intervening life interest which gives rise to the benefit in question.

13.8.2 Examples of Dispositions under which Inheritances are Taken

1. A will by which Joe bequeaths a legacy to Andy.
2. Intestacy where, under the Succession Act 1965, Andy is entitled to a benefit as one of Joe's relations.
3. A gift by Joe to Andy, if Joe dies within two years of the date of the disposition (e.g. the actual date of the gift if it comprised property, e.g. cash, where ownership transferred by delivery or the date the deed of conveyance was executed in the case of land).
4. Joe settles property during his lifetime on Andy for life with remainder to James absolutely.
5. Joe dies and leaves property to Andy for life and then absolutely to James.
6. Joe dies and leaves property in trust to Andy for life and provides that the property is to go absolutely to James two years after Andy's death.

In cases 1 to 3 above Andy takes an inheritance from Joe.

In case 4 Andy takes a gift from Joe on the date the settlement was executed. On Andy's death James is deemed to take an inheritance from Joe.

In case 5 Andy takes an inheritance on Joe's death and, on Andy's death, James is deemed to take an inheritance from Joe also.

In case 6 Andy takes an inheritance from Joe on Joe's death and, when James becomes beneficially entitled in possession to the property two years after Andy's death, James is deemed to have taken an inheritance from Joe also.

13.9   Distinction Between Gifts and Inheritances

The important differences may be summarised as follows:

1.   Inheritance tax applies where the benefit arises *on a death*, while gift tax applies where a benefit is taken otherwise than on a death.
2.   The first **€3,000** per annum in *gifts* made by any one disponer to any one donee is exempt. There is no similar exemption for inheritances.
3.   The conditions to be satisfied for the dwelling house exemption are more onerous if the benefit received is a gift.

13.10 Other General Matters

As in the case of gift tax, inheritance tax does not arise until the beneficiary becomes beneficially entitled in possession to the benefit, i.e. future interests are not taxed until they fall into possession.

13.11 Exemption of Inheritance from a Deceased Spouse or Civil Partner

- An **inheritance**
- taken by a successor who is, **at the date of the inheritance**, the **spouse or civil partner** of the disponer
- is **exempt from inheritance tax, and**
- is not to be taken into account in calculating CAT on later gifts or inheritances (i.e. **no aggregation**).

13.12 Date of the Inheritance

The term **"date of the inheritance"** normally means the date of the death which has to occur in order for a successor to become entitled to a benefit. An exception is where a gift becomes an inheritance because the disponer dies within two years of the date of the disposition and in this case the date of the inheritance is the date of the gift.

> **Example**
> Jack dies on 1 February 2012. Under the terms of Jack's will, he leaves a life interest in a property to his son Joe and provides that the property is to pass absolutely to Joe's son George on Joe's death.
>
> The date of Joe's inheritance from his father is 1 February 2012. The date of George's inheritance from his grandfather will be the date of Joe's death.

Some of the reasons why the date of the inheritance is important are:

- The date determines the rate of tax and the tax-free thresholds which apply. For example, 2012 tax-free thresholds and tax rates will apply to an inheritance receivable under the will of an individual who dies in 2012 even though the beneficiary may not receive the benefit until a later year.

■ An inheritance of foreign property from a non-resident disponer is only within the charge to Irish CAT if the beneficiary is resident or ordinarily resident in the State at the date of the inheritance.

■ For agricultural relief (see **Section 15.7**), business relief (see **Section 15.8**) or dwelling house exemption (see **Section 16.8**) to apply certain conditions must be satisfied at the date of the inheritance and/or at the valuation date. Also clawbacks of the relief or exemption may apply if property which qualified for relief is disposed of within six years (and in certain situations within 10 years) after the date of the inheritance.

13.13 Disclaimers of Benefits

Section 12 CATCA 2003 deals with the effect and consequences of disclaimers of benefits. The section **only applies where the person who disclaims a benefit does not name another person who is to benefit**. Where there is a pure disclaimer the general rules of law (Succession Act 1965) establish who is to benefit. The following points should be remembered:

■ Where a person disclaims a benefit they no longer have a liability to CAT in respect of that disclaimed benefit.

■ A disclaimer is not itself a disposition for CAT purposes.

■ A person can disclaim for consideration. Any consideration is a benefit moving from the original disponer to the person disclaiming (i.e. a substituted gift or inheritance).

■ A **disclaimer in favour of a named person** is considered as an **acquisition and a subsequent disposal** and therefore there is a **double charge to CAT**.

■ A disclaimed legacy falls into residue. If a residuary legatee disclaims, the residue is distributed as if there was intestacy as regards the residue.

■ A person cannot partially disclaim the residue or partially disclaim a share of the residue.

■ If a life interest or other limited interest is disclaimed the remainder interest falls in immediately.

Example 1

John dies testate (i.e. having made a will) on 10 January 2012. He leaves a pecuniary legacy of €60,000 to his brother Michael and the residue of his estate to his daughter Mary. Michael, who is financially well-off, decides to disclaim the legacy to him of €60,000. The legacy falls into the residue of the estate and is inherited by Mary, together with the residue of the estate. Michael has no liability to CAT as he has disclaimed the benefit to him.

Mary has inherited the entire estate from her father John and has taken no benefit from Michael.

Example 2

Maureen, a widow, dies testate in March 2012 and leaves the residue of her estate equally to her three children Noel, John and Mary. Noel, who is living abroad, disclaims his one-third share of the residue under the will, which one-third share then passes by intestacy equally to the three children as to a one-ninth share each. If Noel also disclaims his one-ninth share of the residue passing under the partial intestacy, this one-ninth share then passes equally to John and Mary. John and Mary each end up inheriting a half-share of the estate from Maureen.

Example 3

Paula inherits a house under her Aunt Nora's will but disclaims the inheritance of the house in favour of her brother Tom. As it is not possible to disclaim a benefit in favour of somebody else, this is an inheritance taken by Paula from Nora and then a separate gift of the house by Paula to Tom. Separate claims for CAT on both the inheritance and the gift accordingly arise in this situation.

Example 4

Patrick dies and leaves his farm valued at €350,000 to his son Robert and the residue of his estate to his daughter Sheila. Robert, who has no interest in farming, decides to disclaim the bequest of the farm to him in consideration of a payment to him of €250,000 from the estate.

Robert is treated as taking an inheritance of €250,000 from his father Patrick. Sheila is treated as taking an inheritance from her father Patrick of the farm and the residue of the estate, less the €250,000 passing to Robert.

Questions (to Chapter 13)

Review Questions

(See Suggested Solutions at the end of this textbook.)

Question 13.1

Mary owes John €8,000. John tells her to give €8,000 to Peter, in settlement of the debt.

Requirement
Who is the disponer for the €8,000?

Question 13.2

A mother agrees to give a farm to her daughter when she has her first child.

Requirement
When is the gift taken by the daughter?

Question 13.3

Joyce gives Paddy the family company worth €1 million, subject to Paddy giving €100,000 to Nora.

Requirement
What gifts are taken?

Question 13.4

You are a tax specialist in a firm of Chartered Accountants. The managing partner has asked you to write a memo to him dealing with the following CAT queries:

Requirement
(a)   What is regarded as a "disposition" for CAT purposes?
(b)   What is the "date of the disposition"?
(c)   What does "beneficially entitled in possession" mean?

Territorial Scope

Learning Objectives

After studying this chapter you will have developed the competency to understand that:

- Where the date of the **disposition is on or after 1 December 1999**, the key test in determining whether a gift/inheritance of foreign assets is a taxable gift/inheritance will be the **residence status** of the disposer or the recipient.
- Irish assets are always liable to Irish CAT.
- The general rule is that a gift/inheritance is taxable in the State where:
    1. the disponer is resident or ordinarily resident in the State in the year of assessment in which the disposition giving rise to the gift/inheritance is made; **or**
    2. the donee is resident or ordinarily resident in the State in the year of assessment in which the date of the gift/inheritance falls; **or**
    3. the gift/inheritance is situated in the State.
- The income tax rules for determining residence and ordinary residence generally apply. However, there are special rules for **foreign domiciled persons**, i.e. such people are not treated as resident or ordinarily resident unless:
    1. the date occurs on or after 1 December 2004;
    2. the person has been **resident in the State for five consecutive years of assessment** immediately preceding the year of assessment in which that date falls; **and**
    3. the person is **either resident or ordinarily resident** in the State on that date.

The date is the date of the disposition in the case of the disponer and the date of the gift/inheritance in the case of the beneficiary. As you can see, this is very different to the income tax rules.

14.1 Introduction

The territorial scope of CAT must clearly be limited as is the case for other taxes, such as income tax and CGT. CATCA 2003 therefore sets out a number of rules which determine whether or not a particular gift or inheritance is within the scope of CATCA 2003, i.e. whether a particular gift is a **"taxable gift"** or whether a particular inheritance is a **"taxable inheritance"**. A liability may not necessarily result even where these territorial rules are satisfied. For example, the particular gift or inheritance may be covered by a tax-free threshold or may be exempt altogether.

14.2 Taxable Gifts

14.2.1 Overview

1. Irish property – always taxable

A gift is a taxable gift to the extent that it, or a portion of it, consists of property that is situated in the State at the date of the gift.

2. Foreign property

Foreign property is taxable if the disponer is resident or ordinarily resident or if the donee is resident or ordinarily resident.

This general rule would mean that foreign domiciled people who were only in Ireland for a short time could trigger an Irish CAT liability. In order to ensure that this does not happen, there is a special five year rule for foreign domiciled people.

The current rules apply to gifts where the date of the disposition is on or after 1 December 1999. Before this date, one looked at the domicile of the disponer.

How to Determine Where Property is Situated

CATCA 2003 does not include rules for determining where property is situated. General law determines where property is located. The main rules are as follows:

1. *Land and Buildings*

    Situated where they are physically located.

2. *Debts*

    (i) A simple contract debt is situated where the debtor resides.
    (ii) A speciality debt, i.e. a debt payable under a sealed instrument, is situated where the instrument happens to be.
    (iii) A judgement debt is situated where the judgement is recorded.

3. *Securities/Shares*

    Situated where the share register is kept, if the securities/shares are registered (Irish incorporated companies are required to maintain a register of members in Ireland). Bearer securities/shares are situated where the security/share certificate is physically located.

4. *Tangible Property, e.g. Cars, Furniture, Moveable Goods*

    Situated where they are physically located.

5. ***Cash or Currency of any Kind***
Situated where they are physically located. Bank balances are located in the country where the bank branch is at which the account is kept.

14.2.2 Taxable Gifts

Where the date of the disposition is on or after 1 December 1999, a gift is taxable in the State where:

- the **disponer is resident or ordinarily resident** in the State in the year of assessment in which the disposition giving rise to the gift is made; or
- the **donee is resident or ordinarily resident** in the State in the year of assessment in which the date of the gift falls; or
- the **gift is situated in the State.**

The income tax rules for determining residence and ordinary residence generally apply. However there are special rules for foreign domiciled persons.

14.2.3 Taxable Gifts of Foreign Property – Foreign Domiciled Persons

There are special rules for foreign domiciled persons, i.e. such people are not treated as resident or ordinarily resident unless:

- the date occurs on or after 1 December 2004;
- the person has been resident in the State for **five consecutive years of assessment immediately preceding the year of assessment in which that date falls**; *and*
- the person is either **resident or ordinarily resident** in the State on that date.

The date is the date of the disposition in the case of the disponer and the date of the gift in the case of the beneficiary.

> **Example 1**
> On 1 April 2012, Joe gives Ray one acre of land in Dublin. As this is Irish property it is liable to CAT. It does not matter where either of them is domiciled, resident and ordinarily resident.

> **Example 2**
> On 31 August 2012, Mary who is domiciled, resident and ordinarily resident in Ireland gifts her villa in Spain to her friend Manuel who is Spanish and lives in Spain. As Mary is Irish resident (or ordinarily resident) and domiciled, the gift is subject to Irish CAT, i.e. Manuel must pay CAT.

> **Example 3**
> On 31 August 2012, Martin who is domiciled, resident and ordinarily resident in the US gifts his shares in a US company to his cousin Joe who is domiciled, resident and ordinarily resident in Ireland. As Joe is Irish resident (or ordinarily resident) and domiciled, the gift is subject to Irish CAT, i.e. Joe must pay CAT.

Example 4

On 31 August 2012, Peter who is domiciled, resident and ordinarily resident in the US gifts his shares in a US company to his brother Ivan who moved to Ireland in early 2008. Ivan is US domiciled, but resident and ordinarily resident in Ireland under the income tax rules for 2012. However as Ivan is foreign domiciled, he is only liable on foreign property if he has been **resident in Ireland for the five tax years preceding the year in which he receives the gift, i.e. 2012.** As he has not been so resident, he is not liable to Irish CAT.

Example 5

On 31 October 2012, Joey, who is domiciled, resident and ordinarily resident in the US, gifts his house in Florida to his brother Bart who moved to Ireland in 1998. Bart is US domiciled, but resident and ordinarily resident in Ireland under the income tax rules. As Bart is foreign domiciled, he is only liable on foreign property if he has been resident in Ireland for the five tax years preceding the year in which he receives the gift, i.e. 2012. As he has been so resident, he is liable to Irish CAT on the gift of the house in Florida.

14.2.4 Date of Disposition is before 1 December 1999

If the date of the disposition is before 1 December 1999, the old rules apply. This means that any gift, including a gift of assets situated outside the State, i.e. foreign assets, will be a taxable gift if the disponer is domiciled in the State at the date of the disposition.

Example 6

On 1 November 1999, John, an Irish domiciled but UK resident individual, agrees to give his son, also Irish domiciled and UK resident, a gift of an apartment situated in the UK when he marries. His son marries in October 2012. As the date of the disposition is before 1 December 1999, the gift of the UK apartment is a taxable gift for Irish CAT purposes, as the disponer is Irish domiciled.

As you have seen in **Chapter 12**, CAT on a current gift/inheritance is calculated by deducting CAT payable on all previous taxable gifts/inheritances received on or after 5 December 1991 (Aggregate B) from CAT payable on the current gift/inheritance plus all previous taxable gifts/inheritances (Aggregate A). You need to be aware of the old rules in order to decide whether a gift/inheritance received between 5 December 1991 and 1 December 1999 is a taxable gift/inheritance which needs to be included in Aggregates A and B.

(The above definitions, and those that follow, exclude rules re discretionary trusts as they are *not* examinable.)

14.3 Definitions re Gifts and Inheritances

The above definition of taxable gifts now requires further examination.

14.3.1 Resident

The same tests apply as for income tax.

An individual is resident in the State in any year of assessment in which the individual:

■ spends a total of 183 days or more in the State; or
■ spends more than 30 days in the State in that year and, in that year and the previous year taken together, spends 280 days or more in the State; or

■ elects to be so resident, being in the State in that year with the intention, and in such circumstances, that make it likely, that he will be resident in the following year of assessment.

In respect of the tax years 2009 onwards, an individual is present in the State for a day, if present at any time during that day.

14.3.2 Ordinarily Resident

The same tests apply as for income tax.

An individual is ordinarily resident in the State in any year of assessment in which he has been resident in the State in the three previous years of assessment. Once he becomes ordinarily resident, he remains so until a year of assessment in which he has been non-resident in each of the three previous years of assessment.

14.3.3 Domicile

The same tests apply as for income tax.

Domicile is a legal term. Briefly put, a person's domicile is the country where he is deemed to have his permanent home in law. This is normally the country in which he resides with the intention of remaining permanently. It should be stressed however that an individual may be domiciled in a country without actually residing in it.

14.3.4 Date of the Disposition

In determining whether the old or new rules apply, we see that the date of the disposition is critical. CATCA 2003 defines it to mean:

1. the date of death of the deceased in the case of a benefit taken by will or an intestacy;
2. the date of death of the deceased in the case of benefits derived under the Succession Act 1965 (i.e. basically a widow's legal right or claims of children to a share in the estate);
3. the latest date when the disponer could have exercised the right or power which has been waived, where the disposition consisted of a failure or omission to exercise a right or power;
4. in any other case, the date of the disposition is the date on which the act or, where more than one act is involved, the last act of the disponer was done by which he provided or bound himself to provide, the property comprised in the disposition.

14.3.5 Date of the Gift

We have seen in **Section 13.2** above that the date of the gift is the date of the happening of the event upon which the donee becomes beneficially entitled in possession to the benefit. We have also seen that the **date of the gift** is not necessarily the same date as the **date of the disposition**.

Some of the reasons why the date of the gift is important are:

■ The date determines the rate of tax and the tax-free thresholds which apply. 2012 tax-free thresholds and tax rates will apply where the date of the gift is in 2012.

■ A gift of foreign property from a non-resident disponer is only within the charge to Irish CAT if the beneficiary is resident or ordinarily resident in the State at the date of the gift.

■ For agricultural relief (see **Section 15.7**), business relief (see **Section 15.8**) or dwelling house exemption (see **Section 16.8**) to apply certain conditions must be satisfied at the date of the gift and/or at the valuation date. Also clawbacks of the relief or exemption may apply if property which qualified for relief is disposed of within six years (and in certain situations within 10 years) after the date of the gift.

14.4 Taxable Inheritances

14.4.1 Overview

The rules are the same as for gifts.

1. Irish property – always taxable

An inheritance is a taxable inheritance if the entire property which is to be appropriated to the inheritance or out of which property is to be appropriated to the inheritance, is situated in the Republic of Ireland. If a proportion only of the property mentioned above is situated in the State, then only a similar proportion of the inheritance will be taxable.

2. Foreign property

Foreign property is taxable if the disponer is resident or ordinarily resident or if the successor is resident or ordinarily resident.

This general rule would mean that foreign domiciled persons who were only in Ireland for a short time could trigger an Irish CAT liability. In order to ensure that this does not happen, there is a special five year rule for foreign domiciled people.

The current rules apply to inheritances where the date of the disposition is on or after 1 December 1999. Before this date, one looked at the domicile of the disponer.

14.4.2 Taxable Inheritances

Where the date of the disposition is on or after 1 December 1999, an inheritance is taxable in the State where:

■ the **disponer is resident or ordinarily resident** in the State in the year of assessment in which the **disposition giving rise to the inheritance is made**; or

■ the **successor is resident or ordinarily resident** in the State in the year of assessment in which the **date of the inheritance falls**; or

■ the **inheritance is situated in the State**.

The income tax rules for determining residence and ordinary residence generally apply. However, there are special rules for foreign domiciled persons.

14.4.3 Taxable Inheritances of Foreign Property – Foreign Domiciled Persons

As for gifts, there are special rules for foreign domiciled persons, i.e. such people are not treated as resident or ordinarily resident unless:

■ the date occurs on or after 1 December 2004;

■ the person has been resident in the State for **five consecutive years of assessment immediately preceding the year of assessment in which that date falls**; *and*

■ the person is either **resident or ordinarily resident** in the State on that date.

The date is the date of the disposition in the case of the disporner and the date of the inheritance in the case of the beneficiary.

The term **date of the inheritance** has been dealt with in **Section 13.12** above.

14.4.4   Date of Disposition is before 1 December 1999

If the date of the disposition is before 1 December 1999, the old rules apply, i.e. any inheritance, including an inheritance of assets situated outside the State, i.e. foreign assets, will be a taxable inheritance if the disporner is domiciled in the State at the date of the disposition (normally the date of death).

14.5   Shares in Foreign Incorporated Family-owned Companies

There are anti-avoidance measures to ensure that Irish domiciled non-resident individuals cannot avoid Irish CAT on Irish property by artificially changing the locality of Irish situated assets by transferring the assets into a foreign incorporated, family controlled private company. Shares in a foreign incorporated company would be non-Irish assets. Accordingly a gift of shares in a foreign incorporated company by a non-resident Irish domiciled person would be outside the charge to Irish CAT.

Where the beneficiary, after taking the gift or inheritance, controls a private company incorporated outside the State, the beneficiary is liable to Irish CAT to the extent that the assets of the foreign company are Irish assets.

Questions (to Chapter 14)

Review Questions

(See Suggested Solutions at the end of this textbook.)

Question 14.1

A gift or inheritance of property situated in the State is within the charge to Irish CAT regardless of the domicile/residence position of the disponer or the donee/successor.

Requirement
Outline the general rules which determine where property is situated.

Question 14.2

The following gifts/inheritances were taken during the year ended 31 December 2012:

1. Donal, an Irish domiciled and resident individual, died on 19 April 2012. He left all his assets, consisting of Irish and UK property, to his son Brendan, also Irish domiciled and resident.
2. Gordon, an Irish domiciled and UK resident person, died on 11 July 2012. He left shares in a UK trading company to his Irish resident and domiciled nephew Dermot.
3. Jonathan, a UK domiciled and resident person, died on 15 August 2012 and left land in Cork to his son John, also UK domiciled and resident.
4. Noel, a UK domiciled and resident person, died on 16 September 2012 and left a house in the UK and €20,000 in a sterling bank account in London to his son Nevin also UK domiciled but resident in Ireland since 2002.
5. Michael, an Irish domiciled and resident individual, died on 1 February 2012. He left all his assets equally to his two children, David and Jane. His assets consisted of a house in Clare and €30,000 in an Irish bank account. David and Jane are both Irish domiciled; however, while David is also Irish resident, Jane has been resident in the UK for many years.
6. On 23 August 2012, Maurice, an Irish domiciled and UK resident person, gave shares valued at €10,000 in various UK companies to his nephew Darren, also Irish domiciled and UK resident. Maurice has been living in the UK since 1994. Darren only moved to the UK in June 2011. Prior to moving to the UK, Darren had always lived in Cork.
7. In 1998, Maxine an Irish domiciled and UK resident individual emigrated to Australia. Before she went, by deed she provided that her niece could live in her house in the UK for a period of 14 years but that after that date the house was to be transferred into the absolute ownership of her son Stephen also Irish domiciled and UK resident. The house was transferred to Stephen absolutely in November 2012.
8. Jim, an Irish domiciled and resident individual, gave his daughter Brid, also Irish domiciled and resident, a rental property in the UK by deed dated 12 December 2012.

9. Jean, an individual domiciled in France but resident in Ireland since 2000, gifted her daughter Amelie, also domiciled in France and resident in Ireland since 2000 except for the year 2010 when she was non-resident, shares in an Irish trading company and shares in a French trading company on 31 December 2012.

10. Mark, an Irish domiciled and resident individual, died on 25 June 2012. On his death, his son Declan, also Irish domiciled and resident, inherited land in the UK. Declan's mother, Janet, had died in 1989. Under the terms of Janet's will, Mark received a life interest in the UK land and, on his death, Declan was to become the absolute owner of the land. Janet was UK domiciled and UK resident for many years at the date of her death.

Requirement

(a) Outline the rules for determining whether a gift or inheritance taken during the year ended 31 December 2012 is a taxable gift or inheritance.

(b) For each gift or inheritance outlined above, state whether the gift/inheritance is a taxable gift/inheritance, giving reasons for your answer.

Question 14.3

You are employed in the tax department of a firm of Chartered Accountants and have received a memorandum from an audit partner in the firm. The partner has directed the following queries to you in relation to various CAT issues:

(a) What determines if a gift is a "taxable gift"?
(b) Explain the term "taxable inheritance".
(c) What does "domicile" mean?
(d) What is meant by the term "date of the disposition"?
(e) Explain what is meant by "date of the gift".

Requirement

Write a memorandum to the audit partner setting out your reply to each of the queries raised by him as outlined at (a) to (e) above.

Taxable Value

Learning Objectives

After studying this chapter you will have developed competency in the following:

1. **Valuation Date, Market Value and Taxable Value**

   - The valuation date for a gift is the date of the gift.
   - The valuation date for inheritances is more complex. It can be as early as the date of death. Often, it is much later as the property must be retained for/delivered to the beneficiary for the valuation date to arise. In a complex estate, this could be a considerable time after the date of death.
   - When a gift becomes an inheritance, the valuation date is the date of the gift.
   - The valuation date is key as this is the date when property must be valued and the due date for payment of CAT and filing CAT returns depends on the valuation date. Some of the reliefs have tests which are applied at the valuation date.
   - There are special rules for determining the market value of shares in private controlled companies, i.e. no discount for minority interests.
   - There are special rules for determining the value of a gift or inheritance of an annuity.
   - In calculating the taxable value, liabilities, costs, expenses and consideration paid are deductible.

2. **Agricultural Relief**

   - This is a very important relief. It is available to individuals, who after receiving the agricultural property, have 80% of assets consisting of agricultural property.
   - Agricultural property is all types of agricultural assets.
   - The relief is 90% of the market value of agricultural property, i.e. 10% of the value is taxable.
   - Any related expenses and consideration are only 10% deductible.

- Any non-agricultural property received is fully taxable and related expenses are fully deductible.
- If the agricultural property is disposed of within six years and the proceeds are not re-invested or are only partly re-invested, there is a clawback of all/some of the relief, i.e. increased taxable value and probably CAT payable. If development land is disposed of in the period six to ten years, there is a clawback.

3. Business Relief

- This is a very important relief for Irish business. It is available to beneficiaries of sole trader and partnership businesses and shares in Irish unquoted companies.
- The relief is 90% of the taxable value (net of deductions) of the business/shares, provided that certain conditions have been satisfied and the business/shares have been owned for at least:
    - two years, in the case of inheritances taken on the death of the disponer; or
    - five years, in the case of gifts.
- The trade of the sole trader, the partnership business or company must be a qualifying trade, i.e. all trades, except trades which consist wholly or mainly of dealing in land, shares, securities or currencies or of making or holding investments.
- Shares must generally be unquoted. Also, if the company is not a family-owned company, the beneficiary must satisfy certain minimum shareholding requirements (after receiving the benefit).
- Non-business assets of the business or company are excluded from the relief, i.e. they are fully taxable.
- If the business/shares are disposed of within six years and not replaced, there is a clawback of all/some of the relief. If development land is disposed of in the period six to ten years, there is a clawback.

15.1 General Principles

We have seen that CAT is levied on the **taxable value** of the gift or inheritance concerned. The basic steps involved may be illustrated as follows:

	€
Market value	X
Less: liabilities, costs and expenses payable out of the taxable gift/ inheritance.	(X)
Incumbrance-free value	X
Less: market value of consideration paid by the donee/successor	(X)
TAXABLE VALUE	X

We will now examine in detail the meaning of the above terms:

15.2 Market Value

CATCA 2003 contains specific provisions setting out the method by which the market value of different types of property is to be computed.

15.2.1 Market Value – General Rule

The general rule is that the market value of any property is to be the price, which in the opinion of the Revenue Commissioners, the property would fetch if sold on the **open market, on the valuation date**, in such manner and subject to such conditions as might reasonably be expected to obtain for the vendor the best price for the property.

CATCA 2003 sets out the general market value rule and specifically states that the Revenue Commissioners are not to make any reduction in the estimate of market value on the grounds that the whole property is to be placed on the market at the same time.

Revenue has the power to authorise the inspection of property by any person, they consider fit, at all reasonable times. If Revenue requires a professional valuation, then the cost of such valuation is to be paid for by them.

For the purposes of estimating the market value of unquoted shares or securities if sold on the open market, it is to be assumed that there is available to any prospective purchaser of the shares or securities all the information which a prudent prospective purchaser might reasonably require if he/she were proposing to buy them from a willing vendor at arm's length.

The meaning of the term **valuation date** is dealt with later.

15.2.2 Market Value of Shares in Certain Private Companies

A **private company** is defined to mean a body corporate (wherever incorporated) which:

1. is under the control of not more than five persons; and
2. is not a quoted company which is excluded from the corporation tax close company rules (as adjusted for CAT purposes to counter tax avoidance).

Therefore most companies in Ireland, particularly family-owned companies, are covered by the definition.

CATCA 2003 provides that the market value of each share in a private company, which (after the taking of the gift or inheritance) is, on the date of the gift or inheritance, a company **controlled by the donee/successor**, is to be computed on a market value basis, i.e. each share is valued as if it formed an apportioned part of the market value of the shares in that company. Such apportionment, as between shares of a particular class, is by reference to nominal amount and, as between difference classes of shares, is with due regard to the rights attaching to each of the different classes.

15.2.3 Market Value of Certain Other Property

CATCA 2003 contains specific provision for the valuation of life interests, interests for a period certain (e.g. house for life) and agricultural property. These are dealt with separately in detail later.

15.3 Valuation of Annuities

CATCA 2003 contains special provisions for calculating the value of a gift or inheritance of an annuity. The method of valuation depends on whether the annuity is charged/secured on any property.

Life interests and limited interests are dealt with in **Chapter 18**.

15.4 Free use of Property

A charge to CAT arises where a person has the use and enjoyment of property either for no consideration or for less than full consideration. If the "free" use is ongoing, the benefit is deemed to be taken on 31 December each year. The benefit taken is deemed to be the difference between the consideration given by the person for the use, occupation or enjoyment of the property and the best price obtainable in the open market for such use, occupation or enjoyment. If the free use is of land or a house, the best price obtainable would be the market rent payable for such a property. If the free use is of cash, for example an interest-free loan, the best price obtainable would be the income from the investment of such cash, i.e. the bank deposit rate applicable to such sum and not the rate which a bank might apply to a loan. The following examples explain how the benefit is calculated.

> **Example 1**
> Market value of benefit in "free" use case involving a loan. Joe gives an interest free loan of €100,000 to his nephew John on 1 January. The **bank deposit rate of interest is, say, 2%.** John is deemed to take a gift of €2,000 on 31 December. He is also deemed to take a gift each year, on 31 December, until the loan is repaid and each such deemed gift is taken into account for aggregation purposes. If the loan is repaid during the year, the date of the deemed gift for that year is the date of repayment. If the loan was repaid after six months, the value of the gift for that year would be €1,000.

> **Example 2**
> Market value of benefit in "free" use case involving accommodation. Anne gives the use of her house worth €200,000 to her cousin Colette. The annual market rent is €15,000. Colette pays Anne €5,000 per annum. Colette is deemed to take a gift of €10,000 on 31 December each year that she has the use of the house and each deemed gift is taken into account for aggregation purposes.

Power of Revocation

If a disponer, under a disposition, has **retained the power to revoke a disposition**, then no tax is charged at the date of the disposition on the basis that ownership is deemed to remain with the disponer. CAT will only become payable **when the power to revoke is released** or **when the disponer dies** without revoking the disposition. In the event that the disponer dies without revoking the disposition, the benefit taken will be an **inheritance as it is taken on a death**, i.e. the death of the disponer.

If, as is usually the case, the beneficiary has the free use of the property during the period between the date of the original disposition and the date of death of the disponer, a charge to CAT arises on the annual value of the property, i.e. annual letting value, on the free use basis as described above.

Example

By deed of transfer dated 1 January 2009, Owen transfers his house in Dublin to Declan but reserves to himself a power to revoke the transfer. Owen died on 30 June 2012 without having exercised the power of revocation. At the date of Owen's death, the house is valued at €500,000. The annual value of the market rent is €20,000 per annum. Declan is deemed to take the following benefits:

	€
On 31 December 2009 gift	20,000
On 31 December 2010 inheritance*	20,000
On 31 December 2011 inheritance*	20,000
On 30 June 2012 (6 months "free" use of house) inheritance*	10,000
On 30 June 2012 (house) inheritance	500,000

* Gifts that became inheritances because disponer died within two years. The small gift exemption still applies.

15.5 Valuation Date

The term **valuation date** is critical from the point of view of the following aspects of CAT.

1. The taxable value of property comprised in a gift/inheritance is based on the market value of the property at the valuation date.
2. The valuation date determines when CAT is payable and when a CAT return must be filed. If it is in the period from 1 January to 31 August 2012, CAT is payable and the return must be filed on or before 31 October 2012. If the valuation date is in the period from 1 September to 31 December 2012, CAT is payable and the return must be filed on or before 31 October 2013. Where a return is filed on ROS (the Revenue Online System), the filing date is extended (to 15 November in the case of 2012).
3. Agricultural relief in the valuation of property is only applicable to certain farmers and the tests to be applied in determining whether or not the relief is available is applied as at the valuation date for any particular gift or inheritance. Similarly, the ownership or control test for business relief is applied at the valuation date.

15.5.1 Importance of Valuation Date

Determining the **actual valuation date** is very important as it determines when you value the asset and when CAT is paid.

For example, if a parent is considering gifting shares on 1 April 2012 but actually delays making the gift for say six months until 1 October 2012, then the valuation date is 1 October 2012. If the shares have increased in value by say 20% during that period, then the child has a higher market value, taxable value and probably CAT. Obviously delaying the gift six months has delayed the payment of tax from 31 October 2012 to 31 October 2013, but in this case will probably have increased the amount of CAT as the market value has increased 20%.

15.5.2 Valuation Date of a Taxable Gift

CATCA 2003 sets out the rules for determining the valuation date. The valuation date is normally the **date of the gift**. The valuation date in relation to a **gift which subsequently becomes an inheritance** as a result of the death of the disponer within two years of the disposition is specifically deemed to remain the **date of the gift**.

15.5.3 *Valuation Date of a Taxable Inheritance*

The determination of the valuation date for inheritances is complex. The following are the main rules:

1. For cases not covered by (2) below, the valuation date of a taxable inheritance will be the **earliest** of the following dates:

    (i)   the earliest date on which any person is **entitled** to retain the subject matter of the inheritance for the benefit of the successor; or
    (ii) the date on which the subject matter of the inheritance **is** actually retained; or
    (iii) the date of **actual delivery/payment** of the inheritance to the successor.

2. The valuation date for a gift which has become an inheritance as a result of the disponer dying within two years of the date of the disposition is deemed to be the date of the gift.

Generally speaking, the residue of an estate cannot be regarded as retained for the benefit of the beneficiary until the estate is finally administered. This is, of course, subject to the possibility of interim payments having been made to the legatee in question.

The basic principle therefore to be applied is **that the valuation date will be the date of delivery or payment** of the subject matter of the inheritance to the beneficiary or the date of retainer on his behalf whichever is the earliest.

The valuation date for assets passing under a will or intestacy is usually the date on which the Grant of Representation issues from the Probate Office or District Probate Registry. (The Grant of Representation is the document which allows the people distributing the assets to the beneficiaries to do so.) If assets are passing outside of the will or intestacy, the valuation date will normally be the deceased's date of death.

There can be several valuation dates where multiple benefits are taken from the same estate.

Examples of when date of death is the valuation date include where the beneficiary is in occupation of the property and where there is joint ownership of the property.

Litigation and family disputes may cause the valuation date to be put back to a later time.

Example

Jim dies in 2012. He bequeaths his farm to his wife, a cash legacy to his nephew and the residue of his estate to his son for life with the remainder to his grandson. The valuation dates would be as follows:

(i)   the date of death in the case of the inheritance taken by the wife, as this is probably the earliest date on which the personal representatives are entitled to retain the farm for the benefit of his wife.
(ii) the valuation date in the case of a cash legacy would be the date the personal representative actually paid the legacy to the nephew.
(iii) his son has a life interest in the residue of the estate and the valuation date in this case would be the date of retention of the residue for him by the personal representative. This will be sometime after the issue of the grant of probate when the personal representatives have collected the assets and the liabilities of the estate have been established, but not necessarily paid.
(iv) the grandson's valuation date would probably be the date of the son's death, as the grandson would become beneficially entitled in possession to the benefit at that time.

Example

On 1 November 2012, A, by deed, transfers property to trustees on trust for B for life with remainder to C absolutely. On creation of the trust, B would immediately become beneficially entitled to his benefit and the date of the gift would therefore be 1 November 2012. The valuation date in respect of this gift would be the same date.

The date of C's inheritance is the date of B's death, as that is the date when C becomes beneficially entitled in possession to the benefit. Again, the valuation date is probably the same date.

It is clear from CATCA 2003 that different parts of the same inheritance may have different valuation dates, e.g. if interim payments are made out of a deceased's estate prior to the date of final retainer, the valuation date of each interim payment will be the date on which the advances are actually paid.

The Revenue Commissioners are entitled to determine the valuation date for a particular inheritance but this determination is subject to an appeal by the taxpayer if he/she wishes.

Appendix 15.1 contains a summary of the definitions of the date of the disposition, date of the gift/inheritance and the valuation date.

15.6 Deduction for Liabilities, Costs and Expenses, and Consideration

We have seen that the market value of the taxable gift or inheritance is reduced by any liabilities, costs and expenses that are properly payable out of the taxable gift or taxable inheritance in order to arrive at what is known as the incumbrance-free value.

Any legal or other cost associated with the transfer of property will normally fall under this heading, e.g. solicitors' fees or stamp duty.

The most common examples of expenses that are deductible in calculating CAT are debts owed by the deceased at the date of death, funeral expenses and costs of administering the estate.

Where the property transferred is charged with the payment of a liability, then that liability is properly deductible under this heading also in arriving at the incumbrance-free value.

Example

A transfers a house worth €500,000 to B, subject to a mortgage charged on the house on which there is an outstanding amount due of €150,000. In this case the incumbrance-free value is €500,000 less €150,000, i.e. €350,000. This of course assumes that B takes over the property subject to the mortgage. If B also paid stamp duty and solicitor's costs in connection with the transfer, such expenses would also be deducted.

Example

Joe dies and leaves a business worth €5,000,000 to his son Ray. The executor of Joe's will paid legal expenses of €50,000. These legal expenses are a deductible expense in calculating the taxable value of the benefit taken by Ray, i.e. €5,000,000 less €50,000 = €4,950,000.

Consideration Paid by Donee/Successor

CATCA 2003 permits the incumbrance-free value of the property transferred to be reduced by any "bona fide consideration in money or monies worth paid by the donee or successor," in computing the taxable value of the gift or inheritance.

Consideration is the last deduction to be made in arriving at the taxable value and is deductible in effect from the value of the interest taken by the donee whether absolute or limited. The treatment of limited interest will be dealt with separately.

CATCA 2003 particularly mentions that consideration will *include*:

(i) Any liability of the disponer which the donee/successor undertakes to discharge as his own *personal* liability.

(ii) Any other liability to which the gift or inheritance is subject under the terms of the disposition under which it is paid, e.g. A transfers property to B on condition that B pays €1,000 to C. The €1,000 paid by B to C would represent consideration to be deducted from the incumbrance-free value of the property taken from A in calculating the final taxable value.

Consideration paid by a donee/successor may take many forms:

- a part payment;
- an annuity payable to the disponer;
- a CGT liability of the donor arising out of the disposal which the donee agrees to pay.

Deductions Specifically Prohibited in Arriving at Taxable Values

Set out below are the main deductions not allowable in arriving at taxable values.

1. Contingent liabilities: where the payment of a liability is contingent upon the happening of some future event, no deduction is permitted. If the contingent liability eventually becomes payable by the donee/successor, then an adjustment is allowed.
2. Liabilities, costs, etc., for which reimbursement can be obtained.
3. The tax, penalties or interest payable under CATCA 2003 and any costs of raising money to pay those liabilities.
4. Liabilities connected with exempt assets cannot be used to reduce the taxable value of non-exempt property.

Restriction of Deduction for Consideration in Certain Circumstances

If consideration is paid for a gift/inheritance which comprises both Irish and foreign property, and only the Irish property is subject to CAT, then the amount of consideration deductible in arriving at taxable value is arrived at as follows:

$$\text{Total Consideration Paid} \times \frac{\text{Value of Taxable Gift/Inheritance}}{\text{Total Value of Gift/Inheritance}}$$

We will see also that where agricultural land etc., is valued for CAT at a proportion of its value (i.e. at its agricultural value), then only a corresponding proportion of debts, liabilities and consideration relating to that property may be deducted.

General

CATCA 2003 specifically provides that liabilities which are an incumbrance on specific property are to be deducted as far as possible against the value of the property on which the liability is charged, or by which it is secured.

15.7 Agricultural Relief

15.7.1 Summary Chart of Calculation of Taxable Value where there is Agricultural Relief

- **AGRICULTURAL VALUE**
  less
- **PROPORTION OF LIABILITIES, COSTS, EXPENSES**
  equals
- **INCUMBRANCE-FREE VALUE**
  less
- **PROPORTION OF CONSIDERATION**
  equals
- **TAXABLE VALUE**

15.7.2 The Relief

Provided certain conditions are fulfilled, section 89 CATCA 2003 permits the market value of specified "**agricultural property**" to be **reduced by 90%** in computing the taxable value of the gift/inheritance taken by a "farmer".

Example

Joe received a gift of a farm, livestock and machinery worth €1 million. The value for CAT purposes is calculated as follows:

	€
Market value of agricultural property	1,000,000
Agricultural relief (90%)	(900,000)
Agricultural value	100,000

The relief was lower in the past. The old rules are not examinable.

15.7.3 Definitions

"Agricultural property" is defined as meaning:

1. Agricultural land, pasture and woodlands situated in the EU (for gifts/inheritances taken before 20 November 2008, only the Irish State and not EU was included);
2. Crops, trees and underwood growing on such land;
3. Such farm buildings, farm houses, and mansion houses (together with the lands occupied therewith) as are of a character appropriate to the property.
4. Farm machinery, livestock and bloodstock thereon.
5. A payment entitlement under the EU Single Farm Payment Scheme.

The term **"agricultural value"** refers to the **market value of the agricultural property as reduced by** whatever relief is available – **90% relief** under the current rule.

"Farmer"

The gift or inheritance must consist of agricultural property at the date of the gift or inheritance and at the valuation date.

To qualify for the relief, a donee/successor must qualify as a "farmer" on the valuation date. A **"farmer"** is defined as a donee or successor who is, **on the valuation date and**

after taking the gift or inheritance, an individual in respect of whom **not less than 80% of the market value** of the property to which he is beneficially entitled in possession is represented by the market value of property in the EU which consists of **agricultural property** (as defined above). The gross value of all property is used for the purposes of the 80% test, i.e. no deduction is made for mortgages, etc. except **borrowings on an off-farm principal private residence are deductible for the purpose of the 80% test** provided that, for gifts or inheritances taken on or after 8 February 2012, the borrowings have been used to purchase, repair or improve that residence.

15.7.4 Computation of Relief

In the computation of taxable value, the market value of the agricultural property comprised in the gift or inheritance is reduced to its agricultural value.

Example

◼ **Gift of agricultural property**
John gives the following to his mother, Mary, who has no other assets:

	€
Farmland	300,000
Woodland	100,000
Farm buildings	50,000
Farm machinery	20,000
Bloodstock	30,000
Total	500,000

If there were no agricultural relief, the full gift would be taxable, i.e. taxable value of €500,000. The relief would not be due for example if she had other assets and could not satisfy the 80% test.

She is a farmer as at least 80% of her assets (in this case 100%) are agricultural assets. Therefore agricultural relief is due and the taxable value is reduced. The agricultural value is calculated as follows

	€
Market value of agricultural property	500,000
Relief at 90%	(450,000)
Agricultural value	50,000

◼ **Assume the same facts as in the above example except that Mary has other assets as follows:**

	€
– Bank deposit account	10,000
– Shares	20,000
– Principal Private Residence (PPR)	300,000
– Mortgage to buy PPR	250,000

Gross market value of all Mary's assets (less mortgage re off-farm PPR) is €580,000 (i.e. €500,000 + €10,000 + €20,000 + €300,000 − €250,000)

Gross value agricultural assets €500,000

Is Mary a farmer? $\dfrac{€500,000}{€580,000} = 86\%$

Yes, Mary is a farmer

continued overleaf

Therefore, agricultural relief is due and the taxable value is reduced as follows:

	€
Market value of agricultural property	500,000
Relief at 90%	(450,000)
Agricultural value	50,000

- ■ **Inheritance of Agricultural Property**

  Jack, who has no other assets, inherits the following from his aunt:

	€
–Farmland and buildings	200,000
–Crops	30,000
–Livestock and machinery	20,000
Total	250,000

  If there were no agricultural relief, the full inheritance would be taxable, i.e. taxable value of €250,000.

  Due to agricultural relief, the taxable value is reduced. The agricultural value is calculated as follows:

	€
Market value of agricultural property	250,000
Relief at 90%	(225,000)
Agricultural value	25,000

- ■ **Client may have given you incorrect information**

  If, in the previous example, you deal with Jack's tax affairs and you know that, when you filed his last return on his behalf, he owned property. However, he has stated that he does not have any property in his recent correspondence to your manager. You should advise your manager of the fact that his last tax return showed that Jack had property. Your manager can raise this with Jack to establish whether there was some other explanation, such as having sold the property to pay off debt or whether there was an error made by Jack.

15.7.5 Computation of Relief – Restriction of Deductions

CATCA 2003 also provides that the **allowance for debts, incumbrances and consideration connected with the agricultural property** which has been artificially reduced in value must be **proportionately reduced** to ensure that the final deduction is proportionate to the agricultural value of the property vis-a-vis its market value.

Example

Jim gives agricultural land worth €600,000 to John (who qualifies as a "farmer"). The lands are charged with a mortgage of €100,000. John is required by Jim, in consideration for the transfer, to give Stewart €50,000. The transfer takes place on 1 August 2012.

Computation of Taxable Value:

		€
Market value of agricultural property, i.e. lands		600,000
Less:	Agricultural relief at 90%	(540,000)
"AGRICULTURAL VALUE"		60,000

continued overleaf

Less:	Mortgage charged on land (as restricted):	
	€100,000 × Agricultural Value/Market Value (i.e. 10%)	
	€100,000 × $\frac{60,000}{600,000}$	(10,000)
	IINCUMBRANCE-FREE VALUE	50,000
Less:	Consideration (as restricted)	
	€50,000 × $\frac{60,000}{600,000}$ (i.e. 10%)	(5,000)
	TAXABLE VALUE:	45,000

Example

Colin died on 31 August 2012 and left agricultural land worth €100,000 to Desmond (who qualifies as a farmer). The executors of Colin's will incur legal expenses of €1,400.

Computation of Taxable Value:	€
Market value of agricultural property	100,000
Less: Reduction to arrive at agricultural value (90%)	(90,000)
Agricultural value	10,000
Less: Legal expenses €1,400 × $\frac{10,000}{100,000}$	(140)
Taxable value	9,860

Computation Where Agricultural Property and Other Property Are Involved

Where the gift/inheritance comprises both agricultural and non-agricultural property, then the taxable value of each must be computed separately. This is because:

- any expenses, etc. related to agricultural property will only be 10% allowable;
- any expenses, etc. related to non-agricultural property will be fully allowable; and
- any expenses, etc. related to both will have to be apportioned between agricultural and non-agricultural, and then allowed to the extent of 10% for agricultural and fully for non-agricultural. If there is a mortgage on the agricultural land, Revenue allow this mortgage to be deducted – see next example.

An example will best illustrate the position:

Example

Michael transfers the following assets to his brother Sean:

	Market Value
	€
Agricultural land	1,200,000
Shares	100,000
Total value	1,300,000

The land is mortgaged for €50,000. Sean, in **consideration of the gift, has paid €39,000** to Michael's nephew, Jim.

Sean is a salesman and his only asset is his private residence, which is worth €160,000 (mortgage outstanding of €100,000 for the purchase of the residence).

Legal fees and other costs of the transfer amount to €13,000 and are payable out of the gift.

continued overleaf

Computation

Is Sean a "farmer"?

Yes, as, after taking Michael's gift, more than 80% of his **gross assets** comprise agricultural property, bloodstock and farm machinery, i.e.

$$\frac{€1,200,000}{€1,360,000*} \times 100 = 88\%$$

* €1,300,000 + €160,000 − €100,000

(a) Computation of Taxable Value of Agricultural Property

	€
Market value	1,200,000
Less: Relief	
€1,200,000 × 90%	(1,080,000)
Agricultural value	120,000

Less: Liabilities, costs, etc.

Legal (relates to total property transferred)
Portion applicable to agricultural property only:

$$€13,000 \times \frac{€1,200,000 - €50,000}{€1,300,000 - €50,000} = \quad €11,960$$

Restricted for agricultural value, i.e. allow	1,196	
€11,960 × 10%		
Mortgage (relates to agricultural property only)	5,000	
€50,000 allowable 10%		
		(6,196)
INCUMBRANCE-FREE VALUE		113,804

Less: Consideration (relates to total property)
Portion applicable to agricultural property

$$€39,000 \times \frac{€1,200,000 - €50,000}{€1,300,000 - €50,000} = \quad €35,880$$

Allowable 10%		(3,588)
TAXABLE VALUE OF AGRICULTURAL PROPERTY:		110,216

(b) Computation of Taxable Value of Non-Agricultural Property

	€
Market value	100,000
Less: Liabilities, costs, etc:	
Legal (balance €13,000 − €11,960)	(1,040)
INCUMBRANCE-FREE VALUE	98,960
Less: Consideration:	
Balance €39,000 − €35,880	(3,120)
TAXABLE VALUE OF NON-AGRICULTURAL PROPERTY:	95,840

(c) Computation of Total Taxable Value of Property

Taxable value of agricultural property	110,216
Taxable value of non-agricultural property	95,840
Total	206,056

15.7.6 Other Matters

1. It should be noted that all agricultural land in the EU is within the definition of "agricultural property" where taken on or after 8 November 2008. Prior to this date, for instance, agricultural land situated in Northern Ireland would not qualify for relief.

2. If a taxable gift/inheritance is taken by a donee/successor subject to the **condition that it is to be invested in agricultural property** and this condition is complied with **within two years** of the date of the gift or the date of the inheritance, then the gift/inheritance is deemed to be agricultural property. Therefore, the individual will initially pay the CAT but get a refund of any overpaid CAT, based on availing of agricultural relief.

3. In the case of agricultural property which consists of **trees or underwood**, it is **not necessary for the donee/successor to satisfy the "farmer test"**.

4. Agricultural relief of 90% can be claimed in respect of *all* qualifying gifts and inheritances, i.e. there is no limit on the relief.

5. If an individual does not qualify for agricultural relief (e.g. does not satisfy the test that 80% of assets are agricultural property), the individual **may qualify for business relief** – see **Section 15.8** below. An explanation of the difference between agricultural relief and business relief is set out in **Appendix 15.2**.

Ranking of Agricultural and Business Relief

As it notes in the final paragraph of **Appendix 15.2**, an individual does not have the option of claiming either agricultural or business relief – a claim is made for agricultural relief if the conditions are satisfied.

15.7.7 Clawback of Relief on Disposal or Compulsory Acquisition within Six Years

Agricultural relief previously claimed will be recaptured if the agricultural property (other than crops, trees or underwood) or part of it **is disposed** of or compulsorily acquired within six years from the date of the gift or inheritance, *and* **not replaced by other agricultural property**:

- within a year in the case of a sale; or
- within six years in the case of a compulsory acquisition.

This recapture **does not apply where the donee** or successor **dies** before the property is sold or compulsorily acquired.

If there is **full reinvestment** of proceeds, there is **no clawback**.

If there is **no reinvestment** of proceeds, there is **full clawback**.

Example

Joe inherited a farm, with a market value of €1,000,000 on the valuation date. He qualified for agricultural relief and therefore the taxable value of the inheritance was €100,000. Joe paid CAT at the then rate of 25% on the inheritance as his tax-free threshold was fully utilised. Two years later, Joe sold the farm for €1,400,000. He reinvested none of the proceeds. What is the CAT due as a result?

The CAT on clawback is calculated as follows:

	€
Original relief claimed is clawed back	900,000
Additional CAT payable (at rate that prevailed when inheritance was received) (€900,000 × 25%)	225,000

If a proportion of the proceeds are reinvested, a similar proportion of the relief is clawed back.

15.7.8 Clawback of Agricultural Relief or Business Relief: Development Land

There is a clawback of agricultural and business relief after six years where:

- The gift or inheritance is taken on or after 2 February 2006.
- The gift or inheritance consists wholly or partly of **development land**.
- The development land qualified for either agricultural or business relief (development land has the same meaning as it has for CGT).
- The development land is disposed of in whole or in part by the donee/successor at any time in the period **commencing six years** after the date of the gift or inheritance and **ending 10 years** after that date.

(**Note:** the term "disposed of" has its ordinary meaning (i.e. a transfer of ownership in an asset) and includes a sale, a compulsory acquisition, a gift or a transfer of property occurring on the death of the donee or successor).

Where these conditions are satisfied, then CAT will be recomputed as at the original valuation date of the gift or inheritance. The clawback of relief is calculated by substituting the current use value of the land in place of the development value in arriving at the 90% reduction used for agricultural relief. As the value of the land qualifying for relief is reduced a higher CAT liability will become payable. Interest will be charged from the date of disposal of the land. Previously, interest was charged from the valuation date of the gift/inheritance.

Example

Alan receives a gift of development land of 100 acres from his father on 1 June 2012. The land qualified for agricultural relief. The current use value of the land on the valuation date (i.e. 1 June 2012) is €3 million. The market value of the land on that date is €20 million.

Ignoring small gift exemption and assuming he has used his entire group A threshold, Alan's CAT on his gift on 1 June 2012 is calculated as follows:

	€
Market value of gift	20,000,000
Agricultural relief (90%)	(18,000,000)
Taxable value	2,000,000
CAT @ 30%	600,000

If Alan does not dispose of the land within 10 years, the agricultural relief is never clawed back.

If Alan sells the land within six years, the clawback outlined at **Section 15.7.7** will apply.

If Alan sells the land in 2019 (i.e. seven years later), a clawback will apply in respect of the relief granted on the development value of €17 million (i.e. €20 million less €3 million of current use value).

As before, ignoring small gift exemption and assuming he has used his entire Group A threshold, Alan's CAT on his gift on 1 June 2012 is recalculated as follows:

	€
Market value of gift	20,000,000
Agricultural relief (90% × €3,000,000)	(2,700,000)
Taxable value	17,300,000
CAT @ 30%	5,190,000
Less already paid	(600,000)
CAT payable	4,590,000

15.8 Business Relief

15.8.1 Overview

Under sections 90–102 CATCA 2003, there is a relief for gifts or inheritances of business property if certain conditions are met.

To qualify for the relief, the business concerned must not consist wholly or mainly of dealing in land, shares, securities or currencies or of making or holding investments. The relief extends to all the qualifying activities of the business. In the case of sole traders and partnerships, therefore, the relief applies to the value of the net assets of the business which are used in the course of its qualifying business activities. In the case of companies, the relief applies to that proportion of the value of the shares or securities of the company which derive from qualifying business activities. Assets which are not used for the purposes of a qualifying business activity are excluded. Quoted shares or securities are not eligible for relief, but quoted shares or securities which were unquoted at the time they were acquired by the disponer, can qualify. If an individual does not qualify for agricultural relief (i.e. does not satisfy the 80% test), then he/she may qualify for business relief.

The business property must have been owned by the disponer for a minimum period prior to the gift or inheritance and, where the business property consists of shares or securities in a company, the donee/successor must hold a minimum interest in the business after taking the gift or inheritance.

As can be seen from this overview, there are important conditions to be satisfied if an individual is to benefit from this relief.

The relief may be withdrawn in whole or in part if, within six years after the gift or inheritance, the business ceases to be a qualifying business (other than in the case of a bona fide winding up on grounds of insolvency) or if the relevant business property is disposed of and not replaced within a year by other qualifying business property. Therefore, if the beneficiary disposes of the business within six years and does not replace it, there may be a very significant CAT cost.

The relief applies to both gifts and inheritances.

15.8.2 The Relief

The relief is 90% of the value of qualifying relevant business property. The relief was lower in the past but this is not examinable.

15.8.3 Relevant Business Property

The property that can qualify for relief is "relevant business property", which is as follows:

1. A business or an **interest in a business**.
2. **Unquoted shares** in a company subject to the condition that on the valuation date:

    (a) The **beneficiary** holds **more than 25%** of the voting rights. Or:
    (b) The company is **controlled by the beneficiary**. A company is controlled by a beneficiary if it is controlled by any one or more of the following:

       ■ the beneficiary;
       ■ relatives of the beneficiary;

■ civil partner or children of the civil partner of the beneficiary; and

■ certain nominees and trusts.

"Controlled" generally means holding 50% or more of the nominal value of the shares in a company or more than 50% of the voting share capital. There is no minimum ownership requirement for the beneficiary. The following are relatives of a beneficiary: his spouse, parent, child, aunt, uncle, their children and grand-children, the spouse of any of these relatives (other than the beneficiary's own spouse or civil partner) and his grandparents. For this purpose, a company con-trolled by a beneficiary under the definition above is deemed to be a relative of a beneficiary. Or:

(c) The **beneficiary** holds at least **10%** of the issued share capital of the company **and has worked full time** in the company (or a group company) for the **five years** prior to the date of the gift or inheritance. The % ownership test is carried out **after taking the benefit**.

3. **Land, buildings, machinery and plant** owned by the disponer but **used by a company controlled** by the **disponer** or by a partnership of which the disponer was a partner. The land, etc. must, however, be **transferred to the donee or successor at the same time as the partnership interest or the shares** or securities of the company are trans-ferred, and the partnership interest or shares must be relevant business property.

4. **Quoted shares** or securities of a company where:

(a) they were **owned by the disponer prior** to their becoming **quoted**; and

(b) **one of the ownership tests** set out at (2) above is satisfied.

> ***Examples***
>
> (a) If a sole trader gifts his **business** to a child, this is a gift of relevant business property. If a partner in a partnership leaves the share in the partnership to a child, this is relevant business property.
> 　　If a sole trader gifts **just the premises** in which the trade is carried on (and not the trade itself) to a niece, this is **not relevant business property,** i.e. it is a gift of a premises only and not of a business.
>
> (b) In order to qualify for business relief, the shares generally must be unquoted and **minimum ownership conditions** must be satisfied.
> 　　If a parent gifts shares in AIB plc to a child, this is not relevant business property and business relief will not apply.
> 　　If a parent owns a company and leaves it equally to the three children, then the shares are relevant business property. This is due to the fact that the beneficiary (each child) owns more than 25% of the voting rights. Alternatively, it qualifies as the company is controlled by the beneficiary and relatives.
> 　　A parent owns 30% of an unquoted company. The other 70% is owned by people who are not related to the parent. If the parent gifts these shares to a child, the child receives relevant business property – holds more than 25% of voting power.
> 　　If, alternatively, the parent wants to gift shares equally to two children, then the 15% shareholding received by each child will only be relevant property if the child has worked full-time in the company for the preceding five years.

This means that minority shareholders in a company (which is not their family company), who want a beneficiary to benefit from business relief, must ensure that they give/leave shares to one person who will have:

■ **more than 25% of voting rights** after receiving the shares; or
■ **worked in the business** for five years and will hold **at least 10% of the shares** after receiving the shares.

Non-Qualifying Property

A business or interest in a business, or shares or securities in a company, are *not qualifying property* where the business, or the business of the company, consists wholly or *mainly of dealing in currencies, securities, stocks or shares, land or buildings, or making or holding investments*.

A holding company can qualify provided that its value is primarily attributable, directly or indirectly, to trading activities.

15.8.4 Minimum Period of Ownership by Disponer

The minimum period of ownership by the disponer depends on the type of benefit taken and is as follows:

■ in the case of an **inheritance** taken on the date of death of a disponer, the property must have been owned by the **disponer or his/her spouse or civil partner** for at least **two** years prior to the date of the inheritance; and
■ in the case of a **gift**, or an inheritance taken on the death of a person other than the disponer, the property must have been owned by the **disponer or his/her spouse or civil partner** for at least **five** years prior to transfer.

The two/five-year minimum period of ownership is modified in two situations, namely replacement assets and successive benefits. These are not examinable.

15.8.5 Valuation of Property

1. **Value of a Business**
    The value of the business or an interest in a business (e.g. share in a partnership) is computed on **a net value basis**, i.e. the market value of the *assets used in the business* (including goodwill), reduced by the aggregate market value of any *liabilities incurred for the purposes of the business*.
2. **Valuing Groups**
    There are specific rules for valuing groups but these are not examinable.
3. **Assets Excluded in Determining the Value attributable to Relevant Business Property**
    Having determined that the property is relevant business property, one must then value the property. As noted above, normal market value rules are used. However, CATCA 2003 provides that the value of **certain assets must be excluded** when determining how much of the total value of the business will actually qualify for business relief. The most important are assets used wholly or mainly for **personal use and any non-business assets**.

Example

Harry Porter owned Hogmount Ltd since its formation in 2006 and transferred his 100% shareholding to his son Trevor in October 2012. The company is valued as follows:

	€
Rental property	310,000
Goodwill	300,000
Equipment	70,000
Stock	30,000
Trade debtors	50,000
Trade creditors	(60,000)
	700,000

The company operated a chain of fast food outlets and used surplus funds to invest in rented residential property.

Trevor's CAT liability is as follows

	Qualifying Property	Non-Qualifying Property
	€	€
Market value	450,000	310,000
Less liabilities	(60,000)	
Trade creditors		
Taxable value before relief	390,000	310,000
Business relief	(351,000)	0
Taxable value	39,000	310,000

Total taxable value is €349,000.

15.8.6   Other Matters

■ The relief is deducted from taxable value, i.e. **after deduction of expenses and consideration**. (*Agricultural relief is deducted from market value with a proportionate reduction in expenses and consideration*).

■ Where agricultural relief is claimed, business relief cannot also be claimed. Agricultural relief must be claimed if available.

■ A person carrying on a trade of **farming can qualify for business relief** (where the 80% test has not been met), provided that all the conditions are satisfied.

15.8.7   Withdrawal of Relief

1. **Disposal within Six Years**

There is a clawback of the relief if at any time within six years after the gift or inheritance:

■ the business concerned ceases to be a qualifying business, other than on grounds of insolvency; or

■ to the extent that the relevant business property is sold, leased, redeemed or compulsorily acquired within that six-year period and not replaced within one year by other qualifying business property.

Reinvestment

If there is **full reinvestment** of proceeds, there is **no clawback**.

If there is **no reinvestment** of proceeds, there is **full clawback.**

Example

Albert inherited a business, with a market value of €1 million on the valuation date. He qualified for business relief at 90% of €900,000 and therefore the taxable value of the inheritance was €100,000. Albert paid CAT at the then rate of 25% on the inheritance as his tax free threshold was fully utilised. Two years later, Albert sold the business for €1,400,000. He did not reinvest any of the proceeds in buying another business. What is the CAT due as a result?

	€
Original relief claimed is clawed back	900,000
Additional CAT payable (at rate that prevailed when inheritance was received) (€900,000 × 25%)	225,000

If a proportion of the proceeds are reinvested, a similar proportion of the relief is clawed back.

2. **Disposal of Development Land – 6 to 10 Years after Valuation Date**

As outlined at **Section 15.7.8**, there is a **special clawback** of relief where development land qualifies for business relief and is disposed of at any time in the period commencing 6 years after the date of the gift or inheritance and ending 10 years after that date. As the rules are exactly the same for business relief as they are for agricultural relief, see **Section 15.7.8** for details of this clawback that **only applies to development land**. Interest is charged from the date of the disposal of the land.

Examples

1. Shane Raftery inherited the family business on the death of his mother on 21 February 2012. The taxable value (net of deductions) of the business was €500,000 before relief. The revised taxable value is as follows:

	€
Taxable value before business relief	500,000
Business relief – 90%	(450,000)
Revised taxable value	50,000

2. Jean is a sole trader who runs a travel agency business. The main asset of the business is the shop from which she runs the business. She wishes to transfer the shop to her son Michael. This gift would not qualify for business relief as she is only transferring an asset of the business and not the business itself.

3. Terry owns shares in a company. He wants to know whether business relief would apply if he left the shares in the company to his sister. Set out the questions you would ask in order to establish whether business relief applies.

Solution

The following are the questions to ask:

■ Are the shares quoted and, if so, were they when acquired?
    Reason: relief only applies to unquoted shares or quoted shares which were unquoted when acquired.

■ Is the business of the company wholly or mainly of one or more of dealing in currencies, securities, stocks, shares, land or buildings?
    Reason: If it is, business relief does not apply.

continued overleaf

- ▪ What percentage of the voting rights and total share capital of the company will his sister own after the inheritance? Does she work full-time for the company and if so, for how many years? Also, do the family control the company?
  Reason: If she holds more than 25% of the voting rights, she can qualify. Even if she does not, if she holds 10% or more of the company's total share capital and she worked full-time in the company for the five years up to the inheritance, she can qualify. Finally, she can qualify because the company is controlled by herself and her relatives.
- ▪ How long has he held the shares?
  Reason: Terry or his wife/civil partner must have held the shares for two years (or five years if he decides to give a gift rather than leave the shares in his will).
- ▪ What is the value of the company? What assets does it own and for how long? Were any of the assets used for personal use?
  Reason: To establish the value of the company qualifying for business relief, net of any non-qualifying assets.

4. Brian dies and leaves his share of the family home and his cash to his wife and his Irish retailing business to his two children. His assets were as follows:

	€
Share in family home	80,000
Cash	30,000
Family business	900,000
Total	1,010,000

Legal costs paid on transfer of the business were €18,000.

Wife
Inheritance from spouse – exempt

Each child	€
Share of family business	450,000
Share of legal expenses	(9,000)
Taxable	441,000

Business relief

	€
90%	(396,900)
Liable to CAT (subject to threshold)	44,100

5. Jackie gives 30% of the shares in Patio Ltd, an Irish incorporated paving company, to Jimmy. Jackie had owned all the shares for the last six years. The gift was valued at €150,000.

Jimmy is entitled to business relief as follows:	€
Value	150,000
Relief @ 90%	(135,000)
Taxable	15,000

Appendix 15.1: Summary Chart

GIFT

DATE OF THE DISPOSITION
- ■ The date the person (disponer) does something which binds him to provide the property.
- ■ In the case of failure to act, the latest date when the disponer could have acted.

DATE OF GIFT
- ■ The date the person (donee) becomes beneficially entitled in possession.

VALUATION DATE
- ■ The date of the gift.

INHERITANCE

DATE OF THE DISPOSITION
- ■ Normally the date of death.
- ■ Date when the person (disponer) binds himself to provide the property (including situation where a gift becomes an inheritance).
- ■ In the case of failure to act, the latest date when the disponer could have acted.

DATE OF THE INHERITANCE
- ■ Date of latest death.
- ■ Date of death of life tenant.
- ■ Date of gift where it becomes an inheritance.

VALUATION DATE
- ■ Normally it is the earliest of the following dates:
    - when entitled to retain property
    - retain property
    - property is delivered.
- ■ Gift becomes an inheritance, date of the gift.

Appendix 15.2: An Explanation of Some Differences between Agricultural Relief and Business Relief

■ There is no minimum ownership period for agricultural relief, while there is a two-year (inheritance) or five-year (gift) minimum ownership period for business relief.

■ Agricultural relief applies to the market value of property, while business relief applies to taxable value.

■ Agricultural relief applies to the farmhouse but business relief does not.

■ Non-agricultural assets can be used to purchase agricultural assets, in certain circumstances, and can qualify for relief. There is no such provision for business relief.

■ Unsecured liabilities are apportioned pro rata between agricultural and non-agricultural assets, while in business relief only liabilities applicable to the business are deductible from the business assets and all other liabilities (as far as possible) are deductible from the non-business assets.

■ There must be a farming business for business relief to apply. It is not sufficient that there is an asset that could be used for a business, e.g. property.

■ There is no 80% or residence test for business relief.

■ A beneficiary does not have the option of claiming either agricultural or business relief. If the property is agricultural and the beneficiary qualifies as a farmer, then agricultural relief must be claimed. It is only in the event of failure to qualify for agricultural relief that business relief, may be claimed on agricultural property.

Questions (to Chapter 15)

Review Questions

(See Suggested Solutions at the end this textbook.)

Question 15.1

You are a tax specialist in a firm of Chartered Accountants. The managing partner is meeting with a client who is considering gifting a substantial amount of land and farm assets to his son. The managing partner has asked you to write a memo to him outlining the conditions which would need to be satisfied if his client's son is to qualify for agricultural relief on the transfer.

Requirement
Write a memo to the partner outlining the conditions which must be satisfied if agricultural relief is to be claimed. Your memo should cover the following items:

(a) What relief is given.
(b) The definition of "agricultural property".
(c) The definition of "farmer".
(d) Withdrawal of the relief.

Question 15.2

Amy Smyth died on 1 February 2012 and her estate was administered in accordance with the terms of her will as follows:

(i) To her niece, Margaret:

	Market Value at 1 February 2012 and at the valuation date
	€
Holiday home in France	180,000
Quoted stocks and shares	230,000
€120,000 6% Irish Government Loan Stock	101,500

(ii) To her nephew, Liam:

	€
Farm land	850,000
Farm buildings	90,000
Bloodstock	100,000
Farm machinery	50,000

The farm land was charged with a mortgage of €120,000 and with the payment of farm creditors. Farm creditors amounted to €15,000 at 1 February 2012 and at the valuation date.

(iii) To her daughter, Eva:

100% of the shares in Fine Arts Ltd which were valued at €950,000. Amy owned the shares for few years. The company's net assets at the valuation date were as follows:

	€
Factory premises	130,000
Goodwill	215,000
Investment property	350,000
Plant and machinery	70,000
Inventories	180,000
Receivables	80,000
Net liabilities	(75,000)
Net assets	950,000

(iv) The residue of her estate, charged with the payment of funeral expenses, was also left to her nephew, Liam. The residue consisted of cash on deposit of €50,000. Amy's funeral expenses amounted to €20,000.

Prior to his inheritance from Amy, Liam's only asset was his residence which had a market value of €200,000 on 1 February 2012 and at the valuation date and was subject to a mortgage used to buy the residence of €130,000.

Margaret, Liam and Eva had previously received no gifts or inheritances other than the inheritance received from Amy.

Amy, Margaret, Liam and Eva are all Irish domiciled and resident.

Requirement

Calculate the CAT payable, if any, by Margaret, Liam and Eva.

Question 15.3

You are a tax specialist in a firm of Chartered Accountants. In June 2012, the tax director to whom you report has a telephone conversation with a client to whom your firm has provided tax advice occasionally in the past.

The client, Mr Mark Murphy, owns all the shares in an unquoted company, Murphy Electrical Wholesalers Ltd which carries on a trade as electrical wholesalers. Mr Murphy inherited the shares in Murphy Electrical Wholesalers Ltd from his brother in June 1995. Mr Murphy has many other business interests and has **only been a non-executive director of the company**. Mr Murphy's son Jake works on a full-time basis for the company. Mr Murphy is considering gifting his shares in Murphy Electrical Wholesalers Ltd to Jake. Murphy Electrical Wholesalers Ltd has been valued recently at €3.5 million. The shares were valued at €2 million on the date of Mr Murphy's brother's death in 1995.

Mr Murphy has asked the tax director to advise him on the tax consequences of the proposed gift to his son Jake.

Requirement

Draft a letter in the name of the tax director advising Mr Murphy on the tax consequences of the proposed gift of shares. Your letter should in particular outline the conditions which must be satisfied if any relief from CAT is to be availed of. **(Annual exemption and small gift exemption may be ignored.)**

Question 15.4

Sandra and John are married with one son, James, and all are Irish domiciled, resident and ordinarily resident. On 1 June 2012, Sandra died leaving the following estate:

Assets	Market Value at 1 June 2012 and Date of Retainer
	€
Investment property	520,000
Proceeds of non-exempt life policy	104,000
Bank accounts	60,000

In addition to the above assets, Sandra owned 20% of the issued share capital of the family trading company, Tyrex Ltd, which owns and operates a number of retail outlets. The total issued share capital comprised of 1,000 €1 ordinary shares which, prior to Sandra's death, were held as follows:

John	350	€1 shares
James	50	€1 shares
Sandra	200	€1 shares
Sandra's brother	400	€1 shares
	1,000	

The company has been valued at €1 million on a net assets basis. Included in the company's net assets is a house occupied by Sandra's brother as his main residence that has been valued at €300,000. There is a mortgage charged on the house of €50,000 included in the company's liabilities. This is the only non-trade asset and liability included in the company's net assets. Sandra had owned these shares since 1996.

Sandra's estate had the following liabilities:

	€
Funeral expenses	10,600
Income tax	3,800
Rates on investment property	1,600
	16,000

All these liabilities are to be met from the residue.
Sandra's will contained the following provisions:

■ The investment property was left jointly to her husband, John, and son, James.
■ Her 20% shareholding in the family company was left to her son, James.
■ The residue was left equally to her husband, John, and her son, James.

James has received the following gifts:

- A gift of €15,000 from his aunt on 1 July 1998.
- A gift of €16,000 from his uncle, Sean, on 1 July 2004.
- A gift of 50 shares in Tyrex Ltd from his mother on 1 November 1999. For CAT purposes, the taxable value of these shares was €167,000 on that date. This figure was net of the small gift exemption.

None of the other beneficiaries have previously received gifts or inheritance from any source.

Requirement

Compute the CAT liabilities, if any, in respect of:

(a) The benefits taken by James under Sandra's will.
(b) The benefits taken by John under Sandra's will.

Computation of Tax Payable and Exemptions from Tax

■ If there are prior benefits taken in the same group since 5 December 1991, these must be aggregated in calculating the CAT due on the current benefit. The examples show you the steps and you will see that it is relatively straightforward.

2. Exemptions

These are a range of exemptions, including:

■ The **first €3,000 per annum of** gifts from each disponer is **exempt**.
■ Gifts and inheritances from **spouses or civil partners** are **exempt**.
■ **Non-domiciled and non-ordinarily resident individuals** can receive certain Irish **Government securities tax-free**.
■ Gifts and inheritances of certain **dwelling houses** are exempt provided certain **conditions** are satisfied.
■ There are a range of other exemptions.

COMPUTATION OF TAX

16.1 General

The amount of CAT levied in any situation will depend upon a number of factors, including the following:

■ The **relationship** between the recipient of the gift/inheritance and the person from whom the gift/inheritance is taken.
■ The **taxable value** of the gift/inheritance received.
■ The **aggregate** of the taxable value of all the previous benefits taken by the beneficiary from persons within the same **group threshold** on or after **5 December 1991**.
■ The year in which the gift/inheritance is taken as the group threshold changes each year.

Under Schedule 2 CATCA 2003, CAT payable on a gift or inheritance is calculated as follows:

Step 1: Calculate the CAT chargeable on "Aggregate A", which is the aggregate of:

(i) the taxable value of the current gift or inheritance; and
(ii) the taxable value of all previous taxable gifts and inheritances taken from persons within the **same group threshold** on or after **5 December 1991**.

CAT is chargeable on the group threshold amount at nil and on the excess over the group threshold amount at 30% since 7 December 2011. See **Appendix 16.1** for former rates of CAT.

Step 2: Calculate the CAT chargeable on "Aggregate B", which is the aggregate of the taxable value of all taxable gifts and inheritances taken from persons within the same **group threshold** on or after 5 December 1991 **excluding** the taxable value of the **current gift or inheritance**, i.e. (ii) in Step 1.

CAT is chargeable on the group threshold amount at nil and on the excess over the group threshold amount at the rates shown above.

The excess of the CAT due on Aggregate A over the tax due on Aggregate B is the CAT due on the current gift/inheritance.

The **group threshold** amount depends on the relationship between the provider of the benefit and the recipient of the benefit and the year in which the benefit is taken. The group threshold amounts to be used when taxing a gift or inheritance taken in 2012 are as follows:

Group A **€250,000** where the donee or successor is, on the day the gift or inheritance is taken:

- the child, or the minor child of a deceased child, of the disponer; or
- the child of the civil partner of the disponer, or minor child of a deceased child of the civil partner of the disponer; or
- the minor child of the civil partner of a deceased child of the disponer; or
- the minor child of the civil partner of a deceased child of the civil partner of the disponer.

A child includes an adopted child and a step child. For the purposes of the Group A threshold, it is also deemed to include a natural child who has been adopted by someone else and also a foster child, subject to certain conditions.

This threshold also applies to inheritances taken by a parent on the date of death of his/her child, provided that the inheritance is not a limited interest. (Therefore, an inheritance of a limited interest from a child, or any gift from a child, is within Group B).

Group B **€33,500** where the donee or successor is, on the day the gift or inheritance is taken, a lineal ancestor (other than the above detailed inheritances taken by parents), a lineal descendant (other than a child, or minor child of a deceased child as set out in Group A), a brother, a sister, a child of a brother or of a sister, or a child of a civil partner of a brother or sister, of the disponer.

Group C **€16,750** in all other cases.

The fact that *prior* gifts/inheritances were taken in a different year is irrelevant. **When taxing a benefit taken say in 2012, you only use the group threshold figures and CAT rates for 2012.** These figures are included in the Standard Reference Material given to you when you sit the exam. See **Appendix A** at the end of this book.

The group thresholds have reduced each year, for the last few years. These earlier thresholds are only relevant if you are computing CAT for a year earlier than 2012. You will not be doing such calculations in your exam.

16.2 Aggregation

The aggregate taxable values of all taxable gifts and taxable inheritances taken **on or after 5 December 1991**, by the recipient from all disponers *within the same group threshold*, are taken into account to determine the amount of CAT payable on the current benefit.

(Historical summary of past treatment – for information purposes only: For gifts and inheritances taken before 1 December 1999 gifts and inheritances from all disponers were aggregated in calculating the CAT on a current benefit. In addition for gifts and inheritances taken before 2 December 1998 the aggregate taxable values of all taxable gifts and taxable inheritances taken on or after 2 June 1982 were taken into account. For gifts and inheritances taken before 5 December 2001 the aggregate taxable values of all taxable gifts and taxable inheritances taken on or after 2 December 1988 were taken into account).

For 2012, the maximum total exempt amounts which can be claimed by an individual over his/her lifetime is the total of the three group thresholds, i.e. €250,000 + €33,500 + €16,750 provided that sufficient gifts/inheritances are taken from persons belonging to all three group thresholds. Previously the maximum was €332,084 + €33,208 + €16,604.

While all benefits from persons within the one group threshold are aggregated, there is only one group threshold (i.e. tax-free) amount.

For example, if benefits are received from, a brother, a sister and an aunt, all three benefits are aggregated but the maximum exempt group threshold which can be availed of is €33,500, i.e. one cannot get €33,500 tax-free from each person within the same group threshold. Currently, the maximum amount that may be received tax-free in total from all persons within the same group threshold is the threshold amount, i.e. for 2012:

1. the taxable value of gifts or inheritances which a person may receive from his or her parents in total over a lifetime without giving rise to any CAT liability is €250,000;
2. the taxable value of gifts or inheritances which a person may receive from his or her brothers, sisters, aunts, uncles, grandchildren and grandparents in total over a lifetime without giving rise to any CAT liability is €33,500; and
3. the total taxable value of gifts or inheritances which a person may receive from any other person over a lifetime without giving rise to any CAT liability is €16,750.

16.3 Examples

Example 1

On 7 October 2012, Joan receives a gift of €80,000 from her father. She has received no other benefit since 5 December 1991. (Ignore small gift exemption.)

Requirement Compute the CAT liability on the gift from her father.

Computation 1

There are no prior benefits to aggregate.

	€
Taxable value	80,000
Group threshold	250,000

As the taxable value is less than the Group A threshold, no liability arises.

Example 2

On 1 June 2012, Michael receives an inheritance of €20,000 from his uncle. He has received no other benefit since 5 December 1991.

Requirement Compute the CAT liability on the inheritance from his uncle.

Computation 2

There are no prior benefits to aggregate.

	€
Taxable value	20,000
Group threshold	33,500

As the taxable value is less than the Group B threshold, no liability arises.

Example 3

On 4 April 2012, Mary Ryan received an inheritance with a taxable value of €60,000 from her uncle. She had received no other gifts or inheritances from any source since 5 December 1991.

Requirement Compute the CAT liability on the inheritance from her uncle.

Computation 3

As she has no previous benefits, there is nothing to aggregate.
Therefore, just calculate CAT on the current benefit.

	€
Taxable value	60,000
Group threshold: €33,500 @ Nil	
Balance: €26,500 @ 30% =	7,950
CAT liability	7,950

Example 4

On 28 July 2012, Sean Dunne received a gift with a taxable value of €60,000 from his nephew. He had received no other gifts or inheritances from any source since 5 December 1991.

Requirement Compute the CAT liability on the gift from his nephew. Ignore small gift exemption.

Computation 4

As he has no previous benefits, there is nothing to aggregate.
Therefore, just calculate CAT on the current benefit.

	€
Taxable value	60,000
Group threshold: €16,750 @ Nil	
Balance: €43,250 @ 30% =	12,975
CAT liability	12,975

Example 5

Louise and Ellen are civil partners. On 5 October 2012, Louise's sister Catherine gifts €30,000 to Ellen's daughter Olivia. Olivia has received no other benefit since 5 December 1991. (Ignore small gift exemption.)

Requirement Compute the CAT liability, if any, on the gift taken by Olivia.

Computation 5

As Olivia is the daughter of Ellen, who is the civil partner of Catherine's sister Louise, the Group B threshold applies.

There are no prior benefits to aggregate.

	€
Taxable value	30,000
Group threshold	33,500

As the taxable value is less than the Group B threshold, no liability arises.

Example 6

On 1 February 2012, Mary O'Hagan received an inheritance with a taxable value of €350,000 from her father.

Mary had previously received the following benefits:

- gift of €10,000 on 1 December 1986 from her brother
- inheritance of €5,000 on 20 December 1991 from her sister
- gift of €200,000 on 1 June 1992 from her mother
- gift of €15,000 on 1 November 1998 from her uncle

Ignore small gift exemption.

Requirement Compute the CAT liability, if any, on the February 2012 inheritance from her father.

Computation 6

1. Calculate CAT on Aggregate A, i.e. CAT on gifts and inheritances taken since 5 December 1991 from persons in the Group A threshold.

	€
Aggregate A: Current inheritance from father	350,000
Gift from mother 1/6/92	200,000
Total	550,000
Tax on Aggregate A:	
Group threshold: €250,000 @ Nil	
Balance: €300,000 @ 30% =	90,000
CAT on Aggregate A	90,000

2. Calculate CAT on Aggregate B, i.e. CAT on gifts and inheritances taken since 5 December 1991 from persons in the Group A threshold excluding the current benefit. Aggregate B = €200,000, i.e. gift from mother 1/6/92. As this is less than the group threshold amount of €250,000, CAT on Aggregate B = Nil.
3. CAT on current benefit = CAT on Aggregate A less CAT on Aggregate B, i.e. €90,000 − nil = €90,000.

Example 7

During October 2012 Michael Moran received the following gifts:

1. A gift of a rental property worth €220,000 from his father;
2. A gift of shares worth €30,000 from an aunt; and
3. A gift of €5,000 cash from a cousin.

He had previously received the following benefits:

1. An inheritance of investments valued at €200,000 from his mother on 1 June 1991.
2. An inheritance of shares valued at €30,000 from an uncle on 6 May 1992.
3. An inheritance of a holiday cottage valued at €50,000 from a friend on 11 December 1998.

Ignore small gift exemption.

Requirement Compute the CAT liability, if any, on the gifts received in 2012.

continued overleaf

Computation 7

1. Gift of rental property from father.

    Only one previous benefit taken from a person in this group threshold, his mother, was taken before 5/12/91 and is accordingly ignored. Taxable value of current benefit, €220,000, received from his father is below the group threshold of €250,000. No CAT is therefore payable on the gift from his father.

2. Gift of shares from aunt valued at €30,000.

	€
Current gift	30,000
Previous gift from uncle	30,000
Aggregate A	60,000
Group threshold: €33,500 @ nil	Nil
Balance: €26,500 @ 30% =	7,950
CAT on Aggregate A	7,950
CAT on Aggregate B	
(Previous benefit below group threshold of €33,500)	Nil
CAT on Aggregate A − CAT on Aggregate B =	7,950
CAT on shares from aunt	7,950

3. Gift of cash €5,000 from cousin

	€
Current gift	5,000
Previous gift from friend	50,000
Aggregate A	55,000
Group threshold: €16,750 @ nil	Nil
Balance: €38,250 @ 30% =	11,475
CAT on Aggregate A	11,475
Aggregate B, i.e. previous gift from friend	50,000
Group threshold: €16,750 @ nil	Nil
Balance: €33,250 @ 30% =	9,975
CAT on Aggregate B	9,975
CAT on Aggregate A − CAT on Aggregate B = €11,475 − €9,975 =	1,500
CAT on cash from cousin	1,500

    as the threshold is already used, €5,000 is taxable at 30%

(4) Total CAT payable on gifts taken during 2012:

	€
Rental property from father	Nil
Shares from aunt	7,950
Cash from cousin	1,500

We will see later that these liabilities are payable by 31 October 2013 as the valuation date, i.e. the date of the gift, is during October 2012.

Example 8

Frank and Jonathon are civil partners. On 15 April 2012, Frank died. Under the terms of his will he left property worth €500,000 to Jonathon, cash of €100,000 to his daughter Alexa and cash of €70,000 to Jonathon's son Ryan. None of the beneficiaries have received a gift or inheritance since 5 December 1991, except for Ryan who received a gift of €200,000 from his mother in May 2011.

Requirement Compute the CAT liability, if any, of each beneficiary on the inheritances taken in 2012. *Ignore small gift exemption.*

Computation 8

As Jonathon is the Frank's civil partner, he is exempt from CAT on the benefit of €500,000 which he receives from Frank.

As Alexa is Frank's daughter, the Group A threshold of €250,000 applies. As this is the first benefit she has received in Group A, and the taxable value is less than the threshold, there is no tax payable on the €100,000 she receives.

As Ryan is the son of Frank's civil partner Jonathon, the Group A threshold applies. The prior gift of €200,000 from his mother must be aggregated.

	€
Current inheritance	70,000
Previous gift from mother	200,000
Aggregate A	270,000
Group threshold: €250,000 @ nil	Nil
Balance: €20,000 @ 30% =	6,000
CAT on aggregate A	6,000
CAT on aggregate B	
(Previous benefit below group threshold of €250,000)	Nil
CAT on aggregate A – CAT on aggregate B =	6,000
CAT on cash from Frank	6,000

EXEMPTIONS

There are a large number of exemptions.

16.4 Exemption of Small Gifts

Under section 69 CATCA 2003, the first **€3,000** per annum in **gifts** made by any one disponer to any one donee is exempt, i.e. in computing the amount of a gift to be aggregated, the first €3,000 of total value taken from the *same disponer* in each year is disregarded. For gifts taken before 1 January 2003, the annual exemption was €1,270. (For gifts taken before 1 January 1999, the annual exemption was €635.)

The annual exemption does not apply to inheritances.

However, where a gift subsequently becomes an inheritance, due to the death of the disponer within two years of the date of the gift, then the annual exemption is not recaptured.

The annual exemption applies to gifts taken during **calendar years**.

Example

John receives a gift of €10,000 from his uncle. In consideration of the gift he has to give €1,000 to his sister. John's taxable value is €10,000 – €1,000 = €9,000. The small gift exemption of €3,000 is deducted so that the final taxable value is €6,000.

16.5 Exemption of Gifts and Inheritances taken from a Spouse or Civil Partner and Certain Benefits taken from a Former Spouse or Civil Partner

Inheritances taken by the surviving spouse or civil partner of a deceased spouse or civil partner and gifts taken from a spouse or civil partner are exempt from CAT, and also are not aggregated for the purposes of calculating CAT payable on any other gifts or inheritances taken by that person in the future.

This exemption has been dealt with in detail in **Chapter 13**.

16.5.1 Couples who are Separated

In order for the exemption to apply, the couple must be legally married or be a party to a civil partnership registration. If they are separated (and not divorced or their civil partnership has not been disolved), then they are still legally married or in a civil partnership, and the exemption applies.

> **Example**
> Darren and Tracey signed a deed of separation on 1 July 2012. Under the terms of the deed, Darren agreed to sign over to Tracey his interest in a house he owns. As they are still married, the gift from Darren to Tracey is a gift to a spouse and is, therefore, exempt from CAT. (Note: the transfer is exempt from stamp duty as they are married. For CGT purposes, the disposal is exempt as it is a transfer on foot of a deed of separation. If however, Darren subsequently voluntarily gave Tracey shares for example, while the CAT and stamp duty exemptions would be available, for CGT purposes there would be no relieving provision.)

16.5.2 Married Couples who are Divorcing or are Divorced, and Civil Partnerships which are being Dissolved or have been Dissolved

Where a couple obtains an Irish divorce or a dissolution of a civil partnership, transfers between former spouses or civil partners made on foot of an Irish court order governing the divorce or dissolution of a civil partnership are exempt from CAT. This exemption also applies to a foreign divorce or dissolution of a civil partnership which is recognised as valid under Irish law.

Once divorced or the civil partnership has been dissolved, any transfers made voluntarily between the former spouses or civil partners are not exempt and Group C would be the relevant threshold.

> **Example**
> Grace and Ivan divorced on 1 August 2012. Under the terms of their divorce, Grace agreed to sign over her interest in the family home to Ivan. The transfer of the house from Grace to Ivan is exempt from CAT as it arises under the terms of the divorce. (Note: the transfer is exempt from stamp duty and CGT also.)
> If three years later, Ivan had financial problems and Grace decided to give him €20,000, he would be liable to CAT on this receipt of a gift and the relevant group threshold would be Group C.

> **Example**
> Leopold and Peter registered their civil partnership on 8 April 2011. Towards the end of 2011, they decided that they would separate and get the civil partnership dissolved. They can only get dissolution of their civil partnership if they have been living apart from one another for a period amounting to two out of the previous three years before the application for

continued overleaf

> the dissolution is made. Therefore the earliest this can happen is the end of 2013. When they are granted the decree of dissolution, any provision made under the decree regarding transfer of property, etc. is exempt from CAT, stamp duty and CGT. If say two years after the dissolution, Leopold decided to make a gift of shares to Peter, that gift would be taxable and the Group C threshold would apply.

16.6 Exemption of Certain Government Securities

Irish assets are always liable to Irish CAT. However, to get non-Irish persons to hold Irish Government securities, **certain Government securities are exempt from CAT**, provided the following conditions are satisfied:

1. the **donee/successor** must **neither be domiciled nor ordinarily resident** in the State at the date of the gift or inheritance; and
2. the **disponer was the beneficial owner** of the securities for **15 years** prior to the date of the gift or inheritance. The period of ownership was six years for gifts/inheritances taken before 24 February 2003. Where a disponer already beneficially owns the securities before 24 February 2003, the six-year rule continues to apply. **Therefore, at present, only securities owned at 24 February 2003 can qualify for exemption in 2012**. This **condition does not apply** where the **disponer is neither domiciled nor ordinarily resident** in the State at the date of the disposition.

16.7 Exemption of Certain Inheritances taken by Parents

Inheritances (not gifts) taken by a **parent on the death of a child** are exempt **if the deceased child had taken a non-exempt gift or inheritance from either parent** in the **five-year period prior to the death of the child.**

> **Example**
> On 1 June 2009 Frank gave a gift of €100,000 to his daughter Joanne which she used as part payment to acquire an apartment. Joanne died in 2012 and Frank inherited her entire estate which was valued at €500,000. The €500,000 inherited by Frank is exempt from CAT as Frank had given Joanne a non-exempt gift within five years before her death.

16.8 Exemption of Certain Dwelling Houses

Under section 86 CATCA 2003, a gift or inheritance of a dwelling house or part of a dwelling house taken on or after 1 December 1999 may be exempt from CAT if certain conditions are satisfied.

The conditions that must be satisfied are as follows:

1. The recipient must have occupied the dwelling house continuously as his or her only or main residence for a period of **three years** prior to the date of the gift or inheritance. Where the dwelling house has directly or indirectly replaced other property, this condition may be satisfied where the recipient has continuously occupied both properties as his or her only or main residence for a total period of three out of the four years immediately prior to the date of the gift or inheritance.

2. The recipient must **not,** at the date of the gift or inheritance, be beneficially entitled to any **other dwelling house** or to any interest in any other dwelling house.

3. The recipient must continue, except where the recipient was aged 55 years or more at the date of the gift or inheritance or has died, to **occupy** that dwelling house as his or her only or main residence for a period of **six years** commencing on the date of the gift or inheritance (the **relevant period**). A period of absence working abroad during the relevant period counts as a period of occupation for this purpose.

4. There are **extra conditions** to be satisfied in the case of **gifts** (not inheritances):
   (i) The dwelling house must be owned by the disponer for three years prior to the gift and, where the gifted house has replaced another property, each house must be owned by the disponer for the relevant part of the three-year period that it was occupied by the beneficiary.
   (ii) Any period during which the donee and the disponer occupied the dwelling house as their principal private residence will be disregarded for the purpose of 1. above unless the disponer is compelled by reason of old age or infirmity to depend on the services of the donee during the three-year period of occupancy. This means, for example, that generally co-habiting couples or children living with their parents are excluded from the exemption in the case of gifts (not inheritances).

   Where a gift becomes an inheritance, due to the disponer dying within two years of the disposition, these conditions no longer need to be satisfied as the benefit is now an inheritance and not a gift.

16.8.1 Definition of Dwelling House

A dwelling house means:

1. a building or part of a building which was used or suitable for use for a dwelling; and
2. grounds of up to one acre attaching to the house and where the grounds attaching to the house exceed one acre, one acre of the total area which is most suitable for enjoyment and occupation with the dwelling house.

16.8.2 Clawback of Exemption

The exemption will cease to apply if:

1. The dwelling house is sold or otherwise disposed of before the death of the donee or successor and within the relevant period unless the recipient was aged 55 years or more at the date of the gift or inheritance.
   If, however, the recipient sells or disposes of the dwelling house and invests some or all of the proceeds in a replacement house and continuously occupies both for a total period of six out of the seven years commencing on the date of the gift or inheritance, the clawback will be limited to any proceeds of the sale or disposal not invested in the replacement dwelling house.
2. The recipient ceases to occupy the dwelling house as his only or main residence during the relevant period otherwise than on his death unless he is required to cease to occupy the house as a result of any condition imposed by the employer of the donee or successor requiring him to reside elsewhere.

Where, however, a recipient disposes of the house or ceases to occupy the house as a result of the recipient requiring long-term medical care in a hospital, nursing home or convalescent home, there is no clawback.

Example

Pat and Joe are two brothers, aged 45 and 47, who have lived together in the house they inherited from their parents in December 1998. The house was valued at €100,000 in December 1998. In January 2012, Pat moved out and gave his ½ share in the house to Joe, together with contents valued at €20,000 (in total). The house was valued at €500,000 at the date of Pat's gift. Apart from the inheritance from his parents, Joe has not previously received any other taxable gifts or inheritances.

Requirement

Compute Joe's CAT liability arising from his gift from Pat. Ignore small gift exemption.

CAT computation

½ share in house is valued at €250,000. This is **not exempt,** as Joe has lived in the house with Pat, and Pat has not relied on the services of Joe.

	€	€
Taxable gift		
House	250,000	
1/2 share in contents	10,000	
Taxable inheritance	260,000	
Group threshold:	33,500 @ Nil	Nil
Balance:	226,500 @ 30%	67,950
CAT payable		67,950

Note: No previous gifts or inheritances were taken from persons within the same group threshold. Tax on Aggregate B is, therefore, Nil.

16.9 Exemption of Certain Retirement Benefits

Retirement benefits, redundancy payments or pensions paid to an employee or former employee are generally not treated as gifts or inheritances. Where such benefits are paid to any person other than the employee the benefit is treated as a gift or inheritance taken by the recipient from the person in respect of whose service the benefit arose.

There is an exemption from CAT (as it is liable to income tax) on any balance in an "approved retirement fund" (ARF) or in an "approved minimum retirement fund" (AMRF) which passes on the death of a pensioner, or on the death of the pensioner's spouse or civil partner, to a child or the disponer or the civil partner of the disponer aged 21 years or over (if the child is under 21, it is liable to CAT).

16.10 Exemption of Certain Receipts

There are a large number of exemptions, including:

1. Gifts/inheritances taken by charities.
2. The receipt, during the lifetime of the disponer, by a spouse or civil partner, children, children of the civil partner or dependent relatives, of sums from the disponer for normal support, maintenance or education. These sums must be reasonable having regard to the financial circumstances of the disponer.

3. Post-death support, maintenance or education is exempt where received by a minor child or a minor child of the civil partner of a deceased disponer and the other parent of the minor child is also dead. These sums must be reasonable having regard to the financial circumstances of the deceased disponer.

4. Funds raised by public subscription for permanently incapacitated individuals provided that these monies are held in a qualifying trust.

5. Gift/inheritance, taken exclusively for the purpose of discharging qualifying medical expenses of an individual who is permanently incapacitated by reason of physical or mental infirmity.

6. Bona fide compensation or damages for any wrong or injury suffered by the person or compensation for the death of another person.

7. Gifts or inheritances provided by the disponer to himself, e.g. from a trust created by the disponer.

8. Bona fide winnings from betting, lotteries, Sweepstakes or prizes from games.

16.11 Gifts and Inheritances Taken Free of Tax

The law provides that where a gift or inheritance is taken by direction of the disponer free of CAT, the benefit taken is deemed to include the amount of tax chargeable on the gift or inheritance, but not the amount of tax chargeable on such tax.

Example

Brian receives a gift of €133,500, net of small gift exemption, from his sister Ann in July 2012. Ann has agreed to pay any tax due on the gift, i.e. the gift is free of tax. Brian is regarded as taking two benefits, i.e. the gift of €133,500 and the CAT on that amount. On the basis that Brian has received no previous gift or inheritance, the CAT on the gift is:

	€
Gift	133,500
Threshold amount	(33,500)
Taxable	100,000
Tax @ 30%	30,000
Tax on €30,000 @ 30%	9,000
Tax payable	39,000

Therefore the additional CAT due on the benefit as a result of it being free of CAT is €9,000. There is no further CAT due as a result of Ann paying this €9,000 of tax.

16.12 Relief in Respect of Certain Insurance Policies

There is a valuable relief under section 72 CATCA 2003 whereby the proceeds of **certain insurance policies are exempt from inheritance tax**, where the policy was taken out for the **sole purpose of paying inheritance tax** due in respect of dispositions made by the person insured. The relief, which originally applied to inheritances only, was subsequently extended and also covers **inter vivos dispositions (i.e. gifts)** provided that certain conditions are satisfied (see later).

In the absence of this relief, the proceeds of a life insurance policy, whether taken out to pay inheritance tax or otherwise, are aggregated with the other assets of the deceased and itself subject to inheritance tax in the hands of the beneficiary. Indirectly, therefore, the insurance policy results in an increased tax liability.

16.12.1 Policies to Pay Inheritance Tax Only

To qualify for exemption, the assurance company gets its policy approved by Revenue to ensure Revenue conditions are satisfied. The premiums are payable annually. Obviously a person who is older or has an illness will find that they cannot get insurance or the premiums are too expensive. The policy can cover the life of one or both spouses/civil partners.

The **exemption available is limited to the proceeds of the insurance policy** which are **actually used to pay inheritance tax.** If, for example, the proceeds exceed the inheritance tax liability, then only the portion of the proceeds equal to the inheritance tax liability qualify for exemption. The balance of the proceeds would then become subject to inheritance tax in the normal manner.

Example

Mary died in June 2012. The inheritance tax liability of her estate amounted to €45,000. She held a qualifying life assurance policy which paid €50,000 to her estate on her death. As the proceeds exceed the inheritance tax liability, then only the portion of the proceeds equal to the inheritance tax liability of €45,000 qualify for exemption. The balance of the proceeds, i.e. €5,000 would then become subject to inheritance tax in the normal manner.

This type of exempt policy can also be used to cover the income tax required to be deducted, in certain situations, from an approved retirement fund (commonly known as an ARF). Income tax at 30% must be deducted from assets in an ARF where the beneficiary of those assets is a child of the deceased who is aged 21 years or over.

The policy proceeds are payable on the death of the person insured. For people who are married or in a civil partnership, the policy can be taken out on the joint lives of the insured and his spouse/civil partner. In this case, the annual premiums are payable by either or both spouses/civil partners during their joint lives and the survivor of them during the life of the survivor. The proceeds of the policy are payable on the death of each survivor or the simultaneous death of both such spouses/civil partners.

The following example will illustrate the operation of this exemption:

Example

Pat, a bachelor died on 1st November 2012 and in his will he left the following:

- a legacy of €30,000 to his house-keeper Mrs. Brown, who is unrelated;
- a specific bequest of shares valued at €35,000 to his brother Bart; and
- the residue of his estate valued at €120,000 equally between his two brothers, Bart and Cathal.

None of these three beneficiaries has taken any previous gift or inheritance since 5 December 1991.

Pat had taken out a qualifying insurance policy, the proceeds of which amounted to €20,000. Pat's will had specifically provided that all relevant CAT payable on his death was to be paid pro-rata from this policy.

(**Note:** *The residue of €120,000 **does not** include the qualifying insurance policy*)

continued overleaf

The CAT in connection with Pat's death is calculated as follows:

(i)	**House-keeper Mrs. Brown**	€		€
	Tax on threshold amount of	16,750		nil
	Tax on	13,250	@ 30%	3,975
	Total	30,000		3,975

(ii) **Brother Bart**

Bart takes the specific bequest of €35,000 and half of the residue which will amount to €60,000, making a total inheritance of €95,000.

Tax on €95,000 is as follows:	€		€
Tax on threshold amount of	33,500		nil
Tax on	61,500	@ 30%	18,450
Total	95,000		18,450

(iii) **Brother Cathal**

Cathal takes half the residue valued at €60,000.

	€		€
Tax on threshold amount of	33,500		nil
Tax on	26,500	@ 30%	7,950
Total	60,000		7,950

It will be noted that the total of the CAT liability of the three beneficiaries is €30,375 (€3,975 + €18,450 + €7,950). As Pat directed in his will that the proceeds of the policy of €20,000 were to be paid pro-rata, the CAT will be paid as follows:

(i) Mrs. Brown's liability is paid out of the proceeds in the proportion of

$$\frac{€3,975 \times €20,000}{€30,375}$$ which amounts to €2,617

She pays the balance of tax of €1,358 from her own funds.

(ii) Bart's liability is discharged out of the policy proceeds in the proportion of

$$\frac{€18,450 \times €20,000}{€30,375}$$ which amounts to €12,148

Thus Bart pays the balance of tax of €6,302 from his own funds.

(iii) Cathal's liability is paid out of the policy proceeds in the proportion of

$$\frac{€7,950 \times €20,000}{€30,375}$$ which amounts to €5,235

The balance of €2,715 is paid by Cathal out of his own funds.

16.12.2 Inter Vivos Dispositions

There is a similar relief under section 73 CATCA 2003 (i.e. **exempts from CAT the proceeds of a qualifying policy)** when the policy is taken out to pay CAT arising on inter vivos dispositions made by the insured. The CAT which may be covered by the policy, is the CAT payable in respect of a disposition made by the insured, **within one year after the appointed day.**

The appointed day is:

- a date not earlier than **eight years** after the date on which the policy is taken out; or
- the date on which the proceeds of the policy became payable either on the critical illness or the death of the insured.

16.13 Exemption of Certain Transfers between Qualified Cohabitants

A qualified cohabitant, as defined under the Civil Partnership and Certain Rights and Obligations of Cohabitants Act 2010, has the right to seek a property adjustment order from the Court under which property is transferred to the individual from the other individual or, in the case of a death, the estate of the deceased other individual with whom he/she was cohabiting. This gift or inheritance is exempt from CAT. (It is also exempt from stamp duty and transfers at no gain/no loss for CGT.)

A qualified cohabitant means an adult who was in a relationship of cohabitation with another adult and who, immediately before the time that that relationship ended, whether through death or otherwise, was living with the other adult as a couple for a period:

(a) of two years or more, in the case where they are the parents of one or more dependent children; and

(b) of five years or more, in any other case.

If either was married, the individual must have lived apart from the spouse for four of the previous five years.

Example

Darren and Tracey lived together for ten years in a house in Dublin owned by Darren. They have three minor children and Tracey has no independent source of income. They have decided that they will no longer cohabit. Darren owns a number of assets other than the house. Tracey went to Court and, as she was a qualified cohabitant, she received an Order that the house in Dublin worth €250,000 should be transferred to her. She is exempt from CAT on receipt of this gift from Darren as it is given to her under an Order made under the Civil Partnership and Certain Rights and Obligations of Cohabitants Act 2010.

Appendix 16.1: Rates of CAT since 1 December 1999

From 1 December 1999 to 19 November 2008	20%
From 20 November 2008 to 7 April 2009	22%
From 8 April 2009 to 6 December 2011	25%
From 7 December 2011	30%

Questions (to Chapter 16)

Review Questions

(See Suggested Solutions to Review Questions at the end of this textbook.)

Question 16.1

Calculate the CAT payable in respect of the gift/inheritance taken in 2012 in each of the following cases:

(a) Michael, who is Irish domiciled and resident, gave his daughter, also Irish resident and domiciled, a cash gift of €40,000 on 1 January 2012. His daughter had previously received the following benefits:

    (i)   a house in Sligo valued at €80,000 inherited from her grandmother, also Irish domiciled and resident, in June 1993; and

    (ii) jewellery valued at €20,000 inherited on the death of her mother, also Irish domiciled and resident, in August 1999.

(b) David, who is domiciled and resident in the UK, gave his niece Mary, who is Irish domiciled and resident, shares in a UK trading company valued at €50,000 on 1 June 2012. David had previously given Mary €10,000 worth of UK shares in December 1998. Mary had also inherited €10,000 on the death of a cousin, who was Irish domiciled and resident, in March 2002.

(c) Bridget, who is domiciled in the State but resident in the US, inherited a property in the UK valued at €120,000 from an uncle, who is Irish domiciled and resident, on his death in October 2012. Bridget had previously received the following benefits:

    (i)   a house in the US valued at €200,000 and shares in an Irish quoted company valued at €50,000 inherited on the death of an aunt, US domiciled and resident, in March 1994;

    (ii) a gift of a car valued at €15,000 from a cousin, Irish domiciled and resident, in January 1992; and

    (iii) €25,000 in an Irish bank account inherited on the death of Bridget's grandmother, Irish domiciled and resident, in September 1989.

Note: Business property relief and credit for CGT liabilities may be ignored.

Question 16.2

Sarah and Enda are married with one son, Patrick, and all are Irish domiciled, resident and ordinarily resident. On 1 June 2012, Sarah died leaving the following estate:

Assets	Market Value at 1 June 2012 and Date of Retainer
	€
€18,000 stock of 10% Irish Government National Loan Stock	14,000
€20,000 stock of 12% Irish Government National Loan Stock	16,000

Both Government securities comprised in the estate qualify for exemption from Irish income tax when beneficially owned by individuals not domiciled or ordinarily resident. Sarah has owned these securities since 2000.

Sarah's will contained the following provisions:

- The 10% National Loan Stock was left to Patrick.
- The 12% National Loan Stock was left to Harry, Sarah's cousin, who is domiciled and resident and ordinarily resident in the United States.

Patrick has received the following gifts:

- A gift of €15,000 from his aunt on 1 July 1988.
- A gift of €16,000 from his uncle, Sean, on 1 July 1994.
- A gift of 50 shares in Xbarn Ltd from his mother on 15 May 2001. For CAT purposes, the taxable value of these shares was €467,000 on that date. This figure was net of the small gift exemption.

Requirement

Compute the CAT liabilities, if any, in respect of:

(a) the benefits taken by Patrick under Sarah's will; and
(b) the benefits taken by Harry under Sarah's will.

17

Surrender of Government Securities/Credit for Certain CGT Liabilities

Learning Objectives

After studying this chapter you will have developed competency in the following:

Payment of Inheritance Tax Using Government Securities

■ Certain Government securities can be surrendered at face/par value in settlement of **inheritance tax**, even though their market value is less. This achieves a discount. This is only available if the securities were part of the estate of the deceased for at least three months. **There are no such securities in issue at present**.

This option is not available for gifts.

Credit for Capital Gains

■ For all gifts, and gifts that become an inheritance, there can be a CGT liability for the disponer and a CAT liability for the donee.
■ CGT paid by the disponer is creditable against CAT payable by the donee on the same event, i.e. reduces the CAT.
■ The credit is limited to the lower of the CAT and CGT on the same event. If the CAT relates to more than one benefit, it must be allocated between the benefits.
■ The credit for CGT will be clawed back if the beneficiary disposes of the property transferred within two years of the date of the gift or inheritance.

17.1 Payment of Inheritance Tax by Surrender of Government Securities

Certain qualifying Government securities may be surrendered at par in settlement of inheritance tax liabilities. This provision does not apply to the payment of gift tax liabilities. It should be specifically noted that, **there are no such securities in issue at present**.

Government securities can be issued on the basis that they will be accepted at par value in payment of an equivalent amount of inheritance tax and interest thereon. A benefit will, of course, only arise where the Government securities are quoted at below par value. The ability to surrender such securities at par effectively results in a discount to the person liable for the tax.

Example

Joe dies and leaves his estate worth €145,833 (net of all liabilities) to his nephew Sean. Sean's CAT liability is €43,750. Assuming that included in the estate are qualifying Government securities which can be used to pay inheritance tax. Their par value is €43,750 and market value is €38,000. Sean could use these securities to pay the inheritance tax of €43,750 even though the securities are only worth €38,000. He would effectively get a discount of €5,750.

If qualifying Government securities are issued again in the future, the following are the conditions which must be satisfied:

1. *The typical case*

   Where the liability is CAT in respect of property taken under the **will** or **intestacy** of a deceased person, that person **must have owned the stock for** a continuous period of **at least three months** immediately prior to death.

   Securities passing under particular title can be used to pay CAT on property passing under the same title, i.e. but not necessarily same beneficiary.

Example 1

A dies and leaves by will, a farm to B, with the residue of his estate to C. Assuming that the residue of the estate contains qualifying Government securities, then they may be used in payment of the CAT liability of B on receipt of the farm. **The point is that the securities need not necessarily be used to pay the CAT liability of the person who actually inherits the securities.** Such a person, however, would have to give his consent to such a course of action.

---

2. *The more unusual case*

   If the CAT liability arises as a result of property taken **"on a death"** in any circumstance other than above, (e.g. property passing automatically under joint tenancy rules), then the utilisation of the securities, if in issue, would be restricted.

Example 2

A and B own a property as joint tenants. A dies and B automatically inherits the property under the joint tenancy rules. Assuming A's will also provides that B is to inherit qualifying Government securities, these qualifying securities cannot be used to settle B's liability to CAT in respect of the property which he has inherited from A by virtue of the joint tenancy rules.

It should be particularly noted that if this relief is to be claimed, the qualifying **Government securities must be surrendered as part of the payment of the CAT liability,** i.e. the CAT cannot first be paid and the securities surrendered later as the basis for repayment.

If the securities are quoted at a price above their par value, then this legislation will not be used as it will give no benefit.

Example 3

Assume June inherits an estate which includes qualifying securities whose par value is €100,000 and market value is €105,000. In this case, June would just pay the CAT and not surrender the securities.

17.2 Credit for Certain CGT Liabilities

Certain events can result in the triggering of both a CGT liability and a CAT liability. **Typically an inheritance will not trigger a CGT liability as assets passing on a death do not trigger CGT.**

Gifts frequently trigger both CGT and CAT. If the asset gifted is a capital asset, then the disponer may have a capital gain liable to CGT and the donee receives a gift that may trigger a CAT liability.

For instance, the gift of a farm by a father to a son will result in the following charges to tax:

- a CGT disposal will take place and the liability will be computed by reference to the market value of the land transferred; and
- a CAT liability will arise on the son by reference to the market value of the land acquired by way of gift.

Example 1

On 2 January 2012, a mother gifts shares worth €600,000 to her son Shane. The shares cost €200,000 and the relevant indexation factor is 1.2. Shane had received no prior benefits. Ignore CAT small gift exemption and CGT annual exemption.

Capital Gains Tax

The mother has a CGT liability as follows:

	€
Market value	600,000
Indexed cost €200,000 × 1.2	(240,000)
Gain	360,000
CGT @ 30%	108,000

Capital Acquisitions Tax

	€
Taxable value	600,000
Group threshold	250,000
€250,000 @ Nil	–
€350,000 @ 30%	105,000

The CAT liability is €105,000 subject to credit for CGT. In other words, the CGT credit exceeds the CAT liability so there is no CAT due.

Section 104 CATCA 2003 provides that where the **same event triggers both CAT and CGT liabilities and provided the CGT liability has been paid,** it may be **deducted** as a *credit* **from the net CAT liability arising on the disposition.** This is subject to the limitation that the **maximum amount of credit** is **restricted to the lower of the CGT and CAT arising on the same event**.

The credit for CGT will be clawed back if the beneficiary disposes of the property transferred, within two years of the date of the gift or inheritance.

Example 2

On 5 October 2012, Michael gives his sister Debbie shares worth €80,000. He had bought them for €10,000 on 1 August 1996. What are their CGT and CAT positions, ignoring small gift and annual exemptions?

Under CGT rules, he is treated as disposing of the shares at their market value of €80,000. Therefore, ignoring annual exemption, his CGT liability will be as follows:

	€	€
Market value		80,000
Cost	10,000	
Index – 1996/97 to 2012	1.251	
Indexed cost		(12,510)
Gain		67,490
CGT @ 30%		20,247

Ignoring small gift exemption, Debbie's CAT liability is calculated as follows:

	€	€
Taxable value of gift		80,000
Group threshold amount		33,500
€33,500 @ Nil =	Nil	
€46,500 @ 30% =	13,950	
CAT liability	13,950	
Less: credit for CGT paid by Michael	(13,950)	max
CAT payable	Nil	

Example 3

Assume the same facts as the previous example except that Debbie had previously received €70,000 from Michael. Debbie's CAT liability is calculated as follows:

Aggregate A	€
Taxable value of gifts €80,000 + €70,000	150,000
Group threshold amount	33,500
€33,500 @ Nil =	Nil
€116,500 @ 30% =	34,950
CAT on Aggregate A	34,950

Aggregate B	€
Taxable value of previous gift	70,000
Group threshold amount	33,500
€33,500 @ Nil =	Nil
€36,500 @ 30% =	10,950
CAT on Aggregate B	10,950

continued overleaf

CAT on current benefit =
CAT on Aggregate A − CAT on
Aggregate B = €34,950 − €10,950   24,000
Less: credit for CGT paid by Michael   (20,247)
CAT payable   3,753

In either of the above examples, if Debbie disposes of the shares within two years, the credit for CGT will be clawed back, i.e. she will have to pay €13,950 of CAT in the first example and €20,247 of additional CAT in the second example.

The same event must trigger both the CGT and CAT liability. If the CAT related to two different capital assets, then the CAT and CGT related to each asset must be established and the lower of the two is the creditable amount.

Up to the Finance Act 2012, the law stated that where benefits were taken on the same day, the CAT on a particular asset was calculated by apportioning the total CAT rateably between the assets received based on the taxable value of each. This is now repealed, and there is now no guidance in the law other than where it states in section 104 CATCA 2003 that the CAT is the amount equal to the CAT "attributable to the property which is that asset, or that part of the asset". As there is no guidance in the law, the taxpayer may choose the approach that will minimise his/her tax liability. The taxpayer will choose the approach that will maximise the CGT credit. Depending on the facts of the case regarding the CGT relating to an asset, the taxpayer will treat a particular asset as being received before another asset or that they were all received at the same time. This is illustrated in **Example 4** below.

Example 4

On 28 July 2012 Jack gifts Shane his principal private residence and shares. Information regarding these assets is as follows:

	House	Shares
	€	€
Market value	600,000	100,000
Cost	80,000	20,000
Indexation factor	3	1.5

Shane is his son and has received no other benefits. Shane does not live with Jack.

Capital Gains Tax

House	exempt as it is his principal **private residence**		
			€
Shares	Market value		100,000
	Indexed cost	€20,000 × 1.5	(30,000)
	Gain		70,000
	Annual exemption		(1,270)
			68,730
		CGT @ 30%	20,619

continued overleaf

Capital Acquisitions Tax

		€
Taxable value	€600,000 + €100,000 =	700,000
Small gift exemption		(3,000)
		697,000
Group threshold		250,000
	€	
€250,000 @ 0%	–	
€447,000 @ 30%	134,100	
less credit for CGT	20,619 (Note)	
CAT payable	113,481	

Note: The CAT relates to both the shares and the house. The CGT only relates to the shares. Therefore, the **CGT can only be offset against the CAT on the shares**.

The CAT payable of €114,943 relates to both the house and the shares. From Shane's perspective, he wishes to maximise the CAT associated with the shares as they carry a CGT credit. This is achieved by deciding that the house is the first asset received on 28 July 2012 and then the shares. In that way all of the small gift exemption and the tax free threshold are allocated to the house and therefore the entire gift of the shares of €100,000 is taxable at 30%. Therefore the CAT re shares is €30,000.

The creditable CGT is the lower of:

(i)   CGT on shares €20,619
(ii) CAT on shares €30,000

i.e. €20,619

If the shares are disposed of within two years, the CGT credit is clawed back, i.e. an additional €20,619 of CAT must be paid.

If he decided that it was the shares that were received first, then there would be no CAT on the shares (€100,000 – €3,000 = €97,000, which is below the threshold of €250,000). All the CAT would relate to the house, but he could not claim a CGT credit as the house did not trigger a CGT liability. Therefore, his final CAT liability would be €134,100 (instead of the €113,481 calculated above). If, alternatively, he decided that the CAT should be apportioned between the assets, the CAT on the shares would be €134,100 × €100,000/€700,000 = €19,157, and this would be the maximum CAT against which the CGT would be creditable. Again, this is not as good an approach as it reduces the CGT credit and, therefore, increases the CAT payable.

In certain circumstances, the entitlement to a CGT credit against a CAT liability may need to be apportioned between a number of beneficiaries and, in these circumstances, the Revenue Commissioners are empowered to make any necessary apportionments as appears to them to be "*just and reasonable*". There is, however, a right of appeal to the Appeal Commissioners if the method of apportionment is disputed.

The **CGT must be paid** in order for a credit against CAT to be allowed. If it has not been paid by the due date for payment of the CAT, the full CAT will have to be paid and a refund of CAT sought at a later stage when the CGT has been paid. However, where the due date for payment of CAT on a gift is before the due date for payment of CGT arising on the same event, in practice a credit may be claimed for the CGT payable.

Questions (to Chapter 17)

Review Questions

(See Suggested Solutions to Review Questions at the end of this textbook.)

Question 17.1

You are a tax specialist in a firm of Chartered Accountants. A client of your firm, Mr O'Donovan, owns a substantial portfolio of investment properties. Mr O'Donovan has two daughters, Lorraine and Sheila. Mr O'Donovan is considering transferring an apartment currently valued at €350,000 to Lorraine and an apartment valued at €250,000 to Sheila.

You are given the following additional information:

1. Lorraine has been living rent free in the apartment which her father intends to transfer to her since 1 April 2010. She intends to continue to live in the apartment. She may however be transferred by her employer to work in the UK for a six-month period in 2013. Her father also owns an identical apartment next to hers which he has been letting out at €1,500 a month for the last five years. Mr O'Donovan had acquired the apartment, which Lorraine occupies, in November 1999 for €220,000. (Legal fees and stamp duty associated with the purchase amounted to €15,000).

2. Sheila has been living at home with her father but intends to live in the apartment which her father has bought to give to her. A monthly rent of €1,200 could be charged if this apartment were let at arm's length to a third party. Mr O'Donovan had acquired this apartment in July 2010 for €240,000. (Legal fees and stamp duty associated with the purchase amounted to €28,000).

3. Lorraine and Sheila had each inherited assets on the death of their mother in May 2004. Lorraine received €150,000. Sheila received €215,000. Sheila had also received a gift of Irish quoted shares valued at €20,000 from an uncle in June 2000. Apart from this neither have previously received any taxable gifts or inheritances.

4. Neither Lorraine or Sheila have, or have ever had, any other interest in a residential property.

5. Mr O'Donovan has made no other disposals for CGT purposes during 2011.

Requirement

Write a letter to Mr O'Donovan advising him on the taxation consequences arising from the proposed property transfers to his daughters. (You should assume that the transfers take place on 1 December 2012). In your letter you should also advise Mr O'Donovan on any steps which might be taken by him to mitigate the tax liabilities arising. (Ignore small gift exemption.)

Question 17.2

Janet, a 58-year-old widow, made the following gifts during 2012.

1. **20 April 2012**

   100% of the shares in Fogarty Fabrics Ltd, a company involved in the manufacture of curtains and bed linen, to Janet's son Adam. Fogarty Fabrics Ltd had been incorporated by Janet's husband in 1977 with a share capital of €100. Janet's husband had worked full-time as a director for the company until he died suddenly in March 1997. The shares in Fogarty Fabrics Ltd were valued at €340,000 in March 1997.

   On 20 April 2012, the shares in Fogarty Fabrics Ltd were valued at €950,000. The company's net assets at 1 April 2012 were as follows:

Market Value	€
Factory premises	130,000
Goodwill	215,000
Investment property	350,000
Plant and machinery	70,000
Stocks	180,000
Debtors	80,000
Net liabilities	(75,000)
Net assets	950,000

   Adam has previously received a gift of €100,000 (net of small gift allowance) on 2 May 2001 from his mother.

2. **20 May 2012**

   A house valued at €250,000 to her daughter Julie and her husband Nigel. Janet had acquired this house in December 1989 for €40,000. The house had been let by Janet since then.

   Julie has not previously received any taxable gifts or inheritances. Nigel had previously inherited Bank of Ireland shares valued at €10,000 from an aunt.

3. **30 June 2012**

   An antique vase valued at €3,100 to her niece Sally. Janet had inherited this vase from an aunt in June 1980 when it was valued at €150.

   Sally had previously inherited a house valued at €75,000 from an uncle in November 1999.

4. **30 September 2012**

   Farmland valued at €1.5 million to her son, Kevin. Janet had inherited this land from her mother in August 1968 at which time the land was valued at €50,000. The land was valued at €80,000 on 6 April 1974.

   Kevin has no other assets and has not previously received any taxable gifts or inheritances.

   All persons mentioned above are Irish domiciled and Irish resident.

   Janet had capital losses forward of €10,000 at 31 December 2011.

Requirement

(a)   Calculate Janet's CGT liability for 2012, assuming she made no other disposals other than those listed above.

(b)   Calculate the CAT liabilities arising from each of the above gifts. You may ignore stamp duty.

Question 17.3

On 16 July 2012, on the occasion of his 56th birthday and in order to mark his early retirement, Ronnie Doyle made the following gifts:

Market Value on 16 July 2012

	€
To his sister Janet:	
€35,000 4.5% Exchequer Stock purchased by Ronnie	
in January 2000 and which is exempt from income tax	
where held by a foreign domiciled and ordinarily resident person	€40,000

To his son Jake:

His interest in a van rental business (Note 1)	1,280,000
Cash	20,000

To his son Brendan

Two vans (Note 2):	Van 1	15,000
	Van 2	25,000
An office building (Note 2)		250,000
Cash		50,000

Brendan and Jake had each inherited assets valued at €450,000 on the death of their mother in March 2000. Brendan had also inherited €120,000 on the death of his grandfather in 1999. Apart from this, none of the above had previously received any taxable gifts or inheritances.

   Ronnie, Jake and Brendan are all Irish domiciled and resident. Janet is UK domiciled and UK resident and ordinarily resident.

Notes:

(1)   Ronnie had purchased the van rental business as a going concern in January 2006 for €350,000. He has been involved in running the business on a full-time basis since then.

The value of the business at the relevant dates is made up as follows:

	January 2006	July 2012
	€	€
Vans	175,000	650,000
Stocks of spare parts	30,000	150,000
Net debtors	10,000	180,000
Premises	80,000	0
Goodwill	55,000	300,000
Total	350,000	1,280,000

The cost of all vans exceed their values outlined above. The vans given to Brendan are not included in the above figures.

(2) Brendan is in the process of establishing his own office supplies business. The vans and office building transferred to him had been acquired by his father for his van rental business at the following costs:

	Date of acquisition	Cost
		€
Van 1	6/5/07	20,000
Van 2	20/8/08	45,000
Office building	11/1/06	80,000

Requirement
(a) Calculate the CGT liability, if any, arising from the above gifts.
(b) Calculate the CAT liability, if any, arising on the above gifts.

Note: Small gift exemption and annual exemption and stamp duty may be ignored.

18

Treatment of Limited Interests

Learning Objectives

After studying this chapter you will have developed the competency to understand that:

■ A limited interest is less than a full interest and, therefore, should have a lower taxable value.

■ For limited interests, the calculation of taxable value is:
Market Value
less
Expenses, costs, liabilities
=
Incumbrance free value × **limited interest factor**
less
consideration
=
Taxable value

■ The limited interest factor is some number less than 1. The factor depends on whether it is a life interest or an interest for a particular number of years. The factors are set out in **Appendix 18.1** and **Appendix 18.2**.

18.1 Introduction

Section 2 CATCA 2003 defines 'limited interest' as meaning:

1. an interest (other than a leasehold interest) for the duration of a life, or lives;
2. an interest for a period certain; or
3. any other interest which is not an absolute interest.

Obviously a limited interest is less than a full interest and therefore the taxable value will be lower. This is achieved by applying a factor (i.e. a figure less than 1) to the incumbrance-free value.

18.2 Valuation of Annuities

Section 5 CATCA 2003 contains special provisions for calculating the value of a gift or inheritance of an annuity. The method of valuation depends on whether the annuity is charged or secured on any property.

18.2.1 Annuity Charged or Secured on Property

Where an annuity or limited interest is charged on any property the value of the gift or inheritance is deemed to consist of the **appropriate part** of the property on which the annuity or limited interest is charged. The **appropriate part** is ascertained using the following formula:

$$\text{Entire property} \times \frac{\text{Gross annual value of benefit}}{\text{Gross annual value of entire property}}$$

> **Example**
> Gary gives an annuity of €5,000 to his son Stephen and charges a specific block of investments owned by him with payment of the annuity. The investments have a capital value of €150,000 and produce an annual income of €10,000. The gift given by Gary to Stephen is deemed to consist of the appropriate part of the entire block of investments, i.e.
>
> $$€150,000 \times \frac{€5,000}{€10,000} = €75,000$$
>
> This €75,000 is used as the market value of the gift received by Stephen from his father.

In arriving at the taxable value, as outlined above, from this amount are deducted any liabilities, costs and expenses to give the **incumbrance-free value**. Finally any consideration given is deducted to arrive at the taxable value.

18.2.2 Annuity not Charged or Secured on Property

Where a gift or inheritance of an annuity is given which is not charged on any particular property, the value of the benefit is calculated by deeming the benefit to be equal to the market value of a capital sum required to be invested in the latest Government security issued prior to the date of the gift, which is not redeemable within 10 years, to produce an income equal to the annuity.

> **Example**
> Eoin covenants to pay his mother Bernadette, aged 62, €10,000 per annum. The value of the benefit taken by Bernadette is calculated as follows.
>
> Say, the latest Government stock issued which was not redeemable within 10 years was a 4% Government Bond and this was quoted at €0.90 for €1 of stock.
>
> *continued overleaf*

> In order to produce an annual income of €10,000 by investing in this Government Stock, it would be necessary to buy €250,000 of the stocks, i.e. €10,000/4%. At the current price of €0.90 per €1 of stock it would cost €225,000 to buy €250,000 of this stock, i.e. €250,000 × 0.9. Accordingly the value of the benefit received by Bernadette is deemed to be €225,000.
>
> Again the €225,000 is used as the market value of the benefit received in calculating the taxable value of the benefit received by Bernadette.

In arriving at the taxable value, as outlined above, from this amount are deducted any liabilities, costs and expenses to give the **incumbrance-free value**.

18.3 Life Interest and Interest for a Certain Period

The taxable value of the limited interest is normally based upon the **incumbrance-free value** of the property to which the limited interest relates.

A reminder that the incumbrance-free value is the market value less expenses, costs and liabilities (but before deducting consideration).

If John has received a life interest in his deceased uncle's farm, the taxable value of the inheritance will be based upon the incumbrance-free value of the farm. However, as John's interest is not an absolute interest, the incumbrance-free value will be further reduced to reflect this fact.

The taxable value of John's limited interest is computed by taking a proportion of the capital sum equal to the incumbrance-free value of the farm. The proportion used is determined by Tables A and B which are set out in Part II of the First Schedule to the Act.

Tables A and B are reproduced in **Appendix 18.1 and 18.2**. Table A deals with the valuation of life interests, and Table B deals with the valuation of interest for periods certain. Table A is clearly applicable in the case of John's limited interest in his deceased uncle's farm.

Use of Remainder of Life
If John was aged 45 at the date of his uncle's death, and the incumbrance-free value of the farm was valued at €100,000, the taxable value of his benefit would be computed as follows:

$$€100,000 \times 0.7897, \text{ i.e. } €78,970 \text{ (Table A, Column 3)}.$$

Use for a Fixed Period of Time
If John had instead been **granted the use of the farm for a period of eight years**, his taxable value would have been computed as:

$$€100,000 \times 0.4177, \text{ i.e. } €41,770 \text{ (Table B, Column 2)}$$

If the limited interest is not based upon any specific underlying property then, as we saw at **Section 18.2.2** CATCA 2003 provides an artificial method for determining the notional capital figure in which the limited interest is effectively deemed to subsist.

Example

Eoin covenants to pay his mother Bernadette, aged 62, €10,000 per annum for the remainder of her life. The incumbrance-free value of the benefit taken by Bernadette is calculated as before:

In order to produce an annual income of €10,000 by investing in this Government Stock, it would be necessary to buy €250,000 of the stocks, i.e. €10,000/4%. At the current price of €0.90 per €1 of stock it would cost €225,000 to buy €250,000 of this stock, i.e. €250,000 × 0.9. Accordingly the value of the benefit received by Bernadette is deemed to be €225,000.

As Bernadette has received the annuity for life, she has received a life interest in €225,000. The €225,000, assuming no deductible costs are incurred, must be multiplied by the factor in *Table A for a female aged 62, i.e. 0.6162*, to arrive at the taxable value of the benefit received. The taxable value of the gift received by Bernadette is therefore €138,645 (€225,000 × 0.6162).

There are special rules for valuing interests involving one or more lives and for periods not equal to a year. These are not examinable.

The limited interest factors from Table A and B are given in the standard reference material given out at the exam and set out in **Appendix 18.1** and **Appendix 18.2**.

18.4 Deduction of Limited Interests as Consideration

When a limited interest forms part of the consideration of the gift or inheritance, the amount to be deducted is the **incumbrance-free value of the limited interest** (i.e. before the Table A/B factor is applied).

Example

Ann inherited an investment property valued at €1,750,000 from her father. The property yields an annual income of €125,000. The property was to be charged from the time of his death with the payment of an annuity of €25,000 to his sister Mary, aged 60, for Mary's lifetime.

Taxable value of Mary's inheritance:

$$€1,750,000 \times \frac{25,000}{125,000} = \textbf{€350,000} \times 0.6475 = €226,625$$

Taxable value of Anne's inheritance:

€1,750,000 − **€350,000** = €1,400,000

When Mary dies, Ann will take a further inheritance. The inheritance will be the market value of the property when Mary dies multiplied by €25,000 (Mary's annuity) divided by the annual income from the property at that time.

Appendix 18.1: Limited Interest Factors

TABLE A

1	2	3	4
		*Value of an interest in a capital of €1 for a **male** life aged as in Column 1*	*Value of an interest in a capital of €1 for a **female** life aged as in Column 1*
Years of Age	*Joint Factor*		
0	.99	.9519	.9624
1	.99	.9767	.9817
2	.99	.9767	.9819
3	.99	.9762	.9817
4	.99	.9753	.9811
5	.99	.9742	.9805
6	.99	.9730	.9797
7	.99	.9717	.9787
8	.99	.9703	.9777
9	.99	.9688	.9765
10	.99	.9671	.9753
11	.98	.9653	.9740
12	.98	.9634	.9726
13	.98	.9614	.9710
14	.98	.9592	.9693
15	.98	.9569	.9676
16	.98	.9546	.9657
17	.98	.9522	.9638
18	.98	.9497	.9617
19	.98	.9471	.9596
20	.97	.9444	.9572
21	.97	.9416	.9547
22	.97	.9387	.9521
23	.97	.9356	.9493
24	.97	.9323	.9464
25	.97	.9288	.9432
26	.97	.9250	.9399
27	.97	.9209	.9364
28	.97	.9165	.9328
29	.97	.9119	.9289
30	.96	.9068	.9248

continued overleaf

1	2	3	4
		*Value of an interest in a capital of €1 for a **male** life aged as in Column 1*	*Value of an interest in a capital of €1 for a **female** life aged as in Column 1*
Years of Age	*Joint Factor*		
31	.96	.9015	.9205
32	.96	.8958	.9159
33	.96	.8899	.9111
34	.96	.8836	.9059
35	.96	.8770	.9005
36	.96	.8699	.8947
37	.96	.8626	.8886
38	.95	.8549	.8821
39	.95	.8469	.8753
40	.95	.8384	.8683
41	.95	.8296	.8610
42	.95	.8204	.8534
43	.95	.8107	.8454
44	.94	.8005	.8370
45	.94	.7897	.8283
46	.94	.7783	.8192
47	.94	.7663	.8096
48	.93	.7541	.7997
49	.93	.7415	.7896
50	.92	.7287	.7791
51	.91	.7156	.7683
52	.90	.7024	.7572
53	.89	.6887	.7456
54	.89	.6745	.7335
55	.88	.6598	.7206
56	.88	.6445	.7069
57	.88	.6288	.6926
58	.87	.6129	.6778
59	.86	.5969	.6628
60	.86	.5809	.6475
61	.86	.5650	.6320
62	.86	.5492	.6162
63	.85	.5332	.6000
64	.85	.5171	.5830
65	.85	.5007	.5650

continued overleaf

1	2	3	4
		Value of an interest in a capital of €1 for a **male** *life aged as in Column 1*	*Value of an interest in a capital of €1 for a* **female** *life aged as in Column 1*
Years of Age	*Joint Factor*		
66	.85	.4841	.5462
67	.84	.4673	.5266
68	.84	.4506	.5070
69	.84	.4339	.4873
70	.83	.4173	.4679
71	.83	.4009	.4488
72	.82	.3846	.4301
73	.82	.3683	.4114
74	.81	.3519	.3928
75	.80	.3352	.3743
76	.79	.3181	.3559
77	.78	.3009	.3377
78	.76	.2838	.3198
79	.74	.2671	.3023
80	.72	.2509	.2855
81	.71	.2353	.2693
82	.70	.2203	.2538
83	.69	.2057	.2387
84	.68	.1916	.2242
85	.67	.1783	.2104
86	.66	.1657	.1973
87	.65	.1537	.1849
88	.64	.1423	.1730
89	.62	.1315	.1616
90	.60	.1212	.1509
91	.58	.1116	.1407
92	.56	.1025	.1310
93	.54	.0939	.1218
94	.52	.0858	.1132
95	.50	.0781	.1050
96	.49	.0710	.0972
97	.48	.0642	.0898
98	.47	.0578	.0828
99	.45	.0517	.0762
100 or over.	.43	.0458	.0698

Appendix 18.2: Limited Interest Factors

TABLE B

(Column 2 shows the value of an interest in a capital of €1 for the number of years shown in column 1)

1	2	1	2
Number of years	*Value*	*Number of years*	*Value*
1	.0654	26	.8263
2	.1265	27	.8375
3	.1836	28	.8480
4	.2370	29	.8578
5	.2869	30	.8669
6	.3335	31	.8754
7	.3770	32	.8834
8	.4177	33	.8908
9	.4557	34	.8978
10	.4913	35	.9043
11	.5245	36	.9100
12	.5555	37	.9165
13	.5845	38	.9230
14	.6116	39	.9295
15	.6369	40	.9360
16	.6605	41	.9425
17	.6826	42	.9490
18	.7032	43	.9555
19	.7225	44	.9620
20	.7405	45	.9685
21	.7574	46	.9750
22	.7731	47	.9815
23	.7878	48	.9880
24	.8015	49	.9945
25	.8144	50 and over	1.000

Questions (to Chapter 18)

Review Questions

(See Suggested Solutions to Review Questions at the end of this textbook.)

Question 18.1

Calculate the CAT payable in respect of the gift/inheritance taken in 2012 in each of the following cases:

(a)   Tom, who is Irish domiciled but UK resident and ordinarily resident, executed a deed of covenant on 8 April 2012 for €10,000 per annum for life in favour of his mother, who is Irish domiciled and resident. Tom's mother is a widow aged 59. The latest Government stock issued before 8 April which is not redeemable within 10 years was 5% Government Bonds quoted at €0.92 for €1 of stock.

  Tom's mother had previously received the following benefits:

  (i)   assets valued at €250,000 on the death of her husband, also Irish domiciled and resident, in 1997,
  (ii)   €25,000 in cash on the death of her own mother, Tom's grandmother, also Irish domiciled and resident, in 1996; and
  (iii) jewellery and other assets valued at €30,000 on the death of her sister, also Irish domiciled and resident, in March 1995.

(b)   Martha, an Irish domiciled and UK resident person died in January 1987. Under the terms of her will she left a life interest in a UK property to her brother Jason, Irish domiciled and resident, and on his death absolutely to his son Mark, also Irish resident and domiciled. Jason died on 5 September 2012, at which date the absolute ownership of the UK property reverted to Mark, then aged 56. The market value of the UK property at the date of Jason's death was €300,000.

  Under the terms of Jason's will, Mark also inherited cash in a Dublin bank account of €60,000 and Jason's house valued at €250,000. (Mark had moved in with Jason when Jason became ill four years prior to his death. When Mark moved in with Jason he let out his own house.)

  Apart from the above, the only previous benefit received by Mark was €190,000 worth of savings certificates inherited from his mother, also Irish domiciled and resident, on her death in June 1999 and €10,000 inherited from a nephew in May 1997.

Question 18.2

Calculate the *taxable value* of following gifts/inheritances arising in the year 2012:

1.   Martin a grocer for many years, died on 1 March 2012. He left his entire estate to his brother Dermot, aged 42, for life. His estate consisted of the following at the valuation date:

	€
Grocery business and premises	600,000
House and contents	150,000
Bank accounts	15,000

Funeral expenses and testamentary expenses of €8,000 were outstanding.

2. Jack, a publican for many years, died on 2 June 2012. He left his pub premises and business, valued at €600,000, to his son, John absolutely. The pub produces an annual income of €150,000. Jack charged the premises and business with the payment of an annuity to his sister Margaret, aged 54, of €15,000 for 10 years.

   Jack also left the residue of his estate to his son John. Any liabilities are to be paid out of the residue. These were as follows at the valuation date:

	€
Residue	50,000
Income tax liabilities outstanding	20,000
Funeral expenses and testamentary expenses	9,000

3. In 2007, David inherited an investment property from his father valued at €250,000. The property was charged with the payment of an annuity to David's brother, Larry, for five years of €10,000. In 2007 the property produced an annual rental income of €20,000.

   The last payment was made to Larry in April 2012. In April 2012 the property was valued at €375,000 and produces an annual rental income of €30,000.

4. On 7 August 2012, Alan executed a deed of covenant of €10,000 per annum for life in favour of his widowed mother aged 65.

   The latest Government stock issued before 7 August which is not redeemable within 10 years was 4% Government Bonds quoted at €0.89 for €1 of stock.

5. Tom, a farmer for many years, died on 11 October 2012. He left his entire estate absolutely to his son Fintan. His estate consisted of the following:

	€
Farmland	950,000
Farm stocks and machinery	120,000
Stocks and shares	50,000
Cash	25,000

Funeral and testamentary expenses of €9,500 were also outstanding.

   Under the terms of Tom's will he charged the farmland and farm assets with the payment of an annuity of €15,000 per annum to his daughter Emer, aged 40, for life. Annual income produced by the farmland and farm assets amounts to €50,000. Fintan has no other assets. Emer's only asset is a house valued at €120,000 which she rents to a tenant.

Question 18.3

Andrew McNeill has owned and farmed land for 16 years. On 6 August 2012, he took his son David, into partnership on a 75/25 (25% to David) basis and, at that time, transferred to David 25% of the farm and farm assets. Andrew had made no previous lifetime transfers.

Andrew and David McNeill continued farming in partnership until Andrew's death on 25 November 2012, when all the assets of Andrew, which consisted of the remainder of the farm and farm assets and a number of investments, passed to David. The values of the assets were as follows:-

Assets	Value at 6 August 2012	Value at 25 November 2012 and at valuation date
Farming	€	€
300 acres of farmland	2,200 per acre	3,600 per acre
Farm buildings	28,200	33,600
Machinery	15,600	19,300
Livestock	24,400	31,700
Other investments		95,000

The transfer of the investments to David under Andrew's will was subject to and charged with the payment of an annuity of €5,000 to Andrew's sister, Rachel. The investments produce an annual income of €8,000.

During 2011, David had inherited assets valued at €120,000 from an uncle. By 6 August 2012 David had sold all these assets and had cash in the bank of €126,000. On 10 October 2012 David spent €120,000 on farmland adjoining his father's land. This land was valued at €150,000 on 25 November 2012 and at the valuation date.

Debts and funeral expenses outstanding at the date of death amounted to €15,000. Legal fees associated with Andrew's estate amounted to €10,000.

Apart from the gifts and inheritances outlined above, David had not previously received any taxable gifts or inheritances.

All persons outlined above are Irish domiciled and resident persons.

Requirement
You are required to compute:

(a) the CAT payable by David on the gift from Andrew on 6 August 2012 assuming all available reliefs and exemptions were utilised; and

(b) the CAT payable by David on Andrew's death, assuming that no lifetime transfers had been made after 6 August 2011.

You may ignore stamp duty.

Question 18.4

Shane Murray, a widower, died on 30 June 2012. Under the terms of his will, he provided the following bequests:

	Value at 30 June 2012 And at the valuation date
	€
To his son John:	
100% of the shares in Murray Developments Ltd (Note 1)	1,500,000
Two investment properties (Note 2)	850,000
To his daughter Emily:	
His house (Note 3)	950,000

To his sister Sarah:
An annuity of €10,000 for life (Note 4)

The residue of his estate was left equally between John and Emily and was charged with the payment of funeral and testamentary expenses. The residue consisted of the following:

Cash	146,000
Quoted shares	50,000

Shane had taken out a qualifying insurance policy in 2005 for the sole purpose of paying CAT on dispositions made by him under his will. The proceeds of the policy were €900,000 and Shane's will provided that all inheritance tax payable by John, Emily and Sarah on his death was to be paid pro-rata from this policy.

The Murray family are all Irish domiciled and resident. In November 2004, Shane had transferred an investment property valued at €300,000, with a mortgage of €200,000 charged on the property to John. This transfer gave rise to a gift tax liability to John of €3,800. In 1999 Emily inherited a house from her mother valued at €200,000. Emily has since let the house.

Notes:

1. Shane Murray established Murray Developments Ltd in 1986. It carries on a trade of buying and selling land. The company has employed John for the last five years.
2. The two properties transferred to John were valued at €400,000 and €450,000 with attaching mortgages of €150,000 and €75,000 respectively.
3. Emily who is unmarried had been living, and has always lived, with her father in his house when he died.
4. The annuity payable to Shane's sister is charged on the property valued at €400,000 inherited by John. This property yields an annual rental income of €30,000. Sarah was 63 at the date of Shane's death.
5. Funeral expenses and legal fees associated with the administration of his estate amounted to €3,500 and €8,500 respectively.

(Ignore small gift exemption.)

Requirement
Compute the CAT liabilities, if any, payable by Sarah, John and Emily.

Question 18.5

Peter O'Connor, a farmer aged 57, gifted farmland and farm assets located in Co. Monaghan to his son Stephen valued at €5 million on 18 August 2012 on condition that Stephen would pay him €30,000 per annum for the rest of his life and would take over payment of a mortgage of €350,000 charged on the land. (The latest Government Stock issued before 18 August which is not redeemable within 10 years was 5% Government Bonds quoted at 90c for €1 of stock.)

Peter had inherited this farmland and assets from his own father in January 1999 at which time the lands were valued at €200,000. Peter had farmed this land since he inherited them from his father.

Stephen paid stamp duty and legal fees of €165,000 on the transfer of the land to him.

Stephen had previously inherited a site valued at €45,000 on the death of his mother in May 2004. At the time of his mother's death, the land had planning permission for residential development. Peter subsequently built apartments on the site which are now fully let.

Stephen had also previously inherited land in Co. Antrim (Northern Ireland) from an uncle, Peter's brother, in March 2006 valued at €300,000.

On 18 August 2012, Stephen's assets consisted of the following:

	€
His house (Note)	350,000
A car	20,000
Farmlands in Co. Antrim (Northern Ireland)	500,000
Site inherited from mother, now fully developed	450,000

All the O'Connor family are Irish domiciled. Peter and his wife have always been Irish resident. Stephen's uncle was Irish domiciled and UK resident at the date of his death.

Note
There was a mortgage outstanding in respect of the purchase of the house of €100,000 on 18 August 2012.

Requirement
(a) Calculate the CGT liability, if any, arising on the transfer to Stephen on 18 August 2012.
(b) Calculate the CAT liabilities, if any, arising on the same transfer.

Special Relationship Situations

Learning Objectives

After studying this chapter you will have developed the competency to understand that:

- the group thresholds can be increased in three situations:

    - niece/nephew receiving business assets, provided that individual has worked in the business for the last five years. The Group A threshold of €250,000 applies to gifts/inheritances of *assets of the business* instead of the Group B threshold of €33,500;

    - the surviving spouse or civil partner of a deceased spouse or civil partner takes on the deceased spouse's or civil partner's relationship, where he/she receives a benefit (not where the surviving spouse or civil partner is the disponer);
      The Group A threshold of €250,000 or Group B threshold of €33,500 can apply, instead of the Group C threshold of €16,750.

    - grandchild aged under 18 of a deceased parent. The Group A threshold of €250,000 applies instead of the Group B threshold of €33,500.

19.1 Favourite Nephew/Niece

19.1.1 General Rule

In certain circumstances, under Schedule 2 CATCA 2003, a nephew or niece may be deemed to be the child of a disponer and, therefore, qualify for the Group A threshold of €250,000 rather than the Group B threshold of €33,500.

A niece or nephew means a child of the disponer's brother or sister or a child of the civil partner of the disponer's brother or sister.

The conditions to be satisfied are:

Business

1. the nephew/niece has **worked substantially on a full-time basis for the relevant period** in carrying on, or assisting in the carrying on of a trade, business, or profession of the disponer; and
2. the gift/inheritance consists of property which was used in connection with that trade, business or profession;

   or

Company

1. the nephew/niece **worked substantially on a full-time basis for a company controlled by the disponer** for the **relevant period** in carrying on, or in assisting in carrying on the trade; and
2. the gift/inheritance consists of **shares** in that company.

19.1.2 Conditions

1. The niece/nephew will only satisfy the employment test, i.e. **"worked substantially on a full-time basis"**, if:

   Business

   (a) he/she works **more than 24 hours a week** for the disponer at a place where the business, trade or profession is carried on; or
   (b) where, the business, trade or profession is carried on exclusively by the disponer, his spouse and the niece/nephew, he/she works **more than 15 hours a week** at the place where the business, trade or profession is carried on;

      or

   Company

   (a) he/she works **more than 24 hours a week** for the company at a place where its business, trade or profession is carried on, or
   (b) where, the business, trade or profession is carried on exclusively by the disponer, his spouse and the niece/nephew, he/she works **more than 15 hours a week** for the company at a place where the business, trade or profession of the company is carried on.

2. The **"relevant period"** means:

   (a) the period of **five years** ending on the date of the disposition; or
   (b) in the case where, at the date of the disposition, an interest in possession is limited to the disponer under the disposition, the period of five years ending on the coming to an end of that interest.

Reasonable periods of annual or sick leave are allowed.

3. A **"company controlled by the disponer"** means a company which:

   (a) is a private trading company (as defined in **Chapter 15**);
   (b) has the disponer as one of its directors; and

    (c)   is under the control of:

- the disponer; or
- nominees of the disponer.

"Control" generally means holding 50% or more of the nominal value of the shares in a company or more than 50% of the voting share capital.

Example

June leaves her farm worth €800,000 to her niece Catherine who had worked the farm with her for the last eight years. She also left her shares in Abbey plc worth €50,000.

Firstly, agricultural relief is probably due so that the actual taxable value would be €800,000 × 10% = €80,000.

The group threshold in respect of the farm is Group A of €250,000, as she has worked on the farm for at least five years and it is an inheritance of a trade asset.

The group threshold in respect of the shares is the normal Group B threshold of €33,500.

19.2 Surviving Spouse or Civil Partner of a Deceased Person

CATCA 2003 provides a specialised relief which effectively permits the surviving spouse or civil partner of a deceased person to "stand in the shoes of the deceased person" in certain circumstances. The relief applies where:

- at the date of the gift or inheritance;
- the donee/successor is the surviving spouse or civil partner of a deceased person who at the time of his/her death was of a closer blood relationship to the disponer than the donee/successor.

In these circumstances, for the purposes of a computation of the liability, the donee/successor is deemed to take up the same relationship to the disponer as the deceased spouse or civil partner had at the time of death. This can result in the use of a more favourable tax-free threshold for the computation of any liability due.

Example

Jim died on 28 February 2012 and left €200,000 to his son-in-law, James.

James' wife Ann, (i.e. Jim's daughter) had died some years previously.

In these circumstances, James is deemed to stand in Ann's shoes, vis-a-vis her blood relationship with her father, and, accordingly, the €250,000 group threshold applies. If this rule did not apply, James would be treated as a stranger and a threshold of only €16,750 would apply. If James also received a gift from Ann's aunt, the group threshold would be €33,500 instead of the usual €16,750.

19.3 Minor Child of a Deceased Child

We have already seen that the Group A threshold applies not only from a parent to child, but also to gifts/inheritances taken from a grandparent by the minor child of a deceased child, the minor child of the civil partner of a deceased child, the minor child of a deceased child of a grandparent's civil partner, or the minor child of the civil partner of a deceased child of the grandparent's civil partner. A minor child is defined in CATCA 2003 as a child who is under 18 years of age.

Example

Anthony and Harriet are Jim's parents. Jim is married to Nora. Jim and Nora have a daughter, Emma, who is 5 years old. Jim died on 1 January 2012.

On 2 January 2012, Anthony gave Nora €100,000 and Emma €200,000.

On 1 March 2012, Alan, Nora's father, gave Emma €100,000.

The gift by Anthony to Nora of €100,000 will be dealt with subject to a €250,000 tax-free threshold as **Nora is the surviving spouse** of Jim, who is Anthony's son.

The gift of €200,000 by Anthony to Emma will also be subject to a €250,000 tax-free threshold, as **Emma is a minor child** of a deceased child (i.e. Jim) of Anthony's.

The gift by Alan to Emma is dealt with under the €33,500 tax-free threshold as Alan is Emma's grandparent. Emma is not a minor child of a deceased child of Alan's and therefore the €250,000 class threshold is not applicable.

Questions (to Chapter 19)

Review Questions

(See Suggested Solutions to Review Questions at the end of this textbook.)

Question 19.1

Identify the **group threshold amounts** applicable to the following gifts/inheritances:

1. Gift of investment property by father to daughter on 5/1/2012.
2. Gift of shares by son to father on 20/6/2012.
3. Gift of 25% of shares in trading company by uncle to nephew on 1/4/2012. Remaining 75% of shares owned by unrelated parties. Nephew has worked for company on a full-time basis for last 10 years.
4. Gift of farmland by uncle to nephew on 1/6/2012. Nephew has worked on a full-time basis for uncle farming this land for previous 10 years.
5. Gift of shares by father-in-law to daughter-in-law, son still alive, on 25/12/2012.
6. Gift of shares by grandfather to 19-year-old grandson, grandson's father is deceased on 1/7/2012.
7. Gift of cash from cousin on 1/5/2012.
8. Gift of cash from uncle to niece on 17/3/2012.
9. Gift of cash from nephew to uncle on 20/7/2012.
10. Gift of 75% of shares in trading company by aunt to niece on 1/1/2012. Remaining 25% of shares owned by unrelated parties. Niece has worked for company on a full-time basis for last 10 years.
11. Inheritance received from separated spouse on 25/12/2012.
12. Gift of cash by stepfather to step-child on 1/1/2012.
13. Gift of investment property by grandfather to grandson's wife on 1/9/2012. Grandson is deceased.
14. Gift of 100% of shares in trading company by uncle to nephew on 1/10/2012. Nephew has worked for company on a full-time basis for previous four years.
15. Gift of shares to brother's wife on 7/2/2012. Brother is deceased.
16. Gift of antique vase by granddaughter to grandmother on 5/3/2012.
17. Gift of cash to divorced spouse on 1/12/2012.
18. Gift of cash to adopted child of brother on 15/12/2012.
19. Gift of farmland to wife's nephew on 1/3/2012. Nephew has been working on a full-time basis farming the land for the previous 10 years.
20. Gift of property by uncle to nephew on 19/11/2012. Property had been let to company owned 100% by uncle and nephew has been working on a full-time basis for the company for the last 10 years.

Question 19.2

Jerome Nutley, a widower, died on 26 October 2012. Under the terms of his will, he provided the following bequests:

	Value at 26 October 2012 And at the valuation date
	€
To his nephew Declan:	
55% of the shares in Wiggies Wholesalers Ltd (Note 1)	350,000
To his son Jonathan:	
Property let to Wiggies Wholesalers Ltd (Note 2)	500,000
To his daughter Louise:	
His house (Note 3)	750,000
The residue of his estate was left equally between his son Jonathan and daughter Louise and was charged with the payment of funeral and testamentary expenses. The residue consisted of:	
Cash	65,000

Jerome had taken out a life assurance policy some years ago and had nominated Louise as the sole beneficiary of the policy. Proceeds payable on his death amounted to €350,000.

The Nutley family are all Irish domiciled and resident. Declan had not previously received any taxable gifts or inheritances. Jonathan had previously received a gift of €10,000 from an aunt, an Irish domiciled and resident person, in March 1995. Louise had previously received an inheritance of €179,500 from her father-in-law in 2006.

Notes:

1. Wiggies Wholesalers Ltd carries on the trade of electrical wholesalers. The company was established by Jerome Nutley in 1973. However, he sold 45% of the shares to an unrelated party when he retired in September 1996. Declan has been working full-time for Wiggies Wholesalers Ltd for the past 10 years.
2. The property out of which Wiggies Wholesalers Ltd operates was acquired by Jerome Nutley in 1973 and has been let to the company by him for use in its trade since then.
3. Louise Nutley, a schoolteacher aged 50, had been living with her father in the house which he left to her since her husband died in 1998. Jerome was incapacitated since 2003 and was unable to look after himself. Louise has no other interests in a dwelling house.
4. Funeral expenses and legal fees associated with the administration of Jerome's estate amounted to €2,500 and €4,000 respectively.

Requirement
Compute the CAT liabilities, if any, payable by Declan, Jonathan and Louise.

Administration

Learning Objectives

After studying this chapter you will have developed competency to understand that:

■ A return of any gift or inheritance must be made if the aggregate benefits received within the same group threshold exceed 80% of the group threshold amount. Any CAT due must accompany the return.

■ Most returns must be filed using ROS.

■ The return must be filed with payment:
  ● where the valuation date is in the period from 1 January to 31 August, on or before 31 October in that year; and
  ● where the valuation date is in the period 1 September to 31 December, on or before 31 October in the following year.

■ If the return is filed using ROS, the filing date is extended; for 2012, it is 15 November 2012.

■ The standard interest rules apply, i.e. 0.0219% per day on late payment and, if the necessary conditions are satisfied, 0.011% per day for overpayments.

■ It is possible to pay CAT by instalments in the case of real property and limited interests, subject to the normal interest charge. The interest charge is only three-quarters of the normal daily rate for agricultural and business property.

20.1 Accountable Persons

The person accountable for payment of the CAT is the donee or successor as the case may be. If a donee or successor is deceased, the CAT is recoverable from his/her personal representative.

20.2 Delivery of Returns

Self-assessment applies to CAT. Any return involving claiming an exemption (other than small gift exemption) or a relief must be filed on ROS. All other returns may be filed using a paper tax return, short form IT38, provided the benefit received is an absolute interest without conditions and restrictions. If a paper return is filed, the taxpayer must calculate the CAT due. There are penalties if a return is not filed by the due date.

20.2.1 Persons Accountable

A person who is accountable for CAT is obliged to **deliver a return** by 31 October (see **Section 20.3**) where the aggregate taxable value of all taxable benefits taken by a donee or successor which have the same group threshold exceeds 80% of the group threshold amount.

1. The return must show:

    (i)   every applicable gift/inheritance;
    (ii) all property comprised in such gift/inheritance;
    (iii) an estimate of the market value of the property; and
    (iv) such particulars as may be relevant to the assessment of CAT in respect of such gift.

2. Also, the taxpayer must make on the return, an assessment of such amount of tax as, to the best of his knowledge, information and belief, ought to be charged and paid.

3. Finally, the person must pay any tax which is calculated as due.

20.2.2 Obligation to Make Returns for Capital Acquisitions Tax

The obligation to make self assessment returns for CAT is imposed on persons who are accountable for CAT under CATCA 2003 where the **aggregate taxable values of all taxable benefits taken with the same group threshold exceeds 80% of the group threshold amount** which applies in the computation of tax on that aggregate. Where a taxpayer claims a relief, Revenue expects a return to be filed by the taxpayer, even if the taxable value is less than 80% of the threshold amount.

> **Example**
> December 1992, gift from brother – €10,000.
>
> January 2012, gift from sister – €20,000.
>
> The €33,500 group threshold applies to both of these gifts.
>
> The total aggregate is therefore €30,000.
> The group threshold amount is €33,500.
>
> As the aggregate exceeds 80% of the group threshold amount, a return is required.

Even if no benefit has been received, a person is required to deliver a return if requested to do so by the Revenue Commissioners.

Forms 11 and 12 and CG50 application for a CGT clearance certificate all contain questions designed to act as prompts for the filing of CAT returns in relevant cases.

20.2.3 Expression of Doubt

As with other taxes, there is provision for "an expression of doubt" in the return where an accountable person is uncertain as to the correct application of law to a particular transaction. Interest will not arise on any additional tax arising over and above the tax due per the return on which the expression of doubt was made, provided that the additional tax is paid to the Revenue within 30 days. If the Revenue do not accept the expression of doubt as being genuine, they will notify the taxpayer within 30 days and the additional tax is payable. The taxpayer has a right of appeal within 30 days.

20.2.4 Delivery of Statements

Accountable Person

The accountable person must, where he is required to do so in writing by the Revenue Commissioners, deliver and verify to the Revenue Commissioners:

1.   a statement of such particulars relating to any property; and
2.   such evidence as they require;

as may in their opinion be relevant to the assessment of CAT in respect of the gift. The statement, where appropriate, is to be on a form provided or approved of by the Revenue Commissioners.

The time limit for submitting the statement will be specified in the notice but it is to be not less than 30 days.

The **accountable person must retain records for six years** from the valuation date or the filing date if the return is filed late.

There are penalties for not filing a return and for filing an incorrect return. If there is fraud involved, the penalties are higher.

Disponer

If requested by the Revenue Commissioners in writing, a disponer must deliver to them a return of all property in the gift given to the donee and its value.

20.2.5 Inspection and Assessment

Revenue may authorise a person to inspect any property or accounts etc as may be relevant to the assessment of CAT. Revenue have power to require additional returns from the accountable person if the return made was materially defective and to make any additional assessments. The making of enquiries by Revenue or the making/amending of assessments may not be initiated/done after the expiry of four years from the date the return is received by Revenue. This time limit does not apply where Revenue have reasonable grounds to believe that fraud or neglect has been committed.

20.2.6 Non-resident Beneficiary

Where a non-resident inherits a benefit with a market value of in excess of €20,000 and the personal representative is also non-resident, an Irish resident solicitor must be appointed to act in connection with the administration of the deceased's estate. This solicitor may be assessed and charged in respect of any CAT due by such a non-resident.

Where a non-resident receives an inheritance and the personal representative is resident in the State, and if the beneficiary is required to and does not file a return and pay any CAT due in respect of the inheritance, then the personal representative may be assessed and charged with the payment of the CAT due by the beneficiary.

The personal representative/solicitor will not be liable for CAT due by the beneficiary where the liability arose due to the fact that the beneficiary previously received a taxable gift or inheritance and the personal representative made reasonable enquiries regarding such gifts or inheritances and has acted in good faith.

The personal representative/solicitor will only be held liable to the extent that they have control of the property which is the subject of the inheritance and is entitled to retain funds to cover the CAT liability from the property over which he has control. The personal representative/solicitor is also entitled to raise the funds required to pay any CAT by the sale or mortgaging of any property due to the beneficiary.

20.3 Payment of CAT and Interest, and Filing Returns

There is a fixed pay and file date for CAT of 31 October. **All gifts and inheritances with a valuation date in the 12-month period ending on the previous 31 August will be included in the return to be filed by 31 October**. That means where:

1. the valuation date arises in the period from 1 January to 31 August, the pay and file deadline is 31 October in that year; and
2. where the valuation date arises in the period from 1 September to 31 December, the pay and file deadline is 31 October in the following year.

Similar to income tax and capital gains tax, where the taxpayer files the return and pays tax using ROS, the filing date is extended. For 2012, the date is extended to 15 November 2012.

Example

Ann receives a gift and it has a valuation date of 21 August 2012. The CAT due is €40,222 after claiming agricultural relief. Ann must file and pay €40,222 of CAT on ROS by 5 November 2012.

Terry receives an inheritance and it has a valuation date of 6 November 2012. The CAT due is €30,522. Terry is not entitled to any reliefs or exemptions.

As Terry is not entitled to any reliefs or exemptions, he can file a paper return if he wishes. That return (short form IT38) and payment are due by 31 October 2013. If he files on ROS, the deadline will be some date (not yet known) in mid-November 2013.

A paper return may be filed where the beneficiary is not claiming any reliefs, exemptions, etc., other than the small gift exemption and the benefit received is an absolute interest without conditions or restrictions.

Where any other relief, etc. is being claimed, the return must be filed electronically through ROS.

Provided that CAT is paid by the due date, no interest is payable. However, if the CAT is not paid by the due date, simple interest of 0.0219% per day or part of a day is charged (this is equivalent to an annual rate of approx 8%), from the valuation date until the date of payment.

Provision is made whereby payments on account are applied first by the Revenue Commissioners in settlement of any outstanding interest charges and only then may the balance be set against the principal due.

There is a surcharge for the late filing of a return. The surcharge is calculated as follows:

1. 5% surcharge applies, subject to a maximum of €12,695, where the return is delivered within two months of the filing date (e.g. for 2012, any date between 1 November 2012 and 31 December 2012 inclusive);
2. 10% surcharge, up to a maximum of €63,485, applies where the tax return is not delivered within two months of the filing date.

> **Example**
> Anthony receives a gift on 1 August 2012 and the CAT due is €20,000. He files his form IT38 and makes a payment of €20,000 CAT on 1 December 2012. It was due on 31 October 2012. As a result of late filing, he is subject to a surcharge of 5% of €20,000, i.e. €1,000. He will also be liable to interest on €20,000 from 31 October to 1 December and on €1,000 from 31 October to the date of payment.

A person is deemed to have failed to deliver a return before the due date and will be liable to the surcharge where:

1. the person fraudulently or negligently delivers an incorrect return before the due date and does not correct the error in the return before the due date for filing the return;
2. the person delivers an incorrect return, but does not do so fraudulently or negligently, and it comes to the person's notice that the return is incorrect but the person fails to correct the return without unreasonable delay; or
3. the person files a return before the due date but is served with a notice by the Revenue Commissioners, by reason of their dissatisfaction with the return, to deliver further evidence and that evidence is not provided within the time specified in the notice.

20.4   Payment of CAT by Instalments

The accountable person may elect to pay CAT in respect of a taxable gift or inheritance by means of monthly instalments over a period not exceeding five years in such manner as may be determined by the Revenue Commissioners, the first of which becomes due on 31 October following the valuation date. Interest on the unpaid tax at 0.0219% per day must, however, be added to each instalment and paid at the same time as each instalment.

This option is only open where the taxable gift/inheritance comprises either of:

1. real property, e.g. freehold land and buildings; or
2. a limited interest, e.g. a life interest or interest for a period certain.

The CAT will be regarded as paid under self-assessment where the CAT due and payable is paid by instalments, by the payment of:

1. an amount which includes any instalment which is due prior to or on the date of the self-assessment; and
2. any further instalments of such CAT on the due dates as they fall due.

If a life tenant dies before all instalments have been paid, any instalments due after death cease to become payable. This applies whether or not instalment arrangements were entered into. Accordingly where a life tenant dies and an instalment arrangement was not entered into, any instalments which would have not yet been paid had an instalment arrangement been entered into can be reclaimed.

If the property comprising a gift or inheritance is sold at any time prior to payment of all instalments, then the balance due becomes immediately payable, unless the interest of the donee or successor is a limited interest.

20.4.1 Agricultural and Business Property

If the property is agricultural or business property (except quoted shares) then the daily interest rate is only three-quarters of the normal daily rate, i.e. 0.0164%. Also, the instalment arrangement can continue even if the property is sold or compulsorily acquired within the instalment period, provided that the proceeds are re-invested in other qualifying property within a year of the sale or compulsory acquisition.

20.5 Overpayment of CAT

If CAT has been overpaid, the Revenue Commissioners will repay the excess CAT paid if a valid claim is made within four years commencing on 31 October in the year in which the tax was due to be paid. Interest on CAT overpaid will accrue starting 93 days after the date on which a valid claim is made. In the case where the repayment arises due to a mistaken assumption on behalf of Revenue, interest will accrue from the date of payment of the excess CAT. Interest is payable at the rate of 0.011% per day or part of a day (this is equivalent to an annual interest rate of approx 4%).

20.6 Surcharge on Undervaluation of Property

There is a surcharge, to **penalise accountable persons who underestimate the market value of property** in returns for CAT purposes. The surcharge can be as high as 30%.

Questions (to Chapter 20)

Review Questions

Question 20.1

The managing partner of your firm of Chartered Accountants has asked you as the CAT specialist, to advise him on each of the following matters:

(a)   Who is an accountable person for CAT purposes?
(b)   Under what circumstances is a return required from an accountable person and what is the time frame for the submission of each return?
(c)   What details must be shown on a return and what must accompany a return?
(d)   What action is required of an accountable person who becomes aware that a return which has been lodged is defective in a material respect?
(e)   What are the consequences for the taxpayer of having made a return where the estimated value of the gift or inheritance is materially understated?

Requirement
Write a memorandum to the managing partner setting out your reply to the queries raised by him as outlined at (a) to (e) above.

Question 20.2

Robert Doyle died suddenly on 20 April 2012 without leaving a will. Under the laws of intestacy, his estate was inherited 2/3rds by his wife Sheila, from whom he had been separated for the last 10 years, and 1/3 by his daughters Ruth (21) and Angela (16).

Ruth and Angela had been living with their father when he died. Ruth has a full-time job and Angela is in full-time education and has no income of her own. Robert had taken out a life insurance policy and had nominated Ruth and Angela as the beneficiaries of this policy. The proceeds from the policy amounted to €200,000.

Apart from the insurance proceeds, Robert's assets at the date of his death consisted of the following:

	Value at 20 April 2012 And at the valuation date
	€
His house	600,000
50% share in a newsagents (Note 1)	900,000
€60,000 6% Exchequer Stock purchased by Robert in November 2001	66,000
Cash	45,000
Holiday home in Kerry	150,000
The following debts were outstanding:	
Income tax liabilities	15,000
Mortgage on his house	60,000

Notes:

1. Robert was a 50% owner in a thriving Dublin newsagents which he had established in 1992. Robert's partner will continue to manage the Doyle's 50% share in the newsagents on their behalf.
2. Funeral expenses and legal fees associated with the administration of his estate amounted to €3,000 and €6,000 respectively.
3. Neither Sheila, Ruth nor Angela had previously received any taxable gifts or inheritances. Sheila lives in the US but is Irish domiciled. The rest of the Doyle family are Irish domiciled and resident.

Requirement

(a) Compute the CAT liabilities, if any, payable by Sheila, Ruth and Angela.
(b) If the valuation date is 19 October 2012, outline the latest date by which CAT is payable if interest charges are to be avoided.

Part Four
Corporation Tax

Introduction and General Principles of Corporation Tax

Learning Objectives

After studying this chapter you will have developed the competency to understand that:

- Companies are liable to corporation tax on the profits that they earn.
- The computation of the profits is based on the profits per the financial statements, as adjusted for tax purposes, i.e. all on an actual basis.
- The computation of the profits – income plus gains – uses income tax and CGT principles.
- All types of income and expenses must be separately identified as between Case I (trading), Case II (professions), Case III (certain interest and foreign income), Case IV (certain taxed income and miscellaneous) and Case V (Irish rents). This is achieved by starting with the profit before tax and adjusting it for any non-trade items.
- Chargeable gains are calculated as follows:

$$(\text{Gains} - \text{Losses}) \times \frac{\text{CGT rate, i.e. 30\%}}{\text{Corporation tax rate, i.e. 12.5\% for 2012}}$$

- Even if the financial statements are for a period of longer than 12 months, an accounting period always ends after 12 months.
- Irish resident companies are liable to Irish tax on their worldwide profits.
- The corporation tax rates are:
  - (a) the standard rate of tax (12.5% for 2012) which applies to Case I and II profits (other than an excepted trade) and certain foreign dividends; and
  - (b) the higher rate of tax (25%) which applies to Case III (except certain foreign dividends), IV and V and profits of an excepted trade.

- Companies are required to pay preliminary tax.

  Large companies (i.e. those with a corporation tax liability greater than €200,000 in their previous accounting period) are required to pay preliminary tax in two instalments. The first instalment must amount to 50% of the corporation tax for the preceding year or 45% of the tax payable for the current year. The second instalment of preliminary tax must bring the total preliminary tax paid to 90% of the final corporation tax liability of the current year. The first instalment of preliminary tax must be paid in the 6th month of the accounting period and the second instalment in the 11th month, e.g. a large company with an accounting year end 31 December 2012 will pay its initial instalment by 23 June 2012 and its final instalment by 23 November 2012.

  Small companies (i.e. those with a corporation tax liability equal to or less than €200,000 in their previous accounting period) are only required to make one payment of preliminary tax. This payment must amount to 100% of the corporation tax for the preceding year or 90% of the final corporation tax for the current year and is due in the 11th month, e.g. a small company with an accounting year end 31 December 2012 will pay its preliminary tax liability by 23 November 2012.

  There are special rules to deal with:

  (a) companies that have a chargeable gain after they have paid the preliminary tax, i.e. they can make a top-up payment; and

  (b) companies that have an accounting period of less than one month and one day, i.e. tax is due on day 23 of the month.

- In all cases, the balance of the corporation tax must be paid and the tax return filed within nine months of the end of the accounting period, but not later than day 23 of the month.

- There is an exemption from corporation tax on trading income and trading gains for the first three years for new companies which set up a new trade during the period 1 January 2009 to 31 December 2014, provided that the corporation tax for the year is €40,000 or less and certain conditions are satisfied, including having paid sufficient employer's PRSI. There is marginal relief where the tax exceeds €40,000 but does not exceed €60,000.

The Chartered Accountants Ireland *Code of Ethics* applies to all aspects of a Chartered Accountant's professional life, including dealing with corporation tax issues. As outlined at the beginning of this book, further information regarding the principles in the *Code of Ethics* is set out in **Appendix B**.

21.1 Overview

Under the Taxes Consolidation Act (TCA), corporation tax is charged on the income and chargeable gains, which together constitute the "profits" of companies. The period for which corporation tax is charged is the "accounting period" (see **Section 21.10** below).

Companies produce accounts normally on an annual basis. Included in these accounts are the various sources of income and gains less the expenses incurred by the company. These profits of the company are taxable unless there is a specific exemption. The nature of the profits earned determines under which Case of Schedule D the income is taxable. Capital gains (with the exception of gains arising on development land – these gains are liable to CGT) are also liable to corporation tax.

When taxing the profits of a company, it is essential that the total profits and expenses, are correctly divided between:

Case I	Trading income
Case II	Professions – but actually treated the exact same as Case I. (the only difference is when calculating the professional services surcharge – see **Section 28.11**)
Case III	Untaxed Irish income or foreign income
Case IV	Taxed Irish income and miscellaneous
Case V	Irish rents
Chargeable gains	Capital disposals

This is important because of the different treatments given to these items in the tax code. For example:

- Profits within Case III, IV or V are generally taxed at 25% (certain foreign dividends are taxed at 12.5%).
- Capital gains are taxed at an effective CGT rate which depends on the date of disposal, i.e.:
    - 7/12/11 onwards – 30%
    - 8/4/09 to 6/12/11 – 25%
    - 15/10/08 to 7/4/09 – 22%
    - 3/12/97 – 14/10/08 – 20%.
- The surcharge on undistributed investment and rental income of close companies (see **Chapter 28**) arises in respect of investment (Case III or IV) income and rental (Case V) income but not Case I or gains.

Therefore, unless income/gains and related expenses are properly analysed, the income under the various Cases will not be correct and therefore incorrect calculations could be made in such areas as the rate of corporation tax and close companies surcharge calculations.

For companies, all transactions will be included in the financial statements. Therefore, computation of corporation tax requires the analysis of those profits between the various Cases and gains.

Having prepared the corporation tax computation, tax must be paid and a return filed. As each company has its own accounting year end, the law relates payment of tax and filing returns to that year end.

21.2 Charge to Corporation Tax

Corporation tax is assessed on the profits of companies for accounting periods. Accordingly the concept of basis periods in the income tax code is not carried into the corporation tax system.

The question whether, and how, a company is to be charged to corporation tax depends on whether or not it is resident in the State. The residence of a company is normally located in the place from which it is managed and controlled. However certain Irish incorporated companies are also regarded as resident in the State (see **Section 30.1**).

In the case of a **company resident in the State**, the charge to corporation tax is imposed on **all its income and chargeable gains** wherever arising and whether or not they are remitted to this country.

In the case of a **non-resident company**, the charge is imposed only if the company is carrying on a trade in the State through a branch or agency. Such a company is chargeable to corporation tax on any **income attributable to the branch or agency** and on any chargeable gains on the **disposal of assets** in the State used for the purposes of the trade or **attributable to the branch or agency**.

A brief note on the concept of residence is set out at **Section 21.11**.

There are three special rules in the corporation tax code which should be noted at this stage.

(a) **Corporation tax is not generally charged on dividends or other distributions of an Irish resident company received by another Irish resident company (see Section 27.1). Such income is referred to as Franked Investment Income (FII).**
Such Irish dividends are not liable to corporation tax as they are paid out of profits which have suffered Irish corporation tax.

(b) Corporation tax is charged on the gross amount of any payments, patent royalties, etc. received by a company under deduction of income tax. However, the income tax suffered by deduction may be set off against the corporation tax chargeable (see **Chapter 23**).

(c) No deduction is allowed for dividends paid by a company (or any item treated as a distribution of profits under corporation tax rules), when computing taxable profits.

21.3 Rates of Corporation Tax

Rate	Name	
12.5%	Standard rate	Applies to Schedule D Case I and II profits and to certain foreign dividends (see **Section 31.1.2**).
25%	Higher rate	Applies to Schedule D Case III, IV and V profits and to profits from an "excepted" trade (excepted trades are not examinable).

21.3.1 Standard Rate of Corporation Tax

The standard rate of corporation tax is **12.5%**.

Example 1
Mary Ltd had total profits, all Case I profits from selling clothes, of €700,000 in the year ended 31 December 2012. Corporation tax payable by Mary Ltd is €87,500 (€700,000 @ 12.5%).

21.3.2 Higher Rate of Corporation Tax

A higher rate of corporation tax of **25%** applies to the following income of companies:

(a) **Case III** income, i.e. income from foreign sources, interest income from which tax has not been deducted. Certain foreign dividends are, however, taxable at 12.5% (see **Section 31.1.2**).

(b) **Case IV** income, i.e. interest income from which tax has been deducted, miscellaneous income not taxed under any other Case of Schedule D.

(c) **Case V** income, i.e. Irish rental income.

(d) **Income from an "excepted trade"**, which is one that consists of the following operations:

  (i) dealing in or developing land, which does not include:

 – construction operations; or
 – dealing in fully developed land, e.g. land on which houses or other buildings have been built thereon by or for the company selling the land;

 (ii) mining activities; and
 (iii) petroleum activities.

(Excepted trades are not examinable.)

Example 2
John Ltd, a company involved in the construction of office buildings, has the following income for the year ended 31 December 2012:

	€
Case I – construction operations	800,000
Case III interest	20,000
Case V rental income	150,000
Total	970,000

The corporation tax payable by John Ltd is as follows:

	€
Case I – construction operations	
€800,000 @ 12.5%	100,000
Case III and Case V income	
€170,000 @ 25%	42,500
Total corporation tax payable	142,500

21.4 Dates of Payment of Corporation Tax

21.4.1 Corporation Tax Payable

If preliminary corporation tax and the balance of the corporation tax are paid on/before the due dates, then there is no interest penalty. **Remember that corporation tax includes not only the corporation tax due on profits, but also any income tax payable (see Chapter 23) and any surcharge payable by a close company (see Chapter 28).**

Example
X Ltd has a corporation tax liability on profits of €100,000 and an income tax liability of €3,000. Its year end is 31/12/2012.

Preliminary tax should be calculated on:

	€
CT liability	100,000
Income tax liability	3,000
	103,000

21.4.2 Small Companies

■ **For small companies**, i.e. those with a corporation tax liability **not exceeding €200,000** (in their previous accounting period of a year), preliminary tax is payable in one instalment 31 days before the end of the accounting period, provided that where that day is later than day 21 of the month, the tax will be due and payable not later than day 21 of that month or day 23 of the month where tax liabilities and returns are filed electronically using ROS (21/23 day rule). With effect from 1 June 2011, all companies (small and large) are required to pay corporation tax and file tax returns electronically using the ROS. As all returns will be filed and payments made electronically, they will be due on day 23 of the month at the latest.

    ■ A company may apply for an exclusion from the requirement to file and pay electronically on the grounds that it has insufficient access to the Internet. If a company is excluded from the requirement to pay and file electronically, payments are due on day 21 of the month instead of day 23. It is expected that only a small number of companies will qualify for this exclusion and, accordingly, it is assumed that the normal due date for payment is day 23 rather than day 21. In addition, a company that is not excluded from paying and filing electronically but who pays by some other means is deemed for the purpose of calculating any interest payable to have been required to pay its corporation tax on day 21 of the month instead of day 23.

However, in the case of a small company, interest charges will not arise if the preliminary tax paid amounts to the lower of:

■ 90% of the corporation tax payable by the company for the accounting period; or
■ 100% of the corporation tax payable by the company for the preceding accounting period of the same length.

> **Example**
> A Ltd's corporation tax for the year ended 31 December 2012 is expected to be €120,000. Its liability for 2011 was €90,000.
>
> As it is a small company (corporation tax in 2011 was less than €200,000), preliminary tax should be paid by 23 November 2012 and is calculated as the lower of:
>
> 100% of 2011 final liability   €90,000 Pay this amount
> 90% of final liability for 2012   €108,000

■ Under the 'Pay & File' system, the **balance of corporation tax due** is payable at the **same time** as the company is due to **file its return,** i.e. **within nine months of the end of the accounting period**, but not later than day 23.

21.4.3 Large Companies

■ **For large companies**, i.e. those with a corporation tax liability of more than €200,000 in their previous accounting period, preliminary tax is payable in two instalments.

    ■ The **first instalment is payable in the 6th month** of the accounting period (i.e. 23 June for a company with calendar year accounts) and the amount payable is **50% of the corporation tax liability for the preceding accounting period or 45% of the corporation tax liability for the current accounting period.**

■ The **second instalment is payable in the 11th month** of the accounting period (i.e. 23 November for a company with calendar year accounts) and the amount payable should bring the total preliminary tax paid to 90% of the corporation tax liability for the current accounting period.

Example

B Ltd's corporation tax for the year ended 31 December 2012 is expected to be €220,000. Its liability for 2011 was €230,000. As it is a large company (corporation tax liability in 2011 was greater than €200,000), preliminary tax should be paid in the following instalments:

	€
1st instalment due 23 June 2012	
50% of 2011 final liability (€230,000*50%)	115,000
OR 45% of final liability for 2012 (€220,000*45%)	99,000
The lower amount should be paid, i.e.	99,000
2nd instalment due 23 November 2012	
90% of final liability for 2012 (€220,000*90%)	198,000
Minus amount paid in the 1st instalment	(99,000)
Amount to be paid	99,000

■ Preliminary tax is payable in two instalments by large companies generally where the accounting period is more than seven months in length (for shorter accounting periods, preliminary tax of 90% of tax liability is payable in one instalment as for small companies).

■ Under the 'Pay & File' system, the **balance of tax due** is payable at the **same time** as the company is due to **file its return**, i.e. **within nine months of the end of the accounting period**, but not later than day 23.

21.4.4 Certain Companies Newly within the Charge to Corporation Tax

There is a special rule for companies within the charge to corporation tax for first time. These companies which **do not expect their tax liability** for the first year **to exceed €200,000** are **no longer obliged to pay preliminary tax** in that first year.

Example

D Ltd commenced trading on 1 January 2012 and prepared its first set of accounts to 31 December 2012, showing a corporation tax liability of €195,000. 100% of the corporation tax for the year ended 31 December 2012 will be due on or before 23 September 2013, the filing date for the company's corporation tax return as the exception provided for above applies (corporation tax is less than €200,000).

21.4.5 Late/Default in Payment of Corporation Tax

If a company defaults in the payment of preliminary tax, does not pay sufficient preliminary tax or does not pay its preliminary tax by the due date, interest on late payment arises. In the case of a small company, *all* the corporation tax is deemed to be due on the date that the preliminary tax is due. In addition, preliminary tax is deemed to be due on day 21 of the month instead of day 23. In the case of a large company 45% of its corporation tax is deemed to be due on the date the first instalment of its preliminary tax was due and the remaining 55% on the date the second instalment of its preliminary tax was due. Interest is charged at 0.0219% per day or part of a day on any underpaid corporation tax, including underpaid preliminary tax.

> *Example*
>
> E Ltd's (a large company) corporation tax liability for the year ended 31 December 2012 is €100,000. The company paid its entire liability on 30 December 2013. The company will have an interest liability on the late payment of corporation tax as follows:
>
> €45,000 (€100,000 × 45%) deemed due 21 June 2012 =
>   Interest €45,000 @ 0.0219% × 558 days = €5,499
>
> €55,000 deemed due on 21 November 2012:
> Interest €55,000 @ 0.0219% × 405 days = €4,878
>
> Total interest liability = €10,377

In order to minimise interest exposure where a large company in a group does not meet the 90% preliminary tax payment, any excess preliminary payments made by another large group company can be transferred to the group member who has not met the 90% rule. Both companies must jointly advise Revenue and the claimant company must have paid 100% of its tax by its tax return due date.

21.4.6 Rules for Three Special Situations

1. Corresponding Accounting Periods

As outlined at **Section 21.4.2** above, small companies' preliminary tax payment can be 90% of their current year corporation tax liability or 100% of their corporation tax liability for the preceding accounting period. As outlined at **Section 21.4.3** above, large companies' first instalment of preliminary tax can be 45% of their current year corporation tax liability or 50% of their corporation tax liability for the preceding accounting period. When a company is calculating its preliminary tax payment by reference to the corporation tax liability for the preceding accounting period and the current and the preceding accounting periods are of different lengths, preliminary tax is based on the "corresponding corporation tax" for the preceding accounting period rather than the actual corporation tax liability for the preceding accounting period.

The "corresponding corporation tax" for the preceding accounting period is an amount determined by the following formula:

$$T \times \frac{C}{P}$$

Where T = the corporation tax payable for the preceding accounting period,
       C = the number of days* in the current accounting period, and
       P = the number of days* in the preceding accounting period.

*While the law is drafted on the basis of the number of days in the accounting period, for exam purposes, the examiner will accept calculations based on months.

A "small" company is a company where the corresponding corporation tax liability for the preceding accounting period does not exceed the relevant limit for the current accounting period. The relevant limit is €200,000 but, where the accounting period is less than 12 months, this limit is reduced proportionately.

> *Example*
>
> K Ltd prepares accounts for six months to 31 December 2011 showing a corporation tax liability of €90,000. To check if the company qualifies as a "small" company for 2012:
>
> $T \times \frac{C}{P} = 90,000 \times 366/184 = €179,021 = \text{small company}$
>
> *continued overleaf*

Assuming the company estimates its corporation tax liability for 2012 to be €210,000, the company will satisfy its preliminary tax requirements if preliminary tax of €179,021 is paid by 23 November 2012.

The balance of the corporation tax, i.e. €30,979 (€210,000 − €179,021) must be paid, and the tax return filed, within nine months of the end of the accounting period, but not later than day 23, i.e. not later than 23 September 2013 in this case. For exam purposes, it would be equally acceptable to use months rather than days, i.e. 12/6 rather than 366/184.

Example

Q Ltd prepares accounts to 31 December. Its corporation tax liability for the year ended 31 December 2011 is €140,000. The company changes its accounting date to 30 June and prepares a six-month set of accounts to 30 June 2012 showing a corporation tax liability of €160,000.

The relevant limit for the six-month accounting period ending 30/6/2012 is €99,726, i.e. limit of €200,000 × 182/365.

The company qualifies as a small company as its corresponding corporation tax liability for the period ended 31 December 2011 was €69,808, i.e. €140,000 × 182/365, which is less than the limit of €99,726.

The company will satisfy its preliminary tax requirements for 2012 if preliminary tax of €69,425 is paid by 23 May 2012. For exam purposes, it would be equally acceptable to use months rather than days, i.e. 6/12 rather than 182/365.

The balance of the corporation tax, not paid as preliminary tax, must be paid, and the tax return filed, within nine months of the end of the accounting period 30 June 2012, but not later than day 23, i.e. not later than 23 March 2013 in this case.

Example

M Ltd prepares accounts for the six months ending 31 December 2011 and for the year ending 31 December 2012. M Ltd's corporation tax liability for the six months ended 31 December 2011 is €120,000 and for the year ended 31 December 2012 is €300,000.

The company's corresponding corporation tax liability for the six-month accounting period ending 31 December 2011 is €238,696, i.e. €120,000 × 366/184. As this exceeds the relevant limit of €200,000 for the year ended 31 December 2012, the company is a large company for preliminary tax purposes.

The company will satisfy its preliminary tax requirements for 2012 if preliminary tax is paid as follows:

1st instalment due 23 June 2012
50% of €238,696* = €119,348 or
45% of €300,000 = €135,000
The lower amount should be paid, i.e. €119,348
*corresponding corporation tax liability for the year ended 31/12/2011. For exam purposes, it would be equally acceptable to use months rather than days, i.e. 12/6 rather than 366/184.

	€
2nd instalment due 23 November 2012	
90% of final liability for 2011 (90% of €300,000)	270,000
Minus amount paid in the 1st instalment	(119,348)
Amount to be paid	150,652

---

2. Top-up Payments of Preliminary Tax, Due to Chargeable Gain after Preliminary Tax Due

Where a **chargeable gain arises after the due date for the payment of a company's preliminary tax liability,** the preliminary tax will have to be amended if it has been based on paying 90% of the company's corporation tax for the current year. (If the preliminary tax is based on 100% of the corresponding corporation tax for the preceding year, no amendment is required.) If the company's preliminary tax payment is now less than 90% of its corporation tax liability for that year, and if corporation tax due in respect of the chargeable gain were excluded, the company's preliminary tax payment would not have been less than the necessary 90%. The company may make an additional payment of preliminary tax and not incur interest on late payment of tax. This is provided that:

(a)   the additional payment is made within one month of the end of the accounting period; and

(b)   the aggregate of the additional payment and the preliminary tax paid amounts to at least 90% of the company's corporation tax liability.

If these two conditions are met the company is deemed to have paid its preliminary corporation tax liability by the due date.

Example

N Ltd, not a small company, has a corporation tax liability for the year ended 31 December 2012 of €250,000. Of this liability, €40,000 is in respect of a chargeable gain which arose in December 2012.

The company made preliminary tax payments of €189,000 up to 23 November 2012. This amounts to less than 90% of its liability for 2012. However, excluding the tax arising in respect of the chargeable gain which arose in December 2012, the preliminary tax paid would have amounted to 90% of the company's liability for 2012. If the company makes a top-up payment of preliminary tax of €36,000 by 31 January 2013 (€36,000 + €189,000 = €225,000 which = 90% of €250,000), the company will have satisfied its preliminary tax requirements.

The balance of the corporation tax, i.e. €25,000 (€250,000 − €225,000) must be paid, and the tax return filed, within nine months of the end of the accounting period, but not later than day 23, i.e. not later than 23 September 2013 in this case.

Where the following conditions are satisfied, a large company will be deemed to have paid sufficient preliminary tax by the due date:

1.   the total of the company's first instalment and second instalment of preliminary tax amount to at least 90% of the company's corporation tax liability for the current accounting period;

2.   the company's first instalment of preliminary tax amounts to not less than 45% of the company's corporation tax liability for the current accounting period; and

3.   the company's first instalment of preliminary tax would not have been less than 45% of the company's corporation tax liability for the current accounting period, if no amount were included in the company's profits in respect of chargeable gains arising on the disposal of assets after the due date for the payment of the company's first instalment of preliminary tax.

Example

J Ltd, a large company, had a corporation tax liability for the year ended 31 December 2012 of €500,000. Of this, €100,000 is in respect of a chargeable gain which arose in August 2012.

The company made the following preliminary tax payments:

	€	€
On 23 June 2012 45% of €400,000		180,000
On 23 November 2012 90% of €500,000 = 450,000		
Less first instalment	(180,000)	270,000
Total preliminary tax paid		450,000

continued overleaf

> Although the company's first instalment of preliminary tax is less than 45% of its corporation tax liability for the accounting period, the amount paid would have amounted to 45% of the corporation tax liability for the accounting period if corporation tax in respect of the gain which arose after the due date for the payment of the first instalment of preliminary tax were excluded. In addition, the total preliminary tax paid by the company amounted to 90% of its corporation tax liability for the accounting period. Accordingly the company is deemed to have paid a sufficient first instalment payment of preliminary tax and met its preliminary tax requirements.

3. Accounting period Less than One Month and One Day

Where an accounting period of a company is less than a month and a day in length, preliminary tax will be due and payable not later than the last day of the accounting period, but where that day is later than day 23 of the month, the tax will be due and payable not later than day 23 of that month.

> **Example**
> Q Ltd changes its accounting date from 30 November to 31 December. Accounts are prepared for one month to 31 December 2012. Preliminary tax for the one-month period ended 31 December 2012 will be due on or before 23 December 2012.

21.4.7 Groups of Companies

Excess preliminary tax paid by a group company, which is a large company, may be surrendered to another group member which is a large company (75% relationship) – see **Section 21.4.5**.

21.5 Filing Tax Return and Other Administration

21.5.1 Pay and File

The return of profits form (i.e. **Form CT1**) is submitted to the Revenue.

Where a company is in doubt as regards any matter to be included in a return, the company's obligation with regard to the matter will be fulfilled if it draws the Inspector's attention to the matter, i.e. check/tick the "expression of doubt" box in the return.

Taxpayers must file the corporation tax return electronically through Revenue's on-line service (ROS). *The balance of corporation tax must be paid at the same time as the return is filed*. (**Note:** If the return is filed early, the payment does not have to be made at the same time. It must be paid on or before the deadline date).

A notice of assessment is issued in accordance with the income declared and allowances and reliefs claimed on the return of profits form.

21.5.2 Interest

If there is a default in payment of preliminary tax or the balance of tax (e.g. late payment of tax, payment is too small, or the balance of tax is paid late), interest is charged at 0.0219% per day or part of a day. Interest on late payment of tax is not tax deductible.

Conditions to be satisfied for a company to avoid interest charges for year ended 31 December 2012

Small Companies:

1. preliminary tax of 90% of the corporation tax liability of the current period or 100% of the corresponding corporation tax for the previous accounting period must be paid on/before 23 November 2012; and
2. balance of tax due must be paid on or before 23 September 2013.

Large Companies:

1. preliminary tax of 45% of corporation tax liability of the current period or 50% of the prior period corporation tax must be paid on/before 23 June 2012;
2. preliminary tax of 90% of corporation tax liability must be paid on/before 23 November 2012; and
3. balance of tax due must be paid on/before 23 September 2013.

Remember the special rules for a company that has a chargeable gain in the accounting period, but after the due date for its preliminary tax.

If tax is overpaid, it carries interest at a rate which is currently 0.011% per day. However, the date from which interest runs depends on whether the overpayment is as a result of a mistake made by Revenue or the taxpayer. Where the repayment arises because of a mistaken assumption of the law by Revenue, the interest will be calculated from the end of the accounting period to which the repayment relates or, if later, when the tax was overpaid. In all other cases, including repayments of preliminary tax, interest will run from 93 days (previously six months) after a valid claim to the repayment is made.

Claims for repayment of tax must be made on a timely basis, i.e. the repayment must be subject to a claim being made to Revenue within four years of the end of the period to which it relates (there was a longer time limit in the past). Revenue will only pay interest if it exceeds €10. Interest received on overpayment of tax is not taxable.

Example
Accounts year ended 30 September 2012

Preliminary tax paid
€92,000 on 20/8/2012

Corporation tax for year is €100,000
Corporation tax for preceding year was €150,000.
Company pays balance of €8,000 on 20/6/2013.
Is condition 1 satisfied? Yes – preliminary tax paid of 92% (>90%) by 23/8/2012
Is condition 2 satisfied? Yes – balance of tax paid by 23/6/2013

21.5.3 Annual Tax Returns and Surcharges

The completed Form CT1 must be submitted to Revenue within nine months of the end of the accounting period to avoid a surcharge on the tax liability, provided that where that day is later than day 23 of the month, the return must be filed not later than day 23, i.e. file return and pay the balance of tax on same day – pay and file. With effect from 1 June 2011, all companies are required to pay corporation tax and file their returns electronically (see **Section 21.4.2**). Where a company does not file its return and/or pay its corporation tax electronically, and has not been excluded from electronic pay and file (see **Section 21.4.2**), it will be subject to a fixed penalty. In addition, the due date by which the company is deemed to have been required to file its return is day 21 of the month instead of day 23.

If the return is filed within two months after the filing date, the surcharge is 5%, subject to a maximum of €12,695. If the delay is two months or more, the surcharge is 10%, subject to a maximum of €63,485.

Example

A company had a tax adjusted Case I profit of €500,000 for the year ended 31 December 2012. If the return is filed within nine months, i.e. by 23/9/2013 the liability is €62,500, i.e. €500,000 @ 12.5%.

	€
If it is not filed until say 10/10/2013 the liability is	62,500
+5% surcharge	3,125
	65,625
If it is not filed until, say, 1/12/2013 the liability is	62,500
+10% surcharge	6,250
	68,750

The surcharge payable is treated as part of the company's corporation tax liability for the accounting period which may mean that as a result of having to pay a surcharge the company may have underpaid its preliminary tax.

Example

A "large" company has a corporation tax liability of €200,000 for the year ended 31 December 2012 and €300,000 for the previous year. The company paid preliminary tax for 2012 as follows:

Preliminary tax: €90,000 paid on 23 June 2012.
Preliminary tax: €180,000 less €90,000 paid on 23 November 2012, bringing total to 90% of final corporation tax liability, i.e. €180,000.

The company filed its return for 2012 on 20 December 2013 and accordingly a surcharge of €20,000 (10%) applies. The company's total corporation tax liability for 2012 is deemed to be €220,000. Accordingly the company has underpaid its preliminary tax (amount paid was less than 45% / 90% of €220,000). 45% of the company's corporation tax liability of €220,000 is deemed to have all been due on 21 June 2012 and the balance on 21 November 2012 and interest is charged from these dates to the actual date on which the balance of the tax was paid.

Where a company files its return and fails to include on the return details relating to any exemption, allowance, deduction, credit or other relief the company is claiming (referred to as "specified details") and the return states that the details required are specified details, the company may be liable to a 5% surcharge (subject to the usual maximum of €12,695) and a restriction of loss relief, even if its return has been filed on time. This surcharge and loss relief restriction may only be applied, however, where after the return has been filed it has come to the company's notice or has been brought to its attention that the specified details were not included in the return and the company failed to remedy the matter without reasonable delay. Where a surcharge and/or restriction is applied, it must be included in an assessment so that the taxpayer can appeal to the Appeal Commissioners if the taxpayer is aggrieved with it.

It should be noted that if a company fraudulently or negligently files an incorrect return on or before the due date for the filing of the return, the company is deemed to have failed to file the return before the due date unless the error in the return is remedied on or before the due date for the filing of the return. If a company files an incorrect return on or before the due date for the filing of the return but does so neither fraudulently nor negligently and it comes to the company's attention that the return is incorrect, the company is deemed to have filed the return after the due date unless the error in the return is remedied without unreasonable delay.

21.5.4 Revenue On-line Service (ROS)

The Revenue On-Line Service (ROS) is an Internet facility that allows companies or their agents to file tax returns, pay tax liabilities, claim repayments, pay other taxes such as dividend withholding tax and access their tax details on-line. With effect from 1 June 2011, all companies are required to pay corporation tax and file tax returns electronically using ROS. Returns filed and payments made using ROS are due by day 23 of the month at latest.

ROS also provides companies with access to all of their tax account information including the facility to view details of returns filed and due, payments made, view and amend tax credits, etc.

Certain returns are only available to **upload** to ROS. These have to be created **off-line** via the **ROS Off-line Application**, which has to be downloaded from ROS. Some of the returns can be created off-line using compatible third-party software. Once created and saved, these files can be **uploaded** to ROS. The most important of these for companies is the tax return (Form CT1).

A ROS customer will be provided with a secure ROS Inbox. Correspondence posted to this inbox includes reminders to file returns, copies of returns, statements of account and payment receipts.

21.6 Computation of Income

The basic rule for the calculation of income is that, apart from certain special provisions relevant only to companies, it is to be computed in accordance with income tax principles. The computation will therefore be made for each class of income under the same Schedules and Cases as apply for income tax purposes and in accordance with the law applicable to those Schedules and Cases.

In calculating Case I profits, income earned is included on an accruals basis. The income tax scheme of capital allowances and balancing charges is brought into the corporation tax system. However, **capital allowances** due to trading companies are **treated as trading expenses** for corporation tax purposes and not as a deduction from the assessable income as in the case of income tax. Similarly, balancing charges are treated for corporation tax purposes as trading receipts. Furthermore, **the capital allowances** are calculated by reference to **assets in use/expenditure incurred in each accounting period**. The calculation of capital allowances is not required in your exam.

Also, companies are permitted to open deposit accounts with Irish financial institutions, **the interest on which is not subject to DIRT** provided the company gives its tax reference number to the financial institutions. For the purposes of computing the tax-adjusted profits of a company from its profit and loss account or income statement for an accounting period, the following particular points should be noted:

- Bona fide directors' salaries, fees, benefits payable for directors, etc. are deductible unlike the drawings/salary of a self-employed person. Such income is, of course, assessable in the hands of the individual director under Schedule E.

■ Where a director has a company car available for private use, there is a deduction of the "personal element" for corporation tax purposes unlike the personal element of a self-employed person. Again, a director with the use of a company car for private purposes will of course suffer a benefit in kind assessment.

> **Example**
> Joe and Ann jointly own Deduction Ltd and are both directors on the board of the company. Deduction Ltd pays all the motor expenses incurred in running Joe's car. Only 75% of the expenses are incurred in respect of the business. The balance of 25% is personal. Deduction Ltd will be entitled to a full deduction for all the motor expenses, even though some of the expense is personal; however, Joe will be liable to income tax under Schedule E on the personal motor expenses paid by the company. (If the car cost more than €24,000 for accounting periods ending on or after 1 January 2007 (previously the limit was €23,000) or had CO_2 emissions above 155g/km (if bought on/after 1 July 2008), there would be a restriction on the amount allowable for motor leasing expenses or capital allowances).

■ Dividend payments by a company are not deductible as they are treated as appropriations of profit.

■ Interest on borrowings, which are used for trading purposes (e.g. financing of stock, debtors and fixed assets used for the purpose of the trade), is fully allowable on the **accruals** basis. If, on the other hand, a company has borrowed money and applies the funds for non-trading purposes, e.g. say for the purchase of speculative oil shares or to purchase shares in a subsidiary, then such interest charges are not deductible under Case I. We will see later in **Chapter 23** that certain relief may be available in respect of such interest payments as a charge under the "protected interest" provisions.

A pro-forma corporation tax computation together with notes on important adjustments are set out in **Chapter 22**.

21.7 Computation of Income Assessed under Case III and Case IV Schedule D

The following income is charged under Case III and IV of Schedule D:

■ Case III untaxed interest income and income from foreign sources

■ Case IV income which has been subject to Irish tax at source and miscellaneous income. Companies have the option to receive interest income **without the deduction of DIRT** by simply completing a declaration in writing and providing their Irish tax reference number to the relevant deposit taker that the company is within the charge to corporation tax and interest will be included in the profits on which it is to be charged to corporation tax.

21.7.1 Basis of Assessment

Strictly, tax is charged under Case III and Case IV on the income **received** during the accounting period. In practice, however, interest which is received gross is taxed on an accruals basis.

21.8 Computation of Income Assessed under Case V Schedule D

The following income is charged under Case V of Schedule D:

- rents in respect of any premises or lands in the Republic of Ireland, i.e. offices, shops, factories, land, etc.; and
- certain premiums received for the granting of a lease.

21.8.1 Basis of Assessment

Tax is charged under Case V on the income arising during the accounting period. The rent taken into account is the amount receivable in the accounting period whether or not it is actually received.

21.8.2 Premiums on Short Leases

General

Many years ago, it was possible for a landlord to avoid being taxed on income from let property by letting the property at a large "once-off" premium in the first year and charging a nominal rent thereafter. The "once-off" premium was treated as a capital receipt and was not within the charge to income tax. Legislation was introduced so that a certain proportion of a premium on a "short lease" is taxable under Case V.

Calculation of Taxable Portion of Premium

Where a landlord receives a premium on the creation of a "short lease" (i.e. the duration of the lease does not exceed 50 years), he will be treated as receiving an amount by way of rent (in addition to any actual rent) as computed by the following formula:

$$P \times \frac{51 - N}{50}$$

Where: P = Premium
N = The duration of the lease

Example

A Ltd lets a premises to B Ltd on 1 April 2012 for 21 years at a rent of €18,000 per annum subject to a premium of €20,000. The taxable portion of the premium is:

$$P \times \frac{51 - N}{50} = €20,000 \times \frac{(51 - 21)}{50} = €12,000$$

This is treated as additional rent for the purposes of calculating A Ltd's taxable rental income for 2012.

21.8.3 Allowable Deductions Incurred in Calculating Case V Profits

The following amounts may be deducted from the gross rents:

(a) rent payable
(b) rates (if any)
(c) cost of goods or services which the landlord company is obliged to provide and for which it receives no separate consideration, e.g. gas, electricity, waste disposal, etc.

(d)   Cost of repairs, excluding improvements and items treated as capital expenditure.
(e)   Interest (without restriction) on money borrowed for the purchase, improvement or repairs to the property, but interest charges incurred prior to the first letting are not deductible. There are two additional issues regarding **residential** property namely:

  ■ The taxpayer must have satisfied the registration requirements of the PRTB (Private Residential Tenancy Board) in order to claim interest in their Case V computation.
  ■ Interest relief is no longer available for the full amount of interest on borrowings to purchase/improve residential premises which is let to a tenant. Relief is restricted to 75% of the interest. Interest relief against income from letting of commercial property is not restricted.

(f)   Accountancy fees incurred in drawing up rental accounts and keeping rental records. Strictly such expenses are not allowable as they relate more to the management of the landlord's affairs rather than to the receipt of rent or the management of the premises. In practice, however, Revenue allow a deduction for such expenses as they recognise that the efficient running of a business of letting premises requires that financial accounts should be prepared.
(g)   Mortgage protection policy premiums. Generally financial institutions insist on a mortgage protection policy being taken out by a borrower before they will approve a loan in respect of a property. Like accountancy fees, premiums on such policies would not be strictly allowable being more to do with the landlord's financial affairs than to the management of the property or the receipt of rent. Revenue allow a deduction for such premiums.
(h)   Wear and tear allowances. A wear and tear allowance of 12.5% per annum on a straight-line basis for eight years is available on the cost of furniture and fittings in the case of furnished lettings.
(i)   Revenue do not allow a deduction for the Non Principal Private Residence (NPPR) charge of €200 which is payable by landlords who rent out residential property or for the household charge of €100.

Allowable expenses are normally deducted on an accruals basis rather than on a paid basis. In order to be deductible, the expense must be incurred wholly and exclusively for the purpose of earning the rent and must be revenue rather than capital in nature. Expenses incurred in respect of a property before a lease commences in respect of that property, other than legal and advertising expenses, are not deductible. In the case of interest and rent, no deduction is allowed for either interest or rent payable in respect of a period before the property is first *occupied* by a lessee.

Expenses incurred after the termination of a lease are not deductible. However, expenses incurred after the termination of one lease and before the commencement of another lease in respect of the property are deductible provided the following three conditions are satisfied:

1.   the expenses would otherwise be deductible;
2.   the person who was the lessor of the property does not occupy the premises during the period when the property is not let; and
3.   the property is let by the same lessor at the end of the period.

Example: Rental Computation
A company purchased a rental residential property on 1 January 2012. Between the date of purchase and 31 May 2012 the company spent €25,000 refurbishing the property. On 1 June 2012 the property was leased for €800 per month payable in advance.

continued overleaf

The following expenses were incurred up to 31 May 2012:

	€
Auctioneers and advertising fees for first tenants	800
Repairs and maintenance	600
Light and heat	300
Security and insurance	500
Interest on loan	1,200

The following expenses were incurred in the period 1 June to 31 December 2012

	€
- Water charge	600
- Light and heat	350
- Security	400
- Interest (property was registered with PRTB on 25 June 2012)	3,000
- Repairs/maintenance/PRTB registration costs	870

Solution

	€	€
Gross rents (€800 × 7)		5,600
Less qualifying expenses		
- Pre-letting expenses		
(auctioneers/advertising fees only)	800	
- Water charges	600	
- Light and heat	350	
- Security	400	
- Interest (€3,000 × 75%)	2,250	
- Repairs/maintenance/PRTB registration costs	870	(5,270)
Net Case V income		330

21.9 Computation of Chargeable Gains

Where, for an accounting period, a chargeable gain accrues to a company, the chargeable gain is included in the company's total profit subject to corporation tax. The gain is after deducting both allowable capital losses in the current accounting period and those brought forward from previous years.

The rates of CGT are as follows:

	From 3/12/1997 to 14/10/2008	From 15/10/2008 to 7/4/2009	From 8/4/2009 to 6/12/2011	**From 7/12/2011 onwards**
Rate	20%	22%	25%	30%

21.9.1 Disposals – Other than Development Land

These gains are liable to corporation tax and not CGT. However, this does not change the basic calculation. The gain and tax thereon at 30% (for 2012) are calculated in the normal way. Having calculated the notional CGT, the next step is to calculate the amount to be included in the corporation tax computation. This will be an amount which if it were charged to corporation tax as profits at the standard rate of corporation tax, (i.e. 12.5% for the year 2012) would be equal to the amount of the notional CGT as computed above at 30%.

Example 1

X Ltd prepares accounts to 31 December each year. In the year ended 31 December 2012 the tax-adjusted Case I profit was €20,000. During that year the company bought an asset for €10,000 and sold it for €15,000 in June 2012:

X Ltd
Year ended 31 December 2012

	€
Schedule D Case I	20,000
Chargeable gain €5,000 × 30/12.5%	12,000
	32,000
Corporation tax due @ 12.5% =	4,000

Proof:

	€
Case I €20,000 × 12.5%	2,500
Capital gain €5,000 × 30%	1,500
	4,000

Example 2

Lauren Ltd prepares accounts to 31 December each year.

In December 2012 the company bought an asset for €20,000 and sold it for €30,000. The company also had Case I income of €700,000 and Case V income of €50,000 for that year.

Lauren Ltd
Year ended 31 December 2012

	€
Schedule D Case I	700,000
Schedule D Case V	50,000
Chargeable gain €10,000 × 30/12.5%	24,000
Total profit	774,000

	€
(€700,000 + €24,000) @ 12.5% =	90,500
€50,000 @ 25% =	12,500
Corporation tax due	103,000

Proof:

	€
Case I €700,000 @ 12.5%	87,500
Case V €50,000 @ 25%	12,500
Capital gain €10,000 @ 30%	3,000
	103,000

Example 3

Capital Ltd had the following disposals of fixed assets in its accounts for the year ended 31 December 2012:

1. Freehold premises acquired on 12 December 1974 for €80,000
   Sold for €680,000 on 31 December 2012

2. Plant acquired on 1 May 1992 for €5,000
   Sold for €14,670 on 30 May 2012

3. Fixtures and fittings acquired on 1 February 2006 for €3,000
   Sold for €2,500 on 31 May 2012

4. Leasehold premises acquired on 1 December 2005 under a 60-year lease for €25,000
   Sold for €30,000 on 30 June 2012

continued overleaf

5. Investments acquired on 3 January 1999 for €10,000
   Sold for €8,000 on 30 September 2012

   The company also had capital losses forward of €2,000 from previous accounting periods.

Requirement: Calculate the amount to be included in the corporation tax computation in respect of chargeable gains.

Solution

The amount to be included in the corporation tax computation for the year ended 31 December 2012 would be calculated as follows:

	€	€
1. Disposal of premises		
Cost on 12/12/74	80,000	
Index factor	7.528	602,240
Proceeds		680,000
Chargeable gain		77,760
2. Disposal of plant		
Cost on 1/5/92	5,000	
Index factor	1.356	6,780
Proceeds		14,670
Chargeable gain		7,890
3. Sale of fixtures and fittings		
Cost on 1/2/06		3,000
Proceeds		2,500
Loss		(500)

However no relief is available for the loss of €500 as the assets have, or could have, qualified for capital allowances.

4. Sale of Leasehold Premises

Lease is a long lease as it has more than 50 years to run. Therefore it is not a wasting asset.

	€
Cost on 1/12/2005	25,000
Proceeds	30,000
Chargeable gain	5,000

No indexation due. (Indexation relief was abolished for assets acquired on or after 1 January 2003)

5. Sale of Investments

	€	€
Cost on 3/1/99	10,000	
Index factor	1.212	12,120
Proceeds		8,000
Loss		(4,120)
Restrict to monetary loss		
Cost	10,000	
Proceeds	8,000	
	(2,000)	

Summary of net chargeable gains for the accounting period:

	€	€
Freehold premises	77,760	
Plant	7,890	
Leasehold premises	5,000	90,650
Less: Losses		
Investments	(2,000)	
Loss forward	(2,000)	(4,000)
		86,650

Notional CGT @ 30% = €25,995

continued overleaf

Amount to be included in the corporation tax computation as chargeable gains:

$$€25,995 \times \frac{100}{12.5} = €207,960$$

Notes

1. In the corporation tax computation, the chargeable gain amount is included immediately after the total income has been ascertained as follows:

Schedule D	€
Case I	X
Case III	X
Case IV	X
Case V	X
Total income	X
Chargeable gains	X (i.e. €207,960 in this example)
Profits	X

21.9.2 Disposals of Development Land

Chargeable gains and losses on development land are charged to **CGT** instead of corporation tax. These gains will not therefore form part of the total profits of companies.

The annual exemption of €1,270 does **not** apply to companies.

21.10 Accounting Periods

Corporation tax is assessed on the profits arising in the company's accounting period. The term "accounting period" is given a special meaning for corporation tax purposes. Ordinarily, it is the period for which the company makes up its accounts ("period of account") **but an accounting period cannot exceed 12 months.**

The **first accounting period** for corporation tax purposes of a company begins whenever the company **comes within the charge to corporation tax**. A company may come within the charge to corporation tax in one of several ways:

(a) A company not resident in the State which is carrying on a trade outside the State may become resident in the State. Its first accounting period will start on the day it becomes resident.

(b) A company may acquire for the first time a source of income chargeable to corporation tax, for example, a non-resident company may start to trade in the State through a branch here; at that point an accounting period will start.

(c) A new company may be created and acquire a source of profits.

An accounting period runs for a maximum of 12 months from its start. It will end earlier if the company's own accounting date falls within the 12 months. **An accounting period will end when the company begins to trade** or **first comes within the charge to corporation tax in respect of a trade**, or when a **company ceases to trade** or ceases to be within the charge to corporation tax in respect of its trade. It will end also if the company **begins or ceases to be resident** in the State.

A new accounting period starts immediately at the end of an accounting period unless the accounting period ended because the company ceased altogether to be within the charge to corporation tax.

Example

Start Ltd was incorporated on 1 June 2012. The money subscribed for share capital was put on deposit. The company commenced to trade on 1 September 2012. It prepared its first set of financial statements for the period ended 31 December 2012 and intends to prepare annual financial statements to 31 December each year thereafter.

As Start Ltd acquired a source of income on 1 June, an accounting period commenced. As it commenced to trade on 1 September, an accounting period is deemed to end, even though no actual set of financial statements are prepared. Therefore, Start Ltd has an accounting period of three months, ending on 31 August 2012. Its next accounting period is from 1 September to 31 December 2012. Thereafter it will have accounting periods ending on 31 December each year.

21.10.1 Companies that Prepare Accounts for a Period of Less than 12 Months

The main implications here are as follows:

- If the short accounting period has resulted from a change in the normal annual accounting date of the company, then, unlike the income tax position for a sole trader who changes his accounting date, Revenue have no special powers. For example, if a company has prepared 12-month accounts to 31 December 2010 followed by an 8-month set of accounts to 31 August 2011 followed by a 12 month set of accounts to 31 August 2012, then corporation tax is simply payable for each of these three accounting periods.

- Where the company's **accounting period is less than 12 months long**, then **the normal wear and tear allowances available must be scaled down** appropriately. For example, if an accounting period is eight months long, then the normal wear and tear annual allowances are reduced to 8/12ths.

- The calculation of the **corresponding corporation tax** of the preceding accounting period for a small company and the **carryback period for losses** will have to be reduced to reflect the fact that the company has a short accounting period.

- Preliminary tax payments are based on when an accounting period ends. A shorter than 12 month accounting period results in the earlier payment of preliminary tax.

21.10.2 Companies that Prepare Accounts for a Period Exceeding 12 Months

Corporation tax is payable by reference to accounting periods. The maximum length of an accounting period is 12 months and, accordingly, where a company prepares a set of accounts for a period exceeding 12 months, this "period of account" must be broken down into shorter periods, each a maximum of 12 months long.

Example

X Ltd prepared a set of accounts for 30 months ending on 30 June 2012. In these circumstances corporation tax is payable for the following "accounting periods":

- 12 month accounting period to 31 December 2010
- 12 month accounting period to 31 December 2011
- 6 month accounting period to 30 June 2012 (remember an accounting period is terminated automatically by reference to the date to which a set of accounts is prepared).

As you can see from this example, if the period of account is longer than 12 months, the first accounting period will always be at least 12 months long. In the above example, the profit and loss account was 30 months long. The tax-adjusted profit computation would have to be prepared. This would involve adjusting for the various add-backs and deductions which are normal and, at the end, one would have a tax-adjusted profit computation (ignoring capital allowances for the moment) corresponding to a 30-month period. One would then **time apportion** the tax-adjusted **Case I** profits for this 30-month period to arrive at the relevant Case I income for each of the accounting periods mentioned above.

It should be particularly noted that only the Case I profits are apportioned. **Case III, Case IV, Case V and chargeable gains arising in the 30 month accounting period will be charged by reference to the actual accounting period in which they occur**. For example, if there was only one CGT disposal in the 30-month period, say on 1 May 2012, then the adjusted chargeable gain would be assessed and brought into the computation for the six-month accounting period ending on 30 June 2012.

In the above example, the capital allowances would have to be computed separately for each of the three accounting periods by reference to additions and disposals of assets which occurred during year ended 31 December 2010, 31 December 2011, and six months to 30 June 2012. In the case of the latter six-month period, clearly the wear and tear allowances would have to be restricted appropriately as discussed above. Therefore, in this situation, capital allowances are not allowed as a trading expense until after the Case I income has been time-apportioned.

(**Note:** Past exam questions have required students to deal with companies that have long periods of account and therefore require this type of time apportionment to be done by the student.)

21.11 Residence of Companies

The most important factor in determining a company's liability to corporation tax is the company's **'residence'**. In broad terms, a **resident** company is liable on **all profits**, whereas a **non-resident** company is liable only on profits attributable to an **Irish branch** or agency. How the residence of a company is determined, and the detailed consequences of a company being resident or non-resident, are dealt with in **Chapter 30**.

21.12 Three-year Tax Exemption for Start-up Companies

21.12.1 Overview

Section 486C TCA 1997 provides a new **relief from corporation tax for new companies commencing to trade in the period 1 January 2009 to 31 December 2014**. The exemption is granted in respect of the profits of a new trade and chargeable gains on the disposal of any assets used for the purposes of a new trade. The exemption is granted by reducing the total corporation tax (including the tax referable to capital gains) relating to the trade to nil. **Full relief** is granted where the total amount of **corporation tax** payable by a company for a 12-month accounting period **does not exceed €40,000**. **Marginal relief** is granted where the total amount of corporation tax payable by a new company for a 12-month accounting period exceeds €40,000 but does not exceed €60,000. No relief applies where corporation tax payable exceeds €60,000. For accounting periods beginning on or after 1 January 2011, there is a limit on the relief which is linked to the Employers' PRSI paid or deemed paid. While the concept is straightforward, the calculations are somewhat complex.

The exemption is available for a period of three years from the commencement of the new trade and separate exemptions are available for each new trade. However, the relief will cease if part of the trade is transferred to a connected person. Where an accounting period is less than 12 months, the limits above are proportionately reduced.

21.12.2 Qualifying and Non-qualifying Trades

A qualifying trade for the purposes of this exemption means a trade which is set up and commenced by a new company in the period 1 January 2009 to 31 December 2014 **other than a trade:**

(i)   which was previously carried on by another person and to which the company has succeeded (Note 1);

(ii)   the activities of which were previously carried on as part of another person's trade or profession;

(iii) which is an excepted trade (see **Section 21.3.2**),

(iv) the activities of which, if carried on by a close company with no other source of income, would result in that company being a professional service company (see **Section 28.11**);

(v)   the activities of which are excluded due to an EU Regulation on State Aid (e.g. certain fishery, agricultural, transport, coal and export activities); or

(vi) the activities of which, if carried on by an associated company of the new company, would form part of a trade carried on by that associated company (Note 2). A company is the new company's associated company if one controls the other or both are under the control of the same person or persons.

Note 1: this means that where a sole trader transfers a business to a new company, the company cannot avail of this exemption on income from this trade.

Note 2: this means that an existing company undertaking an expansion of its existing trade cannot avail of the exemption by putting the expansion through a new company.

21.12.3 Calculation of Relief

The relief applies to:

1.   corporation tax payable by the company for an accounting period so far as it is referable to income from the qualifying trade for that accounting period; and

2.   corporation tax payable by the company for an accounting period so far as it is referable to the chargeable gains on the disposal of qualifying assets in relation to the trade. Qualifying assets are assets (including goodwill but not investments) used for the new trade.

Corporation tax referable to income from the qualifying trade is computed based on the "relevant corporation tax", i.e. the total corporation tax for an accounting period apart from corporation tax due to:

■   close company surcharges (see **Chapter 28**);

■   income tax which is withheld by companies (see **Chapter 23**) and paid over at the same time as corporation tax;

■   the corporation tax chargeable on the profits of the company attributable to chargeable gains for that accounting period; and

■   the corporation tax chargeable on the part of the company's profits which are charged to tax at 25%.

(There are some other exclusions but these are not noted here as they relate to areas which are not examinable.)

The profits of a company attributable to chargeable gains for an accounting period is taken to be the amount of its profits for that period on which corporation tax falls finally to be borne exclusive of the part of the profits attributable to income. The part attributable to income is taken to be the amount brought into the company's profits for that period for the purposes of corporation tax in respect of income after any deduction for charges on income, expenses of management or other amounts which can be deducted from or set against or treated as reducing profits of more than one description, i.e. charges, expenses of management, etc. are deductible from income and thereby reduce the trading income which benefits from the tax exemption, if there is no other income against which to offset them.

Limit on Relief – Employers' PRSI

For accounting periods commencing on or after 1 January 2011, there is a limit on the relief, i.e. if the amount of qualifying Employers' PRSI paid by a company in an accounting period is lower than the reduction in corporation tax otherwise applicable, relief is based on this lower amount. The amount of Employers' PRSI paid by a company in an accounting period in respect of each employee or director (the specified contribution), irrespective of whether the employee is an employee of the new or existing (if any) trade of the new company, is the **lower** of:

(i)   the actual Employers' PRSI paid in respect of that employee or director in the accounting period, plus the PRSI which would have been paid, had the company not qualified for relief under the Employer Job (PRSI) Incentive Scheme; and

(ii)   €5,000.

The amount in respect of each employee or director is aggregated to establish **the total of these specified contributions** for the accounting period.

If this is lower than the relief as calculated under normal rules, this lower amount is the relief.

(**Note:** Certain directors, who are not regarded as employees for social insurance purposes, are liable to PRSI under class S and, therefore, there is no Employers' PRSI.)

Full Relief

Provided the total specified contributions (as calculated above) paid by the company in the accounting period amount to at least €40,000, where the total corporation tax payable by the company for that accounting period does not exceed the lower relevant maximum amount (€40,000), then:

(i)   corporation tax payable by the company for that accounting period, so far as it is referable to income from the qualifying trade for that accounting period, and

(ii)   corporation tax payable by the company so far as it is referable to chargeable gains on the disposal of qualifying assets in relation to the trade,

shall be reduced to nil.

Where the total specified contributions paid by the company in the accounting period amount to less than €40,000 then (i) + (ii) are reduced by the lower of (i) + (ii) or the amount of the total specified contributions.

Corporation tax referable to income from a qualifying trade in an accounting period is such an amount as bears to the relevant corporation tax, the same proportion as the income from the qualifying trade bears to the total income brought into charge to corporation tax for that accounting period.

Corporation tax referable to chargeable gains on the disposal of qualifying assets is such amount as bears to the corporation tax payable on the profits of the company attributable to the chargeable gains for the accounting period, the same proportion as the net chargeable gains on qualifying assets disposed of in the accounting period bears to net chargeable gains on all chargeable assets disposed of in the accounting period.

Example 1

Start Ltd was incorporated on 1 November 2009, commenced to trade on 1 January 2010 and had the following income for the year ended 31 December 2012:

Trading income from shop is €100,000.

The company has three employees and one director and the Employers' PRSI is as follows:

Employers' PRSI paid

Employee 1	0	(Exempt from PRSI due to Employer Job (PRSI) Incentive Scheme. Employers' PRSI saved of €2,000)
Employee 2	€4,000	
Employee 3	€6,000	
Director	0	(class S so no Employers' PRSI)

What is the corporation tax payable?

Solution

Corporation tax payable would be €12,500. As this is less than €40,000 and all conditions are satisfied, the exemption is due. The amount of the exemption depends on the amount of Employers' PRSI which has been paid.

Calculation of relief due

	Specified contribution
	€
Employee 1	2,000
Employee 2	4,000
Employee 3	5,000 (max)
Director	0
Aggregate	11,000
Relief due under normal rules	12,500
Relief due	11,000

Final corporation tax payable €12,500 – €11,000 = €1,500

As Start Limited commenced to trade on 1 January 2010, the exemption applies for 2010, 2011 and 2012. The company will not be entitled to the exemption in 2013.

Example 2

Gain Ltd was incorporated on 11 November 2010, commenced to trade on 1 January 2011 and had the following income and gain for the year ended 31 December 2012:
- Trading income from distribution trade €200,000
- Gain on sale of building used for distribution trade €24,000

It has the following employees and directors and Employers' PRSI contributions:

Employers' PRSI paid

Employee	0	(Exempt from PRSI due to Employer Job (PRSI) Incentive Scheme. Employers' PRSI saved of €4,000)
Six employees	€24,000	(each contribution is less than €5,000)
Director 1	0	(class S so no Employers' PRSI)
Director 2	€8,000	

continued overleaf

What is the corporation tax payable?

Solution

Corporation tax payable would be	€
Case I	200,000
Chargeable gain 24,000 × 30/12.5	57,600
Profit	257,600

CT at 12.5% = €32,200

As this is less than €40,000, all conditions are satisfied and this is qualifying trading income and gains only, the exemption is due and the corporation tax payable is nil, provided that the Employers' PRSI paid or deemed to be paid is at least €32,200.

	Specified contribution
	€
Employee 1	4,000
Six employees	24,000
Director 2	5,000
Aggregate	33,000
Relief due under normal rules	32,200
Relief due	32,200

Final corporation tax payable €32,200 − €32,200 = €nil

Example 3
Complex Ltd was incorporated on 14 June 2011, commenced to trade on 1 January 2012 and had the following income for the year ended 31 December 2012.

	€
Case I – existing distribution trade transferred into company	100,000
Case I – new marketing trade	20,000
Case III – interest income	100
Adjusted chargeable gain on disposal of asset used for marketing trade	12,000
Adjusted chargeable gain on disposal of investment	8,000
Income tax withheld when paying interest to non-bank	1,200

It has the following employees and directors and Employers' PRSI contributions:

	Employers' PRSI paid
Two employees	0 (Exempt from PRSI due to Employer Job (PRSI) Incentive Scheme. Employers' PRSI saved of €4,000 per individual)
Six employees	€24,000 (each contribution is less than €5,000)
Director	0 (class S so no Employers' PRSI)

What is the corporation tax payable?

Solution

		€
Case I – existing distribution trade transferred into company		100,000
Case I – new marketing trade		20,000
Case I		120,000
Case III – interest income		100
	€	120,100
Income		120,100
Chargeable gain - marketing trade	12,000	

continued overleaf

Chargeable gain - investment	8,000	20,000
Total profit		140,100
Corporation tax		
€140,000 × 12.5%		17,500
€100 × 25%		25
Total corporation tax before relief		17,525
Less total relief (Note 1)		(4,000)
		13,525
Add income tax		1,200
Total payable		14,725

Note 1 - Calculation of relief

Total corporation tax	17,525
Relevant corporation tax €17,525 − (€100 × 25% − (12.5% of €20,000))	15,000

Corporation tax referable to income from qualifying trade

$$\text{RCT} \times \frac{\text{Qualifying trade income}}{\text{Total income (excl income taxed at 25%)}} \qquad 15,000 \times \frac{20,000}{120,000} = \qquad (2,500)$$

Corporation tax referable to chargeable gains on qualifying assets

$$\text{CT on gains} \times \frac{\text{Net gains on qualifying assets}}{\text{Net gains on chargeable assets}} \qquad 2,500 \times \frac{12,000}{20,000} = \qquad \begin{matrix}(1,500)\\ (4,000)*\end{matrix}$$

*Total relief, provided sufficient Employers' PRSI is paid (see next)

	Specified contribution €
2 employees	8,000
6 employees	24,000
Aggregate	32,000
Relief due under normal rules	4,000
Relief due	4,000

Marginal relief

Where the total corporation tax payable by the company for the accounting period exceeds the lower relevant maximum amount (€40,000), but does not exceed the upper relevant maximum amount (€60,000), then marginal relief applies so that:

(i)   corporation tax payable by the company for that accounting period, so far as it is referable to income from the qualifying trade for that accounting period, and

(ii) corporation tax payable by the company so far as it is referable to chargeable gains on the disposal of qualifying assets in relation to the trade,

the total of (i) and (ii), known as the "aggregate", shall be **reduced to the greater of:**

(i)   The "aggregate" less the "total contribution". The "total contribution" is the lesser of €40,000 or the amount of the Employers' PRSI paid or deemed paid (the total specified contributions), as calculated at **Section 21.12.3**, or

(ii) $3 \times (T - M) \times \dfrac{A + B}{T}$

where—

T   is the total corporation tax payable by the company for that accounting period,

M   is the lower relevant maximum amount (€40,000),

A   is the corporation tax payable by the company for the accounting period so far as it is referable to income from the qualifying trade for that accounting period, and

B   is the corporation tax payable by the company for the accounting period so far as it is referable to chargeable gains on the disposal of qualifying assets of the qualifying trade.

Example

Marginal Ltd was incorporated on 11 November 2011 and commenced to trade on 1 January 2012 and had the following income for the year ended 31 December 2012:

– Trading income from distribution trade €400,000
– Deposit interest of €1,000

The aggregate of qualifying Employers' PRSI contributions paid in 2012 is €42,000.

What is the corporation tax payable?

Solution

	€
Corporation tax payable would be	
Case I	400,000
Case III	1,000
Profit	401,000
Corporation tax at 12.5% =	50,000
Corporation tax at 25% =	250
Total before relief	50,250

As this is more than €40,000 but less than €60,000 and all conditions are satisfied, marginal relief is due, which limits the tax on the trading income (no gain here) to the greater of:

(i) As qualifying Employers' PRSI contributions are greater than €40,000, the total contribution is therefore €40,000.
CT on trading income and trading gains of new trade less total contribution is:
€400,000 × 12.5% = €50,000 − €40,000 = €10,000

(ii) $3 \times (T - M) \times \dfrac{A + B}{T}$

$3 \times (€50,250 - €40,000) \times \dfrac{€50,000 + 0}{€50,250}$

= €30,597

The tax on trading income and trading gains of the new trade is limited to the greater of:

(i) €10,000, and
(ii) €30,597,

i.e. €30,597.

	€
Corporation tax	
CT on Case I after marginal relief	30,597
€1,000 × 25%	250
Total corporation tax payable	30,847

21.12.4 Qualifying Relevant Period

The relief applies for the first three years only – the "relevant period". This commences when the company commences to trade and ends three years later.

21.12.5 Other Issues

Where the accounting period is less than 12 months, all the limits are reduced proportionately.

There are special rules which limit the relief for transport and haulage companies. Also, as the law must comply with the EU *de minimis* State Aid regulations, Revenue are allowed to provide details of relief claimed to other State bodies.

21.13 Appeals and Assessments

A company must file a corporation tax return (known as Form CT1) within nine months (subject to the 21/23 day rule) of the end of its accounting period. An assessment cannot be raised before the due date for the filing of a company's corporation tax return unless the company files its return before the due date.

If a company does not file a return, or if the Inspector is not satisfied with the return filed, the Inspector may raise an estimated assessment. An assessment may not be raised after four years from the end of the accounting period to which the assessment relates unless there has been fraud or neglect by the company.

If a company does not agree with an assessment raised, it can lodge an appeal against the assessment.

A company cannot lodge an appeal against an assessment unless:

(i)   it has filed a return for the period covered by the assessment; and
(ii) it has paid any tax, including any interest and penalties, which would be payable if an assessment were raised which is in agreement with the return which has been filed.

The initial appeal made by a company is heard by the Appeal Commissioners. The company may be represented at the hearing by a barrister, solicitor, qualified accountant or member of the Irish Taxation Institute. Revenue may be represented by a Revenue official or by a barrister.

The Appeal Commissioners may dismiss the appeal where the company or its representative does not attend the hearing or where the company fails to provide information requested by the Appeal Commissioners. If the appeal is dismissed, the assessment made by the Inspector becomes final and conclusive and accordingly the tax assessed becomes due and payable.

The Appeal Commissioners may confirm the assessment or may increase or decrease the amount of income contained in the assessment. If a company is aggrieved by the decision of the Appeal Commissioners, it may apply for a rehearing of the appeal in the Circuit Court. Revenue may not apply for a rehearing in the Circuit Court. Either the company or Revenue may make a further appeal to the High Court but only if the matter under dispute is on a point of law. Either party aggrieved by the decision of the High Court has a right of appeal to the Supreme Court.

Where the company requests a rehearing in the Circuit Court or either party has indicated the intention to make an appeal to the High Court, any additional tax which would be payable or refundable as a result of the decision of the Appeal Commissioners does not become payable or refundable at that point. If neither party indicates the intention to take the appeal further, either the original assessment becomes final and conclusive or, if the decision of the Appeal Commissioners is that the income in the assessment should be increased or decreased, an amended assessment must be issued which becomes final and conclusive.

The Taxes Consolidation Act (TCA) 1997 sets out time limits within which the various appeals must be made, the contents of a notice of appeal, the power of the Appeal Commissioners to issue requests for further information or to summon witnesses, the obligations of the Inspector to issue notices regarding the timing of the hearing. You are not required to know this detail for the purpose of your exam.

21.14 Revenue Audits, Penalities and Qualifying Disclosures

21.14.1 Introduction to Revenue Audit

A Revenue speaker has provided a definition of Revenue Audit as follows:

"A Revenue Audit may be defined as a review, either partial or total, of a company's corporation tax return or declaration of liability, books and records normally for one year to ensure that the major areas of income, deductions and reliefs are correct. It is essentially a check on the accuracy of the corporation tax return or declaration and on the validity of the allowances etc. claimed".

Revenue's *Code of Practice for Revenue Auditors* (to be found at www.revenue.ie) states that the primary objective of a Revenue Audit is to promote "voluntary compliance with tax and duty obligations" and that the audit programme is mainly concerned with "detecting and deterring non-compliance".

A number of years ago, Revenue developed a Risk Evaluation and Analysis Programme (REAP) that systematically analyses their case base by reference to a range of risk criteria to determine which cases should be selected for audit. The system allows for the screening of all tax returns against sectoral and business norms and provides a selection basis for checks or audits. In more recent times, Revenue has started using e-auditing which allows the Revenue auditor to use computer-assisted audit techniques on customer's data as part of its audit process.

Field Audit

Where a business is involved, most audits, whether comprehensive or single tax-head, include **visits** to the business premises. The length of such visits depends on the number and complexity of the points at issue. Notice is generally given in such cases to both the company and its agent. In certain exceptional circumstances (e.g. where it is suspected that records are likely to be removed or altered), a visit may take place unannounced.

Desk Audit

Certain audits (mainly verification of specific claims to expenses, allowances or reliefs) are conducted by letter (post, fax or e-mail), or by telephone, where straightforward issues are involved. This type of audit, known as a desk audit, may also arise in a review of a director's tax affairs or where a company has unearned income. Similarly, CAT and stamp duty audits are normally desk audits. Taxpayers will be informed of the issues being examined in the course of a desk audit.

It should be noted that a desk audit may subsequently involve field work, if this is deemed necessary, including visits to the company's premises to examine records.

Audit Notification

The company will receive a letter from Revenue which will include the wording "Notification of a Revenue Audit". Revenue will specify a date at which they wish to visit the company's premises to examine the books and records of the business. Almost all audits are carried out for a reason, e.g. Revenue will have information or indications that the company may have underpaid tax. Though some audits are carried out on a random basis, Revenue frequently target specific trades or industries.

The Audit Notification will specify the tax-head or heads (corporation tax, VAT, etc.) and the year of assessment or period in question. The Revenue auditor is confined to examining the issues **as notified** and cannot extend the audit without good reason at the time of the visit.

21.14.2 Tax, Interest and Penalties

Tax

Any tax due as a result of the Revenue Audit must be paid.

Interest

Interest is always charged if a failure to pay is identified. Interest **cannot** be mitigated (i.e. reduced).

Application of Penalties

Penalties will apply if, in the course of the audit, tax defaults are identified. Penalties are "tax-geared" which means that the penalty is expressed as a **percentage of the tax** (but not the interest) in question. Penalties will apply in circumstances where there has been:

■ careless behavior; *or*
■ careless behavior with significant consequences; *or*
■ deliberate behaviour.

Careless behaviour The penalty for careless behaviour is **20% of the tax**. Careless behaviour will arise if a person of ordinary skill and knowledge, properly advised, would have foreseen as a reasonable probability or likelihood the prospect that an act (or omission) would cause a tax underpayment, having regard to all the circumstances but, nevertheless, the act or omission occurred. There is also a **materiality test**. The tax shortfall must be **less than 15%** of the tax liability ultimately due in respect of the particular tax.

Careless behaviour with significant consequences The penalty for this category is **40% of the tax**. Careless behaviour with significant consequences is the lack of **due care** with the result that tax liabilities or repayment claims are **substantially incorrect** and pass the 15% test described above. Careless behaviour with significant consequences is distinguished from "deliberate behaviour" by the **absence** of indicators consistent with intent on the part of the company.

Deliberate behaviour The penalty for deliberate default is **100% of the tax**. Deliberate default has indicators consistent with **intent** and includes tax evasion and the non-operation of fiduciary taxes such as PAYE.

Innocent Error

A penalty will not be payable in respect of a tax default if the tax default was not deliberate and was not attributable in any way to the failure to take reasonable care to comply with a company's tax obligations. Factors which will be taken into account in deciding whether a penalty should not be imposed include:

■ Whether the amount of tax was less than €6,000
■ Whether the auditor concludes that the company has provided for, and implemented, the keeping of proper books and records so as to fulfil tax obligations
■ The frequency with which the "innocent error" occurs. Repeatedly making such errors could indicate lack of appropriate care which could put the error into the "careless behaviour without significant consequences" category or higher.
■ The previous compliance record of the company
■ Where the error being corrected is immaterial

Interest will, however, be charged even if no penalty is charged.

Technical Adjustments

"Technical adjustments" are adjustments to a tax liability that arise from differences in interpretation or the application of the legislation.

A technical adjustment will not give rise to a penalty where:

- Due care has been exercised by the company
- The treatment concerned was based on an interpretation of law which could reasonably have been considered to be correct.

Interest will, however, be charged even if no penalty is charged.

Self-correction

This category arises outside of the audit or enquiry process. A return may be self-corrected **without** penalty where:

- Revenue is notified in writing of the adjustments to be made, and the circumstances under which the errors arose.
- A computation of the correct tax and statutory interest payable is provided, along with a cheque in settlement.

Time Limits for Self-Correction

Income Tax	Within 12 months of the due date for filing the return.
Corporation Tax	Within 12 months of the due date for filing the return.
Capital Gains Tax	Within 12 months of the due date for filing the return.
VAT	Before the due date of the IT or CT return for the period in which the VAT period ends, e.g. a self correction of the Jan/Feb 2012 VAT3 for a company with a December year end must occur before 23 September 2013. (For bi-monthly/quarterly/half-yearly remitters of VAT, if the net VAT underpayment is less than €6,000 the amount of tax can be included, without interest, as an adjustment in the next VAT return and there is no requirement to notify Revenue.)
PAYE/PRSI	Within 12 months of the due date for filing the annual return.
Relevant Contracts Tax	Within 12 months of the due date for filing the annual return.

The benefit of self-correction does not apply if Revenue had notified a taxpayer of an audit or if the correction relates to an instance of deliberate behaviour which also featured in a previous period.

Qualifying Disclosures and Reduction of Penalties

Penalties are mitigated in the following circumstances:

- Where there is **co-operation** by the company
- Where a "**Qualifying Disclosure**" is made by the company.

Co-operation

Co-operation includes the following:

- Having all books, records, and linking papers available for the auditor at the commencement of the audit.
- Having appropriate personnel available at the time of the audit.
- Responding promptly to all requests for information and explanations.
- Responding promptly to all correspondence.
- Prompt payment of the audit settlement liability.

Qualifying Disclosures

The company may elect to carry out a review of its own tax affairs and identify where mistakes were made **prior** to their discovery by the Revenue auditor. This type of review is called a "qualifying disclosure", and there are special incentives for companies who wish to make qualifying disclosures. A qualifying disclosure results in the following:

- Non publication of the tax settlement in the list of tax defaulters published by Revenue.
- No prosecution.
- Further mitigation of penalties.

Qualifying disclosures can be either **"unprompted"** or **"prompted"**.

An "unprompted" disclosure is a disclosure that is made **before** the company is notified of an audit, *or* contacted by Revenue regarding an enquiry or investigation relating to its tax affairs.

A "prompted" disclosure is a disclosure made **after** an audit notice has issued but **before** an examination of the books and records or other documentation has begun.

Period to Prepare a Qualifying Disclosure

In order for the company to secure an agreed 60-day period of time in which to prepare and make a qualifying disclosure, **notice of the intention** to make a disclosure must be given.

In the case of an **unprompted disclosure**, the notice of the intention to make a disclosure must be given **before**,

- a notice of audit is issued; *or*
- the company has been contacted by Revenue regarding an enquiry or investigation relating to his tax affairs.

In the case of a **prompted disclosure**, the majority of these will be submitted in the period between the date of the notification of the audit and the commencement of the audit. In the case of a prompted qualifying disclosure, if the company wishes to be given an additional 60 days to prepare the disclosure the notice of intention to make a disclosure must be given **within 14 days** of the day of issue of the notification of audit.

A person, who has given notice within the time allowed of his or her intention to make a qualifying disclosure, will be given 60 days in which to quantify the shortfall and to make the relevant payment. This period of 60 days will begin from the day on which the notice of intention to make a qualifying disclosure was given and will be communicated to the taxpayer in writing by Revenue. The 60-day period allows the company or its agent to contact Revenue to discuss any matters arising, including the category of default on which the mitigated penalty is to be based.

Format of the Qualifying Disclosure

The following conditions must be satisfied for a disclosure to be a **qualifying disclosure** for the purpose of mitigation of penalties:

- The disclosure must be made in writing and signed by or on behalf of the company.
- It must be accompanied by a declaration to the best of that person's knowledge, information and belief, that all matters contained in the disclosure are correct and complete.
- The disclosure must, whether prompted or unprompted, state the amounts of all liabilities to tax, interest and penalties, as respects all tax heads and periods, which were liabilities previously undisclosed by reason of *deliberate behaviour* by the company.
- In the case of a **prompted** disclosure, it must also state the amounts of any liabilities previously undisclosed, for any reason other than *deliberate behaviour*, which are liabilities to tax, interest and penalties within the scope of the proposed audit or audit enquiry.
- In the case of an **unprompted** disclosure, it must state the amounts of any liabilities previously undisclosed, for any reason other than deliberate behaviour, which are liabilities to tax, interest and penalties in respect of the tax types and periods which are covered by the unprompted qualifying disclosure.
- The disclosure must be accompanied by a payment of the total liability arising in respect of the tax and interest in respect of that tax. The qualifying disclosure does not need to make reference to the penalty due.

On receipt of the qualifying disclosure the auditor will agree the penalties with the company and will obtain payment at that stage. Where the company is unable to pay the full settlement amount at this stage, a real, genuine and acceptable proposal to pay the amount due in accordance with the Revenue instalment arrangement procedures will satisfy the payment requirement. If however the company fails to honour the instalment arrangements the company will be regarded as not having made a qualifying disclosure.

Reduction of Penalties

The amount of the reduction available is determined by whether a qualifying disclosure was made in the previous five years. There are three different tables and the table for the first qualifying disclosure is shown below:

Category of Tax Default	Penalty as a % of Tax Underpaid	Net Penalty after Reduction where there is:		
		Cooperation Only	Cooperation AND a Prompted Qualifying Disclosure	Cooperation AND an Unprompted Qualifying Disclosure
Deliberate behaviour	100%	75%	50%	10%
Careless behaviour with significant consequences	40%	30%	20%	5%
Other careless behaviour	20%	15%	10%	3%

For the purpose of your exam, you are not required to memorise the above percentage amounts of penalties. However, you do need to be aware of the different types of default and that the penalty applicable is reduced depending on whether there is co-operation or not and a prompted or unprompted disclosure.

Where a second or subsequent qualifying disclosure is made within five years of a first qualifying disclosure there is still a reduction in penalties. However, the reduction in penalties where the category of tax default falls under "deliberate behaviour" or "careless behaviour with significant consequences" is less than the reduction in penalties for the first qualifying disclosure. The same reduction in penalties applies where the tax default is in the category of "careless behaviour without significant consequences". Where a subsequent qualifying disclosure is made more than five years after a first qualifying disclosure was made, the same reduction in penalties apply as if it were a first disclosure.

21.14.3 Conduct of a Revenue Audit

On arrival at the place of audit, the auditor will show his or her identification and authorisation and explain the purpose of the audit. It is Revenue policy not to disclose the precise reason a company has been selected for audit.

The company is informed about Revenue practice on charging interest and penalties and is offered the opportunity to make a prompted qualifying disclosure. The auditor will advise the company of the benefits of a qualifying disclosure regarding penalties and publication.

After the initial interview the examination of the books and records will begin and the audit commences.

Some of the key points pertaining to the conduct of an audit are as follows:

- The audit will generally take place at the company's place of business unless it would be impractical in which case the audit will take place in the Revenue office. The audit will however always include a visit to the business premises.
- The auditor will try not to retain any records for longer than a month. If more time is required the company will be advised of this.
- A receipt is given for any records removed from the premises.
- The auditor will focus primarily on the years, periods or transactions indicated in the audit notice.
- Issues may arise during the course of the audit that require the auditor to consider opening earlier or later years. If deliberate default/deliberate behaviour is not involved, Revenue may informally draw the company's attention to these issues and the company has the opportunity to make an unprompted qualifying disclosure in relation to these other years.
- If the auditor decides to extend the scope of the audit to other taxes or years not referred to in the audit notice, the company will be given the opportunity to make a prompted qualifying disclosure in respect of those other taxes or years.
- Where during the course of an audit a company representative admits committing an offence, which is not included as part of a qualifying disclosure, the auditor is required to caution the individual that he is not obliged to say anything but anything he says will be taken down in writing and may be given in evidence.

Finalisation of Audit

At the conclusion of the audit the Revenue auditor will:

- Outline the findings of the audit.
- Quantify the tax, interest and penalties due.
- Invite the company to make a written settlement offer.
- If necessary, require the company to confirm that any issues identified have been rectified.

When a settlement has been agreed a final letter have been issued by the Revenue audit setting out:

- The details of the settlement.
- Any inadequacies in the company's records or tax treatments.
- Noting the company's confirmation that any inadequacies have been rectified.

Right to a Review

A company has the right to request a review of the conduct of an audit in particular in relation to:

- Proposed adjustments to receipts or profits figures, claims for reliefs or allowances or to tax computations.
- Penalties to be charged.
- Whether the settlement meets publication criteria.

The initial review is carried out by the local Revenue office; however, if the company is not satisfied with the outcome of this review, it may request a review by the Internal Review Unit.

Questions (to Chapter 21)

Challenging Questions

Question 21.1

Lemmon Ltd

Lemmon Ltd, a distribution company, prepares accounts annually to 31 December. On 1 January 2012, it decided to change its accounting date to 28 February and accordingly a 14-month set of accounts were made up to 28 February 2013. Two brothers, Walter and Jack, who also own a property rental company, Rentco Ltd, own Lemmon Ltd. On 1 July 2012 Lemmon Ltd acquired all the share capital of another distribution company, Distributors Ltd.

Results for the three companies, as adjusted for tax purposes, are as follows:

	Notes	**Lemmon**	**Rentco**	**Distributors**
		14 months ended 28/2/2013	*Year ended 31/12/2012*	*8 months ended 28/2/2013*
		€	€	€
Schedule D Case I		308,000	–	20,000
Schedule D Case III	(1)	5,000	–	–
Schedule D Case V		–	50,000	–
Capital gain	(2)	1,953	–	–

Notes

1. The Case III income was received: €3,000 on 31 December 2012 and €2,000 on 28 February 2013.
2. No adjustment has been made to take account of the difference between the corporation tax rate and the CGT rate. The gain arose on the disposal of quoted shares in June 2012. These shares were acquired in July 2004.

Requirement

(a) Calculate the corporation tax liabilities for all three companies for the above accounting periods.
(b) State the latest date by which all corporation tax liabilities are to be paid. (Assume all companies are "small companies" but ignore the rule that allows "small companies" to base their preliminary tax on its corresponding corporation tax liability for the previous period).
(c) State the latest date for which returns must be filed for the above periods.

Computation of Corporation Tax

Learning Objectives

After studying this chapter you will have developed the competency to understand that:

- The most important point of this chapter is the pro forma tax computation. As you deal with the different chapters, make sure that you understand how they fit into the computation.
- There are many items in the financial statements that require to be adjusted in moving from profit per the accounts to Case I income liable to corporation tax.
- Capital allowances may be claimed in respect of capital expenditure on intangible assets, subject to conditions.
- There is a tax credit for expenditure on R&D and certain expenditure on buildings used for R&D.

22.1 Pro Forma Corporation Tax Computation

COMPLEX COMPANY LTD
CORPORATION TAX COMPUTATION FOR THE 12 MONTH ACCOUNTING
PERIOD TO 31/12/2012 (*Note 1*)

		Notes	€	€
Case I	Tax adjusted trading profits y/e 31/12/2012	2	X	
	Less: Allowable Case I losses forward section 396(1)		(X)	
	Less: section 396A(3) Case I losses	7	(X)	
	Less: Allowable trade charges paid section 243A	8	(X)	X
Case III	Interest on Irish Government Securities	3	X	
	Foreign bond deposit interest		X	
	Irish building society interest		X	
	Irish commercial bank deposit interest		X	
	Income from foreign sources		X	X

Case IV	Income subject to Irish tax at source	4	<u>X</u>	X
Case V	Profit rents from the letting of property			
	in the Republic of Ireland	5		X
Chargeable Gains	(as adjusted, e.g. × 30%/12.5%)	6		<u>X</u>
"Total Profits"				X
Deduct:	Excess Case V capital allowances	7		<u>(X)</u>
				X
Deduct:	Non-trade charges paid during y/e 31/12/2012 (e.g. protected interest)	8		<u>(X)</u>
Profits liable to corporation tax				<u>(X)</u>
Corporation tax Case I, II certain foreign dividends and chargeable gains @ 12.5%		9	<u>X</u>	
Case III, IV and V @ 25%		9	<u>X</u>	
Deduct:	Excess relevant trading charges allowed on a value basis against corporation tax under section 243B	8		(X)
	Loss relief allowed on a value basis against corporation tax under section 396B (3)	7		(X)
Add:	Surcharge (close company)		X	
	Income tax deducted by the company on annual payments		<u>X</u>	X
Deduct:	R&D tax credit	10		<u>(X)</u>
				X
Deduct:	Income tax suffered by deduction	4		<u>(X)</u>
Net corporation tax liability		11		<u>X</u>

Note 1

The computation should always have the name of the company at the top and an appropriate heading, i.e. "corporation tax computation for the 12 month *accounting period* to..........". It is possible for a corporation tax accounting period to be less than 12 months but it can never exceed 12 months.

Note 2

The tax-adjusted trading profits are arrived at after making a number of adjustments. It should be particularly noted that the tax-adjusted trading profits represents the final Case I figure, after capital allowances have been deducted, but before relief for unutilised Case I losses carried forward from the *same trade*.

Note 3

The income here is income received during the accounting period, without deduction of Irish tax. For example, deposit interest earned by a *company* on deposits with an Irish building society or an Irish commercial bank will *not* suffer Deposit Interest Retention Tax (DIRT) provided that the company has provided the financial institution with its tax reference number.

Note 4

Any income which is subject to Irish tax at source is taxable under Case IV, e.g. most patent royalties. In these cases, the appropriate amount to include at this point in the computation is the gross amount before the deduction of the Irish tax and to allow the tax deducted as indicated at the bottom of the computation as a tax credit.

Note 5
This is the actual Case V income arising in the accounting period net of any expenses and capital allowances.

Note 6
A corporation tax computation encompasses not only income but also chargeable gains. There is a special computation method for arriving at the appropriate chargeable gains to include in the computation, which was dealt with in **Chapter 1**. Remember gains on development land are not liable to corporation tax but to CGT.

Note 7
Sections 396A(3) and 396B(3) TCA 1997, which are concerned with the utilisation of relevant trading losses apply to losses from a normal trade, i.e. a trade that would be taxed at the standard rate of 12.5%, if it made a profit.

Trading losses may be offset against trading income only (section 396A(3)). Trading losses which cannot be relieved in this way may be relieved under section 396B(3) on a value basis against corporation tax due on profits. The treatment of corporation tax losses is dealt with in more detail in **Chapter 24.**

Excess Case V capital allowances, i.e. the excess of capital allowances on a building that a company lets out to a tenant over the rental income (net of expenses) of the company. These excess capital allowances may be set off against total profits, i.e. income of all types and chargeable gains – see **Chapter 24.**

Note 8
Relief for allowable charges is given by reference to the actual amount of the charges *paid* during the actual accounting period in question. In certain circumstances, the charges may have to be paid under deduction of standard rate income tax (e.g. patent royalties). In such cases the correct procedure is to allow the gross amount before deduction of the standard rate income tax as a charge. The income tax actually deducted is collected as part of the total corporation tax payable in respect of the accounting period in which the charge was paid – see **Chapter 23.**

A charge that is paid for the purposes of a trade taxed at the standard rate, a "relevant trading charge" such as a patent royalty paid, is allowable against trading income only (section 243A). Excess relevant trading charges are allowed on a value basis against corporation tax under section 243B – see **Chapter 24.**

A charge that is paid and is not for the purposes of the trade, e.g. a non-trade charge such as protected interest, is deductible from total profits and therefore may be set off against income taxable at the higher rate – see **Chapter 23**.

Note 9
The 12.5% rate applies to profits earned in 2012, other than Case III (excluding certain foreign dividends), IV or V profits or profits of an "excepted trade", which are chargeable at 25%. Certain foreign dividends are taxable at 12.5% – see **Chapter 31.1.2.**

Note 10
There is a tax credit of 25% of incremental expenditure on R&D and certain expenditure on buildings used for R&D. This is dealt with at **Section 22.5.**

Note 11 (Assuming Large Company Rules Apply)

The first instalment of preliminary corporation tax, i.e. 50% of prior period or 45% of current period, is due on/before 23 June 2012, with the second instalment due 23 November 2012, bringing the total payment to 90% of the final net corporation tax liability. The balance of the corporation tax is due on/before 23 September 2013.

22.2 Badges of a Trade

Tax is chargeable under Case I of Schedule D on the full amount of the profits or gains of a trade. "Trade" is defined in TCA 1997 as including "every trade, manufacture, adventure or concern in the nature of trade". This definition does not give any guidance on whether a paticular activity constitutes a trading activity. Therefore, a **Royal Commission** was established in the UK to determine the factors which should be taken into account in establishing whether or not there was a trade. Their recommendations have become known as the **"Badges of Trade"**. These factors or badges are as follows:

22.2.1 The Subject Matter of the Realisation

The first factor in determining whether or not a person is trading is the actual property involved. Property which does not generate any income or enjoyment is more likely to have been purchased with a view to selling it than property which produces income or enjoyment. For example, the disposal of a valuable painting may generate a gain of a capital nature rather than trading income. In contrast, the disposal of one million rolls of toilet paper is more likely to be presumed to be a trading transaction.

22.2.2 Length of Period of Ownership

In general, property purchased and sold within a short time period is generally presumed to be of a trading nature. However, there are many exceptions to this standard rule.

22.2.3 The Frequency or Number of Transactions

Transactions which would be treated as being of a capital nature if carried out in isolation, will be treated as trading transactions if there is in fact a succession of such transactions over a period of years or there are several such transactions in or around the same time.

22.2.4 Supplementary Work on or in Connection with the Property

If the property is improved or developed in any way during the ownership so as to bring it into a more marketable condition, or if any special marketing efforts are made to find or attract purchasers, such as the opening of a sales office or a large scale advertising campaign, then this would provide some evidence of trading. Where there is an organised effort to obtain profit, there is likely to be a source of taxable income. However, if nothing at all is done, the suggestion would tend to go the other way.

22.2.5 The Circumstances in which the Property is Realised

There may be some explanation, such as a sudden emergency or opportunity calling for the realisation of cash, which may eliminate the suggestion that any plan of dealing prompted the original purchase, i.e. in the case of "an unsolicited offer that cannot be refused".

22.2.6 Profit Motive

Motive is extremely important in all cases. There are cases in which the purpose of the transaction is clearly discernible. Circumstances surrounding the particular transaction may indicate the motive of the seller and this may in fact overrule the seller's own evidence.

22.3 Adjustments in Arriving at Case I Income

ALWAYS:

1. Deduct non-trading income and gains

Deduct	Taxed Instead
Interest	Generally Case III. If Case IV, tax gross amount with credit for tax deducted.
Rents	Case V (or Case III if non-Irish) – deduct related expenses and capital allowances.
Irish dividends	Not taxable.
Foreign dividends	Case III or IV – method of taxing depends on treaty.
Capital gain	Chargeable gain.
Patent royalties	Case III or IV – Case III if from a foreign patent, Case IV if Irish patent royalties received under deduction of tax, otherwise it is Case III.

2. Add back any expenses not properly associated with the trading activities

Summary of Expenses Commonly Disallowed
(a) Expenses or losses of a capital nature:
  - Depreciation.
  - Loss on sale of fixed assets.
  - Improvements to premises.
  - Purchase of fixed assets.
(b) Payments from which tax is deducted:
  - Annuities and royalties. These may be allowed as a charge.
(c) Expenses not wholly and exclusively laid out for the purposes of the business:
  - Rental expenses re property rented out to a tenant (allowable against Case V rents).
  - Political donations. Most charitable donations are allowed – see (l) below.
  - Fines and penalties and interest on late payment of tax.

Treatment of Certain Specific Items
(a) Bad Debts
Irish GAAP Under Irish GAAP, a company may have general and specific bad debt provisions. Under general tax principles, general provisions are not deductible. Therefore if

there are any movements on the general bad debts provision account, an adjustment must be made, i.e.:

- Increase in a general provision for bad debts - not allowable
- Decrease in a general provision for bad debts - not taxable

There is no difference between the tax and accounting rules in relation to any other movements on bad debts – there is no adjustment required, i.e.:

- Bad debts written off – deducted in P&L account and allowed for tax purposes
- Bad debts recovered – credited to P&L account and is taxable
- Increase in a specific provision for bad debts – deducted in P&L account and allowed for tax purposes
- Decrease in a specific provision for bad debts – credited to P&L account and is taxable.

IFRS Under IFRS, the manner of calculating a provision for doubtful debts is more specific than heretofore. As a result, increases in bad debt provisions are treated as deductible for tax purposes, provided that they are properly calculated in accordance with the new standards.

(b) Entertainment Expenses

General entertainment expenses incurred are completely disallowed, e.g. entertainment of customers and suppliers. Entertainment includes the provision of accommodation, food, drink or any other form of hospitality including the provision of gifts.

Expenditure on bona fide staff entertainment is not subject to the foregoing restrictions provided its provision is not incidental to the provision of entertainment to third parties.

Expenditure incurred in relation to capital assets used for entertainment purposes is subject to similar restrictions.

(c) Legal Expenses are:

- Debt recovery – allowable
- Acquisition of assets – not allowable
- Renewal of short lease – allowable
- Product liability claims and employee actions – allowable

(d) Repairs

Replacement/redecoration, repairs not involving material improvements – expenditure is allowable.

(e) Leased Motor Vehicles

In the case of a leased vehicle, the list price of which exceeds €24,000 (the specified amount) when the car is first registered, the following restriction applies for accounting periods ending in 2011:

The leasing charges are restricted by:

$$\text{Total lease hire charges} \times \frac{\text{List price} - €24,000^*}{\text{List price}}$$

* €24,000 applies for accounting periods ending on or after 1 January 2007.

For cars leased on or after 1 July 2008, the amount of lease hire charges allowed depends on the CO_2 emissions category of the car. The following chart sets out the limits to be used for each CO_2 emissions category:

CARBON EMISSIONS RESTRICTIONS ON MOTOR VEHICLES
bought on/after 1 July 2008

Category A	Category B/C	Category D/E	Category F/G
0–120g/km	121–155g/km	156–190g/km	191g/km+

Category A–C	Use the specified amount regardless of cost

Category D–E	Two steps to calculate the limit:
	   1. Take the lower of the specified limit or cost
	   2. Limit is 50% of this amount

Category F–G	No allowance is available

Example 1

A company which prepares annual accounts to 31 December, leased a car new in March 2012 when its retail price was €35,000. CO_2 emissions category B.

In the annual accounts to 31 December 2012, lease hire charges of €10,000 were incurred.

$$€$$

Disallow

$$€10,000 \times \frac{€35,000 - €24,000}{€35,000} = \underline{€3,143} \text{ Addback}$$

Example 2

A company which prepares annual accounts to 31 December, leased a new car in March 2012 when its retail price was €35,000. CO_2 emissions category D.

In the annual accounts to 31 December 2012, lease hire charges of €10,000 were incurred.

Disallow

$$€10,000 \times \frac{€35,000 - (€24,000/2)}{€35,000} = €6,571 \text{ Addback}$$

If, alternatively, the retail price of the car was €20,000, the addback would be 50% × €10,000 = €5,000.

If, alternatively, this were a category F car, the full €10,000 would be added back.

Example 3

A company which prepares annual accounts to 31 December, leased a car new in March 2012 when its retail price was €20,000. CO_2 emissions category B.

In the annual accounts to 31 December 2012, lease hire charges of €10,000 were incurred.

$$€10,000 \times \frac{€20,000 - (€24,000)}{€20,000} = €2,000 \text{ additional deduction}$$

Where a car is in category A, B or C and its list price is less than €24,000, there will always be an additional deduction.

(f) Interest on Late Payment of Tax

Interest on late payment of any tax (including VAT, PAYE, etc.) is not allowed in computing tax-adjusted profits.

(g) Accountancy/Taxation Fees

■ Normal accounting, auditing and taxation compliance costs are allowable.

■ Special costs associated with Appeal Hearings are likely to be disallowed following the decision of *Allen v. Farquharson Brothers*, where the cost of employing solicitors and counsel in connection with an appeal against income tax assessments were held to be disallowed.

(h) Pre-trading Expenses

Pre-trading expenses, as their name indicates, are incurred before the trade is commenced. As a general rule, pre-trading expenses are not tax deductible. However, tax law was changed so that certain pre-trading expenses are deductible in calculating trading income or losses once the trade commences.

The qualifying expenses are those:

■ incurred within three years prior to the commencement; and

■ which would be allowed as a deduction in calculating trading profits if they had been incurred after trading commenced.

Examples of qualifying pre-trading expenses include, accountancy fees, market research, feasibility studies, salaries, advertising, preparing business plans and rent.

These pre-trading expenses are deductible against income of the trade. If the expenses exceed the income and there is a loss, this loss cannot be offset against other profits of the company nor can it be group relieved, but can only be carried forward against future income of the same trade.

Charges on income incurred before a trade commenced are treated as paid when the trade commences, i.e. are deductible as a charge in the first year of trading.

Example

Ray Ltd commenced to trade on 1 July 2012. It incurred the following pre-trading expenditure:

		€
December 2008	Market research	8,000
December 2011	Director's salary	30,000
January 2012	Business entertainment	5,000
May 2012	Marketing expenditure	17,000

The market research expenditure is not deductible as it was not incurred within three years before the trade commenced. The business entertainment expenditure is never allowable. The expenditure on the director's salary and marketing are allowable. Therefore, Ray Ltd incurs deductible expenses of €47,000 on 1 July 2012. These are fully deductible in calculating the Case I income of the first accounting period. Should this expenditure exceed this income, the excess is only available to offset against future income of this trade. It cannot be offset against other income or gains or used for group relief.

Therefore, the pre-trading loss and any normal trading loss arising in the first accounting period, after commencement of the trade, must be separately identified; the pre-trading loss can only be offset against Case I income, whereas any normal trading loss can be used on a value basis, grouped, etc.

(i) Expenditure on Scientific Research

The full amount of any non-capital expenditure on scientific research is allowable as a deduction in computing the profits of a trade. In addition, sums paid to establishments approved by the Minister for Finance to carry on scientific research and sums paid to Irish universities to enable them to carry on scientific research are also deductible. This rule applies whether or not the payments are related to the existing trade currently being carried on.

(j)   Payments for Intangibles
There are special rules regarding the deduction for payments made to acquire intangibles. These are dealt with at **Section 22.4**.

(k)   Redundancy Payments
Statutory redundancy payments are specifically allowable. Amounts in excess of statutory entitlements are unlikely to be deductible where a cessation of trade has taken place but would be allowed if the trade continued.

(l)   Donations
Companies are entitled to a deduction, as a trading expense, for qualifying donations to eligible charities, educational institutions, schools, churches, research foundations and other approved organisations which satisfy certain conditions. The eligible charity can be established anywhere in the European Economic Area or the European Free Trade Association. To qualify for a tax deduction, the donation(s) to an organisation in a 12-month accounting period must amount to at least €250. If the accounting period is less than 12 months, the €250 minimum is proportionately reduced. There is no upper limit.

Companies are also entitled to a deduction, as a trading expense, for qualifying donations(s) to an approved sports body (most athletics and amateur games or sports bodies) to enable that body to purchase or construct facilities, improve facilities, purchase significant equipment or to repay a loan to carry out any of these activities. As with the other donations, to qualify for a tax deduction, the donation(s) to an organisation in a 12-month accounting period must amount to at least €250. If the accounting period is less than 12 months, the €250 minimum is proportionately reduced. There is no upper limit.

(m)   Lease Payments Re Assets Capitalised in the Balance Sheet
Where a leased asset is capitalised in the balance sheet, the amounts expensed in the P&L are interest expense and depreciation. The lease payment is not expensed to the P&L. Where the burden of the wear and tear of the asset is borne by the lessor – the typical situation – the lessee is not entitled to capital allowances. Instead the lessee is entitled to a deduction for the lease payments made. As only the interest element of the lease payment will have been expensed to the P&L, an adjustment is required, i.e. add back interest and instead allow the full lease payment made.

Example

X Ltd leased a machine from Bank Ltd over a five-year period. Under GAAP, X Ltd is required to capitalise the machine in its books. Under the terms of the lease agreement, the burden of wear and tear in respect of this machine falls on Bank Ltd. Therefore X Ltd has no right to capital allowances.

During 2012, X Ltd paid lease payments of €10,000 of which €3,000 were expensed as interest to the P&L. In preparing the corporation tax computation for 2012, there will be:

- an add-back of €3,000 in respect of interest; and
- an additional deduction allowed for the lease payments made of €10,000.

Also, if there are any upfront payments, e.g. a lump sum paid at the start of the lease, these are allowed over the period of the lease and not in the first year.

If there is a rebate (refund) of lease rentals, typically at the end of the lease, the rebate is taxable when received.

(n) Pension Contributions

Ordinary annual contributions by an employer to a Revenue approved pension scheme for the benefit of his employees are allowable for tax purposes in the year in which they are **paid**. Thus any accruals in respect of ordinary annual pension contributions due, which have been included in arriving at profit in the financial statements, will have to be disallowed.

If an employer makes a special contribution to a Revenue approved pension scheme and the total amount of the special contributions made in the year does not exceed the total ordinary annual contributions paid in the year, relief is given for the special contributions in the year in which they are paid. If, however, the total amount of the special contributions paid exceeds the total ordinary annual contributions paid, relief for the special contributions made is spread forward over a number of years. The number of years over which relief is given is calculated by dividing the total special contributions paid by the total ordinary contributions paid. If the factor produced by this calculation is between one and two, relief is given over two years; otherwise, the factor is rounded to the nearest whole number.

Example

An employer makes the following pension contributions in 2012:

Ordinary annual contribution	€10,000
Special contribution	€27,000

As the special contribution made exceeds the ordinary annual contribution, relief for the special contribution will be spread forward. The number of years over which relief is given is calculated as follows:

$$\frac{\text{Special contribution} \quad €27,000}{\text{Ordinary annual contribution} \ €10,000} = 2.7$$

As 2.7 is between 2 and 3, relief for the special contribution will be given over three years, In the first two years, the amount of relief given will equal the amount of the ordinary annual contribution with the balance of the relief given in the third year. Accordingly relief for the special contribution of €27,000 made in 2012 will be given as follows:

Tax Year	Relief Given
2012	€10,000
2013	€10,000
2014	€7,000

If the amount of the ordinary annual contribution is less than €6,350, in calculating when relief for a special contribution is due, the amount of the ordinary annual contribution may be assumed to be €6,350.

Example

An employer makes the following contributions in 2012:

Ordinary annual contribution	€5,000
Special contribution	€8,000

As the special contribution made exceeds €6,350, relief for the special contribution will be spread forward. The number of years over which relief is given is calculated as follows:

$$\frac{\text{Special contribution} \quad €8,000}{\text{Ordinary annual contribution} \ €6,350} = 1.26$$

continued overleaf

As 1.26 is between 1 and 2, relief is given over two years as follows:	
Tax Year	**Relief Given**
2012	€6,350
2013	€1,650

(o) *Keyman Insurance*

Generally, premiums paid under loss of profits insurance policies are tax deductible and any sums received from the insurance company are taxable under Case I.

Keyman insurance is insurance taken out by a company in its own favour against the death, sickness or injury of an employee (the keyman) whose services are vital to the success of the employer's business.

In general, premiums paid under policies insuring against loss of profits consequent on certain contingencies are deductible for tax purposes in the period in which they are paid. Correspondingly all sums received by an employer under such policies are treated as trading receipts in the period in which they are received. Keyman insurance policies qualify for this treatment where the following conditions are satisfied:

- the sole relationship is that of employer and employee;
- the employee does not have a substantial proprietary interest in the business (i.e. controls not more than 15% of ordinary share capital);
- the insurance is intended to meet loss of profit resulting from the loss of the services of the employee as distinct from the loss of goodwill or other capital loss; and
- in the case of insurance against death, the policy is a short-term insurance providing only for a sum to be paid in the event of the death of the insured within a specified number of years. Short-term generally means five years but, in practice, if all other conditions are satisfied and the policy cannot extend beyond the employee's likely period of service with the business (i.e. not beyond his term of contract or beyond retirement age), then a term exceeding five years is treated as short-term.

If these conditions are not satisfied, there is no tax deduction. Usually any subsequent monies paid on a claim under the policy are not taxable.

(p) *Long-term Unemployed*

Employers may claim a double deduction in respect of certain wages/salaries paid, and the Employers' PRSI thereon, to employees who were long-term unemployed. The double deduction applies for the first three years of employment.

3. Watch out for Receipts Which are Specifically Exempt:

- Interest on tax overpaid.
- Most employment grants/employment-based assistance received from the State and State bodies.

4. Remember Certain Items are Treated Differently for Accounts and Tax Purposes

Fixed assets	**Instead**
Adjust for depreciation, grants amortised, profit/loss on sale of fixed assets	Give capital allowances and do relevant balancing allowance/charge computations

Assets leased under finance leases

Add back finance lease interest	Give a deduction for gross lease payments made, i.e. interest plus capital, during the year

Royalties, etc. which are allowed as a charge

Not deductible on an accruals basis	Allow deduction when paid

Provisions made under IAS 37

Provisions made under IAS 37, which deals with provisions, contingent liabilities and contingent assets, are generally allowable for tax purposes, provided that the provision would be allowable under general rules if it were an expense, e.g. a provision in relation to a capital item would not be deductible.

5. Interest

Interest is deductible on an accruals basis if it is *trade* related, i.e. it is treated the same as the financial statements and therefore no adjustment is required. This is the case even if the money is borrowed to buy capital assets, which is due to a Revenue concession.

There are anti-avoidance rules which deny an interest deduction in certain situations.

Other interest, which is not trade related, must be disallowed in calculating Case I.

- If it is interest on monies borrowed for a property generating rental income, the interest will be allowed as a Case V expense (provided that it is not pre-letting interest).
- If it is interest on monies borrowed to lend to, or invest in, another company, it will either qualify for relief as a non-trade charge (see **Chapter 23** regarding conditions to be satisfied and note where it is claimed in the pro-forma computation) or there is no relief for the expense.

6. Payments to Directors and Other Employees

Remember bona fide directors' salaries, fees, benefits payable for directors are deductible unlike the drawings/salary of a self-employed person. Such income is, of course, assessable in the hands of the individual director under Schedule E. Where a director has a company car available for private use, there is a deduction for the "personal element" for corporation tax purposes unlike the personal element of a self-employed person. Again, a director with the use of a company car for private purposes will of course suffer tax on the benefit in kind. Remuneration paid to directors is tax deductible, provided that it is not excessive.

22.4 Capital Allowances (Including Intangibles)

(**Note:** in the exam you will be given the figure for capital allowances. You will not have to do any capital allowance computations.)

22.4.1 Intangibles

There is tax relief for capital expenditure incurred by companies on the provision of intangible assets for the purposes of a trade. In summary, the scheme provides for capital allowances against taxable income on capital expenditure incurred by companies on the provision of intangible assets for the purposes of a trade. If the expenditure is incurred before trading commences, it will be allowed when the relevant trade commences.

The scheme applies to intangible assets which are recognised as such under generally accepted accounting practice and which are included in the specified categories listed in the legislation.

An asset may be recognised as an intangible asset in a company's financial statements only if:

- the cost of the asset can be reliably measured and
- it is probable that future economic benefits attributable to the asset will flow to the enterprise.

The list of specified intangible assets includes, patents, registered designs, trade marks, brands, copyrights, domain names, know-how and related goodwill to the extent that it relates to these categories of intangible property.

Companies are eligible for a writing down allowance which reflects the standard accounting treatment of intangible assets. However, companies can opt instead for a fixed write-down period of 15 years at a rate of **7% per annum and 2% in the final year.**

The normal rules in relation to balancing allowances/charges apply on the disposal of an intangible asset, with a significant exception.

There is no clawback of allowances where an intangible asset is disposed of more than 10 years after the beginning of the accounting period in which the asset was first provided, provided that the disposal does not result in a connected company claiming allowances in respect of capital expenditure on the asset.

There are a number of restrictions applying so as to ensure that:

1. relief is targeted to business **activities** (amounting to the conduct of a **relevant trade**) in which the specified intangible assets are used;
2. the aggregate amount of capital allowances and related interest which may be claimed in any accounting period is limited to 80% of the trading income of the relevant trade. Related interest for the purpose of this latter restriction is interest incurred as a trading expense on borrowings to fund expenditure on intangible assets for which capital allowances are claimed; and
3. the capital allowances may only be offset against income from a "relevant trade", i.e. a trade consisting of:

   - managing, developing or exploiting the intangible assets; or
   - activities which consist of the sale of goods or services that derive the greater part of their value from the intangible assets or whose value is increased by the use of the intangible assets.

Example 1

	Accounting Period 1	Accounting Period 2
	€	€
Income from relevant trade before allowances:	10 m	11 m
Capital allowances available under scheme:	9 m	9 m
Allowances carried forward from previous AP:	NIL	1 m
Calculation of restriction		
80% of income from relevant trade:	8 m	8.8 m
Computation of income		
Income from relevant trade before allowances:	10 m	11 m
Capital allowances [restricted as above]:	8 m	8.8 m
Income chargeable:	2 m	2.2 m
Allowances carried forward to next AP:	1 m	1.2 m

You will recall that there is a stamp duty exemption for qualifying intellectual property. The definition of intangible assets for this relief is the same as the definition of intellectual property for the purposes of stamp duty.

22.5 R&D Tax Credit

22.5.1 Overview

Section 766 TCA 1997 provides for a tax credit for companies of 25% of qualifying expenditure on research and development (R&D). Where qualifying expenditure is not more than €100,000, the tax credit is 25% of the qualifying expenditure. Where qualifying expenditure exceeds €100,000, the amount which will qualify for the tax credit is €100,000 plus incremental expenditure over the amount spent in the base year, subject to the proviso that the amount which qualifies for the tax credit cannot exceed the actual expenditure on R&D in the year.

There is no minimum spend required and there is no limit. Normal revenue type expenditure (such as consumables, salaries, overheads) and expenditure on plant and machinery qualify. The tax credit is available to all companies within the charge to Irish tax that undertake R&D activities within the European Economic Area (EEA). The tax credit is available for the **first €100,000** R&D spend and thereafter, for **incremental R&D expenditure over a threshold amount, which is the R&D expenditure incurred in a corresponding period in 2003**. The table below sets out examples of the tax credit which would apply depending on a company's R&D expenditure in 2012 and 2003:

Expenditure Incurred In:		Incremental Expenditure	Qualifying Expenditure	Tax Credit @ 25%
2012	2003			
€	€	€	€	€
90,000	100,000	Nil	90,000	22,500
90,000	Nil	90,000	90,000	22,500
140,000	150,000	Nil	100,000	25,000
120,000	80,000	40,000	120,000	30,000
250,000	130,000	120,000	220,000*	55,000

*(100,000 + 120,000)

Expenditure on buildings can also qualify for credit – see **Section 22.5.8**.

The 25% credit can be offset to save or get a refund of corporation tax, or since 1 January 2012 the credit or part of it can be used to reward key employees (excluding directors) working in the R&D activities of the company, i.e. they can receive some tax free emoluments from the company. If the credit or some of it is given to the employee(s), then that part of the credit is not available to the company to offset against corporation tax.

22.5.2 Utilisation of R&D Tax Credit

Any credit, not given to a key employee working in R&D, can be claimed against corporation tax. Claims must be made within 12 months of the end of the accounting period.

- The credit is used to **first reduce** the liability to **corporation tax for that accounting period**.
- The company may then offset any unused portion of the credit against the corporation tax of the **preceding accounting period**.
- Where a company has offset the credit against the corporation tax of the preceding accounting period or where no corporation tax arises for that period, and an excess still remains, the company may make a claim to have the amount of that **excess paid** to them by the Revenue Commissioners in **three instalments**. The three instalments will be paid over a period of at least 33 months from the end of the accounting period in which the expenditure was incurred. Students are required to do a computation involving claiming the credit against corporation tax payable but are not required to do a calculation involving a repayment of the credit.
- There is a limit on the amount of tax credits payable to a company by Revenue. The limit refers to expenditure on R&D activities and on buildings which qualify for the credit. The amount cannot exceed the greater of:
  - The corporation tax payable by the company for the 10 years prior to the accounting period preceding the period in which the expenditure was incurred, or
  - The amount of PAYE, PRSI, USC and levies, which the company is required to remit in the period in which the expenditure was incurred and in the previous accounting period, as adjusted for prior claims.
- Any credit which has not been offset against corporation tax or refunded is available to offset against corporation tax of future accounting periods.

Example

In the accounting period ended 31/12/2012 PQR Ltd incurred €400,000 of qualifying expenditure (after deduction of the threshold amount) on R&D.
The following shows the company's corporation tax liability.

Accounting Period Liability

12 months ended 31/12/2011 €30,000
12 months ended 31/12/2012 €10,000
12 months ended 31/12/2013 €15,000
12 months ended 31/12/2014 €10,000

Tax credit due in respect of the accounting period ended 31/12/2012
       €400,000 @ 25%   =   €100,000.

Of this €100,000, €20,000 is surrendered to key employees working in R&D.

Offset of tax credit as follows:

	CT Liability	Order	Tax credit
12 months ended 31/12/2011	€30,000	2	€30,000
12 months ended 31/12/2012	€10,000	1	€10,000

The unclaimed credit of €100,000 − €20,000 − €10,000 − €30,000 = €40,000 may be reclaimed from Revenue over the next three years or so to the extent it has not been used to offset against CT of subsequent accounting periods. This repayment assumes that the company has paid sufficient CT, PAYE, PRSI, USC and other levies.
The credit is **in addition to the normal tax relief at 12.5% for the expenditure.**

22.5.3   Qualified Company

The company must be a "qualified company" in order for the credit to apply, i.e. a company that satisfies the following conditions:

■ the company itself must carry on a trade, *or* be a 51% subsidiary of a trading company *or* be a member of a trading group (i.e. a 51% subsidiary of a holding company of a trading company);
■ it must carry out R&D activities;
■ it must maintain a record of its R&D expenditure; and
■ it must maintain separate records if it has R&D activities in separate geographical locations.

22.5.4   Qualifying R&D Activities

R&D activities means systematic, investigative or experimental activities in the field of science or technology, being one or more of the following:

■ basic research;
■ applied research; and
■ experimental development.

Each of these is defined in tax law.

In addition, activities will not be R&D activities unless they:
■ seek to achieve scientific or technological advancement; and
■ involve the resolution of scientific or technological uncertainty.

22.5.5 Qualifying R&D Expenditure

The law is drafted in terms that are applicable to groups of companies. A single company is treated as a group of one company. Expenditure incurred by a company on R&D activities carried out by the company in an EU Member State or an EEA Member State qualifies. However, in the case of an Irish tax resident company, the credit is available only if the expenditure on the R&D does not otherwise qualify for a tax benefit elsewhere. Also, this law does not apply to expenditure on a building or structure – see **Section 22.5.8** for the rules on buildings used for R&D.

Before expenditure can be regarded as expenditure on R&D for the purposes of the tax credit, it must qualify for tax relief in the State under *one* of the following:

- An amount which is an allowable deduction of a trade or as a charge on income (or would be but for accounting rules); this does not include capital allowances.
- Expenditure which is allowable as capital allowances on plant or machinery, or under special rules that provide for an allowance for capital expenditure on scientific research.
- Other expenditure that qualifies for scientific research allowance.

Where plant or machinery will not be used wholly and exclusively for R&D activities, a proportionate allocation, as appears to the Inspector (or on appeal to the Appeal Commissioners) to be just and reasonable, will be made of the expenditure on such plant and machinery for the purposes of determining the amount that will be treated as wholly and exclusively incurred on R&D activities.

In general, the cost of sub-contracting or outsourcing R&D will not qualify for the tax credit. However, an amount of up to €100,000, or up to 5% of total R&D expenditure, whichever is higher, which is paid to a university or institute of higher education to carry on R&D activity, may qualify. Expenditure incurred by companies subcontracting R&D activities to unconnected parties may qualify for the tax credit to a limit of up to 10% of qualifying R&D expenditure in any one year, or €100,000, whichever is higher.

Interest payments do not qualify as expenditure on R&D.

22.5.6 Groups

As pointed out at **Section 22.5.1**, where expenditure on R&D exceeds €100,000, the amount which will qualify for the tax credit is €100,000 plus incremental expenditure over a threshold amount, which is the R&D expenditure incurred in a corresponding period in 2003 (subject to the proviso that the amount which qualifies for the tax credit cannot exceed the actual expenditure on R&D in the year).

Where a company is part of a group of companies the threshold amount is calculated on a group-wide basis and compared with current qualifying expenditure incurred by all members of the group. However, the law provides that where a group has different R&D centres in separate geographical locations (not less than 20 kms apart) and subsequently ceases to use one of those centres for the purposes of a trade, the expenditure on R&D activities in respect of that centre may be excluded in the calculation of the "threshold amount". There are anti-avoidance provisions accompanying this provision.

The definition of a group is the same as that for loss relief purposes as outlined in **Chapter 25**, except that the shareholding requirement is only 51%, i.e. a parent and its 51% subsidiaries form a group. In addition, companies are treated as being in the same group, for the purposes of this credit, if they are under common control. The members of the group that incur expenditure on R&D in the current period may allocate the expenditure between them in such manner as they wish. Any such allocation is to be specified in writing to the Inspector of Taxes. If no allocation is made by the group members, the relief is allocated between the group members who incurred qualifying expenditure in the current period in the same proportion as the amount of total group expenditure the company incurred, i.e. if a group member incurred 50% of the group qualifying R&D expenditure in the current period, that group member will be allocated 50% of the relief available to the group.

Corporation tax of an accounting period of a company can be reduced by 25% of so much of the qualifying expenditure of the group on R&D as has been allocated to the company.

Where in an accounting period, the amount of the credit exceeds the corporation tax against which it can be offset, the excess is to be carried back for offset against corporation tax payable in the preceeding accounting period and a refund of any unused credits may be claimed as outlined at **Section 22.5.2**. Unused credits can be carried forward indefinitely.

22.5.7   Other Issues

Expenditure that is met by any direct or indirect EU or EEA grant assistance is not considered to be expenditure incurred by the company and will therefore not be eligible for the credit.

Expenditure incurred under cost sharing or pooling arrangements will qualify for the tax credit only to the extent that the expenditure is incurred by the qualified company in the carrying on by it of qualifying R&D activities. If the company carrying on the R&D in Ireland receives a cost-sharing contribution from another company in the international group, this receipt is ignored, i.e. it is the gross expenditure on R&D which is taken into account. Reimbursements or sharing of costs incurred *by* another company in the carrying on of R&D activities would not qualify.

Companies claiming the R&D tax credit are not required to hold the intellectual property rights resulting from the R&D work. Also, the R&D does not have to be successful. Documentary evidence must be maintained in respect of this credit claim. This includes details of the technical aspects of the project, the skills of the R&D team, as well as the basis for the actual costs and time incurred on the project.

22.5.8   Buildings Used for R&D

Relevant expenditure qualifies for the credit, i.e.:

- expenditure on the construction, reconstruction, repair or renewal (including the provision of water, sewage or heating facilities in the course of restoration or repair) of a "qualifying building". A "qualifying building" is a building or structure used for the purposes of R&D activities in the EU or EEA. At least 35% of the use of the building must be for R&D purposes. Expenditure on the acquisition of land, machinery or plant and expenditure which qualifies for relief as outlined in **Section 22.5.5** is not included;
- expenditure that qualifies for industrial buildings allowance; and
- does not qualify for tax relief in another EEA country.

Under section 766A TCA 1997, credit is available in respect of expenditure on the construction, including refurbishment, of a building or structure, where the R&D activities carried on by a company in that building or structure over a period of four years (referred to as the "specified relevant period") represents at least **35% of all activities** carried on in the building or structure. The credit is calculated by reference only to the portion of the building or structure to be used for R&D activities. (The rules were different in the past.)

Where a qualified company (see **Section 22.5.3**) incurs relevant expenditure on a qualifying building the corporation tax of the company may be reduced by 25% of the "specified relevant expenditure". "Specified relevant expenditure" means the same proportion of relevant expenditure as the R&D activities carried on by the company for the specified relevant period bears to the total of all activities carried on by the company in that building for that period, e.g. if a company incurs expenditure on the construction of a building and 50% of the building is to be used for R&D activities, then only 50% of the construction expenditure will be "specified relevant expenditure".

The tax credit is utilised in the same manner as set out in **Section 22.5.2**.

Example

Rev Ltd constructed a building in Kildare in the accounting period ended 31/12/2012 at a cost of €1 million. The R&D activities to be carried on by the company in that building over the specified relevant period will represent 40% of all activities carried on in the building or structure. The tax credit is calculated as follows:

Specified relevant expenditure	€1,000,000 @ 40% =	€400,000
Tax credit	€400,000 @ 25% =	€100,000.

The full amount of the tax credit of €100,000 is used to reduce the corporation tax liability in respect of the accounting period ended 31/12/2012. If any excess remains it may be carried back to reduce the corporation tax of the preceding accounting period. A refund of any unused credits may be claimed as outlined at **Section 22.5.2**. Unused credits may be carried forward indefinitely.

Example

High Tech Ltd, a technology company, is an Irish subsidiary of a US multinational. It has had an R&D programme for a number of years. During the year ended 31 December 2003, it spent €400,000 on revenue and capital expenditure (excl. buildings) on its R&D programme. During 2012, it significantly expanded its R&D programme. Its R&D spend was as follows:

- a new building at a cost of €2 million, of which €200,000 was the cost of the site;
- €200,000 on new machinery; and
- €500,000 on salaries, overheads, etc.

High Tech Ltd has a cost sharing agreement with its US parent company and fellow subsidiaries. As a result, High Tech Ltd received a contribution of €350,000 from these companies towards the cost of its R&D programme. High Tech Ltd satisfies the conditions regarding genuine R&D, maintaining records, etc. High Tech Ltd's corporation tax payable for the year ended 31 December 2012, before R&D credit, is €582,000.

What is the R&D tax credit due to High Tech Ltd for the year ended 31 December 2012 and what is the final corporation tax payable, assuming that €25,000 of the credits are surrendered to key employee(s) working in R&D?

continued overleaf

Tax credit due on Qualifying R&D expenditure	€
Machinery	200,000
Salaries, overheads, etc.	500,000
	700,000
First €100,000 qualifies	100,000
Qualifying on an incremental basis	
€700,000 − €400,000	300,000
Qualifying for credit	400,000
R&D tax credit at 25%	100,000
Less: surrendered to key R&D staff	25,000
Credit due against CT	75,000
Tax credit due on R&D building	
Expenditure on building	2,000,000
Less site cost	(200,000)
	1,800,000
Total credit due re building at 25%	450,000
Corporation tax payable	€
Originally due	582,000
Less R&D tax credits	(75,000)
R&D tax credit on building	(450,000)
Corporation tax payable	57,000

22.5.9   Clawback

If the building or structure is sold or ceases to be used by the company for R&D activities or for the purpose of the same trade that was carried on by the company at the start of the "specified relevant period", within 10 years of being incurred for the purposes of R&D, no further credit is to be given and any credit already given is to be withdrawn. The withdrawal is by way of a Case IV assessment of four times the credit granted. This amount is then taxed at 25%, i.e. the credit given is clawed back.

Questions (to Chapter 22)

Review Questions

(See Suggested Solutions to Review Questions at the end of this text.)

Question 22.1

Telstar Ltd. a company which commenced to trade in 2001 makes up its accounts each year to 31 December. The Income Statement to 31 December 2012 is as follows:

		€	€
Gross profit			239,800
IDA grant for extension of premises			10,000
IDA employment grant			1,000
Patent royalty (net) (1)			1,600
Discount received			3,300
Dividends from Irish quoted shares			1,300
Profit on sale of van (2)			1,000
Profit on sale of shares (3)			2,000
Bank deposit interest (paid gross)			600
			260,600
LESS:	Discount given	3,000	
	Goods stolen	3,000	
	Business overdraft interest	5,800	
	Depreciation	15,149	
	Van expense	3,400	
	Motor expenses (4)	6,800	
	Bad debts	2,300	
	Obsolete stock - written off	2,600	
	Salaries and wages	95,840	
	Telephone	311	
	Entertainment (5)	2,700	
	Finance lease charges (6)	1,300	
	Legal fees (7)	2,400	144,600
	Profit before tax		116,000

Notes

1. The patent royalty was received in December 2012.

2. Profit on sale of van
   The van was acquired second hand on 3/2/07 for €12,000. It was sold on 5/5/2012 for €4,000. The net book value of the van at 31/12/2011 was €3,000.

3. Profit on sale of shares

   These shares were acquired on 31/3/2001 for €4,000 and sold on 30/4/2012 for €6,000.

4. There are two cars

	€
Mercedes purchased second-hand on 30/6/2012	
Cost	28,000
Expenses	800
Category B car leased on 1/2/2010	
Cost	25,000
Operating lease payments	6,000

5. The charge for entertainment is made up as follows:

	€
Prizes for top salesperson of the year	900
Christmas party for staff	750
Christmas gifts for suppliers	150
Reimbursement of managing director for costs incurred entertaining customers at home	350
General customer entertainment	550
	2,700

6. Finance lease charges

   These relate to a machine leased in 2010, the cost of which is capitalised in the company's accounts. The lease agreement states that the burden of wear and tear remains with the lessor. Total repayments made during the year ended 31 December 2012 were €9,400, which included both capital repayments and finance charges.

7. The legal fees relate to the extension of the premises.

8. Capital allowances for the year are €7,272.

9. The company paid €80,000 of corporation tax on its 2011 profits.

Requirement

Calculate the corporation tax liability for the year ended 31 December 2012 and show the dates on which it is payable.

Question 22.2

The Profit and Loss Account of **Zaco Ltd** for the year ended 30 September 2012 is as follows:

	€	€
Sales		2,450,000
Cost of sales		(1,959,750)
Gross profit		490,250
Less: Salaries and wages	62,500	
Rent and rates	5,400	
Repairs (1)	16,100	
Insurance	1,720	
Professional fees (2)	1,600	
Depreciation	13,000	

Audit Fees	1,000	
Subscriptions (3)	2,400	
Entertainment (4)	600	
Staff award (5)	1,000	
Discount allowed	320	
Bank interest	7,060	
Light and heat	12,250	(124,950)
Add: Dividends (6)	3,600	
Bad debts recovered	300	
Profit on sale of investments (7)	5,200	
Interest on tax overpaid	1,200	
Profit on sale of fixtures and fittings (8)	4,300	14,600
Profit before Tax		379,900

Notes

1. Repairs
   Includes improvements to offices €5,200.

2. Professional fees
   Includes debt collection fees €200, architects fees re office improvements €300.

3. Subscriptions
   Includes political donations of €750 and staff race sponsorship of €1,000.

4. Entertainment
   This is made up as follows:

	€
Customer entertainment	450
Supplier entertainment	150
	600

5. Staff award
   A special award of €1,000 was made to an employee who achieved first place in Ireland in his engineering examinations during the year.

6. Dividends

Irish dividends	–	cash amount	€3,000
UK dividends	–	cash amount	€600

   The UK dividends are from trading profits and Zaco Ltd owns less than 1% of the shares. (Therefore, as we will see later, they are taxable @ 12.5%.)

7. Sale of investments

	€	€
Irish National Loan Stock		
Cost May 2007	2,148	
Proceeds June 2012	2,800	652

   Shares in quoted investment company

Cost June 1997	1,000	
Proceeds July 2012	5,548	4,548
		5,200

8. Profit on sale of plant

   Cost €8,000 in August 2010 and sold for €11,100 in September 2012. Net book value was €6,800 on 30/09/2011.

9. The capital allowances (including balancing allowances and charges) are €9,846.

10. There are capital losses forward of €10,000.

Requirement

Calculate the company's corporation tax liability for the year.

Question 22.3

From the following information you are required to calculate the corporation tax liability of **ALPHA LTD** for the year ended 31 December 2012.

Profit and Loss Account

		€	€
Sales			3,450,000
Cost of sales			(2,850,000)
Gross profit			600,000
Less: Salaries and wages	(1)	71,300	
Rent and rates	(2)	7,600	
Repairs	(3)	18,500	
Insurance	(4)	1,350	
Loss on sale of investments	(5)	600	
Legal expenses	(6)	2,700	
Commissions		9,209	
Depreciation		13,260	
Audit fees		1,550	
Subscriptions	(7)	3,400	
Discounts allowed		900	
Bank interest	(8)	3,300	
Other interest	(9)	7,000	
Light and heat		11,234	
Motor expenses	(10)	33,126	
Sundry	(11)	3,740	
Entertainment expenses	(12)	1,191	
Finance lease charges	(13)	1,700	(191,660)
Add: Irish dividends	(14)	4,500	
Gain on sale of Irish shares	(15)	1,000	
Amortisation of IDA grant	(16)	240	

Interest on tax overpaid	475	
Interest on national loan stock	2,500	
Rent received	6,000	
Deposit interest (received gross)	1,500	
Bad debts	50	16,265
Profit before tax		424,605

Notes:

1. Salaries and wages include €25,000 in respect of staff bonuses relating to the year ended 31 December 2012 which were not paid until 5 January 2013.
2. Rent and rates include an amount of €1,000 relating to part of the company's premises which has been let to a sub-tenant.
3. Repairs include an amount of €15,000 for an extension to the factory premises.
4. Insurance includes an amount of €350 relating to the let premises.
5. Loss on sale of investments

   UK shares purchased 2007

	€	€
Cost		10,000
Proceeds		9,400

6. Legal expenses

Debt collection	700
Extension to factory	2,000
	2,700

7. Subscriptions

Chamber of commerce	430
Local football club	20
Trade association	1,135
Political	1,815
	3,400

8. Bank interest
   Bank interest includes an amount of €1,500 relating to borrowings taken out to finance the extension to the factory premises.

9. Other interest
   Interest on monies borrowed from bank to acquire shares in a trading subsidiary, where Alpha Ltd is represented on the board and there has been no recovery of capital. €7,000 gross was paid during the year (this issue is dealt with in **Chapter 23**). The interest is allowed as a charge.

10. Motor expenses
    The company leased six new motor cars on 1 April 2011, CO_2 emissions category B. The retail price of each, at the time the lease contracts were entered into, was €25,000.

The motor expenses can be analysed as follows:

	€
Leasing charges on leased cars	21,126
Running costs of leased cars	12,000
	33,126

11. Sundry

	€
Interest on late payments of VAT	1,630
Parking fines	30
Christmas party	500
Gifts to customers	541
General office expenses	1,039
	3,740

12. Entertainment

	€
Hotel and accommodation for overseas Customers	1,191

13. Finance lease charges

These relate to new machinery leased in 2010, the cost of which is capitalised in the company's accounts. The lease agreement states that the burden of wear and tear remains with the lessor. Total repayments made during the year ended 31 December 2012 were €12,200, which included both capital repayments and finance charges.

14. Irish dividends

	€
Dividend on quoted shares	1,500
Dividend from subsidiary	3,000
	4,500

15. Sale of Irish quoted shares

	€
Cost (July 2007)	19,000
Proceeds (January 2012)	20,000
Gain	1,000

16. IDA grant

An IDA grant of €1,200 was received on 2 April 2012 in respect of the factory extension. This is being amortised over a five-year period.

17. Capital allowances for the accounting period are €26,006.

18. The company has a trading loss of €20,000 carried forward from the year ended 31 December 2011. (This issue is dealt with in **Chapter 24**)

19. There is a capital loss forward of €215 from year ended 31 December 2011.

Income Tax on Annual Payments and Charges on Income

23

Learning Objectives

After studying this chapter you will have developed competency in the following:

Annual Payments

- A company can either make or receive an annual payment.
- An annual payment is a payment from which income tax at the standard rate, currently 20%, must be withheld. There are some exceptions to this withholding requirement, e.g. payments can be made gross within groups.
- If a company makes an annual payment, it must withhold 20% tax and pay it over to Revenue when it is paying corporation tax.
- Where a company receives an annual payment net, it will receive an amount net of 20% tax. The company is taxable on the gross amount. The tax withheld is creditable against the company's corporation tax payable for the accounting period.

Charges

- A charge is deductible either against total profits if it is a non-trade charge or against trading income if it is a relevant trading charge. The most common examples of non-trade charges are covenants and protected interest (which are deductible against total profits). Patent royalties are an example of a relevant trading charge (which are deductible against Case I).
- Where interest is deductible against a particular source of profits, deduct it (e.g. trade interest is deductible Case I; interest on loan to purchase rental property is deductible Case V). Where interest is not deductible against a particular source of profits, then the interest is not deductible unless the company satisfies the conditions to have it deductible as protected interest.
- Expenses which are allowed as charges must be added back in the calculation of Case I income and instead allowed as a charge when paid.

23.1 Annual Payments

23.1.1 Relevant Payments

A company must deduct income tax when making relevant payments. Relevant payments include:

- Annual interest (subject to exceptions – see below)
- Patent royalties
- Covenants
- Rents paid to non-residents in respect of property in the State
- Health insurance payments for employees
- Loans to participators in close companies

The following annual interest may be paid without deduction of tax:

- interest paid to a bona fide bank or building society in the State and other companies that carry on a trade of lending and satisfy certain conditions;
- interest paid to a resident of a country with which Ireland has a tax treaty, the terms of which provide that withholding tax is to be reduced to nil;
- interest paid, in the ordinary course of a trade or business, to a company resident in the EU or a country with which Ireland has signed a tax treaty where that country imposes a tax that generally applies to interest receivable in that country by companies from sources outside that country;
- interest which is treated as a distribution, e.g. interest in excess of a certain amount paid to a director of a close company (see **Chapter 28**);
- annual payments made by a member of the 51% same tax group (see **Chapter 25**) to another member of that group are made without deduction of tax; and
- interest and royalty payments made by a company to its associated company (25% direct shareholding relationship) resident in the EU or Switzerland, subject to certain conditions being satisfied.

23.1.2 Payment of Tax Deducted from Annual Payments

Income tax, at the standard rate of 20%, is deducted from any relevant payment and must be paid over to Revenue. For collection of tax purposes, this **income tax is treated as corporation tax and is included as part of the company's corporation tax liability**. Because it is treated as corporation tax, it is taken into account when establishing the amount of the preliminary tax and the balance of tax which has to be paid.

23.1.3 Credit for Tax Suffered on Annual Payments Received

Where, in an accounting period, a company receives an annual payment from which Irish income tax has been deducted, the tax withheld at source is deductible against its corporation tax liability.

23.2 Charges on Income

23.2.1 General

Certain payments, such as interest, annual payments and patent royalties, rank as "charges on income" and are allowed as deductions of the accounting period in which they are **paid**.

If they are **non-trade charges**, they are allowed **against the total profits** (including chargeable gains); if they are **trade charges**, they are allowed **against trading income**.

Frequently, income tax has to be withheld when charges are paid (as they are annual payments). If income tax is withheld from the payment, it is the **gross** amount that is deductible. The income tax withheld in paying the charge is paid over to Revenue as part of the corporation tax liability of the accounting period in which the payment is made.

A payment does not rank as a charge on income in so far as it is deductible in computing income from a particular source. Thus, if a company pays interest wholly and exclusively for the purposes of its trade, such interest will be deductible in computing the profits of its trade and will therefore not fall to be treated as a charge on income.

Likewise, interest on borrowed money employed in the purchase, improvement or repair of let premises, which is allowable as a deduction in computing the amount for assessment under Case V in respect of rents receivable, would not rank as a charge on income.

However, patent royalties and covenants are specifically disallowed in arriving at income from any source for corporation tax purposes. Accordingly, such amounts can only be allowed by way of a "charge on income" and only if they satisfy the necessary conditions.

23.2.2 Amounts Treated as Charges

The following amounts, subject to the above, are treated as "charges on income":

1. Yearly interest (other than interest allowable in computing profits chargeable under Case I and Case V of Schedule D).
2. Annuities or other annual payments, e.g. certain covenants.
3. Patent royalties.
4. Any other interest payable in the State on an advance from a bona fide bank or a bona fide discount house or bona fide stock exchange member in the EU.

All of the above items may be paid under deduction of income tax at 20%. However, it is the gross amount which will be allowed as a charge on income.

23.2.3 Interest Qualifying as a Charge

This type of interest is commonly known as "protected interest". The term "protected interest" is used to denote interest on borrowings used for the acquisition of shares in, or for lending to, certain companies. There are a number of conditions to be satisfied before interest can be regarded as "protected interest".

1. The investing company must use the proceeds of the loan:
    (a) in acquiring any part of the ordinary share capital of:
        (i) a company, the business of which consists wholly or mainly of the carrying on of a trade or trades, or a company the income of which consists wholly or mainly of profits or gains chargeable under Case V of Schedule D; or
        (ii) a company the business of which consists wholly or mainly of the holding of stocks, shares or securities of a company referred to in (i);
        and where the loan is used to subscribe for shares in a company, the company into which the investment is made must use the funds received for the purposes of its trade or purchase, improvement or repair of Case V premises or holding of stocks, etc. whichever is appropriate; or

(b) to lend to a company referred to in (a) where the money is used wholly or mainly for the purposes of its trade or the purchase, improvement or repair of Case V premises, or for the purpose of holding such stocks, whichever is appropriate; or

(c) to lend to a company referred to in (a) where the money is used wholly and exclusively by a connected company, where the connected company exists wholly or mainly for the purpose of carrying on a trade or trades, or the income of which consists wholly or mainly of profits or gains chargeable under Case V of Schedule D and the money is used for the purposes of its trade or the purchase, improvement or repair of Case V premises, whichever is appropriate; or

(d) in paying off another loan where relief could have been obtained for interest on that other loan under (a) or (b) above if it had not been paid off.

2. The investing company at the time the interest is paid must have a "material interest" in the company that uses the money. "Material interest" means the beneficial ownership of, or the ability to control, directly or through a connected company, **more than 5%** of the ordinary share capital of the company in which it has invested.

3. At least one **director** of the investing company must be a director of the company that uses the money throughout the period from the application of the proceeds of the loan until the interest is paid.

4. During the period referred to in (3), the investing company must **not have recovered any capital** from the company. If the investing company recovers any capital and does not use the capital recovered to repay its loan, for the purpose of calculating the interest relief due, the investing company is deemed to have repaid a portion of the loan made. An investing company is regarded as recovering capital from the company if:

- the investing company sells any of its shares or the company repays any share capital;
- the company or a connected company repays a loan to the investing company; and
- the investing company receives consideration for the assignment of any debt due to it by the company.

There are also anti-avoidance provisions in the law to stop perceived abuses of the relief.

23.2.4 Relation of "Charges on Income" to Other Reliefs

Relief depends on whether the charge is a relevant trading charge, or a non-trade charge.

Relevant Trade Charges
Relevant trade charges (i.e. charges that are related to a trade, other than an excepted trade, e.g. patent royalties) are deductible against trading income of the accounting period in which the charges are paid. They can also be **relieved on a value basis**, or used to create or augment a **trading loss forward** (see **Chapter 24**).

Non-trade Charges
Charges, other than relevant trading charges, may be offset against a company's total profits of the period in which the charges are paid. As outlined in **Chapter 21**, Case III, IV and V income, and income from an excepted trade, are taxed at 25%, whereas Case I income is generally taxed at the standard rate of corporation tax, i.e. 12.5%. Where a

company has income taxed at the standard rate and at 25% and has paid non-trade charges, the legislation does not specify the order in which the non-trade charges are to be offset. Accordingly the company may choose how to offset the charges. Generally, therefore, a company will offset its non-trade charges against income taxed at 25% firstly. In Tax Briefing, a Revenue publication, they advised that they accept that such charges may be claimed against income chargeable at the highest rate.

Protected interest is an example of a non-trade charge. (Charges of an excepted trade, which is not examinable, are also dealt with in this way.)

Example

In the year ended 31 December 2012, a company had the following results:

	€
Case I (not an excepted trade)	100,000
Case V	50,000
Trade charges (patent royalties paid under deduction of tax)	10,000 (gross)
Non-trade charges (interest paid under deduction of tax)	30,000 (gross)
Corporation tax liability:	€
Case I	100,000
Trade charges	(10,000)
	90,000
Case V	50,000
Total Profits	140,000
Non-trade charges	(30,000)
Taxable	110,000
€90,000 × 12.5% =	11,250
(€50,000 − €30,000) €20,000 × 25% =	5,000
	16,250
Income tax withheld from charges	
€40,000 × 20%	8,000
Corporation tax due	24,250

Questions (to Chapter 23)

Review Questions

(See Suggested Solutions to Review Questions at the end of this text.)

Question 23.1

Nifty Investments Ltd had the following results for the year ended 31 March 2012:

	€
Trading profits	90,000
■ after charging the following amounts:	
Depreciation	10,000
Patent royalties (paid August 2011)	8,000 (Net)
Interest paid to an Irish bank on monies borrowed to invest in a company – conditions satisfied to qualify as protected interest	9,000
■ after crediting:	
Loan interest received October	6,000 (Net €4,800 actually received)
Bank interest received October	1,000 (Gross)
Chargeable gain before adjustment (January 2012)	11,000

Requirement

Compute the corporation tax payable by Nifty Investments Ltd for the year ended 31 March 2012.

Corporation Tax Loss Relief

Learning Objectives

After studying this chapter, you will have developed competency to understand that:

- The utilisation of losses depends on the type of loss and when it was incurred.
- All losses of a relevant trade can only be offset against trade profits of a relevant trade of the current year and prior year, i.e. they cannot be offset directly against income taxed at 25% and gains. However, relevant trading losses, which cannot be used against relevant trading income, are available on a value basis to reduce the corporation tax on total profits of the current year and prior year.
- Where a loss is carried back, it can only be offset against a profit arising or taxation in a period of the same length.
- All other "income" losses may only be offset against income from the same Case. Capital losses may only be offset against capital gains. Excess Case V capital allowances may be offset against total profits of the current year and prior year.
- Excess relevant trading charges (over relevant trading income) may be offset on a value basis against corporation tax of the current accounting period or carried forward as a Case I loss.
- Non-trade charges may be offset against total profits of the current accounting period. If they exceed total profits, the excess cannot be utilised by the company itself.
- Losses arising from pre-trading expenses can only be offset against future trading income. They cannot be utilised on a value basis.
- Normally trading losses can only be carried back one year, but they can be carried forward indefinitely against income of the same trade. On a cessation of the trade, there is no future trading income. Therefore, unused trading losses of the final 12 months may be carried back against trading income of the three preceding years.
- Where there is a change of ownership of the company, the trading losses will not be available to carry forward if there is a significant change in the trade.
- If a tax return is filed late, the amount of loss relief is restricted.

24.1 Relief for Losses in a Trade (other than Terminal Losses)

A company which incurs a "relevant trading loss" may obtain relief for the loss in one of the following ways:

(a)   By carry forward (section 396(1) TCA 1997).
(b)   By set off against relevant trading income in the same accounting period (section 396A(3) TCA 1997). This only arises if the company has more than one trade.
(c)   By set off against relevant trading income in the immediately preceding accounting period of the same length (section 396A(3) TCA 1997).
(d)   By claiming relief for the loss in the same accounting period on a "value" basis (section 396B(3) TCA 1997).
(e)   By claiming relief for the loss in the immediately preceding accounting period of the same length on a "value" basis (section 396B(3) TCA 1997).

A claim for loss relief under (b) to (e) must be made within two years of the end of the accounting period in which the loss occurs.

A section 396A claim must be made before a claim can be made under section 396B.

A "relevant trading loss" is a loss incurred in a trade other than an "excepted" or leasing trade. An excepted trade is one which consists of the following operations:

1.   Dealing in or developing land. This does not include:

   ■   construction operations;
   ■   dealing in fully developed land, e.g. land on which houses or other buildings have been built thereon by or for the company selling the land.

2.   Mining activities
3.   Petroleum activities

Most trading losses which you encounter in general, and at CAP 2 level, will be relevant trading losses. Accordingly, in the balance of these notes, losses are assumed to be relevant trading losses, unless otherwise stated (losses in an excepted trade are not examinable).

24.1.1 Carry Forward

A trading loss in an accounting period may be carried forward under section 396(1) indefinitely and set off against income from the **same trade** in succeeding accounting periods.

The loss must be set off in computing the trading income for an earlier accounting period in priority to a later accounting period.

Example 1
ABC Ltd, a distribution company, had the following results for the years ended 31 December 2011 and 2012.

	2011	2012
	€	€
Case I profit/(loss)	(50,000)	60,000
Taxable income		
Case I	Nil	60,000
Less section 396(1) relief		(50,000)
Taxable income	Nil	10,000

24.1.2 Relief by Offset against Relevant Trading Income

A trading loss may be offset against relevant trading income arising in:

(a)   the accounting period in which the loss was incurred and, if the loss has not been fully utilised in this fashion, against

(b)   the immediately preceding accounting period of the same length.

Any loss relieved by way of set off is not available for offset under section 396B on a value basis or for carry forward. The relevant trading income of an accounting period against which a loss is to be set off are those as first reduced by losses brought forward from earlier accounting periods.

Example 2
DEF Ltd, a distribution company, had the following results for the years ended 31 December 2011 and 2012.

	2011	2012
	€	€
Case I profit/(loss)	30,000	(50,000)
Taxable income		
Case I	30,000	Nil
Less section 396A(3) relief	(30,000)	
Taxable income	Nil	Nil

Relief may be obtained for the remaining loss of €20,000 by carrying it forward for offset against profits arising from the same trade in future accounting periods. (If the company had income taxable at 25%, the remaining loss could be used on a value basis).

Examples: Accounting Periods of Different Lengths
Example 3
GHI Ltd, a distribution company, had the following results for the year ended 31 December 2011 and for the nine-month accounting period ended 30 September 2012.

	2011	2012
	€	€
Case I profit/(loss)	30,000	(60,000)
Taxable income		
Case I	30,000	Nil
Less section 396A(3) relief (Note)	(22,500)	
Taxable income	7,500	Nil

Relief may be obtained for the remaining loss of €37,500 by carrying it forward for offset against profits arising from the same trade in future accounting periods. (If the company had income taxable at 25%, the remaining loss could be used on a value basis).

Note: As the loss arose in an accounting period nine months long, it may only be offset against 9/12ths of the relevant trading income for the year ended 31/12/2011.

Example 4

MNO Ltd, a distribution company, had the following results for the year ended 31 March 2011, the nine months ended 31 December 2011 and for the year ended 31 December 2012.

	Y/E 31/3 2011	P/E 31/12 2011	Y/E 31/12 2012
	€	€	€
Case I profit/(loss)	30,000	20,000	(60,000)
Taxable income			
Case I	30,000	20,000	Nil
Less section 396A(3) relief (Note)	(7,500)	(20,000)	
Taxable income	22,500	Nil	Nil

Note: The loss-making period was 12 months long. Accordingly, the loss to the extent not utilised against relevant trading profits of the nine-month period ended 31/12/2011 may be offset against relevant trading income arising in the three months to 31/3/2011, i.e. against 3/12ths of Case I income for the year ended 31 March 2011.

Relief may be obtained for the remaining loss of €32,500 by carrying it forward for offset against profits arising from the same trade in future accounting periods. (If the company had income taxable at 25%, the remaining loss could be used on a value basis).

24.1.3 Relief for Relevant Trading Losses on a Value Basis

Where in any accounting period a company incurs a relevant trading loss, as outlined above, the company may offset this loss against relevant trading income arising in the same accounting period or a preceding accounting period under section 396A(3). A company may also claim relief for relevant trading losses on a "value basis". The amount of the relevant trading loss for which relief may be claimed on a value basis is reduced by any relief which could have been claimed under section 396A(3), i.e. a full section 396A claim must be made before a claim can be made under section 396B. Even if a claim for relief has not been made under section 396A, the amount of the relevant trading loss for which relief may be claimed on a value basis is reduced by the amount for which relief *could have* been claimed under section 396A.

Relief is given for relevant trading losses on a value basis by reducing the "relevant corporation tax" payable by the company by an amount equal to the following formula:

Trading Company Taxed at the Standard Rate

In the case of a loss arising from a trade which would be taxable at the standard corporation tax rate, reduce "relevant corporation tax" by:

$$L \times \frac{R}{100}$$

where L = the excess of the relevant trading loss, i.e. the relevant trading loss as reduced by any relief claimable under section 396A, and

R = the standard rate of corporation tax applicable for the accounting period, i.e. 12.5%

The **"relevant corporation tax"** payable by a company is the corporation tax on profits which would be payable by the company if no relief for losses on a value basis were claimed, i.e. **corporation tax, not including any withholding taxes and any surcharge liability of a close company**.

Relief may be claimed on a value basis against relevant corporation tax arising in:

(a) the accounting period in which the loss was incurred and, if the loss has not been fully utilised in this fashion, against

(b) the immediately preceding accounting period of the same length. If the loss is carried back from a short accounting period to a longer accounting period, then only a proportion of the relevant corporation tax of the preceding accounting period may be relieved. See **Example 6** below.

Remember: Open a loss memo into which you record the amount of the loss and show how the loss is used.

Example 5

PQR Ltd, a distribution company, had the following results for the years ended 31 December 2011 and 2012.

	2011	2012
	€	€
Case I profit/(loss)	30,000	(55,000)
Case V income	10,000	10,000
Corporation tax computation		
Case I	30,000	Nil
Less section 396A(3) Relief (1)	(30,000)	
Taxable Case I income	Nil	Nil
Case V income	10,000	10,000
Corporation tax @ 25%	2,500	2,500
Relief on a value basis (2) (Note)	(625)	(2,500)
Corporation tax payable	1,875	Nil

Note

Losses available for relief on a value basis:

	€
Total loss	55,000
Offset under section 396A	(30,000)
Losses available for relief on a value basis	25,000

"Value" of losses:

$$€25,000 \ (L) \times \frac{12.5(R)}{100} = €3,125$$

Offset against relevant corporation tax 2012	2,500
Offset against relevant corporation tax 2011	625
	3,125

Examples – Accounting Periods of Different Lengths
Example 6
STU Ltd, a distribution company, had the following results for the year ended 31 December 2011 and for the nine-month accounting period ended 30 September 2012.

	2011 (12)	2012 (9)
	€	€
Case I profit/(loss)	30,000	(200,000)
Case V income	20,000	20,000
Corporation tax computation		
Case I	30,000	Nil
Less section 396A(3) relief (Note 1)	(22,500)(i)	
Taxable Case I income	7,500	Nil
Case V income	20,000	20,000
Taxable income	27,500	20,000
Corporation tax payable		
@ 12.5%	937	Nil
@ 25%	5,000	5,000
	5,937	5,000
Relief on a value basis (Note 2)	(4,453)(iii)	(5,000)(ii)
Corporation tax payable	1,484	Nil

(i) to (iii) show the sequence of the loss claims.

Note 1: As the loss arose in an accounting period nine months long, it may only be offset against 9/12ths of the relevant trading income for the year ended 31/12/2011.

Note 2: Relief on a value basis may only be claimed against 9/12ths of the corporation tax payable for the year ended 31/12/2011. The corporation tax for the year ending on 31/12/2011 is €5,937. Therefore, the relief is €5,937 × 9/12ths, i.e. €4,453.

Losses available to carry forward and offset against profits arising in subsequent years from the same trade are as follows:

	€
Total loss	200,000
Utilised by way of 396A(3) relief	(22,500)
Utilised by way of 396B(3) relief:	
Against 2012: €40,000 @ 12.5% = €5,000	(40,000)
Against 2011: €35,624 @ 12.5% = €4,453	(35,624)
Losses available to carry forward	101,876

Example 7

VWX Ltd, a distribution company, had the following results for the year ended 31 December 2011, the nine months ended 30 September 2012 and for the year ended 30 September 2013.

	Y/E 31/12 2011	P/E 30/9 2012	Y/E 30/9 2013
	€	€	€
Case I profit/(loss)	30,000	20,000	(250,000)
Case V	20,000	15,000	20,000

Corporation Tax computation

Case I	30,000	20,000	Nil
Less section 396A (3) relief (Note 1)	(7,500)	(20,000)	
Taxable Case I income	22,500	Nil	Nil
Case V income	20,000	15,000	20,000
Taxable income	42,500	15,000	20,000

Corporation Tax Payable

@ 12.5%	2,812	Nil	Nil
@ 25%	5,000	3,750	5,000
	7,812	3,750	5,000
Relief on a value basis (Note 2)	(1,953)	(3,750)	(5,000)
Corporation tax payable	5,859	Nil	Nil

Claims for loss relief are made:

■ first against trading income of 2012 and 2011; and
■ then against corporation tax, on a value basis against 2013 then 2012 and 2011.

Note 1: The loss-making period was 12 months long. Accordingly the loss to the extent not utilised against relevant trading income of the nine month period ended 30/9/2012 may be offset against relevant trading income arising in the three months to 31/12/2011, i.e. against 3/12ths of Case I income for the year ended 31 December 2011.

Note 2: Relief may be claimed on a value basis against corporation tax arising in the nine-month period ended 30/9/2012 and against 3/12ths of corporation tax of the year ended 31/12/2011. Corporation tax for the year ended 31/12/2011 is €7,812. 3/12ths of €7,812 = €1,953.

"Value" of 2013 losses:

$$€250,000 - €20,000 - €7,500 = €222,500 \text{ (L)} \times \frac{12.5 \text{ (R)}}{100} = €27,812$$

Losses available to carry forward and offset against profits arising in subsequent years from the same trade are as follows:

	€
Total loss	250,000
Utilised by way of 396A(3) relief:	
Against P/E 30/9/2012	(20,000)
Against Y/E 31/12/2011	(7,500)
Utilised by way of 396B(3) relief:	
Against Y/E 30/9/2013:	
€40,000 @ 12.5% = €5,000	(40,000)

continued overleaf

Against P/E 30/9/2012:
€30,000 @ 12.5% = €3,750   (30,000)
Against Y/E 31/12/2011:
€15,624 @ 12.5% = €1,953   (15,624)
Losses available to carry forward   136,876

i.e. €27,812 − €5,000 − €3,750 − €1,953 = €17,109 × 100/12.5% = €136,872
(Difference due to rounding.)

Example 8

A company's results are as follows:

	Year ended 31/12/2011	Year ended 31/12/2012
	€	€
Relevant trading profit/(loss)	100,000	(120,000)
Chargeable gains (non-development land)- adjusted	7,680	–
Chargeable gain 1/5/12 – development land	–	20,000
Deposit interest (received gross)	1,600	3,400

The company must firstly claim to have the loss of €120,000 set off as far as possible against the trading income of the accounting period to 31 December 2011 and then used on a value basis.

Accounting period 12 months to 31 December 2012

	€
Case III	3,400
Corporation tax @ 25%	850
Less relief on a value basis	(850) (ii)
Corporation tax payable	Nil

Losses may not be offset against the chargeable gain arising on the disposal of development land, as it is liable to CGT. Therefore, CGT of €20,000 × 30% = €6,000 is due.

Accounting period 12 months to 31 December 2011

	€
Case I	100,000
Less section 396A(3)	(100,000) (i)
Case I	–
Case III	1,600
Chargeable gains	7,680
Profit	9,280
Corporation tax	
€1,600 × 25% =	400
€7,680 × 12.5% =	960
	1,360
Less relief on a value basis	(1,360) (iii)
Corporation tax payable	Nil

(i) to (iii) show the sequence of the loss claims.

continued overleaf

	€
Loss Memo	
Relevant trading loss	120,000
Utilised by way of	
- section 396A(3) against y/e 31/12/2011	(100,000)
Utilised by way of	
- section 396B(3) against y/e 31/12/2012	
€6,800 × 12.5% = €850	(6,800)
Utilised by way of	
- section 396B(3) against y/e 31/12/2011	
€10,880 × 12.5% = €1,360	(10,880)
Loss forward to 2013	2,320

24.1.4 Set Off Against Total Profits

Trading losses on excepted trades can be offset against total profits, including chargeable gains, arising in:

(a) the accounting period in which the loss was incurred and if the loss has not been fully utilised in this fashion, against,

(b) the immediately preceding accounting period of the same length.

Losses from an excepted trade are not examinable.

24.2 Relief for Excess Charges

24.2.1 Relevant Trading Charges

As outlined in **Chapter 23**, relief is given for relevant trading charges under section 243A TCA 1997 (i.e. charges paid wholly and exclusively for the purposes of a trade other than a trade the profits of which are taxed at 25%), by deducting the amount paid in the accounting period from the company's Case I income. Where the amount of the relevant trading charges exceed Case I income, relief for the excess is given in two ways:

(a) by claiming relief for the excess in the same accounting period on a "value" basis (section 243B); or

(b) by carrying the excess forward as a trading loss (section 396(7)).

Claim for Relief on a Value Basis

Relief on a value basis for excess relevant trading charges is calculated in a similar manner to relief on a value basis for relevant trading losses.

Relief is given for excess relevant trading charges on a value basis by reducing the "relevant corporation tax" payable by the company by an amount equal to the following formula:

$$C \times \frac{R}{100}$$

where C = the excess relevant trading charges, i.e. the amount of the relevant trading charges which have not been used by offset against trading income, and

R = the standard rate of corporation tax applicable for the accounting period in which the loss arises.

The "relevant corporation tax" payable by a company is the corporation tax which would be payable by the company if no relief for excess relevant trading charges or relief under section 396B were claimed.

The sequence of claims is:

- **section 396(1), i.e. trading losses forward against income of the same trade;**
- **section 396A, i.e. trading losses against trading income;**
- **section 243A, i.e. trading charges against trading income;**
- **section 243B, i.e. trading charges against corporation tax on a value basis; and**
- **section 396B, i.e. trading losses against corporation tax on a value basis.**

Example 9

YZA Ltd, a distribution company, had the following results for the years ended 31 December 2011 and 2012:

	2011	2012
	€	€
Case I profit/(loss)	30,000	(70,000)
Relevant trading charges	20,000	15,000
Case V income	15,000	20,000
Corporation tax computation		
Case I	30,000	Nil
Less 396A(3) relief	(30,000)	–
Taxable Case I income	Nil	Nil
Case V income	15,000	20,000
Corporation tax @ 25%	3,750	5,000
Relief on a value basis:		
Excess trading charges (section 243B) (Note 1)	(2,500)	(1,875)
Losses (section 396B) (Note 2)	(1,250)	(3,125)
Corporation tax payable	Nil	Nil

Note 1: Excess 2011 charges are:

	€
Case I	30,000
Less section 396A relief	(30,000)
Less relevant charges	(20,000)
Excess charges	20,000

Value of excess charges: $€20,000 \times \dfrac{12.5\%}{100} = 2,500$

Excess 2012 charges are €15,000 as Case I is nil.

Value of excess charges: $€15,000 \times \dfrac{12.5\%}{100} = €1,875$

Note 2: section 396(B) relief is claimed after relief for excess charges "Value" of 2012 losses:

$€70,000 - €30,000 = €40,000 \text{ (L)} \times \dfrac{12.5\%}{100} = €5,000$

continued overleaf

Losses available to carry forward and offset against profits arising in subsequent years from the same trade are as follows:

	€
Total loss	70,000
Utilised by way of section 396A(3) relief:	
Against Y/E 31/12/2011	(30,000)
Utilised by way of section 396B(3) relief:	
Against Y/E 31/12/2012: €25,000 @ 12.5% = €3,125	(25,000)
Against Y/E 30/12/2011: €10,000 @ 12.5% = €1,250	(10,000)
Losses available to carry forward	5,000
i.e. €5,000 − €3,125 − €1,250 = €625 × 100/12.5% = €5,000	

Claim to Carry Excess Forward

If the amount of the relevant trading charges exceed Case I income, the excess may be treated as a Case I loss to be carried forward under section 396(1) for offset against future profits from the same trade. A claim for relief for excess charges on a value basis (section 243B) is not compulsory. If, however, a claim is made for relief under section 243B, the amount of the excess charges carried forward as a Case I loss is reduced by the amount of the charges for which relief has been claimed under section 243B.

Example 10

BCD Ltd, a distribution company, had the following results for the years ended 31 December 2011 and 2012:

	2011	2012
	€	€
Case I profit	10,000	80,000
Relevant trade charges	40,000	25,000
Case V income	10,000	10,000
	€	€
Corporation Tax computation		
Case I	10,000	80,000
Less section 396(1) loss (Note 2)	–	(10,000)
Less relevant trade charges	(10,000)	(25,000)
Taxable Case I income	Nil	45,000
Case V income	10,000	10,000
Total profits	10,000	55,000
Corporation tax @ 12.5%	–	5,625
Corporation tax @ 25%	2,500	2,500
Relief on a value basis:		
Excess charges (section 243B) (Note 1)	(2,500)	–
Corporation tax payable	Nil	8,125

continued overleaf

Note 1: Excess 2011 charges are:

	€
Case I	10,000
Less relevant charges	(40,000)
Excess charges	30,000

Value of excess charges: $\dfrac{€30,000 \times 12.5\%}{100} = €3,750$

Note 2: Excess charges carried forward as a loss:

$€3,750 - €2,500 = €1,250 \times \dfrac{100}{12.5} = €10,000$

24.2.2 Non-trade Charges

As outlined in **Chapter 23**, charges other than relevant trading charges may be offset against a company's total profits. Where non-trade charges exceed a company's total profits no relief may be obtained for the excess. In addition, where relief is claimed for losses under section 396B (i.e. relief for losses on a value basis), in calculating trading losses available for carry forward to subsequent years, the company is deemed to have used up any additional loss relief under 396B instead of claiming any relief for non-trade charges, expenses of management and other amounts deductible against total profits (except excess Case V capital allowances).

24.3 Pre-trading Losses

As outlined in **Chapter 22**, pre-trading expenses are deductible against income of the first accounting period of the company. However, if the pre-trading expenses exceed the income and thereby create a loss or if part of a loss arises from pre-trading expenses, they **may not be offset on a value basis** against corporation tax of the company for that accounting period. (Also, if the company has an existing trade, the pre-trading losses could not be offset against income of that other trade). In addition, the losses **may not be group relieved**. They can, however, be **carried forward** and offset against future income from the same trade.

24.4 Relief for Terminal Losses (Section 397)

A company may claim "terminal loss relief" in respect of trading losses which can be attributed to the whole or part of the 12-month period up to the date of cessation of trade, provided such losses have not, or cannot, otherwise be relieved from tax.

It is not necessary that the results of the final 12 months trading as a whole should show a loss. A terminal loss may arise if there is a loss in any other accounting periods which fall either wholly or partly within the final 12 months.

Where the accounting period which ends on the date of cessation is less than 12 months (i.e. the typical situation), the terminal loss is computed by reference to that accounting period and the part of the penultimate accounting period which begins 12 months prior to the date of cessation. The calculation of the amount of terminal loss will be in accordance with the following table:

Final accounting period less than 12 months	Part of penultimate accounting period commencing 12 months before cessation	Calculation of terminal loss
(1)	(2)	(3)
Loss	Loss	Add the losses
Loss	Profit	Take loss at (1) only
Profit	Loss	Take loss at (2) only

A company may claim to have a terminal loss set off against trading income of the same trade in accounting periods falling wholly or partly within the three years (or shorter period throughout which the company has carried on the trade) immediately preceding the terminal 12 month period. The maximum period for which the trading profits may be relieved is the three years preceding the final 12 months of trading.

The relief is not allowable in respect of losses which have been, or can be, otherwise relieved, e.g. by set off against trading income or on a value basis.

In calculating terminal loss relief, charges paid wholly and exclusively for the purposes of the trade in the final 12 months of trading are included in the terminal loss claim, to the extent that they have not already been claimed. The terminal loss is to be set against income of a later period in priority to an earlier period and is not to displace relief already given for losses carried forward from earlier periods.

Example

A Ltd ceases to trade on 31 January 2013. The accounts show the following results:

	Trading Profit/ (loss) €	Other Income €
Year to 31 December 2009	12,000	3,000
Year to 31 December 2010	10,000	2,000
Year to 31 December 2011	15,000	2,560
Year to 31 December 2012	(75,000)	3,840
1 month to 31 January 2013	4,000	1,000

It will be remembered that a loss can only be utilised as a terminal loss if it has not or cannot be otherwise relieved. The loss for the period to 31 December 2012 can be relieved as follows:

	€
By set off: against trading profits of the preceding accounting period to 31 December 2011	15,000
By carry forward: against trading income of the accounting period to 31 January 2013	4,000
On a value basis	
2012: Against CT – €3,840 × 25% = €960	
Loss used €7,680 × 12.5% = €960	7,680

continued overleaf

2011: Against CT − €2,560 × 25% = €640

Loss used €5,120 × 12.5% = €640   5,120

Loss used   31,800

The unrelieved loss of the accounting period is thus €43,200 (i.e. €75,000 − €31,800) of which the amount attributable to the 11 months to 31 December 2012 is €39,600, i.e. 11/12 × €43,200.

Terminal loss relief is due as follows against the trading profits of the three-year period commencing on 1 February 2009 and ending on 31 January 2012

	€
1. Against trading income of the period from 1 January to 31 January 2012	Nil
2. Against trading income of the accounting period to 31 December 2011 (profits absorbed by loss carried back)	Nil
3. Against trading income of the accounting period to 31 December 2010	10,000
4. Against trading income of the period 1 February 2009 to 31 December 2009 i.e. 11/12ths × 12,000	11,000
	21,000

The balance of the loss, i.e. €18,600 (€39,600 − €21,000) cannot be relieved in any way.

24.5 Disallowance of Trading Losses following a Change of Ownership

Losses forward are potentially valuable. If a company makes profits from the trade, it will not pay tax on those profits until all losses forward are utilised. Equally another company may find it attractive to buy a company, ensure that the company's trade is profitable when the new shareholder is running it (e.g. by transferring in some business) and thereby have losses to offset against trading profits and reduce tax.

There are anti-avoidance rules that limit the ability to do this type of planning.

There are provisions in TCA 1997 to disallow the carry forward of trading losses incurred before a substantial change of ownership of a company's shares. The disallowance will apply:

1. if a major change in the nature or conduct of the company's trade and the change in ownership both occur within any period of three years; or
2. where the activities of the trade have become small or negligible and there is a change of ownership before any considerable revival of the trade.

The provisions were introduced with the intention of attacking the practice of purchasing shares in a company to obtain the benefit of accumulated losses.

In applying the provisions to the accounting period in which the change of ownership occurs, the part of the period occurring before the change of ownership and the part occurring after the change are treated as separate accounting periods. Apportionments are to be made on a time basis.

A "major change in the nature or conduct of the trade" includes:

(a) a major change in the property dealt in, services or facilities provided, in the trade; or

(b) a major change in customers, outlets or markets of the trade.

It should be noted however that this definition is not exhaustive.

Such a change will be regarded as occurring even if the change is the result of a gradual process which began outside the three-year period.

There have been a number of cases which dealt with the meaning of a "major change in the conduct of the trade" which gives some guidance on the meaning of the term as follows:

Cases where it was held that there had been **no major change** in the nature or conduct of the trade:

1. A company which had sold its products direct to customers, mainly wholesalers, then commenced to do the same through distribution companies.

2. A company ceased to slaughter pigs and manufacture meat products and, for a temporary period of 16 months, distributed the same products manufactured by its parent company. After the 16-month period, it recommenced slaughtering and manufacturing meat products.

Cases where it was held that there had been a **major change** in the nature or conduct of the trade:

1. A company which carried on a business of minting coins and medallions from precious metals purchased its principal supplier's entire stock of gold and then purchased gold directly from wholesalers. This resulted in substantial increases in stock levels.

2. A company which operated a retail chain of shops changed its promotional policy by discontinuing the issue of trading stamps and reducing prices. The change resulted in a substantial increase in turnover.

There are rules for determining whether there has been a change in ownership and generally these are such as to ensure that if there is a new person or persons controlling the company, then there is a change of ownership.

24.6 Losses in Foreign Trades

A foreign trade is one which is carried on wholly outside of the State by a company resident in the State, e.g. a company managed and controlled in this country but exercising a trade wholly in Germany would be regarded as carrying on a foreign trade. It is taxable under Case III.

A loss on a foreign trade is only available for carry forward against future profits from the same trade. There is no right to set off losses in foreign trades against other profits.

24.7 Case IV and Case V Losses

Case IV losses may be set off against the amount of any other income assessable to corporation tax under Case IV for the same accounting period.

Case V losses (which are defined as losses after offset against any Case V income of the accounting period) may be set against corresponding income of a previous accounting period of the same length. A claim for this relief in respect of a Case V loss must be made within two years after the end of the accounting period of loss.

Both Case IV and Case V losses, so far as unrelieved, may be carried forward and set against corresponding income of subsequent accounting periods.

Example

A Ltd makes up accounts to 31 December.
Recent results are as follows:

	2009	2010	2011	2012
	€	€	€	€
Trading income	100,000	110,000	120,000	130,000
Interest on Government securities	10,000	11,000	12,000	13,000
Rental income (loss)	20,000	(30,000)	5,000	20,000

2009

Case I		100,000
Case III		10,000
Case V	20,000	
Less: Loss	(20,000)	Nil
		110,000

2010

Case I	110,000
Case III	11,000
Case V	Nil
	121,000

2011

	€	€
Case I		120,000
Case III		12,000
Case V	5,000	
Less: Loss forward	(5,000)	Nil
		132,000

2012

	€	€
Case I		130,000
Case III		13,000
Case V	20,000	
Less: Balance of		
loss forward	(5,000)	15,000
		158,000

24.8 Case IV and Case V Capital Allowances

Capital allowances in relation to non-trading income, i.e.:

- capital allowances available to lessors of plant and machinery (Case IV allowances); and
- capital allowances available to lessors of industrial buildings (Case V allowances),

are to be treated primarily as deductions from the relevant income, i.e. the lease rentals.

Any excess of such allowances over the relevant income may be:

■ Carried forward and treated as an allowance for a later accounting period.
■ Set off against total profits (including chargeable gains) for the same accounting period or for an immediately preceding period of the same length. A claim must be made within two years of the end of the accounting period in which the excess occurs.

(The utilisation of capital allowances on certain leased assets under Case IV are subject to restrictions).

Example

Takeaway Ltd has the following income and allowances:

Year Ended	Case I	Case III	Case V	Case V Capital Allowances
31 December 2011	20,000	40,000	80,000	30,000
31 December 2012	100,000	20,000	25,000	160,000

Corporation Tax Year Ended 31 December 2011

			€	€
Case I				20,000
Case III				40,000
Case V			80,000	
Less	Case V allowances		(30,000)	50,000
				110,000
Less	Excess Case V			
	allowances in 2012			(15,000)
				95,000

Corporation Tax

€20,000 × 12.5% =	€2,500
€75,000 × 25% =	€18,750
Total	€21,250

Note: The excess Case V capital allowances are offset against total profits. The taxpayer will choose to offset them against the profits taxed at the highest rate, i.e. 25%.

Corporation Tax Year Ended 31 December 2012

			€	€
Case I				100,000
Case III				20,000
Case V			25,000	
Less	Case V allowances		(25,000)	Nil
				120,000
Less	Excess Case V allowances			(120,000)
				Nil

Balance of Case V capital allowances available for set off against 2011 profits:
€160,000 − €25,000 − €120,000 = €15,000

24.9 Capital Losses

While trading losses may be set off against trading profits and utilised on a value basis, capital losses can only be set off against current chargeable gains on other assets or carried forward against chargeable gains in subsequent accounting periods.

24.10 Restriction of Loss Relief on Late Submission of Returns

The due date for submission of a company's accounts to the Inspector of Taxes is within nine months after the end of the accounting period provided that if the last day of that period is later than day 21 of the month, the return must be filed on day 21 (extended to day 23 if using ROS).

If a company fails to submit its return of income for a chargeable period on or before the specified return date for the chargeable period, then claims to offset trading losses against trading income or on a value basis or to offset excess allowances against profits or any claim under group relief are reduced by 50%.

The 50% restriction or reduction referred to above is subject to a maximum amount in any particular case. There is a maximum of €158,715 in each case for those restrictions or reductions. In cases where the delay in filing a return is *less than two months*, the amount of the restriction is effectively reduced from 50% to 25% subject to a maximum amount restricted of €31,740.

Example

Lana Ltd had the following results for the year ended 31 December 2012:

	€
Case I	100,000
Case V income	60,000
Case V capital allowances	80,000

If Lana Ltd files its return for the year ended 31 December 2012 on 21 October 2013, one month late, its taxable profits for the year ended 31 December 2012 will be as follows:

	€	€
Case I		100,000
Case V	60,000	
Capital allowances	(80,000)	
Excess Case V capital allowances	20,000	
Restricted to 75%		(15,000)
Taxable profits		85,000

If Lana Ltd files its return for the year ended 31 December 2012, on 21 December 2013, three months late, its taxable profits for the year ended 31 December 2012 will be as follows:

	€	€
Case I		100,000
Case V	60,000	
Capital allowances	(80,000)	
Excess Case V capital allowances	20,000	
Restricted to 50%		(10,000)
Taxable profits		90,000

Example

HIJ Limited, a distribution company, had the following results for the years ended 31 December 2011 and 2012:

	2011	2012
	€	€
Case I profit/(loss)	60,000	(100,000)
Case V income	45,000	50,000
Corporation Tax Computation		
Case I	60,000	Nil
Less section 396A(3)	(60,000)	–
Taxable Case I income	Nil	Nil
Case V income	45,000	50,000
Taxable profits	45,000	50,000
Corporation tax @ 12.5%	Nil	Nil
Corporation tax @ 25%	11,250	12,500
Relief on a value basis (section 396B) (Note)	–	(5,000)
Corporation tax payable	11,250	7,500

Note

€100,000 − €60,000 = €40,000. €40,000 @ 12.5% = €5,000

If HIJ Ltd files its return more than two months after the due date for filing its return, relief under sections 396A and 396B will be restricted as follows:

	2011	2012
	€	€
Case I profit/(loss)	60,000	(100,000)
Case V income	45,000	50,000
Corporation Tax Computation		
Case I	60,000	Nil
Less section 396A(3) (Note 1)	(30,000)	–
Taxable Case I income	30,000	Nil
Case V income	45,000	50,000
Taxable profits	75,000	50,000
Corporation tax @ 12.5%	3,750	Nil
Corporation tax @ 25%	11,250	12,500
Relief on a value basis (section 396B) (Note 2)	–	–
Corporation tax payable	15,000	12,500

Note 1: Relief under section 396A: Profits to be reduced by relief restricted to 50% of the amount they would have been, i.e. €60,000 × 50% = €30,000.

Note 2: Relief under section 396B: The trading loss is reduced by 50% (€100,000 x 50% = €50,000). Then from this must be deducted the claim which could have been made under section 369A if the return had been filed on time, i.e. €60,000. Therefore as this amount of €60,000 exceeds €50,000, no relief may be claimed under section 396B. The loss available for carry forward to 2013 against future income of this trade is €100,000 − €30,000 = €70,000.

Questions (to Chapter 24)

Review Questions

(See Suggested Solutions at the end of this textbook.)

Question 24.1

Using the figures shown below for ENYA Ltd show how the Case V (rents) and Case I (trade, all non-manufacturing) losses may be used. Assume a tax rate of 12.5% on trading income and 25% for Case III and V for all years.

		Rents	Trading profits / (losses)	Case III
		€	€	€
y/e	31/3/2009	5,000	60,000	10,000
y/e	31/3/2010	(4,000)	70,000	5,000
y/e	31/3/2011	6,000	(130,000)	10,000
y/e	31/3/2012	8,000	10,000	3,500

Question 24.2

Hells Bells Ltd shows the following results:

	Year ended 31 March 2012	Nine months ended 31 December 2012
	€	€
Trading profit/(loss) (non-manufacturing)	167,000	(190,000)
Rents	4,000	(4,000)
Chargeable gains/(losses) (non-development land)	(19,000)	10,000
Case III	10,000	20,000

Requirement
Calculate the tax payable for each accounting period claiming the earliest possible relief for losses.

Question 24.3

Monk Ltd prepares annual accounts to 31 December each year. Recent results were as follows:

	Year Ended 31/12/2011 €	Year Ended 31/12/2012 €
Adjusted Case I profit/(loss) (Note 1) (before capital allowances)	360,000	(310,000)
Case I capital allowances	20,000	90,000
Interest on Government Stocks	5,000	30,000
Rental income	15,000	20,000
Capital gains as adjusted for CT (non-development land)	12,000	26,000
Capital gain on development land (1 June)	–	100,000

The following additional information is available:

1. Monk Ltd has an agreed unutilised Case I loss forward from the year ended 31/12/2010 of €20,000.
2. The company wishes to claim the loss reliefs available so as to maximise the benefit of the losses.

Requirement
Compute the corporation tax payable for each of the above years and indicate the amount (if any) of unutilised losses available for carry forward to year ending 31/12/2013.

Question 24.4

Monaghan Limited prepares annual accounts to 30 June each year. Recent results were as follows:

Year Ended 30 June

	2010 €	2011 €	2012 €
Adjusted Case I profit/(loss) (before capital allowances)	200,000	(450,000)	150,000
Case I capital allowances	20,000	80,000	10,000
Trade charges paid (Note)	10,000	10,000	6,000
Interest on Government Stocks	5,000	30,000	10,000
Rental income	10,500	20,000	20,000
Capital gains as adjusted for CT	10,200	40,000	50,000
Cash dividend received from subsidiary	10,000	30,000	Nil
Non-trade charges paid	–	–	50,000

Monaghan Limited has an unutilised Case I Loss forward from the year ended 30/6/2009 of €20,000.

Note: Trade charges of €4,000 relating to the year ended 30 June 2012 were paid in July 2012 and are not included in the figures above.

Requirement

Compute the net profits assessable to corporation tax for each of the above years and indicate the amount (if any) of unutilised losses available for carry forward to year ending 30/6/2013.

Group Relief

25.1   Introduction

Tax law has special relieving provisions for member companies of certain qualifying groups.

Broadly speaking, these reliefs may be broken down under the following headings:

1.   Payments relief;
2.   Loss relief; and
3.   Relief from tax on capital gains (dealt with in **Chapter 26**).

By far the most important relief is loss relief, i.e. if one company in a group has a loss, it can surrender the loss to another group member and thereby reduce the taxable profits of and tax payable by that other group company.

25.2   Payments Relief – Groups

Certain payments made by companies are generally required to be made under deduction of income tax at the standard rate. These include:

■   yearly interest;
■   annuities;
■   annual payments; and
■   patent royalties.

A company making any of the above payments would, in the normal course of events, be required to deduct income tax at the standard rate from the gross amount due and pay this over to the Revenue Commissioners as part of its corporation tax payments. Under section 410 TCA 1997 all such payments can be made gross within a group provided certain conditions are satisfied.

25.2.1   Conditions to be Satisfied

1.   A 51% (direct or indirect) shareholding relationship between paying and recipient company, i.e. more than 50% of its ordinary share capital (any issued share capital other than fixed rate preference shares) is owned.

This requirement is satisfied where either:

(i)   The paying company is a 51% subsidiary of the recipient company; or
(ii)   The recipient company is a 51% subsidiary of the paying company; or
(iii) Both companies are 51% subsidiaries of another company.

2.   Both the paying and the recipient company must be resident in an EU Member State or an EEA country which has a tax treaty with Ireland (i.e. Norway and Iceland).
3.   It is not permitted to utilise a shareholding in a company which is not resident in an EU Member State or an EEA country which has a tax treaty with Ireland (i.e. Norway and Iceland) or to use a shareholding in a share dealing company to establish the necessary 51% relationship.
4.   If the recipient of the payment is not resident in the State, the payment must be taxable in the other country.

Example 1

A Ltd

100 %

B Ltd

90 %

C Ltd

60 %

D Ltd

Interest paid by D Ltd to A Ltd will qualify for relief, as there is a 54% relationship between these two companies. Equally, interest paid by D Ltd to B Ltd or C Ltd will qualify for relief, as there is at least a 51% relationship between the companies.

Example 2

X Ltd

51 %   51 %

Z Ltd   H Ltd

Qualifying payments from Z Ltd to H Ltd, or H to Z would qualify for relief, as both companies have a 51% relationship with the same parent.

In determining whether two companies have the necessary 51% relationship, shareholdings by EU resident companies and shareholdings by companies resident in an EEA country which has a tax treaty with Ireland (i.e. Norway and Iceland) may be taken into account. Accordingly, in this example, if X Ltd were resident in France, then Z and H would have the necessary 51% relationship. If however X Ltd were resident in the US, Z and H would not have the necessary 51% relationship and payments between them would have to be made under deduction of tax.

25.3 Loss Relief – Groups

25.3.1 Introduction

Briefly put, the provisions relating to relief for trading losses and trade charges in qualifying groups in sections 411 to 429 TCA 1997 permit a profit-maker within the group to take relief for losses incurred by other members of the group **during the same accounting period**, either by deduction against trading income or on a value basis. Other "losses" in a single company are deductible against total profits; we will see that the same applies within a group – they are deductible against total profits of other group members.

25.3.2 Losses which may be Grouped

1. **Trading losses**, excluding trade losses attributable to pre-trading expenses. There are other restrictions, but these arise infrequently.

Example

Parent Ltd has a trading profit of €100,000. Subsidiary Ltd is in a group for loss relief purposes with Parent Ltd. Subsidiary Ltd has a trading loss of €50,000. The trading loss of Subsidiary Ltd can be grouped against the trading profits of Parent Ltd.

Example

New Company Ltd incurs qualifying pre-trading expenses of €50,000. It commenced to trade and earned income of €10,000. New Company Ltd's tax computation would show a Case I loss of €40,000 (i.e. €10,000 – €50,000). If New Company Ltd is a member of a group, that loss of €40,000 cannot be grouped, it can only be carried forward and offset against future trading income of New Company Ltd.

Please note that capital allowances are automatically included in the trading loss available for group relief as capital allowances are a deductible expense in arriving at adjusted Case I profit for corporation tax purposes. However, trading losses forward from a previous accounting period may not be grouped.

Relevant trading losses may only be offset against relevant trading income (i.e. trading income taxed at the standard rate of 12.5%) of another group member or relief can be given on a value basis for the "relievable loss" against the corporation tax payable by the other group company. The relievable loss is the loss not already claimed against relevant trading income either by the company itself (under section 396A) or by another group company (under section 420A) – see examples later.

2. **Excess Case V capital allowances** exclusive of capital allowances carried forward from a previous period.

It should be noted that the excess allowances available for group relief are those claimed for the current accounting period in excess of the Case V income for that period **before any reduction of that income for previous periods' capital allowances or losses forward.**

Excess Case V capital allowances may be grouped against total profits of other group members.

Example

	€
Current period Case V income	20,000
Current period capital allowances	50,000
Current period Case V balancing charge	5,000
Case V capital allowances forward	7,000
Case V losses forward from previous period	3,000
Computation:	
Case V tax-adjusted income (current period)	20,000
ADD: Case V balancing charge (current period)	<u>5,000</u>
	25,000
DEDUCT: Current period Case V capital allowances	<u>50,000</u>
Excess Case V capital allowances available for group relief:	<u>(25,000)</u>

These excess Case V capital allowances may be grouped against total profits of the other group company.

Excess Case V capital allowances which arise due to wear and tear allowances claimed on rented residential accommodation may not be surrendered by way of group relief.

3. **Excess management expenses** of current accounting period (excluding those of a previous accounting period which have been carried forward and are deemed to be management expenses of the current accounting period). Management expenses are claimed by investment companies – see **Chapter 29**.

These excess management expenses may be grouped against total profits of the other group company.

It is not necessary for the claimant company to be an investment company for group relief to be claimed.

4. **Excess Charges Paid:**
Non-trade charges
Non-trade charges paid in an accounting period which are in excess of that period's total profits (before any deduction has been made in arriving at those total profits for losses, capital allowances or management expenses of other accounting periods) may be surrendered and set against the total profits of the claimant company.

Relevant trading charges
Relevant trading charges may only be offset against relevant trading income of another group member or claimed against relevant corporation tax on a value basis. As with relevant trading losses, relevant trading charges must be claimed against relevant trading income firstly and only then on a value basis.

Note:

1. You can only group the four categories of loss/excess detailed above
2. You cannot group capital losses, or Case III, IV or V losses
3. You can only group a loss of the current accounting period. You cannot group a loss forward.

25.3.3 Examples

Example 1

A Ltd owns 80% of B Ltd. The following are the results for the year ended 31 December 2012

	A Ltd	B Ltd
	€	€
Relevant trading income/(loss)	10,000	(25,000)
Case III	8,000	6,400

Calculate the tax payable by each company.

B Ltd

Case I	–
Case III	6,400
Corporation tax @ 25%	1,600
Relief on a value basis	(1,600)
Corporation tax payable	Nil

A Ltd

Case I	10,000
Group relief section 420A	(10,000)
Case I	Nil
Case III	8,000
Corporation tax	
8,000 @ 25% =	2,000
Relief on a value basis	(275)
Corporation tax payable	1,725

Loss Memo

Relevant trading loss for y/e 31/12/2012	25,000
Utilised by way of	
– section 396B(3) against CT of B Ltd	
€12,800 × 12.5% = €1,600	(12,800)
Utilised by way of	
– section 420A(3) against trading income of A Ltd	(10,000)
– section 420B(3) against CT of A Ltd	
€2,200 × 12.5% = €275	(2,200)
Loss forward to 2013	Nil

A claim must be made under section 420A (trading losses) against relevant trading income of A Ltd before a claim can be made under section 420B on a value basis.

A claim does not have to be made by B Ltd under section 396B before a claim can be made by A Ltd under section 420A or section 420B. However a claim must be made by B Ltd under section 396A, if possible, before A Ltd can make a claim under section 420B.

Example 2

C Ltd owns 90% of D Ltd. The following are the results for the year ended 31 December 2012:

	C Ltd	D Ltd
	€	€
Relevant trading income/(loss)	(10,000)	30,000
Case III	5,000	6,000
Case V	8,000	
Case V capital allowances	15,000	

Calculate the tax payable by each company.

C Ltd

	€
Case I	–
Case III	5,000
Case V	–
Income	5,000
Excess Case V capital allowances (Note 1)	(5,000)
Taxable	nil

Note 1:	Case V	8,000
	Capital allowances	(15,000)
	Excess Case V capital allowances	7,000
	Utilised by C Ltd	5,000
	Available for grouping	2,000

D Ltd

	€
Case I	30,000
Section 420A(3)	(10,000)
	20,000
Case III	6,000
	26,000
Excess Case V capital allowances from C Ltd	(2,000)
Taxable	24,000
Corporation tax	

	€
20,000 × 12.5% =	2,500
4,000 (Note) × 25% =	1,000
Corporation tax payable	3,500

Note: The excess Case V capital allowances are claimed against the profits taxable at the highest rate, i.e. Case III @ 25%.

25.3.4 *Qualifying Group – Irish Resident Companies*

To avail of group relief, the profit maker must be in the same "75% group" as the loss maker. Under section 411 TCA 1997, this condition is satisfied in relation to two companies if one company holds, directly or indirectly, not less than 75% of the ordinary share capital of that company or both companies are 75% subsidiaries of a third company. To establish the 75% relationship, the following shareholdings are ignored:

■ shares held in a share dealing capacity either directly or indirectly; and
■ shares held directly through a company which is not resident in an EU Member State or a country which has signed a tax treaty with Ireland or is not listed on a recognised stock exchange or a 75% subsidiary of a company so listed.

A company may establish the 75% holding by aggregating any ordinary shares held directly in that company and also those held indirectly through a third company. See examples of qualifying loss groups on next page.

Examples: Qualifying 75% Loss Group

1. The loss maker is a 75% subsidiary of profit maker or vice versa:

2. Both are 75% subsidiaries of a third company:

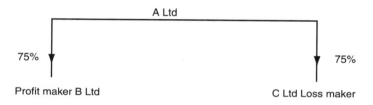

If A Ltd is resident in Germany (an EU country) or the US (a country with which Ireland has a tax treaty), then B Ltd and C Ltd are in an Irish loss group.

If A Ltd is resident in Bolivia, a country with which Ireland does not have a tax treaty, then for a group to exist, A Ltd must be quoted on a recognised stock exchange or be the 75% subsidiary of a company quoted on a recognised stock exchange.

3. Establishing a 75% relationship through a third company:

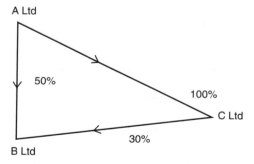

A, B and C Ltd are all members of the same 75% loss group.

For the purposes of the 75% test, "ordinary share capital" is defined as meaning all the issued share capital (by whatever name called) of the company other than capital where the holders have a right to a dividend at a fixed rate but have no other right to a share in the profits of the company. It should be noted that this definition would include participating preference shares as "ordinary share capital".

In addition to the "share capital test" there is also a profit and an asset test to be satisfied, i.e. the parent must be entitled to 75% of the profits available for distribution and 75% of assets on a winding up, in addition to owning 75% of the ordinary share capital. In most situations, a parent will satisfy all three conditions. The profits and assets tests can be failed when there are unusual financing structures into a subsidiary so that, for example, the parent is entitled to less than 75% of profits.

25.3.5 Qualifying Group – Non-resident Companies

In the past, all members of the group had to be Irish tax resident. This rule was changed as a result of the decision of the European Court of Justice (ECJ) in 1998 in the case of *Imperial Chemical Industries plc v. Colmer*. The ECJ held that the UK legislation (on which the Irish equivalent was based) discriminated against companies which had exercised their right of freedom of establishment under the Treaty of Rome (the founding treaty for what is now the EU) and which controlled companies resident in other Member States. As a result, Irish tax law was amended to provide that companies resident in an EU Member State could be taken into account in determining if the group (or consortium) relationship existed and to allow an Irish resident company form a group with an Irish branch of an EU company so that losses could be surrendered between the Irish resident company and the Irish branch of the EU resident company. Subsequent legislation extended the definition further to include Irish branches of companies resident in EEA States that have a tax treaty with Ireland.

Finance Act 2012 provides that companies in non-EU/non-qualifying EEA countries can be taken into account in determining whether a group exists, if they are resident in a treaty country, quoted on a recognised stock exchange or a 75% subsidiary of a company so listed. However, losses of these companies may not be offset against Irish profits.

Following the ECJ decision in the *Marks & Spencer plc v. Halsey* case, Irish law was amended to provide that trading losses incurred by its non-Irish subsidiaries resident in EU Member States or EEA Member States with which Ireland has a double taxation agreement can be group relieved against profits of the Irish parent. It must be proven that the loss cannot be otherwise used by the foreign subsidiary, the 75% relationship must exist between the companies and the claim must be made within two years.

25.3.6 General Conditions and Rules for Group Relief

1. In a qualifying group, relief may be passed upwards, downwards or sideways.
2. It is permissible for two or more profit makers to avail of relief from any one loss maker.
3. It is not necessary for the profit maker to make a claim for the full amount of the loss maker's loss, i.e. the claim may be tailored to suit the individual company's needs. It is not necessary for the profit maker to make a payment to the surrendering company when claiming group relief.
4. Even if the relationship between the companies is only 80%, all of the loss may be grouped.
5. There is no rule in group relief which requires that losses of the surrendering company must first be applied in reducing other profits arising in the accounting period of the loss. The surrendering company may accordingly choose to be liable to corporation tax on any non-trading income or gains of the period while surrendering the full amount of the loss sustained in the period.
6. It is vital to remember that before availing of group relief the profit maker concerned must claim all other reliefs except set off of losses for a subsequent accounting period and

cessation relief. Thus, while excess Case V capital allowances, excess management expenses and non-trade charges of the loss maker are available for set off against the profit maker's total profit, it is the profit maker's total profit after all claims have been made for charges paid in the accounting period, unutilised losses and capital allowances coming forward from a previous accounting period and any losses incurred and capital allowances claims for the accounting period for which group loss relief is being claimed.

As in a single company, relevant trading losses must be claimed firstly against relevant trading income of the other group company and only then used on a value basis against corporation tax of the other group company.

In relation to relief on a value basis, the order of claiming relief is:

(i)   relevant trading charges;

(ii) trading losses; and

(iii) group relief.

7.   Group relief is only available where the accounting period of both the loss maker and profit maker corresponds wholly or partly. Where they correspond partly the relief is restricted on a time-apportionment basis.

Example

Group Limited has a wholly owned subsidiary, Sub Limited. In the year ended 31 December 2012, Group Limited incurs a Case I loss of €240,000. In the year ended 30 September 2012, Sub Limited has Case I income of €120,000.

The corresponding accounting period is the period 1 January 2012 to 30 September 2012, i.e. nine months. Therefore, the maximum group relief available is the lower of:
— loss of €240,000 × 9/12 = €180,000
— profit of €120,000 × 9/12 = €90,000

Sub Limited can make a claim to utilise €90,000 of the losses incurred by Group Limited, thereby reducing its taxable income in the year ended 30 September 2012 to €30,000. Group Limited will have unused losses of €240,000 less €90,000 = €150,000 and some of these losses may be available for group relief against Sub Ltd's trading income for the year ended 30 September 2013, i.e. the period 1 October to 31 December 2012.

---

8.   Group relief is only given if the surrendering company and the claimant company are members of the same group throughout the whole of the surrendering company's accounting period and the claimant company's corresponding accounting period. Where a company joins or leaves a group, all of the companies in the group are deemed to end an accounting period at that date for the purposes of establishing any group relief due. The corresponding accounting period rules referred to at 7 above apply.

Example

Owner Limited acquired 100% of the share capital of Acquired Limited on 30 June 2012. Both companies make up their financial statements to 31 December. In the year ended 31 December 2012, Owner Limited has Case I income of €100,000, while Acquired Limited has a Case I loss of €60,000. Only losses incurred since 1 July 2012 may be grouped, i.e. the corresponding accounting period is the period 1 July 2012 to 31 December 2012, i.e. six months. Therefore, the maximum group relief available is the *lower* of:
— profit of €100,000 × 6/12 = €50,000
— loss of €60,000 × 6/12 = €30,000

Owner Limited can make a claim to have €30,000 of the losses incurred by Acquired Limited to be offset against its trading income thereby reducing its taxable income for the year ended 31 December 2012 from €100,000 to €70,000. Acquired Limited will have unused losses of €60,000 less €30,000 = €30,000.

Example

A Ltd owns 80% of B Ltd. The following are the results for the each company:

	A Ltd y/e 31/12/12	B Ltd y/e 30/6/12
	€	€
Relevant trading income/(loss)	10,000	(50,000)
Case III	8,000	6,400

Calculate the tax payable by each company.

B Ltd

	€
Case I	–
Case III	6,400
Corporation tax @ 25%	1,600
Relief on a value basis	(1,600)(1)
Corporation tax payable	Nil

A Ltd

	€
Case I	10,000
Group relief section 420A	(5,000)(2)
Case I	5,000
Case III	8,000
	13,000

	€
Corporation tax	
5,000 @ 12.5% =	625
8,000 @ 25% =	2,000
Relief on a value basis	(1,000)(3)
Corporation tax payable	1,625

Loss Memo

Relevant trading loss for y/e 30/6/2012		50,000
1	Utilised by way of <u>section 396B</u> against CT of B Ltd (Note 1) €12,800 × 12.5% = 1,600	(12,800)(1)
2	Utilised by way of <u>section 420A</u> against trading income of A Ltd (Note 2)	(5,000)(2)
3	Utilised by way of <u>section 420B</u> against CT of A Ltd (Note 3) €8,000 × 12.5% = €1, 000	(8,000)(3)
	Loss forward to 2013	24,200

Note 1: Typically a company will make a claim under section 396B. However, there is no legal requirement to make a claim under section 369B in B Ltd, before surrendering the loss to A Ltd to use under section 420A against relevant trading income of A Ltd. A claim must be made under section 420A against relevant trading income of A Ltd, before a claim can be made under section 420B on a value basis.

Note 2: Section 420A claim

Claim is for lower of
- trading loss of surrendering company for overlap period; and
- trading income of claimant for overlap period.
  Trading loss 6/12 × (€50,000) = (€25,000)
  Trading income 6/12 × €10,000 = €5,000. Therefore, claim €5,000

Note 3: Section 420B claim

Claim the unclaimed loss of the overlap period on a value basis – the unclaimed loss is €25,000 – €5,000 = €20,000; its value is €20,000 × 12.5% = €2,500. Relief may be claimed against the CT on profits of the overlap period which have not already been relieved. All the Case I of the overlap period has been relieved, so it is the CT on the Case III income of the overlap period (6/12 × €8,000 × 25% = €1,000).

9. The profit maker must lodge a formal claim to avail of group relief from the loss maker within two years of the end of the loss maker's accounting period.
10. The loss maker must give formal consent for the surrender of the loss.
11. Payments to the loss maker by the profit maker for availing of the losses are ignored for corporation tax purposes provided they do not exceed the amount of the loss surrendered, i.e. no tax deduction is available to the profit maker in respect of the payment and the receipt by the loss maker is not taxable.
12. The loss maker and the profit maker must be resident in an EU/qualifying EEA Member State or must be EU/qualifying EEA resident subsidiaries of a third company which is resident in an EU/qualifying EEA Member State. However the losses to be surrendered must be losses incurred in a trade in respect of which the surrendering company is within the charge to Irish tax.

Example

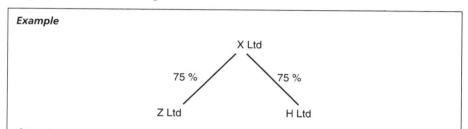

If X Ltd is resident in France and not trading in Ireland and both Z Ltd and H Ltd are resident in Ireland, losses may be surrendered between Z and H. If Z Ltd were resident in Italy but trading in Ireland through a branch whose profits are liable to Irish corporation tax, losses could still be surrendered between Z and H. However, losses may never be surrendered by X to either Z or H as X is not within the charge to Irish tax on its trading profits.

Following the amendment of Irish law subsequent to the ECJ decision in the *Marks & Spencer plc v. Halsey case*, trading losses incurred by its non-Irish subsidiaries resident in EU Member States or EEA Member States with which Ireland has a double taxation agreement can be group relieved against the Irish parent's income. It must be proven that the loss cannot be otherwise used by the foreign subsidiary, a 75% relationship must exist between companies and the claim must be made within two years. The loss can only be surrendered **to the parent** by a subsidiary. A loss of the parent cannot be used by a subsidiary. For example, the loss of a French parent company could never be used by an Irish resident subsidiary.

13. Shares held as trading stock (i.e. by share dealing companies) and shares in non-EU/non-DTA resident companies, other than quoted companies or 75% subsidiaries of quoted companies, are excluded for the purposes of calculating the necessary shareholding relationship.

25.4 Consortium Relief

Where a company decides to enter into a joint venture with a third party, the investment is often structured via a new company in which each of the investors has a shareholding, e.g. a 50:50 joint venture where each owns 50% of the shares in the new company. Clearly the new company is not a "75% subsidiary" and therefore the group relief rules in this chapter do not apply.

There is a form of group relief, known as consortium relief, which applies in these situations. It is not examinable.

Questions (to Chapter 25)

Review Questions

(See Suggested Solutions to Review Questions at the end of this textbook.)

Question 25.1

B Ltd has the following results for year ended 31/12/2012

Tax-adjusted trading profits (i.e. after current year capital allowance claim)	€180,000
Interest on Government Stocks (Case III)	€4,000
Profit rent (Case V)	€20,000

Unutilised trading losses forward from year ended 31/12/2011 amount to €16,000.

Z Ltd is a 100% trading subsidiary of B Ltd. During the year ended 31/12/2012 it incurred tax adjusted trading losses of €96,000. It also had taxable Case III income of €20,000.

Requirement

Compute B Ltd's corporation tax liability for the year ended 31/12/2012 after allowing for any group relief for losses of Z Ltd.

Question 25.2

A Ltd owns 80% of B Ltd's issued share capital and 75% of C Ltd's issued share capital. Results for year ended 31/3/2012 were:

	A Ltd	B Ltd	C Ltd
	€	€	€
Tax-adjusted Case I profit/(loss)	(90,000)	56,000	48,000
Case III income	1,000	2,000	3,000
Case V income	20,000	25,000	2,000
Case I trading losses forward	(4,000)	–	(26,000)

A Ltd wishes to arrange its affairs to ensure that it pays no corporation tax, if possible, before it surrenders any loss relief to its subsidiaries.

Requirement

Calculate the tax payable by each company for the year ended 31/3/2012.

Question 25.3

Queen Ltd has two wholly-owned subsidiaries, Pawn Ltd and Rook Ltd. Queen Ltd, Rook Ltd and Pawn Ltd are trading companies. Accounts for the year to 31 December 2012, show the following results:

	Queen Ltd	Pawn Ltd	Rook Ltd
	€	€	€
Gross operating profit	297,463	81,000	47,437
Less: Depreciation	12,000	10,000	16,000
Entertaining (customers)	1,350	1,200	1,650
Administration	73,650	61,110	107,373
Interest	11,150	10,720	3,000
Capital grant release	(3,000)	–	–
	95,150	83,030	128,023
Net profit/(loss) before investment income	202,313	(2,030)	(80,586)

Notes:

1. Rook Ltd was incorporated and commenced to trade on 1 January 2012.
2. (i) Interest is analysed as follows:

	Queen Ltd	Pawn Ltd	Rook Ltd
	€	€	€
Accrued 1 January 2012	(1,250)	–	–
Paid	10,000	9,000	2,750
Accrued 31 December 2012	2,000	1,750	250
Interest on overdue tax	400	–	–
	11,150	10,720	3,000

(ii) Pawn Ltd has used its loan to purchase 7% of the share capital of Bridge Ltd, whose income consists mainly of rental income from commercial properties. None of the directors of Bridge Ltd is also a director of Pawn Ltd. Interest incurred by Queen Ltd and Rook Ltd were in respect of borrowings taken out for the purpose of their trades.

3. (i) Queen Ltd received dividends of €7,500 from other Irish resident companies. These dividends have not been included in the profit figures above.

(ii) Queen Ltd also received deposit interest of €23,846 which was not subject to DIRT.

4. Capital allowances

	Queen Ltd	Pawn Ltd	Rook Ltd
	€	€	€
Capital allowances	7,375	3,000	5,627

5. Pawn Ltd had trade losses brought forward of €80,000 at 1 January 2012.
6. Queen Ltd intends to pay a dividend of €10,000 on 9 January 2013.
7. Queen Ltd is a wholly owned subsidiary of a UK company quoted on the London Stock Exchange.
8. The companies paid the following corporation tax on profits of 2011:

	Queen Ltd	Pawn Ltd
	€	€
Corporation tax	55,000	10,000

Requirement

(a) Compute the corporation tax liabilities (if any) of each of the three companies for the year ended 31 December 2012, on the assumption that all available reliefs are claimed to the benefit of the group as a whole.
(b) State the amount of any losses available to carry forward at 31 December 2012 for each company.
(c) State the due date of payment of any tax payable.
(d) State the tax consequences for the company of paying the dividend of €10,000. This part of the question can only be answered after you have studied **Chapter 27**.

Company Capital Gains

26

Learning Objectives

After studying this chapter you will have acquired the competency to know that:

- Most gains are liable to corporation tax. **Gains on development land** and gains on **specified assets disposed of by non-resident companies are liable to CGT**.

- There is a very important **exemption from corporation tax on gains on disposal of certain shareholdings**. There are a number of conditions which must be satisfied, the most important being that the seller owned at least 5% of the shares, the shares had been held for at least a year and the shares are in a company resident in the EU (including Ireland) or tax treaty country.

- There is a **capital gains group** when a company is an effective **75% subsidiary** of another company. If that subsidiary has effective 75% subsidiaries, then they are also part of the group.

- The main benefit of the group rules is that **assets may be transferred from one group member to another without triggering a capital gain**, i.e. move at no gain/no loss.

- When the asset is sold outside the group, the **base cost is the original cost** to the first member of the group to own the asset.

- Where **a member of a group leaves the group with an asset that it had acquired from another group member**, then the **company leaving the group is liable to tax on the gain not triggered** when the asset was transferred to it.

- **Capital losses cannot be grouped**.

- There are a range of anti-avoidance rules in relation to **pre-entry losses** and gains realised by certain non-resident companies.

Companies can be liable to Irish tax on capital gains. The rules which determine if the gain is actually liable, and whether it is liable to corporation tax (most common) or CGT, are set out below.

Please note that a gain is either liable or not liable. There is no remittance basis for companies.

26.1 Gains Liable to Corporation Tax

Irish Resident Companies

Such companies are liable to corporation tax in respect of **all** capital gains wherever arising, excluding disposals of development land. Thus gains on disposal of foreign assets by an Irish resident company are liable to Irish corporation tax.

Non-resident Companies

A non-resident company is only liable to corporation tax on its capital gains if all of the following conditions are satisfied:

1. it must carry on a trade within the State through a branch or agency;
2. the gain must have arisen as a result of the disposal of an asset which was either used, or had been acquired, or held for the purposes of the branch or agency; and
3. the asset which is the subject of the disposal must fall within the category of assets chargeable to tax on persons who are neither resident nor ordinarily resident, namely:

    (i)   land and buildings in the State;
    (ii) minerals, mineral rights, exploration and exploration rights in the State and assets related to mining or the searching for minerals;
    (iii) unquoted shares deriving their value or the greater part of their value from assets mentioned at (i) and (ii) above; and
    (iv) assets used in connection with a trade carried on through a branch/agency.

Therefore, non-resident companies are not liable to corporation tax on most disposals, e.g. disposals of foreign assets, other Irish assets.

26.2 Gains Liable to Capital Gains Tax

Irish Resident Companies

Capital gains arising on the disposal of development land are specifically charged to CGT and are therefore excluded from the charge to corporation tax.

Non-resident Companies

CGT applies to the following disposals:

(i) disposals of development land in the State; and
(ii) disposals of assets specifically chargeable on non-residents (see 3 above), where the gain is not liable to corporation tax because no trade is carried on in the State through a branch or agency.

Tax Residence Status of a Company

This is determined by reference to the place where the **central management and control of the company is exercised**. However certain Irish **incorporated** companies may be resident in the State even if the central management and control of the company is exercised abroad. See **Chapter 30** for consideration of the concept of corporate residence.

26.3 Exemption from Tax on Disposal of Certain Shareholdings (Also Known as the Participation Exemption)

Section 626B TCA 1997 provides for an exemption from tax in certain circumstances, in the case of gains from the disposal of shareholdings by "parent companies". While any gains are not taxable, equally if there is a loss on disposal, there is no relief for the loss. A number of conditions must be met before a gain can be exempt:

- Firstly, the investor company must be a 'parent' company at the time of disposal, i.e. the investor company must have a **minimum shareholding in the investee company at the time of disposal**. That holding, directly or indirectly, must have been **at least 5%**, i.e.
  - it must hold not less than 5% of the company's ordinary share capital;
  - it must be beneficially entitled to not less than 5% of the profits available for distribution to equity holders of the company; **and**
  - on a winding up, it must be beneficially entitled to not less than 5% of the assets available for distribution to equity holders.
- The investor is required to have the minimum holding in the investee company for a **continuous period of at least 12 months**.
- The **investee company must carry on a trade**, or the business of the investor company, its investee company and their "5%" investee companies, taken as a whole, must consist wholly or mainly of the carrying on of a **trade** or trades.
- Finally, at the time of the disposal the **investee** company must be resident in a **Member State of the EU** or a country with which **Ireland has a tax treaty**.

The exemption continues to apply for two years after the 'parent' company minimum shareholding is no longer satisfied. **The exemption does not apply where the shares derive the greater part of their value from land in the State or from minerals, or rights or interests in relation to mining or minerals or the searching of minerals in the State or exploration and exploitation rights of the seabed**. A similar exemption applies to assets related to shares, e.g. options, but this is not examinable.

> *Example*
> Owner Ltd owns 100% of Irish Ltd, a trading company, for the last 10 years. Acquisition Ltd wishes to acquire Irish Ltd. This disposal by Owner Ltd will generate a profit of €5 million. Due to the exemption, Owner Ltd will pay no tax on this gain.
>
> If the facts were the same except that it is shares in French Ltd, a French resident company, the exemption would be available also to Owner Ltd.
>
> However, if it were a disposal of shares in a Jersey company, then the gain would be fully taxable as the investee company is not resident in a Member State of the European Communities or a country with which Ireland has a tax treaty.

26.4 Method of Taxation

Where, for an accounting period, chargeable gains accrue to a company, a notional amount of CGT must be calculated as if CGT fell to be charged on the company in respect of those gains and as if accounting periods were years of assessment. The amount of CGT is computed on the net gains after deducting both allowable losses in the current accounting period and those brought forward from previous years.

Having calculated the notional CGT, the next step is to calculate the amount to be included in the corporation tax computation. This will be an amount which, if it were charged to corporation tax as profits at the normal rate, would be equal to the amount of the notional CGT as computed in the previous paragraph.

Example

X Ltd prepares accounts to 31 December each year. In the year ended 31 December 2012 the tax-adjusted Case I profit was €20,000. During that year the company bought an asset for €10,000 and sold it for €17,000 in October 2012. The company had a capital loss forward of €1,000.

X Ltd	Year ended 31st December 2012
	€
Schedule D Case I	20,000
Chargeable gain	
▪ current year €7,000	
▪ loss forward (€1,000)	
Chargeable gain €6,000 × 30/12.5%	14,400
	34,400
€34,400 @ 12.5%	
Corporation tax due	4,300

You have done this tax computation for X Ltd and are satisfied that you have done the calculations correctly. However, you are uncomfortable as you know that your father bought a property for €80,000 from X Ltd on 1 February 2012, and there is no mention of this disposal in the information which was sent to your manager by the client. What should you do?

You should advise your manager of this purchase by your father and, therefore, disposal by the client, so that your manager can raise it with the client.

However, chargeable gains on development land are charged to CGT instead of corporation tax. These gains will not therefore form part of the total profits of companies for corporation tax purposes. The normal CGT rules apply to such gains. The fact that these gains are not subject to corporation tax means that:

▪ non-development land capital losses cannot be offset against them; and
▪ other reliefs including deductions which can be offset against total profits (e.g. management expenses) and loss relief on a value basis are not available.

CGT payable in respect of such gains is due on the due date for the payment of CGT (i.e. 15 December and 31 January – see **Section 1.10.2**) rather than on the due dates for the payment of corporation tax.

Note: The "annual" exemption of €1,270 available to individuals does not apply to companies.

26.5 Capital Gains Group – Introduction

A company may be part of a group for CGT purposes. This can give important benefits to the companies within the group, namely assets can be transferred from one group company to another without triggering a capital gain.

Definition of a Group

Section 616 TCA 1997 provides that a principal company and its effective 75% subsidiaries form a capital gains group and, where a principal company itself is a member of a group (as being itself an effective 75% subsidiary), that group comprises all of its effective 75% subsidiaries.

A principal company means a company of which another company is an effective 75% subsidiary (directly or indirectly). A company is an effective 75% subsidiary of another company, the parent, if:

1. the company is a 75% subsidiary of the parent, i.e. the parent owns, directly or indirectly, not less than 75% of its ordinary share capital;
2. the parent is beneficially entitled to not less than 75% of any profits available for distribution; and
3. the parent would be beneficially entitled to not less than 75% of the assets of the company available for distribution on a winding up.

The definition of "company" above means a company resident in an EU Member State or resident in an EEA country which has a tax treaty with Ireland (i.e. Norway and Iceland). Accordingly both Irish and non-Irish EU/qualifying EEA companies may be part of a capital gains group.

(In the examples that follow, it should be assumed that a company is entitled to the same % of profits and assets as its shareholding %, e.g. where the example indicates 75% shareholding it should be assumed that there is an entitlement to 75% of profits and assets also).

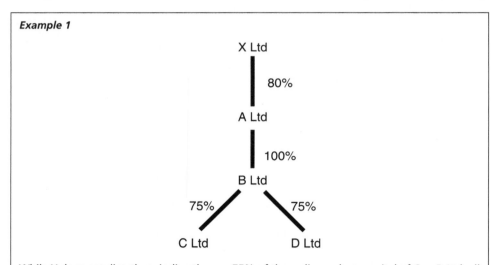

Example 1

While X does not directly or indirectly own 75% of the ordinary share capital of C or D Ltd, all the companies X, A, B, C and D are members of the one capital gains group. This is because B, C or D are clearly 75% subsidiaries of A, and A itself is an effective 75% subsidiary of X.
It should be noted, however, that all of the above companies do not form a single group for loss relief purposes, i.e. X, A, B, and A, B, C, D groups form separate groups for loss relief purposes, as X is not common to both these groups.

Although only companies resident in an EU country or resident in an EEA country which have a tax treaty with Ireland (i.e. Norway and Iceland) may be members of a capital gains group, shareholdings held through non-EU resident companies may be taken into account in determining whether the necessary 75% relationship exists.

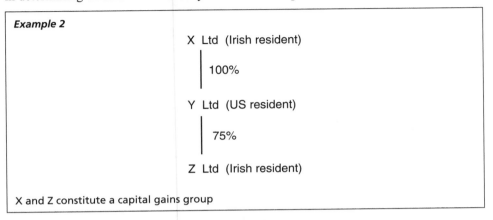

Example 2

X Ltd (Irish resident)

100%

Y Ltd (US resident)

75%

Z Ltd (Irish resident)

X and Z constitute a capital gains group

Groups Incorporating Non-resident Companies

For many years, the capital gains relief (transfer of assets without triggering a chargeable gain) for groups only applied to Irish resident companies.

The relief can also apply to an Irish branch of an EU resident company or of a company resident in an EEA country which has a tax treaty with Ireland (i.e. Norway and Iceland) if it is a member of a group and the asset is used by the Irish branch, i.e. it is a chargeable asset. Therefore, any transfers between the branch and group members qualify for relief.

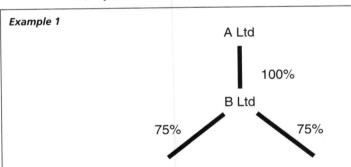

Example 1

A Ltd

100%

B Ltd

75%   75%

A,B,C,D, form a capital gains group.

If A, C and D are Irish resident and B is resident in the UK (but has no branch in Ireland), A, B, C and D still form a capital gains group but the reliefs applying on transfer of assets between group members only apply to transfers between A, C and D. However, if B had an Irish branch and if the asset were used by the Irish branch, then a transfer of the asset between B and A,C or D would qualify.

If A, C and D are Irish resident and B is resident in the US, only A, C and D form a capital gains group, i.e. B can be taken into account to determine whether C or D are effective 75% subsidiaries of A, but not for actually claiming any relief in its own right.

The distinction between a group for loss relief purposes and for CGT purposes is that where a principal company is itself an effective 75% subsidiary, it and all its effective 75% subsidiaries will be part of the same capital gains group as its parent.

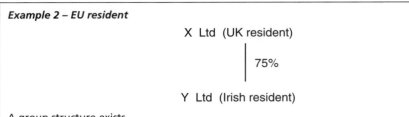

Example 2 – EU resident

X Ltd (UK resident)

75%

Y Ltd (Irish resident)

A group structure exists.

If the UK resident company has an Irish branch operation, capital assets can be transferred between Y Ltd and the Irish branch of X Ltd without triggering a gain. However, if an asset was transferred by Y Ltd to the head office of X Ltd in the UK, then Y Ltd is liable to corporation tax on the gain.

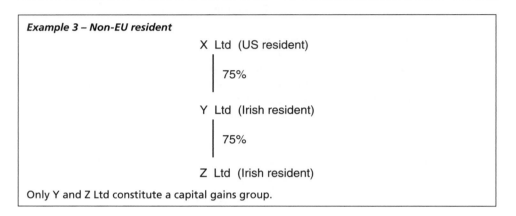

Example 3 – Non-EU resident

X Ltd (US resident)

75%

Y Ltd (Irish resident)

75%

Z Ltd (Irish resident)

Only Y and Z Ltd constitute a capital gains group.

26.6 Disposal of Capital Assets within a Group

In general, a transfer of an asset from one member of the group to another is deemed to be for a consideration of such amount that neither a gain nor a loss accrues.

The group is effectively treated as one taxpayer so that a chargeable gain does not arise until the asset is sold outside the group or the company holding the asset leaves the group.

Example: Irish resident companies
X Ltd owns a building which it bought for €1 million, nine months ago. It disposes of it to its parent Y Ltd when it is worth €1.25 million. Therefore, a gain of €0.25 million arose. Normally this gain would be adjusted and included in the profits of X Ltd. However, this rule ensures that the asset moves at no gain/no loss, i.e. €1 million. So X Ltd has no chargeable gain and Y Ltd's base cost is €1 million.

Example: Transfers between an Irish resident company and an Irish branch of an EU resident company or a company resident in an EEA country which has a tax treaty with Ireland

A Ltd, an Irish resident company is owned by B Ltd, a French resident company that has a branch in Ireland. A Ltd owns a building which it bought for €1 million, nine months ago. It disposes of it to the Irish branch of its parent B Ltd, when it is worth €1.25 million. Therefore, a gain of €0.25 million arose. Normally, this gain would be adjusted and included in the profits of A Ltd.

continued overleaf

> However, as the asset is being transferred to an Irish branch of an EU resident company, the asset continues to be a chargeable asset and, again, the rule ensures that the asset moves at no gain/no loss, i.e. €1 million. So A Ltd has no chargeable gain and B Ltd's base cost is €1 million.
>
> If the sale were from the Irish branch of B Ltd to A Ltd, again the sale would be at no gain/no loss.

The same rule applies to transfers of capital assets between Irish branches of EU resident companies. **Relief for sales between group companies is granted automatically and is compulsory**. There are no provisions for making elections or time limits.

Capital Losses

There are no provisions for transferring chargeable losses between group companies.

Planning: If one member of a group has a capital loss which it is unable to utilise, and another company in the group wishes to sell an asset (to a non-group company) which will realise a gain, then to utilise the loss, the asset must first be sold to the group company holding the loss and then sold by that company to the non-group company.

> **Example**
>
> A Ltd has a capital loss of €100,000. L Ltd, its subsidiary, wishes to sell quoted shares in November 2012 which will generate a gain of €50,000. If L Ltd just sells the shares, it must pay tax on the gain of €120,000 @12.5%, i.e. include a chargeable gain of €50,000 × 30/12.5% in its corporation tax computation.
>
> Alternatively, if L Ltd sold the shares to A Ltd which then sold them to the third party:
>
> ■ L Ltd would have no gain as it sold the shares to A Ltd, a member of the group; and
> ■ A Ltd would have a gain of €50,000 but it would have a loss of €100,000 to offset. Therefore, it would have no gain and a reduced loss forward of €50,000.

Trading Stock

An asset may be held as a capital asset by one company and as trading stock by another, e.g. a property could be held as an investment or as trading stock by a property dealer. Because of this, there are special rules which apply where an asset is transferred within a group and one company holds it as a capital asset and the other holds it as trading stock. These rules are not examinable.

26.6.1 Pre-entry Losses

Because of the above planning possibilities, in the past, companies who anticipated a future gain on the disposal of an asset would acquire a company with capital losses forward. The asset, with the gain, would be transferred, before the sale, into the company with the losses forward so that the losses forward could be used to shelter the gain. The term "pre-entry losses" refers to losses accruing to the company before entry to the group as well as losses on the sale of assets brought in. Anti-avoidance provisions were introduced to prevent use of such pre-entry losses. While the provision ensures that these losses cannot be used subsequently by a group which had no previous commercial connection with the company when those losses accrued, that company will be allowed to use those losses itself in the same way that it could have had it never entered the group.

What is a Pre-entry Loss?
The term applies to losses:

■ that have arisen to a company prior to it becoming a member of the group; and
■ the pre-entry proportion of a loss arising on an asset held at the date a company became a member of a group (even though the loss is crystallised after it became a member).

Calculation of the Pre-entry Loss
The pre-entry loss is the lower of:

■ a loss calculated with reference to the market value at the date on which the company became a member of the group; and
■ the amount of the loss which arose on disposal.

Pre-entry Loss before Joining Group: Gains from which it is Deductible
Pre-entry losses which actually accrued to the company before it joined the group can be set against:

■ gains on assets disposed of after entry but which were held by the company before entry; or
■ a gain arising on the disposal of an asset which was acquired from a non-group member and which has been used for the purpose of the company's trade.

Loss on Pre-entry Asset: Gains from which it is Deductible
The loss on a pre-entry asset must be split as between that which is pre-entry and can only be offset against the gains specified in the previous paragraph and that part which is post-entry and can be offset under the normal rules.

26.7 Disposal of Capital Assets Outside the Group

If there is a disposal of an asset by a member of a group to a person outside the group, and the asset had been acquired by the company making the disposal from another group member, then **the period of ownership for the purpose of both indexation relief and determining the appropriate rate of tax to be applied to the gain (currently there is only one rate) is arrived at by reference to the length of time the asset had been owned by the group as a whole**. Of course, if the asset had originally been acquired prior to 6 April 1974, then the market value at that date will form the base cost for indexation purposes from 6 April 1974 to the date of sale.

Example

A Ltd and Y Ltd are Irish resident members of a capital gains group. Both companies prepare accounts to 31 December each year. Y Ltd acquired an asset in 1973 at a cost of €10,000 and transferred it to A Ltd in August 1979. On 31 December 2012 A Ltd sold the asset to a non-group company for €200,000. The market value of the asset at 6 April 1974 was €20,000.

When the asset was disposed of by Y Ltd to A Ltd in 1979, no gain arose to Y Ltd.

continued overleaf

A Ltd has a disposal in y/e 31 December 2012 of an asset with a base cost of €20,000, i.e. 6 April 1974 valuation.

Computation of A Ltd's liability:	€
Proceeds	200,000
Base cost (M.V. at 6 April 1974) €20,000	
Indexed at 7.528	(150,560)
Gain	49,440

Regross to include in corporation tax computation:

$$€49,440 \times \frac{30}{12.5} = €118,656$$

26.8 Company Leaving Group – Anti-avoidance Measure

Where a company ceases to be a member of a group of companies (otherwise than because of a genuine liquidation), the CGT deferred on any **asset transferred** between the companies since 6 April 1974 and **within 10 years of the company ceasing to be a member of the group** shall become payable.

In effect, the asset is treated as sold and immediately re-acquired by the company leaving the group, at its market value at the time of its original acquisition from the other member of the group, i.e. **the gain arising on the original transfer between the group members is triggered**. Indexation relief is applied by reference to that date and not by reference to the date the company actually leaves the group. It should be particularly noted that the gain and corresponding **liability is that of the company leaving the group**. The cost of future disposals of the assets in question by the company leaving the group will, of course, be the market value attributed to the earlier transfer.

If the asset was acquired by the company more than 10 years prior to the date the company leaves the group, this anti-avoidance rule is not triggered.

Example

Groups Ltd has owned the €2 issued share capital of Feeley Ltd since its incorporation on 3 January 1979. Both are Irish resident companies. Feeley Ltd commenced to trade on 1 February 1979. On 1 March 2002, Groups Ltd sold Feeley Ltd its shareholding in Wheels Ltd for €9,000.

Groups Ltd had purchased the shares in Wheels Ltd for €1,000 on 3 January 1979. The market value of the shares at 1 March 2002 was €10,000.

On 3 January 2012, Groups Ltd sold its shareholding in Feeley Ltd for €100,000.

Requirement
Calculate the chargeable gains arising in respect of the above transactions.

Solution
Groups Ltd

2002: No chargeable gain arises on the sale of shares in Wheels Ltd as they are sold to another group member.

2012: If Feely Ltd is a trading company or the business of Groups Ltd and its 5% subsidiaries taken as a whole, consists of trading, then the gain on the sale of the shares will be exempt, as all other conditions are satisfied.

continued overleaf

Feeley Ltd

2002: Acquired asset on a no gain/no loss basis

2012: Feeley Ltd is leaving the group and, therefore, is treated as having sold and immediately re-acquired the shares in Wheels Ltd at the market value at the time of their acquisition from Group Ltd.

	€	€
Market value on transfer at 1 March 2002		10,000
Cost 3/1/79	1,000	
Index	3.956	
Indexed cost		(3,956)
Gain		6,044

Note 1   This would be taxable at the relevant rate in 2002.

Note 2   If Groups Ltd did not sell its shares in Feeley Ltd until March 2012, then no CGT would arise on Feeley Ltd, as it would have held the shares in Wheels Ltd for 10 years and, therefore, would be exempt from the anti-avoidance provisions.

26.9   Chargeable Gains of Non-resident Companies

The law makes provision to prevent persons avoiding CGT by transferring property to closely controlled companies abroad, i.e. to a company that would be a close company if resident in the State. It enables Revenue to look through the non-resident closely controlled company to its resident or ordinarily resident participators (shareholders) and, subject to certain exceptions, to assess them to CGT on their share of the gains made by the company. If the participator is an individual, the person must be Irish domiciled. The exceptions are:

- gains on tangible property, on certain intangible assets or on a lease of such property, used only for a trade carried on by a company, or by another company which is in a group with a trading company, wholly outside the State;
- gains on the disposal of foreign currency or a credit in a foreign bank if used for a trade carried on wholly outside the State; and
- gains chargeable on the company itself as, for instance, gains on the disposal of specified assets such as land or mineral rights in the State.

A chargeable gain is not treated as accruing to a participator if the aggregate of the amount which would be so treated as so accruing, and the amount which is treated as accruing to persons connected with the participator, does not exceed 1/20th of the gain accruing to the company.

Where any amount of CGT is paid by a participator as a result of the charge to tax arising under this legislation, and an amount in respect of the gain charged is distributed (either by way of dividend or capital or on the dissolution of the company) within two years from the time when the gain accrued to the company, that amount of tax (so far as not reimbursed) can be used to reduce or eliminate any liability to tax in respect of the distribution.

Any CGT paid by a participator in a non-resident company under this section (so far as neither reimbursed by the company, nor used to reduce a liability to tax on a distribution) is treated as allowable expenditure in the CGT computation of the gain arising on the disposal of the asset representing the participator's interest in the company.

Distributions and Dividend Withholding Tax

Learning Objectives

After studying this chapter you will have developed competency in the following:

Distributions

■ There is no tax deduction for distributions. Therefore, if they have been expensed in the Income Statement or P&L, they must be added back.

Dividend Withholding Tax

■ Dividend Withholding Tax (DWT) is payable in respect of all distributions (cash and non-cash) made by an Irish resident company, with certain exceptions.

■ DWT is payable at 20% of the distribution and must be paid to Revenue within 14 days of the end of the month in which the distribution is made.

■ DWT does **not apply** to distributions:

● to Irish resident companies, pension schemes and charities;
● to an EU company which owns at least 5% of the Irish company; and
● out of tax exempt profits.

■ DWT does **not apply** to distributions to non-resident companies who are resident in an EU or a tax treaty country and not controlled by Irish residents.

■ A declaration is required from a non-resident company in order to quality for the DWT exemption.

■ DWT does not apply to distributions to non-resident individuals who are resident in an EU or a tax treaty country provided the necessary declaration of non-residence is made and a certificate from the taxing authority in the country of residence is provided.

27.1 Distributions

For corporation tax purposes, no deduction is allowed in computing income from any source in respect of dividends or other distributions. When doing a computation for a trading company, one always starts with "Profit before taxation" and, therefore, there is no need to adjust for dividends as they will not have been deducted. Regarding other distributions such as certain interest paid to directors by close companies, the interest will have been expensed in the Income Statement or P&L account and therefore will have to be added back.

Corporation tax is not chargeable on dividends or other distributions of a company resident in the State, i.e. if an Irish resident company receives a distribution from another Irish resident company, it is not liable to corporation tax on the income. (Anti-avoidance legislation exists which provides that the exemption from tax for dividends received from an Irish company does not apply in certain circumstances where an Irish company receives a dividend from a company which had been previously non-Irish resident. However, in general, dividends received by a company from another Irish resident company are exempt from corporation tax). However, individuals are liable to income tax under Schedule F in relation to dividends or other distributions.

The following constitute distributions:

(a)   dividends paid by a company, including a capital dividend;

(b)   scrip dividends – where a shareholder in a quoted resident company opts to take shares instead of a cash dividend;

(c)   redemption of bonus securities;

(d)   any distribution out of assets in respect of shares, except any part of it which represents a repayment of capital;

(e)   sale of assets by a company at undervalue or purchase of assets by a company at overvalue from a shareholder;

(f)   certain interest paid to non-resident parent companies;

(g)   interest paid to certain directors of close companies which exceeds a prescribed limit is treated as a distribution (see **Chapter 28**); and

(h)   certain expenses, incurred by a close company in the provision of benefits for a participator, which are treated as a distribution (see **Chapter 28**).

27.2 Dividend Withholding Tax (DWT)

27.2.1 Introduction

Chapter 8A of **Part 6 TCA 1997** sets out the law in relation to Dividend Withholding Tax (DWT). Under section 172B, DWT is payable in respect of all "relevant" distributions made by an Irish resident company with certain exceptions. The amount of the DWT due is tax at the standard rate, currently 20%, on the distribution made.

> **Example**
> ABC Ltd, an Irish resident company, is owned by three Irish resident individuals. ABC Ltd is to make an interim dividend payment of **€10,000** to each of its shareholders for the year ended 31 December 2012 on 1 October 2012. ABC Ltd must deduct DWT of €2,000 from each of the dividend payments made. Each shareholder will receive a **net payment of €8,000.**

27.2.2 Returns and Payment of DWT

DWT due must be paid to Revenue, and a DWT return filed, within 14 days of the end of the month in which the distribution is made. Such returns and payments must be made electronically via ROS. In the above example, ABC Ltd would have to pay the DWT deducted from the dividend payments made of €6,000 (3 × €2,000) by 14 November 2012. There is a four-year time limit for making repayment claims.

27.2.3 "Relevant" Distributions

DWT applies to all "relevant" distributions made by an Irish resident company. Relevant distributions are all dividends and distributions made by a company including:

(a)   cash dividends;
(b)   any non-cash distributions;
(c)   expenses incurred by close companies in providing certain benefits for a participator in the company (see **Chapter 28**);
(d)   interest in excess of a specified amount paid by close companies to directors (see **Chapter 28**); and
(e)   any amount taxable under Schedule F or Schedule D Case IV in respect of shares issued in lieu of dividends.

DWT applies to all distributions outlined at **Section 27.1** and to additional shares taken by shareholders in unquoted companies instead of a dividend, which are taxable under Case IV. However, there are a large number of exemptions from DWT in TCA 1997 – see below.

The amount of the relevant distribution to which the DWT applies is the cash amount, where a cash payment is made, or the market value of the distribution where a non-cash distribution is made.

Example
DEF Ltd, which is owned by three Irish resident individuals, owns shares in another company, XYZ Ltd. DEF Ltd distributes all its shares in XYZ Ltd to its own shareholders. At the time the shares in XYZ Ltd are distributed, they have a market value of €90,000. DEF Ltd is required to pay **DWT of €18,000** (€90,000 × 20%) to Revenue. DEF Ltd is entitled to recover the €18,000 from its shareholders.

27.2.4 Exemptions from DWT

Distributions made to persons not subject to tax on the distribution are exempt from DWT. These include:

(a)   an Irish resident company;
(b)   a pension scheme, approved minimum retirement fund and approved retirement fund;
(c)   a charity; and
(d)   under section 831 TCA 1997 a company resident in another EU Member State which owns 5% or more of the share capital of the distributing company (a "parent" company). However, if more than 50% of the voting rights in the parent company are controlled directly or indirectly by persons who are neither resident in an EU Member

State nor a treaty country then the exemption will not apply unless the EU parent company exists for genuine commercial reasons and not for the purpose of avoiding tax, including withholding tax.

In order to qualify for exemption from DWT, the persons listed at (a) to (c) above must make a declaration of entitlement to relief to the company making the distribution. This declaration confirms that the declarer is beneficially entitled to the distribution and is entitled to exemption falling under one of the categories (a) to (c) above.

However, in the case where an Irish resident company makes a distribution to its Irish resident parent (i.e. it is a 51% subsidiary), then a declaration is not required. Also note that companies qualifying under (d) above do not have to make a declaration.

In addition to (d) above, certain other non-resident persons are exempt from DWT. The **main** non-resident persons who are exempt include:

Non-resident Companies

A company which is not resident for tax purposes in the State and which:

(a)   is resident for tax purposes in an EU Member State or in a country with which Ireland has a tax treaty including where a treaty has been signed but has not yet come into force (a "tax treaty country");

(b)   is not under the control, whether directly or indirectly, of a person or persons who is/ are resident in the State; and

(c)   before the distribution is made, has submitted a declaration to the paying company confirming that it is a qualifying non-resident person and stating where it is resident for tax purposes.

Where a declaration has been made by the non-resident shareholder, it is treated as a current declaration from the date it is made to 31 December in the fifth year following the year in which it is made, i.e. the shareholder self-assesses its entitlement to the exemption and this continues to be valid for at least five years. If the shareholder's circumstances change and it is no longer entitled to the exemption, it must advise the paying company accordingly.

Example

Cusker Limited, an Irish resident company, is a wholly owned subsidiary of Cusker (US) Limited, a US resident company. Cusker (US) Limited is in turn owned by Cusker (IOM) Limited, an Isle of Man resident company. Cusker (IOM) is owned by four US resident individuals. Provided the appropriate declaration is made, Cusker Limited may pay dividends to Cusker (US) Limited without deduction of DWT.

There are exemptions for distributions made to other foreign companies. These other companies are ones which are ultimately under the control of persons resident in EU or treaty countries and not under the control of non-EU or non-treaty resident persons or whose shares are quoted on a stock exchange in the EU or a treaty country. These are required to reflect the fact that foreign investment into Ireland is not always held directly, but may be made through intermediary companies.

Non-resident Individuals

A non-resident person, other than a company, is exempt from DWT provided that the following conditions are satisfied:

(i)   the person must not be resident or ordinarily resident in the State;

(ii)   the person must be resident in an EU or a tax treaty country; and

(iii)   before the distribution is made, a declaration must be made by the recipient of the dividend to the paying company confirming that the individual is not resident in the State and is beneficially entitled to the dividend. The declaration must be accompanied by a certificate from the tax authorities of the country in which the person is resident, confirming that the person is resident in that country. Where a certificate from the relevant tax authorities has been submitted by the non-resident shareholder, it is treated as a current certificate from the date of issue to 31 December in the fifth year following the year in which it is issued.

Example
Harrison Ltd, an Irish resident company, has the following shareholders:

Mr Murphy, Irish resident
Mrs Murphy, Irish resident
Mr Muller, German resident
Mr Matthews, Swiss resident (treaty country)

Dividends may be paid to Mr Muller and Mr Matthews without deduction of DWT provided the appropriate declarations are made.

Dividends Paid Out of Exempt Profits

Dividends which are not liable to income tax in the hands of the recipients, e.g. dividends out of profits or gains from the occupation of woodlands, are also exempted from DWT. However, paying companies are still obliged to return details of such distributions in their DWT returns.

27.2.5   Shares Issued in Lieu of Dividend

Where an Irish resident company issues shares in lieu of a dividend in order to satisfy the DWT liability arising, it is required to issue a reduced number of shares with a value equal to the cash dividend foregone less DWT due on a cash dividend.

Example
On 1 October 2012 ABC Limited, an Irish unquoted resident company gives its shareholders an option to receive one ordinary share for every €20 of dividend. Each shareholder is entitled to receive a dividend of €5,000. If shares are taken, the position will be as follows:

	€
Amount of dividend receivable in cash	5,000
Less DWT @ 20%	(1,000)
Value of shares to be issued to each shareholder	4,000

Each shareholder that elects to receive shares will receive 200 shares valued at €20 each, i.e. €4,000. For each shareholder that elects to receive shares, the company will be required to pay DWT of €1,000 to Revenue.

Questions (to Chapter 27)

Review Questions

(See Suggested Solutions to Review Questions at the end of this textbook.)

Question 27.1

Lance Investments Ltd, an Irish resident company is to pay a dividend of €500,000 on 1 November 2012. Its shareholders are as follows:

	Number of Ordinary Shares
Mr C (resident in the State)	3,000
Mr A (resident in UK)	2,000
Mr R (resident in US)	1,000
UK Investments Ltd (resident in UK)	7,000
Spanol Investments Ltd (resident in Spain)	8,000
Thailand Investments Ltd (resident in Thailand)	1,000
Local Investments Ltd (resident in the State)	3,000
Total share capital	25,000

Notes:

1. All of the foreign companies which own shares in Lance Investments Ltd are controlled by individuals living in that country.
2. Ireland does not have a tax treaty with Thailand.

Requirement
(a) Compute the DWT payable by Lance Investments Ltd assuming all declarations necessary to obtain exemption are given.
(b) Indicate when the DWT is payable assuming the dividend is paid on 1 November 2012.
(c) Indicate the declarations to be made and the certificates to be provided by shareholders of Lance Investments Ltd in order to obtain exemption from DWT.

Close Companies and the Disadvantages

Learning Objectives

After studying this chapter you will have developed the competency to understand that:

■ Most Irish companies are close companies, as family companies are effectively under the control of one person. As this is anti-avoidance legislation, the definitions are complex.

■ There are the following negative tax consequences for close companies and their shareholders:

Expenses of Participators and their Associates

■ Expenses of shareholders or associates who are not employees/directors are treated as a distribution and must be added back in the tax computation but, since they are a distribution, they reduce any surcharge on undistributed investment or estate income or professional services income.

■ Expenses treated as a distribution give rise to a DWT liability for the company of 20% of the amount of the expenses paid.

Interest Paid to Directors and their Associates

■ Interest paid to directors or associates who own more than 5% of the shares is not fully deductible. The amount deductible is limited to the *lower* of 13% of

- such loans; or
- the nominal value of share capital plus share premium.

The excess is a distribution and must be added back in the tax computation, but since it is a distribution, it can reduce any surcharge on undistributed investment or estate income or professional services income.

■ The interest which continues to be treated as interest is subject to income tax withholding of 20%.

■ The interest, which is treated as a distribution, gives rise to a DWT liability for the company of 20% of the amount treated as a distribution.

Loans to Participators and their Associates

■ Where a company makes a loan to a shareholder or associate, it must also make a payment to Revenue, i.e. the loan to the shareholder is treated as a net annual payment. Therefore, the payment to Revenue is 20/80ths of the loan. Revenue repays this amount when the loan to the shareholder is repaid.

■ There is an exception for small loans, i.e. loans of €19,050 or less to employees/directors who work full-time in the company and do not own more than 5% of the shares. There is also an exception for financial institutions.

■ The receipt of the loan has no consequences for the shareholder. However, if it is at a preferential rate – which it typically is – the income tax benefit-in-kind rule will apply.

Repayment or Write Off of Loans to Participators

■ For as long as the loan is on the balance sheet of the company, the income tax payment made to Revenue stays with Revenue. There are two possible ways of the loan ceasing to be on the balance sheet, namely:
  ● write off loan; or
  ● shareholder repays loan.

■ If the loan is written off, the shareholder is deemed to receive income. The shareholder is taxable on the gross payment received, i.e. loan × 100/80ths, with a credit for the tax withheld at source.

■ The income tax paid by the company to Revenue is not repaid by Revenue.

■ The company is not allowed a deduction for the loan written off, i.e. it must be added back if the shareholder is not an employee or director of the company.

■ If the shareholder repays the loan, Revenue repays the tax. This is done by deducting the refund from the corporation tax due on profits of the year in which the loan is repaid.

Surcharge on Undistributed Estate and Investment Income

■ If a company does not distribute its franked investment income (FII) and its after-tax investment (Case III, IV) and rental (Case V) income to its shareholders, it is subject to a surcharge.

■ The steps in preparing a computation of the surcharge are set out in the notes. Typically, the amount subject to the surcharge is:
  ● For a trading company, it is 92.5% of [FII plus 75% (estate and investment income)]
  ● For an investment company, it is:
    (a) FII plus estate and investment income less management expenses, less
    (b) Tax at 25% on [(a) – FII]

If there are current year trading losses, Case V losses or relevant trading charges, then these must be deducted.

■ From this amount, you deduct all distributions made during the year (including excess interest and expenses that are treated as distributions) and dividends paid for the year, either during the year or within 18 months of the end of the accounting period. If the figure is €635 or less, there is no surcharge. If it is greater than €635, the surcharge is **20%** of the figure.

■ The paying and recipient companies may jointly elect to have a distribution ignored for the surcharge.

Surcharge on Certain Services Companies
- These are mainly professional services companies.
- The surcharge applies to the undistributed Case II income, as well as undistributed estate and investment income.
- The surcharge applies to:
  - 50% of the distributable trading income; plus
  - 100% of the distributable estate and investment income; less
  - any distributions made/dividends paid.

The surcharge rate is 20% on undistributed estate and investment income (i.e. net of distributions/dividends). The balance (net of distributions/dividends) is liable at 15%.

28.1 Meaning of Close Company

Under section 430 TCA 1997, a **close company** is one which is **under the control of**:

- **five or fewer participators**; or
- **participators who are directors**.

A resident company will also be regarded as close if, **on a full distribution of its income, more than half of it would fall to be paid to five or fewer participators, or to participators who are directors**.

Most Irish private companies are close companies, whereas almost all publicly quoted companies are not close companies. As most private companies are close companies, the anti-avoidance rules applying to close companies are very important.

28.2 Definitions

Because this is anti-avoidance legislation, all words used are very widely defined so as to deter people finding a loophole and avoiding the rules.

28.2.1 Participator

A **shareholder** is the most common example of a participator. A participator is a person having a share or interest in the capital or income of the company. However, because this is anti-avoidance legislation, the definition is very widely drafted. A participator includes any person having a present or future share or interest in the capital, assets or income of the company and also includes a "loan creditor" of the company. A "loan creditor" is a creditor of the company because of money lent to the company or a capital asset sold to the company. A normal bank would not however be regarded as a loan creditor.

28.2.2 Control

A person is regarded as having control of a company if he exercises, or is able to exercise, or is entitled to acquire, control over the company's affairs and, in particular, if the person possesses or is entitled to acquire more than 50% of the company's share capital, income if it were distributed, or assets in a winding up.

Importantly, in determining if an individual satisfies any of the above tests the rights and powers of his associates and any company over which he, or he and his associates, have control are attributed to him.

28.2.3 Associate

An associate of a participator means:

(a) a relative of the participator (i.e. spouse, civil partner, ancestor, lineal descendant, brother or sister); it does not include an aunt, or uncle, or cousin;
(b) a partner of the participator; or
(c) a trustee of a settlement established by the participator or a relative.

28.2.4 Director

In order to be regarded as a director, a person need not actually have the title of director. A director includes a person:

(a) occupying the position of director by whatever name called,
(b) in accordance with whose directions or instructions the directors are accustomed to act,
(c) who is a manager of the company or otherwise concerned in the management of the company's trade or business, and who is, either on his own or with one or more of his associates, the beneficial owner of, or able, directly or through the medium of other companies or by any other indirect means, to control, **20% or more** of the ordinary share capital of the company.

Example

Shares in Alphabet Limited, an Irish resident company, are held as follows:

	Status	Shareholding
Mr A	Director	10%
Mrs A		2%
Mrs C (Mr A's aunt)		2%
Mrs B		10%
B Ltd (Shares in B Ltd held 50% each by Mr and Mrs B)		5%
Mr J (Mrs B's cousin)		4%
Mr D	Director	10%
Mrs D		2%
Ms D (Mr and Mrs D's daughter)		2%
Mrs E (Mr D's sister)		2%
Mr F		6%
Mr G		5%
Other shareholdings (Unrelated parties all holding <5%)		40%
		100%

Is Alphabet Limited under the control of five or fewer participators?

Shares held by Mr A:		
Mr A	10%	
Mrs A	2%	12%
Shares held by Mrs B:		
Mrs B	10%	
B Ltd	5%	15%

continued overleaf

Shares held by Mr D:

Mr D	10%	
Mrs D	2%	
Ms D	2%	
Mrs E	2%	16%
Mr F		6%
Mr G		5%
		54%

In determining the shares controlled by each participator, shares held by associates are included. Spouses, civil partners, children, siblings and parents are included as associates; however, shares held by cousins or aunts are not included.

Alphabet Limited is under the control of five or fewer participators and is, therefore, a close company.

28.3 Excluded Companies

Certain companies that would be regarded as close companies under the above definitions are not regarded as close companies. The *main* excluded companies are:

(a) a company which is controlled by a company which is not a close company or by two or more companies who are not close companies, and the company could only be regarded as close if one of these companies were included in the five or fewer participators;

(b) a company not resident in the State;

(c) a company controlled by or on behalf of the State, a Member State of the EU or government of a tax treaty country and not otherwise a close company; and

(d) "public" companies: for this purpose, a company is regarded as a public company if the following two tests are satisfied:

- at least 35% of the voting share capital is held by "the public"; and
- these shares are quoted on a recognised stock exchange and in the previous 12 months there have been dealings in those shares on the stock exchange.
  Where the total percentage of the voting power in the company possessed by all the company's principal members exceeds 85%, the company is not a public company.

In this context "the public" does not include:

- directors or their associates;
- a company under the control of directors and/or their associates;
- an associated company of the company;
- a fund for the benefit of employees or directors (past or current); and
- a principal member, which means a person who holds more than 5% of the voting share capital and who is one of the five largest shareholders. In determining a principal member's shareholding, shares held by an associate are taken into account.

28.4 Consequences of Close Company Status

Close companies are subject to special anti-avoidance rules which have negative tax consequences for the company and/or its shareholders.

The reason for the special anti-avoidance rules contained in the law dealing with close companies, is to deal with the fact that closely held companies generally can take decisions so as to minimise tax in a way that would not be feasible for a publicly quoted company.

For example, a publicly quoted company would have so many shareholders that generally it would not be feasible to fund itself with loans rather than share capital. However if it were tax-efficient for a closely held company with just a few shareholders, it could easily do so. In the absence of the anti-avoidance rules applying to close companies, it would be more tax-efficient to pay shareholders interest which would be tax deductible, rather than dividends, which would not be tax deductible.

Again, in the absence of the close company anti-avoidance rules, companies would lend money to shareholders rather than pay a dividend. Such a loan would not be income and therefore the loan would not be taxable income. (There may be a liability on the preferential interest rate, but not the loan itself). To stop this type of planning, the close company is subject to a tax penalty if it makes a loan to a participator, i.e. a shareholder.

Without close company rules, more individuals would incorporate. The top income tax rate is 41% plus PRSI (4%) and Universal Social Charge (up to 10% for self-employed). This marginal rate of up to 55% compares with the corporation tax rates of 12.5% and 25%. Therefore incorporation would save money. However, the close company surcharges (i.e. additional tax) on service company income and investment and rental income, make incorporation significantly less attractive.

28.5 Disadvantages of Close Company Status

The disadvantages of close company status are as follows:

1. Certain **expenses** for participators and their associates are treated as distributions.
2. **Interest** paid to certain directors and their associates, which exceeds a prescribed limit, is treated as a distribution.
3. There is a tax penalty for close companies making **loans** to participators or their associates.
4. Loans to participators or their associates which are subsequently **written off** will be assessable to income tax in their hands.
5. A **surcharge** of **20%** is levied on the **distributable estate and investment income** of close companies, to the extent that it is not distributed.
6. In the case of **certain** closely held **service companies**, a **surcharge** of **15%/20%** is levied on:
   - 50% of the distributable trading income; and
   - 100% of the distributable estate and investment income.

   Obviously a publicly quoted company which is not a closely held company is not subject to these rules.

   We will now examine each of the above.

28.6 Certain Expenses for Participators and their Associates

Any expenses incurred by a close company in providing benefits or facilities of any kind for a participator or an associate of the participator, will be treated as a distribution.

Where an item is treated as a distribution, there are three consequences:

1. the **expense** will be **disallowed** to the company;
2. the company will have dividend withholding tax (**DWT**) liability equal to 20% of the market value of the distribution. The company can recover this tax from the participator and, accordingly, the DWT is a cost to the participator; and
3. the recipient will be **assessed** under **Schedule F** on the distribution, i.e. liable to income tax at the marginal rate (most likely 41%), liable to the Universal Social Charge (USC) at the marginal rate (typically at 7%) and may also be liable to PRSI at 4%, e.g. if the individual is liable under Class S.

The following expense payments are **not** treated as distributions:

(a) any expense made good to the company by the participator;
(b) any expense incurred in providing benefits or facilities to directors or employees, as such expenses are already assessable as benefits in kind under Schedule E; and
(c) any expense incurred in connection with the provision for the spouse, civil partner, children or dependants or children of a civil partner of any director or employee of any pension, annuity, lump sum or gratuity to be given on his death or retirement.

The legislation also contains anti-avoidance measures to counter two or more close companies from arranging to make payments to one another's participators.

Example

Mr A holds 2% of the ordinary share capital of X Ltd a close company. Mr A is not an employee or director of X Ltd.

X Ltd pays the rent on Mr A's house of €3,000 per annum. The amount is charged each year in X Ltd's accounts under rental expenses.

As X Ltd is a close company and Mr A, a participator, the expense will be treated as a distribution. Accordingly, the €3,000 will be disallowed to X Ltd in arriving at its profits assessable to corporation tax.

X Ltd will be required to pay DWT of €600 (€3,000 × 20%) to Revenue within 14 days of the end of the month in which the rent is paid. X Ltd can recover this €600 from Mr A.

Mr A will be assessed under Schedule F on €3,000 with a credit of €600 given against his total tax liability. However, if Mr A does not pay the DWT to X Ltd, he will not get a credit for DWT.

Mr X will be liable to income tax at his marginal rate – most likely 41%. He will also be liable to the USC. This will typically be at 7%. (However, for self-employed taxpayers and others whose non-PAYE income is greater than €100,000, the USC is charged at 10% on income above that limit.) He may also be liable to PRSI at 4%.

28.7 Interest Paid to Directors and their Associates

The legislation is concerned with interest on loans in excess of a prescribed limit paid to, or to an associate of, a director of the company (or of any close company which controls, or is controlled by it), if he has a "material interest" in the company or in any company that controls it.

A person has a material interest if he/she, either on his own or with any one or more of his associates, or if any associate(s) of his with or without any such other associates, is the beneficial owner of, or is able to control, directly or indirectly **more than 5%** of the ordinary share capital.

The prescribed limit is calculated in the first instance as an overall limit. The overall limit is then apportioned between the various directors affected according to the amounts of interest paid to them.

The overall limit is **13%** per annum on the **smaller** of:

1. the total of all **loans** on which interest to directors (or their associates) with a "material interest" was paid by the company in the accounting period. Where the total of the loans was different at different times in the accounting period, the average total is to be taken; and
2. the **nominal** amount of the issued **share capital** of the company plus the amount of any **share premium** account at the **beginning of the accounting period**.

If the total amount of interest paid to a director in the accounting period exceeds this limit the excess will be treated as a distribution.

Example 1

Zoey Ltd has an issued share capital of €100. It has two shareholders who are both directors and who each lent the company €10,000 at an interest rate of 10% per annum.

The interest expense is €10,000 × 10% × 2 = €2,000. As both are directors with a material interest, then the limit on this interest is the *lower* of:

(a) 13% × €20,000 = €2,600; and
(b) 13% × €100 = €13

Therefore, only €13 is deductible. As €2,000 has been expensed, €1,987 must be added back in the tax computation.

Zoey Ltd will be required to deduct DWT of €397 (€1,987 × 20%) from the interest paid, and pay this amount within 14 days of the end of the month in which the interest is paid, to Revenue. Also, assuming that the interest is annual interest, Zoey Ltd will have to withhold income tax from the interest, i.e. withhold €13 × 20% = €3.

From each director's perspective, they are taxed on a gross distribution of 1/2 × €1,987, under Schedule F and on interest income liable under Case IV of 1/2 × €13 with a credit for DWT of 1/2 × €397 and for income tax of 1/2 × €3, against his income tax liability.

Each will be liable to income tax at his mariginal rate – most likely 41%. Each will also be liable to the USC at his marginal rate – typically at 7%. Each may also be liable to PRSI at 4%.

Example 2

XYZ Ltd has an issued share capital of €30,000. The shares are held as follows:

	€
Mr A (Director)	3,000
Mr B (Director)	1,200
Mrs B	400
Mr C (Director)	1,500

continued overleaf

Mr D (Director)	4,000	
Mr E (Director)	3,500	
Mr F (Director)	1,500	
Mr G	1,000	
15 unrelated shareholders each holding less than 1,000 shares	13,900	
	30,000	

The following loans were made to the company:

Mr A   €8,000 @ 20% per annum

Mr B   €7,000 @ 10% per annum for the first six months increased to €9,000 @ 10% per annum for the last six months of the year

Mr C   €6,000 @ 15% per annum

Mr E   €5,000 @ 12% per annum for the first six months and

@ 16% per annum for the last six months

Mr F   €5,000 @ 15% per annum

Mr G   €2,000 @ 15% per annum

The interest charge in XYZ Ltd's Profit and Loss account was made up as follows:

				€	€
Mr A	€8,000 @ 20%				1,600
Mr B	€7,000 @ 10% × 1/2	=	350		
	€9,000 @ 10% × 1/2	=	450		800
Mr C	€6,000 @ 15%	=			900
Mr E	€5,000 @ 12% × 1/2	=	300		
	€5,000 @ 16% × 1/2	=	400		700
Mr F	€5,000 @ 15%	=			750
Mr G	€2,000 @ 15%	=			300
					5,050

The share capital of the company was the same at the start of the year. There was no share premium account.

1. **Is the company close? Yes**

It is under the control of participators who are directors, i.e.:

	€	€
Mr A		3,000
Mr B	1,200	
Mrs B	400	1,600
Mr C		1,500
Mr D		4,000
Mr E		3,500
Mr F		1,500
		15,100

continued overleaf

2. Identify **directors** who made loans to the company and who, together with their associates, **own more than 5%** of the shares

	€
Mr A	3,000 (10%)
Mr B	1,600 (5.33%)
Mr E	3,500 (11.67%)

3. **Calculate the overall limit**

The lower of:

(a) 13% of share capital, i.e.: 13% × €30,000 = €3,900

(b) 13% × loans from directors with material interest

	€
Mr A	8,000
Mr B (average)	8,000
Mr E	5,000
	21,000

13% × €21,000 = €2,730
The overall limit is €2,730

4. **Apportion limit** to relevant directors by reference to interest paid

	Interest Paid	Limit	Excess treated as a Distribution
Mr. A	€1,600	$\frac{€1,600}{€3,100} \times €2,730 = €1,409$	€191
Mr. B	€800	$\frac{€800}{€3,100} \times €2,730 = €705$	€95
Mr. E	€700	$\frac{€700}{€3,100} \times €2,730 = €616$	€84
	€3,100	€2,730	€370

€370 will be disallowed to XYZ Ltd in computing its profits for corporation tax. DWT @ 20% must be deducted from the portion of the interest treated as a distribution. Each of the directors will be assessed under Schedule F to income tax, USC and possibly PRSI on the proportion of the excess referable to him with a credit given against their total tax liability for the DWT deducted.

5. The company paid €5,050 of interest of which €370 is treated as distribution. The balance of the interest, i.e. €4,680, is deductible. However, as with any other annual payment, the company must deduct tax at the standard income tax rate when paying this interest and pay this tax to Revenue. Each of the directors will be assessed under Schedule D Case IV, to income tax, USC and possibly PRSI, on the proportion of the €4,680 referable to him with a credit given against their total tax liability for the income tax deducted.

28.8 Loans to Participators and their Associates

Where a close company makes a loan to an **individual** who is a participator or an associate of a participator, the company will be required to pay income tax in respect of the amount of the loan grossed up at the standard rate (i.e. 20%) as if that grossed-up amount were an annual payment. A close company is to be regarded as making a loan to any person who incurs a debt to the company or where a debt due from a person to a third party is assigned to the company.

There are **three exceptions** to the above, which means that the following are not treated as loans to participators:

1. Where the business of the company is, or includes, the lending of money and the loan is made in the ordinary course of that business.
2. Where a debt is incurred for the supply of goods or services in the ordinary course of the business of the close company, unless the credit given exceeds six months or is longer than the period normally given to the company's customers.
3. Loans made to directors or employees of the company (or an associated company) if:

    (a) the amount of the loan, together with all other loans outstanding made by the company (or its associated companies) to the borrower (or his spouse or civil partner), does not exceed €19,050;

    (b) the borrower works full time for the company; and

    (c) the borrower does **not** have a "material interest" in the company or an associated company – a person has a material interest if he, either on his own or with any one or more of his associates, or if any associate(s) of his with or without any such other associates, is the beneficial owner of, or is able to control, directly or indirectly **more than 5%** of the ordinary share capital.

It should be noted that, in relation to 3.(c), if the borrower subsequently acquires a material interest, the company will be required to pay income tax in respect of all the loans outstanding from the borrower at that time.

When the loan or part of the loan is repaid by the participator (or associate), the tax, or a proportionate part of it, will be refunded to the company provided a claim is made within 10 years of the year of assessment in which the loan is repaid. However, the tax will not be refunded with interest.

Although the legislation is primarily concerned with loans to individuals, there is a similar provision for close companies making loans to a non-resident company which is a participator or an associate of a participator. However, this legislation does not generally apply to loans made to companies resident in EU Member States.

Example 3

ABC Ltd, a close company, made interest-free loans to the following shareholders in the accounting period to 31 March 2012.

	€
Mr A (Director owning 10% of the share capital)	16,000
Mr B (Director owning 4% of the share capital)	10,000
Mr C	8,000

continued overleaf

What are the tax consequences for the company assuming that no other loans had been made to the three individuals in the past? You may also assume that Mr A and Mr B work full-time for the company.

Solution

The company will be required to pay income tax in respect of the loans to Mr A and Mr C grossed up at the standard rate as if the grossed-up amount were an annual payment.

The tax penalty for the company is calculated as follows:

	€
Mr A	16,000
Mr C	8,000
	24,000 × 20/80ths = €6,000

The loan to Mr B is not caught as Mr B:

(i)   is a director who works full-time;
(ii) does not have a "material interest" in the company; and
(iii) the loan is less than €19,050.

This tax of €6,000 is added to the corporation tax on profits and must be paid over to the Collector General at the same time as the corporation tax on profits, i.e. preliminary tax due on/before 23 February 2012 and the balance due on/before 23 December 2012.

28.9   Write Off of Loans to Participators

Where a company makes a loan to a participator and subsequently releases or writes it off, the shareholder receives income at the time of writing off the loan, i.e. a debt is released. The participator will be treated as though his total income for the year in which the release or write off occurs were increased by the amount released or written off grossed up at the standard rate of income tax.

However, no repayment of income tax will be made in respect of the grossed-up amount and it will not be treated as taxed income available to cover charges.

Example 4

Assume that in the previous example Mr A repays his loan of €16,000 on 31 December 2012 and at the same time the company writes off the loan to Mr C.

What are the tax consequences for the company and the shareholder?

Company

The company will be repaid the tax on Mr A's loan, i.e. €4,000 (20/80 × €16,000) However, it will lose the tax paid on Mr C's loan, i.e. €2,000 (20/80 × €8,000)

Shareholders

There are no tax consequences for Mr A.

Mr C, however, will be assessed to tax under Case IV Schedule D on the grossed-up amount of the loan, i.e. €10,000 (8,000 × 100/80)

continued overleaf

Assume Mr C has other income of €30,000, is liable to PRSI under Class A, has personal tax credits of €3,300, is single and the tax bands are as outlined below. The grossed-up loan of €10,000 would be taxed at current rates of tax as follows:

	€
Other income	30,000
Case IV loan	10,000
Total/Taxable Income	40,000
Tax: €32,800 @ 20% =	6,560
€7,200 @ 41% =	2,952
	9,512
Less: Personal tax credits	(3,300)
	6,212
Less €10,000 @ 20%	(2,000)
Tax payable (before PRSI and USC)	4,212
USC	
€10,036 @ 2% = €201	
€5,980 @ 4% = €239	
€23,984 @ 7% = €1,679	€2,119

PRSI will be charged at 4% on reckonable earnings only, which would not include the loan written off as it does not relate to his employment (he is not employed by the company).

Where the company writes off the loan, it will not get a refund of the income tax paid to Revenue when the loan was made.

As the loan is written off, there is an expense in the Income Statement. The expense is not deductible and must be disallowed in the corporation tax computation.

28.10 Surcharge

Where a company has cash surplus to its trading requirements, it can invest the cash itself or dividend it to the shareholders. If the company invests itself, it will be liable at 25% on most investment income. If it pays a dividend to its shareholders, the shareholder must pay tax – probably 52% (i.e. 41% income tax plus 7% USC plus 4% PRSI) – on the dividend and can only invest the dividend net of tax. Therefore, unless the shareholder needs the cash, it would generally be left in the company to avoid shareholder tax. The close company anti-avoidance rule, known as the surcharge, reduces some of the benefit of leaving cash in a company.

A surcharge of 20% is levied on a close company which does not distribute its after tax estate (rental) and investment income. (**Note:** There is no surcharge on the base Case I income, but there is a surcharge on Case II income of professional services companies – see **Section 28.11.**)

28.10.1 Surcharge Calculation – Trading Company (No Losses, etc.)

Remember that this is a surcharge on undistributed estate and investment income, i.e. not trading income and not gains. The calculation of the surcharge for a trading company is summarised below. Please note that:

- The figures below are only in respect of income of the current accounting period, i.e. before any claim for losses, etc. back or forward.
- Irish dividends (FII) are not liable to corporation tax, just the surcharge.
- The approach below is only for companies that have no current year trading losses, Case V losses, relevant trading charges, or relevant charges.

The computation may be summarised as follows:

		€
Case III		X
Case IV		X
Case V		X̲
		Y
FII		X̲
		X
Less: Corporation tax (usually @ 25%) on "Y" only		(X̲)
		Z
Less: 7.5% of "Z"		X̲
Liable to surcharge		X
Less		
Dividends declared for or in respect of the accounting period and paid during or within 18 months of the end of the accounting period	X	
All distributions made in the accounting period (other than dividends)	X̲	X̲
Amount on which surcharge will be levied @ 20%		X̲

There will be no surcharge if the excess of the distributable estate and investment income over the distributions is €635 or less. Where the accounting period is less than 12 months, the €635 will be reduced proportionately. If there are associated companies, the €635 will be reduced by dividing it by one plus the number of associated companies.

In preparing this computation, it is essential to note that:

Case III Foreign dividends are generally taxable under Case III. In relation to foreign dividends, there are two key points:

- If the dividends are paid by a foreign company, a gain on disposal of whose shares would qualify for exemption (see **Section 26.3**), then that dividend is exempt from the surcharge and will not be included in Case III for the surcharge.
- Case III income is generally taxed at 25%. However, many foreign dividends are taxable at 12.5% (see **Section 31.1.2**) and, therefore, for this Case III income, the tax rate used will be 12.5%.

Case V It is the Case V profit of the current accounting period, i.e. before Case V losses carried forward or back and before capital allowances.

FII/distributions Two Irish resident companies may elect to pay distributions so that the distributions are not treated as distributions for the purposes of the surcharge – see **Section 28.10.4**.

Example 5

Shop Ltd, a close company, runs a shop in Dublin. It had the following income in the year ended 31 December 2012:

Case I	100,000
Case III	2,000
Case V	6,000

The company pays no dividends.

What is the surcharge?

The surcharge is payable on distributable estate and investment income, to the extent that it is not distributed.

	€
Estate and investment income (2,000 + 6,000)	8,000
Corporation tax @ 25%	(2,000)
	6,000
Trading company: deduct 7.5%	(450)
	5,550

As no dividends were paid, the surcharge is €5,550 @ 20% = €1,110.

Example 6

Trumps Ltd, a close company, has the following results for the year ended 31 December 2012:

	€
Trade income	480,000
Deposit interest	2,000
Rental income	40,000
Rental loss forward from 2011	(10,000)

Notes
1. The company had a loss forward relating to the trade of €20,000.
2. The company had chargeable gains in the accounting period of €2,000, after adjustment.
3. A cash dividend of €700 was received from another Irish company in the accounting period.
4. An interim dividend of €14,000 in respect of the accounting period was paid on 1 October 2013. A final dividend of €9,580 will be paid on 10 October 2014.

Calculate the amount of the surcharge (if any) arising in respect of the estate and investment income of the accounting period ended 31 December 2012 and state when the tax is payable.

continued overleaf

Solution

Distributable estate and investment income

	€
Case III	2,000
Case V	40,000
	42,000
FII	700
Estate and investment income	42,700
Less: Corporation tax at 25% on €42,000	(10,500)
	32,200
Less 7.5% × 32,200	(2,415)
Distributable estate and investment income	29,785

Note: Ignore any non-estate and investment income (e.g. Case I) and any losses forward (i.e. only estate and investment income of the current accounting period is relevant) and chargeable gains.

Calculate amount on which surcharge is levied

	€
Distributable estate and investment income	29,785
Less: Dividends paid within eighteen months	(14,000)
	15,785

The surcharge is €15,785 @ 20% = €3,157.

The surcharge of €3,157 is an additional corporation tax liability which is charged as part of the corporation tax payable in respect of the accounting year ended 31 December 2013, the preliminary tax on which is payable on/before 23 November 2013, and the balance of which is payable on/before 23 September 2014.

If the final dividend were paid on, say, 30 June 2014, the surcharge could have been as follows:

	€
Excess (as above)	15,785
Less: Dividends paid on 30/6/14	(9,580)
	6,205

The surcharge is €6,205 @ 20% = €1,241.

28.10.2 Surcharge Calculation – Trading Company (with Losses, etc.)

Where a company has current year trading losses, Case V losses, relevant trading charges (trade charges), or relevant charges (non-trade charges), then these must be deducted in arriving at the amount liable to the surcharge.

Example 7: Trading Loss
Loss Limited, a close company, runs a garage in Dublin. It had the following income in the year ended 31 December 2012:

	€
Case I	(10,000)
Case III	2,000
Case V	16,000
FII	5,000

The company pays no dividends.

continued overleaf

What is the surcharge?

	€
Estate and investment income (2,000 + 16,000)	18,000
Less current year trading losses	(10,000)
	8,000
Add FII	5,000
	13,000
Corporation tax @ 25% on €8,000	(2,000)
	11,000
Trading company: deduct 7.5%	(825)
	10,175

As no dividends were paid, the surcharge is €10,175 @ 20% = €2,035.

Example 8: Non-trade Charge

Interesting Limited, a close company, has a business in Dublin. It had the following income and charges in the year ended 31 December 2012:

Case I	100,000
Case III	2,000
Case V	16,000
FII	5,000
Non-trade charge paid	4,000

The company pays no dividend in respect of the year.

What is the surcharge?

	€
Estate and investment income (2,000 + 16,000)	18,000
Less non-trade charge paid	(4,000)
	14,000
Add FII	5,000
	19,000
Corporation tax @ 25% on €14,000	3,500
	15,500
Trading company: deduct 7.5%	1,162
	14,338

As no dividends were paid, the surcharge is €14,338 @ 20% = €2,868.

The situation for trade charges is a little different, as part of the trade charge has to be allocated to the trading income. The next example illustrates how to deal with trade charges.

Example 9: Trade Charge

Patent Ltd, a close company, runs a manufacturing business in Dublin. It had the following income and charges in the year ended 31 December 2012:

	€
Case I	10,000
Trade charges paid	600
Case III	2,000
FII	17,000

On 9 January 2013, the company pays a dividend of €10,000 in respect of the year.

What is the surcharge?

	€
Estate and investment income	2,000
Less *share* of trade charges, i.e. E&I income/Total income	
€600 × €2,000/€12,000	(100)
	1,900
Add FII	17,000
	18,900
Corporation tax @ 25% on €1,900	(475)
	18,425
Trading company: deduct 7.5%	(1,382)
	17,043
Less dividends paid	(10,000)
Liable to the surcharge	7,043

The surcharge is €7,043 @ 20% = €1,409.

28.10.3 Surcharge Calculation – Investment Company

Investment companies are dealt with at **Chapter 29** and the calculation of the surcharge for those companies is dealt with at **Section 29.7**.

28.10.4 Election – Not a Distribution for Surcharge

A company making a distribution (e.g. dividend) and a company receiving a distribution may jointly elect that the distribution will not be treated as a distribution for the purposes of the surcharge calculation.

As a result, an Irish holding company and an Irish subsidiary that pays or makes a distribution to the holding company can elect not to treat the distribution as coming under the close company surcharge provisions. Where such an election is made, the distribution will be treated as not being a distribution received by the holding company and as not being a distribution made by the subsidiary.

Note: for the purposes of the examples throughout the chapter, the election has not been made and the distribution, i.e. FII received, has been taken into account for the purposes of the surcharge calculation. In Example 9, if the election been made in respect of the dividend paid, then Patent Ltd would not have been allowed a deduction in respect of the dividend paid by it. In example 9, if the election been made in respect of the dividend *received*, then Patent Ltd would not have been liable to the surcharge on that dividend.

28.10.5 Other Matters

The following points should be noted in relation to the surcharge:

(a) The surcharge will not apply to any income, which a company is by law precluded from distributing.
(b) The surcharge is only ever levied on a source of income, it is never levied on a gain.
(c) There will be marginal relief where the excess over the distributions of the distributable investment and estate income is slightly in excess of €635. The marginal relief will restrict the tax to 4/5 (total − 635).
(d) **Close company distributions** (i.e. expenses for participators and associates and excess interest to directors and associates) can be taken into account to **reduce the amount on which the surcharge is levied**.
(e) If the amount liable to the surcharge is more than the accumulated undistributed income at the end of the accounting period, then the surcharge is levied on the lower accumulated undistributed income.

28.10.6 Payment of Surcharge

The surcharge is treated as corporation tax on the earliest accounting period which ends on or after a day which is 12 months after the end of the accounting period in which the investment or rental income arises, e.g. a company has a potential surcharge liability of say €5,000 in respect of the accounts year ended 30 September 2012. If it does not make the necessary distribution within 18 months, i.e. before 31 March 2014, the surcharge liability is treated as corporation tax of the accounts year ended 30 September 2013.

If, instead, the next accounting period were only nine months long, i.e. period ended 30 June 2013, the surcharge would be treated as corporation tax of the accounts year ended 30 June 2014.

This delay in paying the surcharge is necessary as the company has up to 18 months after the end of the accounting period to pay a dividend to reduce/eliminate the surcharge.

28.11 Service Company Surcharge

A service company is a close company, the principal part of whose income chargeable under Cases I and II of Schedule D and Schedule E is derived from:

(a) carrying on directly a profession or providing professional services or the having, or exercising of, an office or employment; or
(b) providing services or facilities of any nature;
    (i) to a company within (a):
    (ii) to an individual or partnership carrying on a profession;
    (iii) to a person who holds or exercises an office or employment; or
    (iv) to a person or partnership connected with any person in (i) to (iii) above.

Services provided to an unconnected person or partnership are, however, ignored.

For a service company to be liable to the surcharge under this legislation, the main part of its income must come from a profession, provision of professional services, an employment or provision of the services or facilities to a connected person. Therefore, it is important to understand what is a profession. There is no definition in the law as to what is a profession. The UK case of *CIR v. Maxse* sets out the determining factors to be taken into account. A profession involves the idea of an occupation requiring either purely intellectual skill or of a manual skill controlled by the intellectual skill of the operator, e.g. painting or sculpture or surgery. This is distinguishing from an occupation which is substantially the production or sale, or arrangement for the production or sale, of commodities, which would not be a profession.

The issue of whether an activity is a profession has been considered in a number of cases, particularly in the UK. The Revenue have set out in a Tax Briefing lists of what in Revenue's view, are and are not professions, taking into account case law. These are set out below and give practical examples of what Revenue **regard as professions**:

- Accountant
- Actor
- Actuary
- Archaeologist
- Architect
- Auctioneer/estate agent
- Barrister
- Computer programmer
- Dentist
- Doctor
- Engineer
- Journalist
- Management consultant
- Optician
- Private school
- Quantity surveyor
- Solicitor
- Veterinary surgeon

The Tax Briefing also sets out practical examples of what Revenue regard as not being professions, with the following activities generally **not considered** to constitute the carrying on of a **profession**:

- Advertising agent
- Auctioneers of livestock in a cattle mart
- Insurance brokers
- Operation of a retail pharmacy
- Public relations company
- Stockbrokers
- Book-keeping

The differences between this surcharge and the surcharge on undistributed estate and investment income are that **half the after-tax Case I/II income** is also liable to surcharge but **a rate of only 15%** applies to this part of the income.

The amount on which the surcharge is levied is arrived at as follows:

1. Calculate the "trading income" of the company, i.e. "the income of the company for the accounting period" less estate and investment income before deduction of relevant charges, i.e. non-trade charges. However, if these charges actually exceed the estate and investment income, then the excess charges may be deducted from the income. "The income of the company for the accounting period" is computed without regard to any losses, deficiencies, expenses of management or charges carried forward from an earlier accounting period, or any losses carried back from a later accounting period and group relief, but after deducting any trading losses, Case V losses and relevant trading charges of the company in the current accounting period.

2. Calculate "distributable trading income", i.e. the trading income as calculated at 1 above less corporation tax on that income, i.e. 12.5% for 2012 and later years.

3. Calculate "distributable estate and investment income" as per **Section 28.10**.

4. Calculate the amount on which the surcharge is levied:

50% × distributable trading income (DTI)	A	
100% × distributable estate and investment income (DEII)	B	
	X	
Less:		
Dividends declared for, or in respect of, the accounting period and paid during or within 18 months of the end of the accounting period	X	
All distributions made in the accounting period (other than dividends)	X	(X)
Amount on which surcharge will be levied		X

5. As distributable estate and investment income (DEII) is taxed at 20%, and distributable trading income (DTI) at 15%, the amount calculated at 4 above needs to be divided between DTI and DEII. All distributions are treated as firstly offset against DEII.

DEII	B	
less: Distribution	X	
Balance	Y	(could be €Nil)

If distributions exceed DEII, then offset excess against DTI.

6. Calculate the surcharge as follows:

Y (per step 5) @ 20%	X
A (per step 4) less any unutilised distributions @ 15%	X
Total Surcharge	X

If this figure is €635 or less, there is no surcharge. As before, if it is slightly higher, there is marginal relief – see **Section 28.10.5** above. Where the accounting period is less than 12 months, the €635 will be reduced proportionately. If there are associated companies, the €635 will be reduced by dividing it by one plus the number of associated companies.

As for the surcharge on estate and investment income, the service company surcharge is treated as corporation tax of the earliest accounting period which ends on or after a day which is 12 months after the end of the accounting period in which the service income arose.

Example 10

Good Advice Ltd a closely held firm of management consultants had the following income for the year ended 31 December 2012:

	€
Professional income	100,000
Interest on Government Securities	30,000
Rental income	20,000
Irish dividend received (cash amount)	14,000

The company declared and paid a dividend of €50,000 for the accounting period on 6 July 2012.

As the principal part of the company's income is derived from carrying on a profession, the company is a service company.

The amount on which the surcharge is levied is calculated as follows:

1. Calculate the "trading income" of the company

	€
Case II professional income	100,000
Case III interest on Government Securities	30,000
Case V rental income	20,000
	150,000
Less: estate and investment income	
(€30,000 + €20,000)	(50,000)
Trading income	100,000

2. Calculate "distributable trading income"

	€
Trading income	100,000
Corporation tax @ 12.5%	12,500
Distributable trading income	87,500

3. Calculate "distributable estate and investment income" (DEII)

	€
Case III interest on Government Securities	30,000
Case V rental income	20,000
	50,000
Franked investment income	14,000
Estate and investment income	64,000
Corporation tax €50,000 × 25%	(12,500)
	51,500
Less 7.5% × €51,500 =	(3,862)
Distributable estate and investment income	47,638

continued overleaf

4. Calculate amount on which surcharge is levied   €

50% × distributable trading income 87,500 =	43,750
100% × distributable estate and investment income	<u>47,638</u>
	91,388
Dividend paid	<u>(50,000)</u>
Liable to surcharge	<u>41,388</u>
Surcharge levied at 15% (as DEII is less than dividends)	<u>6,208</u>

The surcharge of €6,208 is an additional corporation tax liability which is charged as part of the corporation tax payable in respect of the accounting year ended 31 December 2013, the preliminary tax for which is payable on/before 23 November 2013 and the balance of which is payable on/before 23 September 2014.

Questions (to Chapter 28)

Review Questions

(See Suggested Solutions at the end of this textbook.)

Question 28.1

(a) State the tax effect on a close company arising out of a loan made to a participator in that company. Indicate the circumstances in which the loan would have no tax consequences for the company.

(b) Size Ltd is a close company and has the following adjusted profits for the year ended 31 December 2012:

	€
Trading profits	500,000
Rents	30,000
Deposit interest	3,000
	533,000

It has declared the following dividends payable out of the year ended 31 December 2012 profits and payable on the dates shown:

Date	€
30/1/2013	6,300
30/9/2013	3,000
10/7/2014	4,000

Requirement
Show its corporation tax liability for the year ended 31 December 2012 and the additional corporation tax payable for the year ended 31 December 2013 due to the surcharge.

Question 28.2

Close Ltd is a family owned distribution company with no associated companies. Results to 31 December 2012 are as follows:

	€	€
Gross profit	50,000	
Other income	10,000	
		60,000
Depreciation	15,000	
Salaries	10,000	

Rent and rates	1,000	
Sundry	1,100	(27,100)
Net profit		32,900

The directors do not recommend the payment of a dividend.

Other Income

	€
Interest on Government Securities	8,500
Capital grants	1,500
	10,000

Sundry

Miscellaneous office expenses	300
Expenses of majority shareholder's	
brother Y, who does not work for	
Close Ltd, paid to him	
on 1/7/2012	800
	1,100

Capital allowances due are €4,000.

Requirement
(a) Compute corporation tax payable.
(b) Compute surcharge arising.
(c) Indicate treatment of specific items.

Question 28.3

Maxi Ltd is a family-owned company, with no associated companies, dealing in farm machinery. The results for the year ended 31 December 2012 were as follows:

	€	€
Sales		6,300,000
Opening stock	1,100,000	
Purchases	5,650,000	
	6,750,000	
Closing stock	1,450,000	
		(5,300,000)
		1,000,000

Less: **Expenses**

Administration	220,000	
Financial	200,000	
Distribution and sales (Note 1)	270,000	
Depreciation	100,000	(790,000)
Trading profit		210,000
Loss on sale of plant (Note 5)	(20,000)	
Profit on sale of building (Note 2)	1,480,000	
Rents (Note 3)	200,000	
		1,660,000
Net Profit		1,870,000

Note 1: The following items were included in distribution and sales:

(a) Entertainment

	€
Entertaining customers	6,000
Entertaining suppliers	5,000
Staff Christmas party	10,000
Christmas gifts for suppliers	900
Cost of MD attending trade fair in London	850
	22,750

(b) Lease payments

The company leases equipment, the cost of which is capitalised in the company's accounts. The lease agreement states that the burden of wear and tear remains with the lessor. Total repayments made during the year ended 31 December 2012 were €15,000, which included both capital repayments and finance charges.

The company also leases two vans, the cost of which are not capitalised in the company's accounts. Total repayments made during the year ended 31 December 2012 were €10,000, which included both capital repayments and finance charges.

Total amounts included in distribution and sales in respect of these items were as follows:

	€
Equipment – finance charges	2,000
Vans – lease payments	10,000
	12,000

Note 2: The building, which was sold in October 2012, had been acquired in May 1974 for €50,000. The building was located on a site on which planning permission had been granted for the construction of a shopping centre. Proceeds received for the building were €1.5 million. The current use value of the building at the time of sale was €750,000. Legal fees of €18,000 were incurred in connection with the disposal. The company acquired a

new site in November 2012 for €200,000 on which it intends to build a replacement factory during 2012. €15,000 in respect of architects' fees for drawings for the new factory have been included in distribution expenses above.

Note 3: On 1 June 2012, the company re-let its investment property under a 20-year lease. A premium of €50,000 was received on the sub-letting. This premium is included in rental income in the Profit and Loss Account.

Note 4: In June 2012, the Managing Director (and principal shareholder) borrowed €550,000 from the proceeds from the sale of the building to purchase a new residence for himself in his own name.

Note 5: 100% capital allowances had been claimed in respect of the plant sold. Total capital allowances, including balancing allowances and charges, for the year were agreed at €50,000.

Note 6: Maxi Ltd has €210,000 of trading losses forward at 31/12/2011.

Requirement
Calculate in respect of Maxi Ltd:

(a) the corporation tax payable
(b) the CGT liability, if any, and
(c) any surcharge which might become payable.

Note: The CGT consequences arising from the granting of the lease may be ignored.

Question 28.4

Servisco Ltd, a closely held company trading as management consultants, had the following income for the year ended 31 December 2012:

	€
Professional income	430,000
Rental income	100,000
Interest on Government Stocks	50,000
Chargeable gains before adjustment (October 2012)	54,000

The company had a loss forward of €9,000 on its professional activities from the year ended 31 December 2011.

In the year ended 31 December 2013, the company sustained a loss on its professional activities of €10,000 all of which was claimed for set off against the 2012 income.

The company received dividends of €7,500.

Dividends of €70,000 were paid within 18 months.

Requirement
Compute the company's corporation tax liability for the year and the surcharge which will be payable as part of the corporation tax liability for the year ended 31 December 2013.

Question 28.5

Machinery Ltd was incorporated in the Republic of Ireland on 1 June 1990 and since that date has been engaged in providing machinery to companies. The founder members of the company were Mr V Duffy and his wife Fanny and the company was formed to take over their existing business which they previously conducted in partnership. Mr and Mrs Duffy have actively encouraged members of their immediate family and other relatives to take up employment within the company and have endeavoured to ensure that the control of the company remains, as far as possible, within the family. The company's Profit and Loss Account for the year ended 31 December 2012 showed the following results:

	€	€
Sales		1,660,000
Inventories at 31/12/2012	450,000	
Inventories at 1/1/2012	360,000	90,000
		1,750,000
Purchases		(805,000)
		945,000
Less: Depreciation	59,790	
Rent	79,710	
Light and heat	17,500	
Distribution costs	39,000	
Bank and loan interest	65,000	
Motor expenses (all vans)	44,000	
Sundry expenses	13,000	(318,000)
Net profit from trading		627,000
Add: Bank deposit interest	10,000	
Rents from let property		
(after allowable deductions)	50,000	60,000
Profit for year		687,000

The shareholdings in, and loans made to, the company as at 31 December 2012 were:

	Ordinary €1 shares	Loans Made	Interest Paid
Mr V. Duffy (Director)	3,000	€4,000 @ 15%	€600
Mrs V. Duffy (Director)	1,250	€5,000 @ 12%	€600
G. Duffy (mother of V. Duffy)	2,900	€5,000 @ 15%	€750
S. Duffy (father of V. Duffy)	2,000	€5,000 @ 15%	€750

D. O'Connell (Director)	2,750	€5,000 @ 15%	€750
Mrs K. Moran (aunt of V. Duffy)	500	–	–
L.T. Smith (Director)	2,100	€10,000 @ 13.21%	€1,321
Louise Hare (Company Secretary and sister of Paul Hare)	3,000	€3,000 @ 12%	€360
Paul Hare (husband of V. Duffy's sister)	2,500	€3,000 @ 9.3%	€279
	20,000		€5,410

Notes:
1. The loan interest was paid in addition to bank interest of €59,590, thus reconciling with the amount shown in the Income Statement.
2. For the accounting period ended 31 December 2011, capital allowances were €10,700.
3. None of the shareholders are related except as shown above.
4. The share capital at 1 January 2012 was the same as at 31 December 2012.

Requirement
Compute the corporation tax liability of the company for the accounting year ended 31 December 2012 and the surcharge which will be payable as part of the corporation tax liability for the year ended 31 December 2013.

Question 28.6

Tax Advisors Ltd, a professional services company, had the following sources of income and charges for the year ended 31 December 2012:

	€
Case II income	100,000
Case III income	100,000
Trade charges paid during 2012	(60,000)
Non-trade charges paid during 2012	(50,000)

Tax Advisors Ltd paid an interim dividend on 1 December 2012 of €30,000.

Requirement
Calculate the surcharge payable by Tax Advisors Ltd in respect of the above figures.

Investment Companies

Learning Objectives

After studying this chapter you will know that:

- An investment company is a company which makes investments. Therefore, its profit is mainly from Case III, Case IV, dividends and capital gains.
- It is entitled to a deduction, against total profits, for its expenses of managing its investments. However, there is a limit on directors' remuneration:
  - 10% of gross income; or
  - 15% of gross rents in the case of a property rental company where the directors devote a substantial part of their time to the management of the company's properties and there is not a separate management charge.
- If management expenses exceed profits then they can be:
  - grouped against profits of another group member; or
  - carried forward to offset against total profits of future accounting periods.
- The corporation tax rates are as follows:
  - 12.5% on certain foreign dividends.
  - 25% on Case III, Case IV and Case V.
  - chargeable gain is grossed up at $\frac{30}{12.5}$ and taxed at 12.5%.
  - FII is exempt.
- Investment companies earn passive income. As most are closely held, the surcharge on undistributed estate and investment income will apply to most investment companies.

29.1 Background

After studying this chapter you will have developed the competency to understand that up to now, we have dealt with companies that just held shares in another company, i.e. a holding company, and companies that carried on a trade.

A holding company does not trade and, therefore, is not entitled to claim the type of expense deductions that a trading company could. By its nature, a holding company merely holds investments.

This is in contrast to a subsidiary of say a bank, which actively trades shares and securities daily so as to derive a profit from share dealing. Such a company carries on a trade and, therefore, is entitled to a deduction for its trading expenses.

An "investment company" lies somewhere between a holding company and a share dealing company.

Investment companies are often established by individuals. By establishing an investment company, expenses, i.e. management expenses, which would not otherwise be deductible for an individual, are deductible for a company.

29.2 Definition

Under section 83 TCA 1997, an "investment company" is any company:

■ whose business consists wholly or mainly in the **making** of investments; and
■ the principal part of whose income is derived therefrom; and includes a savings bank.

The key issue is that there is active involvement by the company in making investments.

This first requirement was addressed in the tax case of *Casey (Inspector of Taxes) v. The Monteagle Estate Company,* where it was held that the company which acquired and managed the Monteagle estate was not engaged in the making of investments. The judge made it clear that in his judgement that what was to be looked to is the **nature of the operations or functions of the company**. An investment company is not a company making investments, but a company whose main business is the making of investments. Therefore, a certain level of activity on the company's part is required as opposed to a company making a single once-off investment.

There is no specific guideline as to what level of activity a company needs to engage in to establish its "investment company" status. One would, however, expect an "investment company" to have **regular meetings to review existing investments** and decide on possible new investments.

In another tax case, *Howth Estate Company v. Davis,* the company held certain investments and estates for their entire period. The judge held that the company was in the business of **holding, rather than making, investments.**

29.3 Relief for Management Expenses

An "investment company" resident in the State is entitled to deduct its expenses of management in computing its total profits (including chargeable gains) for corporation tax purposes.

29.4 Management Expenses

The term "management expenses" is not defined in law. The law allows a deduction for "… any sums disbursed as expenses of management....except any such expenses as are deductible in computing income for the purposes of Case V…". The law specifically provides that lump sums paid under the Redundancy Payments Act 1967, and an employer's contributions under an approved superannuation scheme, are deductible. The law provides no further guidance. Therefore, there have been a number of cases where the courts in Ireland and the UK have considered whether payments are allowed as "expenses of management". In the *Sun Alliance Assurance Co v. Davidson* case the judge expressed the view that the term "expenses of management" was not susceptible to precise definition and there must be a borderline or twilight area. Indeed, this is reflected in the judicial opinions, where there is significant divergence. However, there are expenses which are clearly within the definition. These are listed at (d) on the list that follows.

The courts have either taken the broad view or the narrow view of what are "expenses of management". The broad view is that *any* expenses incurred by management are deductible, whereas the narrow view is that only expenses of management are deductible, i.e. only the expenses of management in shaping policy and in other matters of managerial decision. While the UK case of *Capital & National Trust Ltd v. Golder* supported the narrower view, in the Irish case of *Stephen Court Ltd v. Browne*, Mr. Justice McWilliam in the High Court adopted the broader view.

However, in the later case of *Hibernian Insurance Company Ltd v. MacUimis*, the Supreme Court supported the narrower view. The issue was whether abortive acquisition costs incurred by Hibernian on a proposed acquisition qualified as "expenses of management". The company argued unsuccessfully that the expenses were deductible as they were not of a capital nature and also that management expenses were deductible, irrespective of their nature. Mr. Justice Murphy held that the very substantial costs incurred by the group in getting advisors to evaluate three investment opportunities did not constitute "expenses of management". He held that the expenditure was capital in nature and, therefore, was not management expenses. *A subsequent UK case Camas v. Atkinson allowed as "expenses of management" all costs up to the time when a company makes a definitive decision to acquire a business, i.e. allowing the broad view again.* **While this UK case is persuasive, the *Hibernian* case is binding as it is an Irish case.** Therefore, monies spent on evaluating new investment opportunities are not deductible as management expenses.

The list set out below mainly reflects case law and practice. Management expenses:

(a) include lump sums paid under the Redundancy Payments Act 1967 or an employer's contribution under an approved superannuation scheme;

(b) do not include expenses which are deductible in computing income from rents, etc. under Case V;

(c) are to be reduced by any income not subject to tax other than franked investment income (such income is relatively rare);

(d) include rent, rates, interest on loans to finance day-to-day running of the company, stationery, accountancy, secretarial and audit fees;

(e) include stockbrokers' fees, but not fees spent on new investments, as these would relate to capital expenditure;

(f) include directors' fees subject to the limit outlined below (Revenue practice); and

(g) include donations to charities, etc. and approved sports bodies, where the donation to the charity/sports body is at least €250 (for a 12-month accounting period).

29.4.1 Directors' Remuneration

In the UK case of *Berry (LG) Investments Ltd v. Attwooll*, it was held that directors' salaries and fees were only deductible to the extent that they were commensurate with the services provided. Rather than deal with each investment company on a case by case basis, there is a Revenue practice, i.e. the amount of directors' remuneration that is deductible is fixed at either 10% or 15% – see below.

Property Rental Companies

With regard to property rental companies, Revenue take the view that directors' remuneration is deductible to the extent that it is reasonable, having regard to the services rendered or the duties performed. In practice, no objections will be raised to payments which do **not exceed 10% of the gross rents**. Where the directors devote a substantial part of their time to the management of a company's properties and there is **not a separate management charge**, payments which **do not exceed 15% of gross rents** will not be questioned.

Investment Companies Generally

In relation to investment companies generally, it has been a long standing Revenue practice to accept as admissible directors' remuneration which does not exceed **10% of the company's gross income**, including franked investment income. Where the income of an investment company includes rental income to which the 15% limit applies, the 15% limit will apply to the rental income only, while the 10% limit will apply to the other income of the company.

Example

Thornton Properties Limited is an investment company. It has been established that its directors devote a substantial part of their time to the management of the company's properties. The company's income is as follows:

		€
Gross rents		400,000
Loan interest		25,000
Deposit interest, received gross		15,000
Irish dividends		35,000
Chargeable gains		6,000
Maximum deduction for directors remuneration:		
Gross rents	€400,000 @ 15% =	60,000
Other income:		
Loan interest	25,000	
Deposit interest, received gross	15,000	
Irish dividends	35,000	
	75,000 @ 10% =	7,500
Maximum deduction for directors remuneration		67,500

If the actual amount paid to directors were only €59,000, then only €59,000 would be deductible.

29.5 Carry Forward of Unutilised Management Expenses

If the management expenses of an accounting period, together with any charges on income paid in the period wholly and exclusively for the purpose of the company's business, cannot be wholly allowed by way of a deduction in that period, the balance may be carried forward to the succeeding period and treated as management expenses of that period, qualifying for allowance in that period or, if needs be, in subsequent periods.

29.6 Rates of Corporation Tax

The corporation tax rates are as follows:

- 12.5% on certain foreign dividends – see **Section 31.1.2**
- 25% on other Case III, Case IV and Case V;
- for 2012, a chargeable gain is grossed up at 30%/12.5% and taxed at 12.5%; and
- FII (franked investment income – dividends from Irish resident companies) is exempt.

29.7 Surcharge on Undistributed Income

You will recall from **Chapter 28** that there is a surcharge on the undistributed estate and investment income of closely-held companies. If an investment company is a closely-held company, then a surcharge will have to be calculated. The calculation for an investment company is similar, except for an investment company:

- it is not a trading company, so there is no 7.5% deduction; and
- it has management expenses, and these need to be deducted.

As before, please note that:

- The figures below are only in respect of income of the current accounting period, i.e. before any claim for losses, etc. back or forward, or management expenses carried forward.
- Irish dividends (FII) are not liable to corporation tax, just the surcharge.
- The approach below is only for companies that have no current year Case V losses or relevant charges.
- All the other issues re timing of payment, elect to have distribution not to be a distribution for the surcharge, etc. apply here also.

The computation may be summarised as follows:

	€
Case III	X
Case IV	X
Case V	<u>X</u>
	Y
FII	<u>X</u>
	X

Less: Management expenses		(X)
		Z
Less: Corporation tax @ 25% on "Z" less FII		(X)
Liable to surcharge		X
Less		
Dividends declared for, or in respect of, the accounting period and paid during or within 18 months of the end of the accounting period	X	
All distributions made in the accounting period (other than dividends)	X	X
Amount on which surcharge will be levied @ 20%		X

There will be no surcharge if the excess of the distributable estate and investment income over the distributions is €635 or less. Where the accounting period is less than 12 months, the €635 will be reduced proportionately. If there are associated companies, the €635 will be reduced by dividing it by one plus the number of associated companies.

Example

Investment Limited is a closely-held Irish resident investment company. It had the following in the year ended 31 December 2012:

	€
Case III	2,000
Case V	30,000
Case V capital allowances	3,000
FII	17,000
Adjusted chargeable gain	5,000
Management expenses	12,000

On 9 February 2013, the company pays a dividend of €10,000 in respect of the year.

What is the surcharge?

The surcharge is payable on distributable estate and investment income, to the extent that it is not distributed. (Remember, it is the Case V before capital allowances.)

	€
Estate and investment income (2,000 + 30,000)	32,000
Add FII	17,000
	49,000
Less management expenses	(12,000)
	37,000
Corporation tax @ 25% on €32,000 − €12,000	5,000
	32,000
Less dividends paid	10,000
Liable to the surcharge	22,000

The surcharge is €22,000 @ 20% = €4,400.

Summary Chart of Offset of Management Expenses

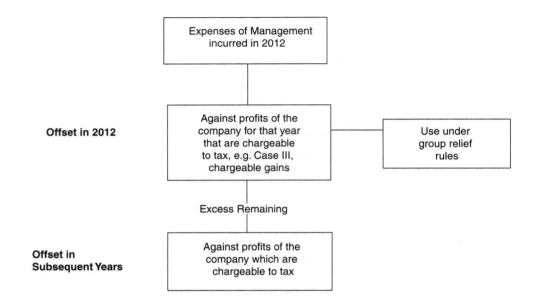

Questions (to Chapter 29)

Review Questions

(See Suggested Solutions at the end of this textbook.)

Question 29.1

Equities Ltd, a company whose business is the making of investments, had the following Income Statement for the year ended 31 December 2012:

Income:	€
Irish dividends	140,000
Interest on National Loan Stock	35,100
	175,100

Expenditure:	
Accounting fees	1,000
Secretarial fees	12,000
Auditors' remuneration	6,000
Directors' remuneration	20,000
Stockbroker's charges for advice	3,000
	(42,000)

Net income:	133,100

Requirement
Calculate the corporation tax liability for the period claiming all possible reliefs.

Taxation of Resident and Non-resident Companies

Learning Objectives

After studying this chapter you will have developed competency to understand that:

- If a company is managed and controlled in Ireland, it is Irish tax resident. An Irish incorporated company is Irish tax resident unless it can avail of a trading or treaty exemption. Irish tax resident companies are liable to Irish tax on their worldwide profits.
- Non-resident companies are liable to corporation tax only on profits of the Irish branch.
- Other income may be liable to income tax.
- Gains on disposal of specified assets are typically liable to CGT.

30.1 Residence of Companies and Charge to Tax

The most important factor in determining a company's liability to corporation tax is the company's residence. If a company is Irish tax resident, it is liable to Irish tax on its worldwide profits. At **Section 30.3** is set out the charge to tax for non-resident companies.

30.1.1 Summary of the Rules to Establish Residence of a Company

The chart below summarises the rules used to establish whether a company is resident or non-resident in Ireland for tax purposes.

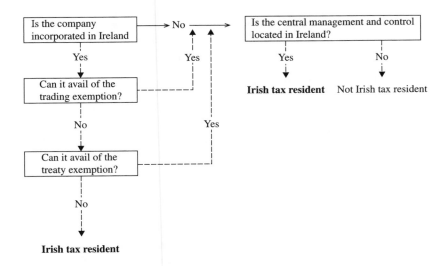

As can be seen from this chart, a company **may** be Irish tax resident if it is:

- managed and controlled in the State; or
- Irish incorporated.

Companies Managed and Controlled in the State

The rules for determining the residence of a company have evolved from UK case law, which has been followed in Ireland. A company, irrespective of where it is incorporated, is Irish tax resident if it is "managed and controlled" in the State. Again, UK case law has provided guidance on what constitutes "managed and controlled". Based on these cases, the *key* factors which have been taken into account in determining where a company is "managed and controlled" are the following:

- Where are the questions of important policy determined?
- Where are the directors' meetings held?
- Where do the majority of the directors reside?
- Where are the shareholders' meetings held?
- Where is the negotiation of major contracts undertaken?
- Where is the head office of the company?
- Where are the books of account and the company books (minute book, share register, etc.) kept?
- Where are the company's bank accounts?

As you can see, control is to do with where the directors hold their meetings and **'whether real decisions affecting the company are taken at those meetings'**. In each case, one needs to look at the facts of the case to determine where the company is actually managed and controlled.

Irish Incorporated Companies

As can be seen from the chart, Irish incorporated companies are tax resident in Ireland unless they can avail of the:

- trading exemption; or
- treaty exemption.

Trading Exemption

The trading exemption is available if the company or a related company carries on a trade in the State **and** the company is controlled by persons resident in a treaty or EU country or its shares (or a related company's shares) are regularly traded on a stock exchange in a treaty country or the EU.

Treaty Exemption

The treaty exemption applies where the Irish incorporated company is regarded as resident in another country, i.e. managed and controlled in that other country, under the terms of the double taxation agreement (tax treaty) between Ireland and that country. The rules for determining where a company is managed and controlled are set out above.

30.1.2   Implications of Residence

- Resident companies are liable to corporation tax on worldwide profits.
- Non-resident companies are liable to corporation tax only on Irish branch profits. If a non-resident has other taxable Irish income, this will be subject to income tax.
- Resident companies are liable to corporation tax on all capital gains other than disposals of development land. Non-resident companies are only liable to corporation tax on gains from the disposal of specified assets (e.g. land in the State) used for the purpose of an Irish trading branch (see **Section 26.1**).
- Certain tax reliefs are only available to resident companies.

Example

R Ltd is a UK incorporated company that manufactures clothes in England, France and Germany. It has a warehouse and offices in Ireland. All of its directors are Irish residents. All directors' and shareholders' meetings take place in Ireland. It has the following sources of income:

- UK profits
- French profits
- German profits
- New Zealand deposit interest
- Rental income in the USA

Therefore, as its controlling body and management is located in Ireland, its place of residence is Ireland. ALL sources of profits are liable to Irish corporation tax.

30.2   Uses of Non-resident Companies

Non-resident companies can be found in the group structures of both Irish-owned multinationals and foreign-owned multinationals investing into Ireland.

30.2.1 Irish Multinationals

Where an Irish company expands into international markets, it will generally establish a separate subsidiary company in the foreign country. Often the foreign subsidiary is managed and controlled in that foreign country and therefore is not Irish tax resident. Such foreign subsidiaries of Irish companies are non-resident in Ireland and are only liable to Irish tax on the profits detailed at **Section 30.3**, i.e. certain Irish source profits. However, these foreign subsidiaries typically do not generate Irish profits (they are established to generate foreign profits) and, therefore, no Irish tax is payable by the foreign subsidiary. Obviously, foreign tax may arise.

30.2.2 Foreign Investment into Ireland

Where a foreign company establishes an operation (e.g. factory in Ireland), the operation will be run by a company in the multinational group. This company is normally an Irish resident company established specifically to run the Irish operation. Sometimes, for international tax planning reasons, a non-resident company is used. Where a non-resident company runs the Irish operation, its liability to Irish tax is as set out in **Section 30.3**.

30.3 Non-resident Companies' Charge to Tax

A non-resident company is chargeable to Irish *corporation tax* only if it carries on a trade here through a "branch or agency", *which is defined as any factorship, agency, receivership, branch or management.*

   If the non-resident company does carry on a trade here through a branch or agency, corporation tax will be charged on:

1. any trading income arising directly or indirectly through or from that branch or agency;
2. any income wherever arising from property or rights used by, or held by or for, the branch or agency, e.g. income from patent rights held by the branch; and
3. chargeable gains accruing on assets situated in the State as used for the purpose of the branch trade.

Where a foreign multinational sets up a factory in Ireland and uses a non-resident company, the non-resident company would be liable to Irish tax on the manufacturing income and any other income/gains of the branch, e.g. deposit interest.

   Income from sources *within* the State that is not subject to corporation tax (because it is not attributable to the branch or agency) may be subject to *income tax*.

   Thus, the difference between a non-resident and a resident company is that any profits not attributable to the Irish branch, e.g. foreign interest, foreign trading income, are not liable to Irish corporation tax.

Note: profits are either liable or not. There is no remittance basis concept.

30.4 Non-resident Companies – Income Tax

A non-resident company may be liable to **income tax on income received which is not income of an Irish branch**. For example, a non-resident company may own shares in an

Irish company. If the non-resident company receives a dividend or other distribution from that Irish company, it will be liable to DWT unless it is exempt – see **Chapter 27**. This DWT is the final tax to settle all income tax due, if any. Similarly where a non-resident company receives interest on an Irish deposit account, it may or may not have an Irish income tax liability. If the company is resident in a treaty country, there will be no DIRT withheld and therefore no income tax. Withholding tax will settle any tax due.

30.5 Capital Gains

30.5.1 Branch Assets

In relation to capital gains, the charge to corporation tax on a non-resident company carrying on a trade in the State through a branch or agency falls on chargeable gains accruing on the disposal of assets in the State which at, or before, the time when the chargeable gain accrued **were used in, or for, the purposes of the branch or agency**.

Where it is a branch of an EU resident company, then assets can be transferred tax-free to/from the branch to other Irish resident members of the group or to other group members for whom the asset would be a chargeable asset, i.e. within the charge to CGT on disposal of the asset – see **Chapter 26**.

30.5.2 Other Assets

Chargeable gains on the disposal of land in the State, minerals in the State or any rights, interests or other assets in relation to mining or minerals or the searching for minerals, which were not used in or for the purposes of the trade or used or held or acquired for the purpose of the branch or agency, will be chargeable to CGT. Gains on development land are subject to CGT rather than corporation tax even if the gain arises on an asset which was used for the branch trade.

Questions (to Chapter 30)

Review Questions

(See Suggested Solutions to Review Questions at the end of this textbook.)

Question 30.1

Overseas Limited

Overseas Limited, a distribution company which is resident in Taxland and under the control of individuals resident in Taxland, has been trading in Ireland for many years through a branch.

The company has the following income during the year ended 31 December 2012:

	€
Trading profits	900,000
(including branch trading profits of €600,000)	
Interest income from surplus funds invested by branch	20,000
(received gross)	
Dividends received from:	
▪ Australian subsidiary	10,000
▪ Irish quoted company (net of DWT)	8,000

The Irish branch had chargeable gains, before adjustment, on the sales of premises of €32,000 in December 2012.

The company also owned development land in the State, not used for the purposes of the branch, which was sold in August 2012 to a manufacturer and realised a capital gain of €50,000. This land had been acquired in 1976.

Requirement

Calculate the relevant Irish tax liabilities of the company.

Double Taxation Relief

Learning Objectives

After studying this chapter you will have developed the competency to understand that:

■ Where an Irish company earns profits outside the State, it may also have a liability to foreign tax. If it pays such foreign tax, there are three possible ways of relieving the tax. The most common is for Ireland to allow a credit for the foreign tax.

■ A credit will apply either because a **tax treaty allows a credit**, or the company can benefit from the **unilateral credit relief rules which are in Irish domestic tax law**.

■ **Foreign tax (treaty) credit** A treaty can provide credit relief in respect of tax on any type of income or gain.

■ **Unilateral credit relief** This mainly applies to dividends. Because the unilateral credit relief requires the Irish company to only **own 5% of the foreign company** and some treaties require the Irish company to own more, dividends from both treaty and non-treaty countries will benefit from the unilateral credit relief rules.

■ Unilateral credit is now available on profits of branches located in countries where Ireland does not have a double tax agreement. The Irish company can reduce its tax liability by the foreign tax paid for that branch. Where the foreign tax exceeds the Irish tax, then the excess can be 'pooled' and credited against the Irish tax or other foreign branch profits.

■ The foreign tax is only creditable against the Irish tax on the same income. Therefore, the income, net of foreign tax, is grossed up at the lower of the Irish and foreign effective rates.

$$\frac{\text{Income net of foreign tax}}{100 - \text{lower of:}} \times 100$$
$$\text{- the Irish tax rate}$$
$$\text{- foreign tax rate}$$

■ The Irish rate on foreign dividends is 12.5%, provided conditions are satisfied.

31.1   Introduction to Double Taxation Relief and Rate of Tax

31.1.1   Introduction

It is common for the laws of two countries to levy tax on the same income and capital. This arises because a resident company is normally taxed on its worldwide profits and a non-resident company is taxed on its profits in that country only.

> **Example**
> An Irish resident company carries on business through a branch in a foreign country. The branch profits would be subject to corporation tax in Ireland as a resident company is liable to tax on its worldwide profits. The branch profits would also be subject to tax in the foreign country as the income arises in the foreign country.
>
> Where an Irish company takes the decision to generate income from another country, it must firstly decide whether the income is earned by the company itself or another company.
>
> If the foreign income is earned by an Irish tax resident company, then that income is liable to Irish tax. It may also be liable to tax in the foreign country in which it arises. This depends on the laws of that foreign country and the tax treaty between Ireland and the foreign country.
>
> Alternatively, the Irish company may establish a wholly owned subsidiary in the foreign country or make an investment (e.g. 20% shareholding) in a foreign company. In this case, the foreign company typically will not be managed and controlled in Ireland and will not have Irish source income. Therefore, the foreign company has no Irish tax liability. The Irish parent or investor company will not receive any income from this foreign company until a dividend is paid to it. Therefore, the Irish parent/investor company does not have an Irish tax liability until it receives a dividend. Generally, this dividend will have been paid out of profits which have suffered foreign tax. When the dividend is actually paid, it may also suffer withholding tax in the foreign country.
>
> When the Irish company receives the dividend, the dividend is taxable in Ireland. Generally there is a credit for foreign tax suffered, be it the withholding tax and/or an appropriate share of the tax on profits of the foreign company. Sometimes there is only relief by deduction – see **Section 31.2.1.**

31.1.2   Rate of Tax

If the foreign income is trading income from a foreign branch of the Irish company, then provided the trade is not carried out wholly abroad – and, generally, this is the case – this income is taxable at 12.5% (unless it is from excepted operations – this is not examinable). If the trade is carried out wholly abroad, it is regarded as a foreign trade and the income therefrom is Case III income, subject to corporation tax at 25%.

If the income is interest or rental income from a foreign deposit or property, the income is taxable at 25%.

Previously, all foreign dividends were taxable at 25%. Now certain foreign dividends are taxable at 12.5%. The dividends concerned are dividends received by a company out of the **trading profits** of a non-resident company that is resident in:

- an EU Member State;
- a country with which Ireland has signed a tax treaty;
- a company quoted on any stock exchange in the EU or a tax treaty country;
- a 75% subsidiary of a company quoted on any stock exchange in the EU or a tax treaty country; or

- a country which has ratified the Convention on Mutual Assistance in Tax Matters (non-EU/tax treaty countries which have ratified this convention include Azerbaijan and Ukraine).

Where the dividend is received by a company that is a **portfolio investor** (holds no more than **5%** of the dividend-paying company), there is no need for the dividend-paying company to satisfy the trading test.

In all other cases, where a dividend for a period is paid partly out of trading profits and partly out of non-trading profits, the dividend is to be apportioned by reference to the amounts of trading profits and other profits of the dividend-paying company for that period. The part attributable to trading profits will then be subject to the 12.5% rate. There is a "safe harbour" that allows the full amount of a dividend received by a company to be charged at the 12.5% rate where two conditions are met, notwithstanding that a part of the dividend may not be paid out of trading profits:

1. 75% of the dividend paying company's profits must be trading profits or dividends received from trading profits of companies resident in EU Member States or in countries with which Ireland has signed a double tax treaty, and
2. 75% of the assets of the group must be trading assets.

31.2 Methods of Relief

Relief is given for double taxation in one of the following ways:

- Deduction
- Credit
- Exemption

31.2.1 Deduction Method

In the absence of credit relief or an exemption, under general Irish tax law, foreign profits are reduced by the foreign tax borne on these profits.

Example

X Ltd, an Irish resident company, was in receipt of the following income for the year ended 31 December 2012:

	€	€
Irish trading profits		500,000
Argentinian bank deposit interest	€10,000	
Less Argentinian withholding tax	(€1,500)	8,500

Corporation Tax Computation		€
Schedule D Case I		500,000
Schedule D Case III		8,500
		508,500

Corporation tax		
€500,000 @ 12.5% =	€62,500	
€8,500 @ 25% =	€2,125	
Corporation tax due		64,625

The effective rate of tax suffered on the Argentinian interest is:
(€1,500 + €2,125)/ €10,000 = 36.25%

The **deduction method applies:**

- in the case of dividends from **shareholdings of less than 5%**; and
- in the case of other income (e.g. interest, rental income), if there is **no double taxation agreement** (DTA) with the foreign country. There is no DTA with Argentina. The list of countries with which we have a DTA is outlined in **Section 31.4**.

31.2.2 Credit Method

Credit relief is allowed either because it is provided for **under a tax treaty** (double taxation agreement) between Ireland and another country, or because Irish domestic tax law allows it (known as **unilateral credit relief**).

If there is a DTA with the foreign country then either the credit or exemption method will apply. To determine which applies it is necessary to examine the particular.

Example – the operation of credit relief

Ladder Ltd has a branch in a country with which Ireland has a tax treaty. In the year ended 31 December 2012, the branch had profits of €120,000 on which tax was paid at 10%. Ladder Ltd's total Case I profits, including the branch profit, for the year ended 31 December 2012 were €400,000.

	€
Irish corporation tax	
Schedule D Case I	400,000
Corporation tax @ 12.5%	50,000
Less: credit relief €120,000 @ 10%	(12,000)
Tax due	38,000

Irish effective rate of tax $\dfrac{50,000}{400,000} \times 100 = 12.5\%$

(Note: *Branch profits are taxable under Case I rather than Case III where the trade is not carried out "wholly" abroad.)*

Credit relief is far more beneficial than relief by deduction as it can fully relieve any liability to Irish tax, e.g. if the foreign tax rate had been 12.5%, then no Irish tax would have been payable.

If the foreign income is a dividend, credit relief is normally available not only for any foreign withholding tax but also in respect of *tax paid on the profits out of which the dividend has been paid (underlying tax)*. Under many of Ireland's tax treaties, there is a minimum shareholding requirement as a condition of obtaining credit relief for underlying tax on dividends. However, unilateral credit relief rules also apply and can be more beneficial in the case of dividends.

There is a formula for the calculation of underlying tax. However, for the purposes of your exam, you will be told the effective rate of tax in the foreign country and, therefore, you do not need to know this formula.

The Irish corporation tax liability will be on the aggregate of the dividend received and the amount of credit relief.

Example

In the year ended 31 December 2012, Ludo Ltd received a dividend of €10,000 from Jenga Ltd, a trading subsidiary resident in a *treaty country where the tax rate is 10%*, out of its profits for the year ended 31 December 2011. No withholding tax was deducted on payment of the dividend. The following information is relevant to Jenga Ltd for the year ended 31 December 2011:

Accounts profit after tax   €100,000

Effective rate of tax in treaty country 7.4%

Dividend received of €10,000 has been paid out of profits which suffered tax at 7.4%. Underlying tax relating to dividend is, therefore:

$$\frac{€10,000}{100\% - 7.4\%} - €10,000 = €799.$$

Ludo Ltd is taxed on the dividend received plus the amount of the underlying tax, i.e.

	€
Case III	10,799
Corporation tax @ 12.5% (see **Section 31.1.2**)	1,350
Credit for underlying tax	(799)
Irish CT due	551

Unilateral Credit Relief

In addition to relief under a tax treaty, unilateral credit relief rules apply under domestic legislation. Unilateral credit relief rules apply where relief is not available for the foreign tax under tax treaty – frequently because there is no treaty. This relief applies where the foreign income is a dividend from a foreign company and the company in Ireland **owns 5% or more of the ordinary share capital**. The company in Ireland can be Irish resident or a branch of an EU resident company or a branch of a company resident in an EEA country which has a tax treaty with Ireland (i.e. Norway and Iceland).

Unilateral credit is now available on profits in branches located in countries where Ireland **does not have a double tax agreement**. The Irish company can reduce its tax liability by the foreign tax paid for that branch. Where the foreign tax exceeds the Irish tax then the excess can be 'pooled' and credited against the Irish tax or other foreign branch profits.

Limit on Credit Relief

The credit for foreign tax in respect of any income is typically limited to the corporation tax attributable to that income (but see **Section 31.3** regarding on-shore pooling for dividends; this is not examinable). The corporation tax attributable to the foreign income is basically the foreign income, as calculated for Irish tax purposes, multiplied by the rate of tax payable by the Irish company on that income in Ireland. If the foreign income is taxable under Case III or IV, the corporation tax attributable to that income will be corporation tax at the 25% rate. If the foreign income is taxable under Case I or is a foreign dividend satisfying the conditions set out at **Section 31.1.2**, the corporation tax attributable to the foreign income will be at the 12.5% rate. For the purpose of determining the Irish effective rate, the **gross foreign income** should be used.

The credit for foreign tax in respect of a chargeable gain is limited to the corporation tax attributable to that gain determined by applying the general corporation tax rate for the period to the amount of the gain before credit for foreign tax is given.

Unilateral Foreign Tax

Any foreign tax which cannot be allowed by way of credit relief due to the above limitations is to be allowed by way of deduction in taxing the income or gains. **This can be achieved by "grossing up" the foreign income (net of foreign tax) at the lower of the Irish and effective foreign tax rates and giving credit relief at the same rate.**

$$\frac{\text{Income net of foreign tax}}{100 - \text{lower of the Irish tax rate or foreign tax rate}} \times 100$$

The effect of grossing up at the lower of the two rates is that:

- if the foreign rate is lower, you gross up at that rate and Irish tax is payable; and
- if the foreign rate is higher, you gross up at the Irish rate and no Irish tax is payable.

Two examples are required to illustrate the point.

Example 1

A Ltd receives a foreign dividend of €160,000 (net of foreign tax of €40,000). Assume Irish effective rate is 25%.

The foreign effective rate is:

$$\frac{40,000}{200,000} \times 100 = 20\%$$

Grossing up the net foreign income at the lower of the two rates:

$$\frac{€160,000}{100 - 20} \times 100 = €200,000$$

This is the amount to be included in the Irish corporation tax computation.

	€
Schedule D Case III	200,000
Corporation tax @ 25%	50,000
Less credit relief €200,000 @ 20%	(40,000)
Net corporation tax payable	10,000

It will be noticed that credit relief has been allowed for the full amount of foreign tax as it is lower than the Irish rate.

Example 2

B Ltd receives a foreign dividend of €24,000 (net of foreign tax of €20,000).
Assume Irish effective rate is 25%.
The foreign effective rate is:

$$\frac{20,000}{44,000} \times 100 = 45\%$$

Grossing up the net foreign income at the lower of the two effective rates

$$\frac{€24,000}{100 - 25} \times 100 = €32,000$$

continued overleaf

This is the amount to be included in the Irish corporation tax computation.

	€
Schedule D Case III	32,000
Corporation tax @ 25%	8,000
Credit relief (restricted) €32,000 @ 25%	(8,000)
Net corporation tax due	Nil

Effectively relief for the €20,000 of foreign tax is given by:

■ reducing <u>taxable</u> income by €12,000 (i.e. taxing €32,000 and not €44,000); and
■ reducing corporation tax by €8,000.

Clearly reducing taxable income is not as attractive as reducing tax.

Please note that the €12,000 for which credit relief was not allowed in this example, is actually allowed under "on-shore pooling" for dividend rules. However, on-shore pooling for dividends is not examinable at CAP 2 level – see **Section 31.3**.

31.2.3 Exemption Method

This simply exempts the profits from tax in one of the two countries. The most common example of this is that, under many DTAs, **interest is not liable to tax in the country of origin**, only in the country of residence.

Example 1
A Ltd., an Irish resident company, was in receipt of the following income for the year ended 31 December 2012:

	€
Irish trading profits	800,000
UK deposit interest	10,000

Under the terms of the Irish/UK DTA, UK deposit interest earned by an Irish resident company is only taxable in Ireland.

	€
Schedule D Case I	800,000
Schedule D Case III	10,000
	810,000
€800,000 × 12.5% =	100,000
€10,000 × 25% =	2,500
Corporation tax due	102,500

31.3 Ireland as a Holding Company Location

Irish tax law contains provisions designed to make Ireland an attractive location for holding companies and, thereby, attract holding companies and the related headquarter activities to Ireland.

■ There is the very low holding of 5% to avail of unilateral credit relief.
■ There is on-shore pooling of excess foreign tax credits in relation to qualifying foreign dividends. This topic is not examinable.
■ There is the exemption from tax in the case of capital gains from the disposal of holdings in "subsidiaries" – this is dealt with in **Chapter 26** on company capital gains.
■ There is an exemption from the close company surcharge on dividends from these shareholdings, but only where they are shares in a foreign company. This is dealt with in **Chapter 28**.

31.4   Double Taxation Agreements

Ireland has concluded double taxation agreements with the following countries. You do not need to know whether Ireland has an agreement with a particular country, as you will be told this in the exam:

Albania	Greece	New Zealand
Armenia*	Hong Kong	Norway
Australia	Hungary	Pakistan
Austria	Iceland	Panama*
Bahrain	India	Poland
Belarus	Israel	Portugal
Belgium	Italy	Romania
Bosnia & Herzegovina	Japan	Russia
Bulgaria	Korea (Rep. of)	Saudi Arabia*
Canada	Kuwait*	Serbia
Chile	Latvia	Singapore
China	Lithuania	Slovak Rep.
Croatia	Luxembourg	Slovenia
Cyprus	Macedonia	South Africa
Czech Rep	Malaysia	Spain
Denmark	Malta	Sweden
Egypt*	Mexico	Switzerland
Estonia	Moldova	Turkey
Finland	Montenegro	United Arab Emirates
France	Morocco*	United Kingdom
Georgia	Netherlands	United States of America
Germany		Vietnam
		Zambia

*not effective yet

Given the possibility of delay in bringing treaties into force with relevant foreign countries, the treaty requirement has been relaxed to mere signing of the treaty, i.e. once the treaty has been signed with the country, companies dealing with that country may avail of its provisions as they impact on Irish tax.

31.5   Double Taxation Agreement Contents

A double taxation agreement (or tax treaty) determines how taxing rights will be divided between two countries so as to ensure that companies/individuals are not subject to double taxation, e.g. a company may suffer the higher of the tax rates applying in Ireland and the U.K, but never a rate greater than that higher rate. Most tax treaties follow the international standards set down by the OECD, but every treaty will have its own special provisions.

These special provisions generally reflect one country's policy in a certain area, or its concern about protecting some aspect of its taxation rights.

A tax treaty determines whether a country will tax a particular type of income at source. For example, an Irish resident company earning deposit interest from a bank in a tax treaty country is liable to Irish tax only. However an Irish company earning rents from a property in a tax treaty country may be subject to foreign tax also. In either case, Irish tax is payable on the income. Obviously the issue of giving a credit foreign tax only arises with the rental income.

Where an Irish company trades with a tax treaty country, it may have a foreign tax liability. If it mainly sells products to that country without any presence there, then there is no foreign tax. If, alternatively, it establishes an office there, then that foreign branch is liable to foreign tax while the Irish company is also liable to Irish tax on those branch profits, but with a credit for the foreign tax suffered. The treaty assists in determining whether an Irish company's presence abroad is sufficiently small to ensure that no foreign tax is payable.

31.6   EU Parent – Subsidiary Directive

The EU Parent Companies and Subsidiaries Directive, which has been incorporated into Irish law, was designed to reduce tax barriers to flows of profits between corporate entities resident in different Member States of the EU. Where the flow of profits is from a "subsidiary" to a "parent company" owning 5% or more of the subsidiary's share capital, a number of reliefs, as set out below, apply to distributions of profit in respect of the shareholding of 5% or more, subject to transitional arrangements.

- No withholding tax is to be deducted from the distributions by the subsidiary's country of residence (e.g. no DWT in Ireland).
- The parent company's country of residence is either to exempt, or as applies in Ireland allow credit for the "underlying" corporation tax or equivalent foreign tax suffered by the subsidiary on the profits out of which the distribution is made (the credit method).

While Switzerland is not a member of the EU, the provisions of this law apply to Switzerland also.

Questions (to Chapter 31)

Review Questions

(See Suggested Solutions to Review Questions at the end of this textbook.)

Question 31.1

Foreign Income Limited is in receipt of the following sources of income for the year ended 31 December 2012.

	Notes	€
Trading income		700,000
Dividend from UK Subsidiary Ltd	1	87,500
Dividend from UK Company Ltd	2	80,000
Dividend from Monaco Ltd	3	94,342
Dividend from Irish Maniacs Ltd	4	75,000

Notes

1. The dividend of €87,500 was received from its 100% subsidiary in the UK, which paid the dividend out of trading profits taxed at an effective rate of 26%.
2. The dividend of €80,000 was received from UK Company Ltd, out of trading profits. Foreign Income Ltd owns 2% of the company and is not entitled to credit relief.
3. The company owns 4% of Monaco Ltd. The dividend from Monaco Ltd is after deduction of Monaco withholding tax at 3%. Ireland does not have a tax treaty with Monaco, it is not in the EU and it has not signed the Convention on Mutual Assistance in Tax Matters.
4. The company owns 20% of the shares of Irish Maniacs Ltd.
5. Foreign Income Ltd paid a dividend of €54,000 in total to its three shareholders, all of whom are Irish resident individuals, on 1 February 2012.

Requirement

Calculate the corporation tax payable for the accounts year ended 31 December 2012. Also indicate the taxation consequences for the company arising from the payment of the dividend in February 2012.

Question 31.2

Templemore Ltd had the following income for the year ended 31 December 2012.

	€
Trading income	50,000
Investment income	
Interest from the UK (Note 1)	10,000
Dividend from UK subsidiary (Note 2)	37,500

Dividend from UK company (Note 3)	20,000
Dividend from Peruvian company (Note 4)	5,950

Note 1: The UK interest is received and shown gross.

Note 2: The dividend was paid out of the trading profits for the year ended 31 December 2010. The effective rate of UK tax is 20%.

Note 3: Templemore Ltd owns 4% of the share capital of this trading company and is not entitled to credit relief.

Note 4: The dividend from the Peruvian company is shown net of Peruvian tax of 15%. Ireland does not have a tax treaty with Peru. Templemore Ltd owns **30%** of the Peruvian company.

Requirement

Calculate the corporation tax liability for the year.

Question 31.3

Touchdown Limited has the following Income and Expenditure Account for the year ended 31 December 2012.

	€
National loan interest	41,400
UK dividend	10,000
Irish dividend	1,240
	52,640
Less	
Directors' salaries	(10,000)
Bank interest (Note 1)	(15,000)
Qualifying charitable contribution	(800)
Stockbrokers' fees for advice	(250)
Accounting and secretarial	(3,750)
Surplus	22,840

Note 1: Bank interest is paid on a loan used for the purpose of investing in the UK company. There are common directors.

Note 2: Touchdown's investment in the UK company represents less than 5% of the voting power in that trading company and no credit relief is due.

Note 3: The company's business is the making of investments.

Requirement

Calculate the company's corporation tax liability for the year.

32

Companies in Liquidation

Learning Objectives

After studying this chapter you will have developed competency to understand:

- The responsibilities of a liquidator in a liquidation in the context of corporation tax
- Revenue's position as a preferential creditor of the company in liquidation
- Distributions received by shareholders on the liquidation of a company are liable to CGT

32.1 Liquidation/Winding up of a Company

There are two types of liquidations or winding up of companies:

1. compulsory winding up by a court; and
2. voluntary winding up initiated by the shareholders or creditors.

When a company commences to be wound up, it ceases to be the beneficial owner of its assets and the **custody and control of those assets pass to the liquidator.**

32.2 Status of Liquidator

A liquidator is not an agent of the company or of the creditor, nor is the liquidator an officer of the company.

Prior to liquidation, a company is both the legal and beneficial owner of its assets. When the company is put into liquidation, it ceases to be the beneficial owner and it no longer retains control of the assets. The liquidator holds the assets for the purposes of distributing them or what remains of them to the ultimate beneficial owners.

32.3 Corporation Tax Consequences of a Liquidation

32.3.1 Liquidator's Responsibilities

A company is chargeable to corporation tax on profits arising in the winding up of a company. *During the course of the winding up the liquidator has the responsibility of accounting for corporation tax on income received and on capital gains arising on disposal of chargeable assets.* Therefore, the liquidator must pay the corporation tax by the due date and submit any corporation tax returns.

32.3.2 End of an Accounting Period for Corporation Tax

When a company commences to be wound up, **an accounting period ends** and a new one begins; thereafter, an accounting period may not end otherwise than on the expiration of twelve months from its beginning or by the completion of the winding up. The ending of an accounting period can affect the following:

- the due date for payment of corporation tax;
- the date the company's corporation tax return must be submitted; and
- the extent to which trading losses may be offset against the total profits of the immediately preceding period, or against fellow group member's total profits on a claim to group relief.

As regards the due date for the corporation tax return and the balance of tax, where an accounting period ends on or before the date of commencement of the winding up of a company and the specified return date in respect of that period would fall on a date after the commencement of the winding up but not within a period of three months after that date, then the specified **return date becomes the date which falls three months after the date of commencement of the winding up**, but in any event not later than day 23 of the month in which that period of three months ends.

Example

Bond Ltd was trading for a number of years and had a 31 December year end. On 30 June 2012 a liquidator was appointed and the company commenced to be wound up.

This results in the end of an accounting period (i.e. 1 January 2012 to 30 June 2012). Assuming Bond Ltd is a "small" company for preliminary tax purposes, 90% of the corporation tax liability for that period (or 100% of the CT for the corresponding accounting period) would have to be paid by 23 May 2012.

The corporation tax return for the period to 30 June 1012 together with the balance of tax must be submitted on or before 23 March 2013.

Regarding the year ended 31 December 2011, its return must be filed by 23 September 2012. As this is within three months of the commencement of winding up on 30 June 2012, the return date is not changed. If the commencement of winding up were on, say, 30 April 2012, then the return for the year ended 31 December 2011 would be due on 23 July 2012 (three months later), instead of 23 September 2012.

32.3.3 *Ranking of Creditors and Revenue Priority*

On the occasion of a company being put into liquidation, the ranking of creditors in respect of payments due to them may be summarised as follows: creditors with a fixed charge (proceeds from that particular asset), liquidation costs, preferential creditors, creditors with a floating charge, unsecured creditors and finally shareholders. The main preferential creditors are Revenue, employees and Local Authorities in respect of rates due. There is legislation outlining the exact periods for which taxes are preferential.

32.4 Liquidations and Taxation of Shareholders who are Individuals

Where a company is liquidated and the company is not solvent, then the individual shareholders will receive no payment from the liquidator. As a result, the individual shareholder will have a loss. While there is no actual disposal, a loss may be claimed under the rule that a claim may be made when an asset has negligible value – see **Section 1.13.8**.

Where the company is solvent and the shareholder receives a payment in excess of the amount paid for the shares, the gain is liable to CGT in the normal way.

Appendices

Useful Taxation Reference Material for Tax Year 2012

INCOME TAX RATES

Lone parents (single widowed, or surviving civil partner) with qualifying children	Rate	Single/Widow(er) or surviving civil partner without qualifying children	Rate	Married or in civil partnership	Rate
First €36,800	20%	First €32,800	20%	First €41,800/€65,600*	20%
Balance	41%	Balance	41%	Balance	41%

* Depending on personal circumstances of a married couple

INCOME TAX CREDITS

	Non-Refundable Tax Credits €
Basic personal tax credit	
Single person	1,650
Married person or civil partner	3,300
Widowed person or civil partner (year of bereavement)	3,300
Widowed person or surviving civil partner – no qualifying children	2,190
One-parent family tax credit (additional)	1,650

Widowed person or surviving civil partner
(with qualifying child)

Year 1 after the year of bereavement	3,600
Year 2 after the year of bereavement	3,150
Year 3 after the year of bereavement	2,700
Year 4 after the year of bereavement	2,250
Year 5 after the year of bereavement	1,800
Age tax credit – single, widowed or surviving civil partner	245
Age tax credit – married or in civil partnership	490
Incapacitated child tax credit	3,300
Dependent relative (maximum)	70
Dependent relative – income limit €13,837	–
Home carer's credit (maximum)	810
Income limit of home carer €5,080	
Blind person	1,650
Both spouses or civil partners blind	3,300
Employee tax credit	1,650

Rent Tax Credit	Over 55 Years of Age	Others
Single	480	240
Married or in a civil partnership, or widowed or surviving civil partner	960	480

Rent-a-room relief (maximum) – €10,000

INCOME TAX ALLOWANCE

Employed person taking care of incapacitated person   €50,000 (max.)

INCOME TAX EXEMPTION LIMITS 2012

PERSONS under 65 years	*Maximum Allowable*
	€
Single, widowed or surviving civil partner	0
Married or in a civil partnership	0

PERSONS aged 65 and over	*Maximum Allowable*
	€
Single, widowed or surviving civil partner	18,000*
Married or in a civil partnership	36,000*

* Qualifying children: Increase exemption by €575 for each of first two, and by €830 for each additional child.

UNIVERSAL SOCIAL CHARGE (USC)

EMPLOYEES

For the year 1 January 2012 to 31 December 2012:

The rates of USC are:

Rate of USC	Annual Income	Monthly Income	Weekly Income
2%	Up to €10,036 per annum	Up to €837 per month	Up to €193 per week
4%	Next €5,980	Next €498	Next €115
7%	Balance	Balance	Balance

- Persons over 70 years are not liable at the rate of 7% but instead pay at 4%.
- Persons who hold a full medical card are not liable at the rate of 7% but instead pay at 4%.

Exempt Categories:

- Where an individual's total income for a year does not exceed €4,004.
- All Department of Social Protection payments.
- Income already subjected to DIRT.

SELF-EMPLOYED

For the year 1 January 2012 to 31 December 2012:

The rates of USC are:

	Under 70 and NOT in receipt of a Medical Card	Over 70 OR in receipt of a Medical Card
Up to €10,036	2%	2%
Next €5,980	4%	4%
Next €83,984	7%	
Balance (>€100,000)*	10%	7%

* The 3% surcharge is only levied on income derived from self-employment.

Motor Benefit-in-Kind Scale

Annual Business Kilometres	Cash Equivalent (% of OMV)
24,135 or less	30%
24,136 to 32,180	24%
32,181 to 40,225	18%
40,226 to 48,270	12%
48,271 and over	6%

Pension Contributions

The maximum amount on which tax relief may be claimed in respect of qualifying premiums are as follows:

Age	% of Net relevant Earnings
Under 30 years of age	15%
30 to 39 years of age	20%
40 to 49 years of age	25%
50 to 54 years of age	30%
55 to 59 years of age	35%
60 years and over	40%

Earnings limit for 2012 €115,000

PREFERENTIAL LOAN – BENEFIT-IN-KIND

Specified rates 2012
5% in respect of qualifying home loans.
12.5% in all other cases.

RESTRICTED COST OF PASSENGER MOTOR VEHICLE FOR CAPITAL ALLOWANCES AND MOTOR LEASES EXPENSES RESTRICTION PURPOSES

	€
From 1 January 2002	22,000
From 1 January 2006	23,000
From 1 January 2007	24,000

CARBON EMISSIONS RESTRICTIONS ON MOTOR VEHICLES bought on/after 1 July 2008

Category A	Category B/C	Category D/E	Category F/G
0–120g/km	121–155g/km	156–190g/km	191g/km+

Category A–C	Use the specified amount regardless of cost
Category D–E	Two steps to calculate the limit: 1. Take the lower of the specified limit or cost 2. Limit is 50% of this amount
Category F–G	No allowance is available

PRSI 2012

EMPLOYEES

Tax Year 2012

Employee's income chargeable as below:	Employee rate	Employer's rate
Income up to and including €356 per week	4%	4.25%
Income greater than €356 per week	4%	10.75%

Note 1: Employees are exempt from PRSI on the first €127 per week.

SELF–EMPLOYED

Tax Year 2012

All Income is subject to PRSI at 4%.*

* Individuals in receipt of income of less than €5,000 in 2012 will not be subject to PRSI. A minimum contribution of €253 is required.

CORPORATION TAX – RATES

	Standard Rate %	Higher Rate %
Year ended 31 December 2012	12.5	25

STAMP DUTY – RATES

Shares – 1%

Rates of duty for residential property (for instruments executed on or after 8 December 2010)
The rates of duty applicable for residential property (whether new or second-hand) are as follows:

Consideration	Rate
First €1,000,000	1%
Balance	2%

Non-residential property – 2% (For instruments executed on or after 7 December 2011)

CAPITAL GAINS TAX

The rates of CGT are as follows:

	From 3/12/1997 to 14/10/2008	From 15/10/2008 to 7/4/2009	From 8/4/2009 to 6/12/11	From 7/12/11 onwards
Rate	20%	22%	25%	30%

CAPITAL GAINS TAX ANNUAL EXEMPT AMOUNT

€1,270

Capital Gains Tax – Indexation Tables

Year of Assessment in which Expenditure was Incurred	*Multiplier for Disposal in Period Ended*							
	5th April 1997	*5th April 1998*	*5th April 1999*	*5th April 2000*	*5th April 2001*	*31st Dec 2001*	*31st Dec 2002*	*31st Dec 2003 et seq.*
1974/75	6.017	6.112	6.215	6.313	6.582	6.930	7.180	7.528
1975/76	4.860	4.936	5.020	5.099	5.316	5.597	5.799	6.080
1976/77	4.187	4.253	4.325	4.393	4.580	4.822	4.996	5.238
1977/78	3.589	3.646	3.707	3.766	3.926	4.133	4.283	4.490
1978/79	3.316	3.368	3.425	3.479	3.627	3.819	3.956	4.148
1979/80	2.992	3.039	3.090	3.139	3.272	3.445	3.570	3.742
1980/81	2.590	2.631	2.675	2.718	2.833	2.983	3.091	3.240
1981/82	2.141	2.174	2.211	2.246	2.342	2.465	2.554	2.678
1982/83	1.801	1.829	1.860	1.890	1.970	2.074	2.149	2.253
1983/84	1.601	1.627	1.654	1.680	1.752	1.844	1.911	2.003
1984/85	1.454	1.477	1.502	1.525	1.590	1.674	1.735	1.819
1985/86	1.369	1.390	1.414	1.436	1.497	1.577	1.633	1.713
1986/87	1.309	1.330	1.352	1.373	1.432	1.507	1.562	1.637
1987/88	1.266	1.285	1.307	1.328	1.384	1.457	1.510	1.583
1988/89	1.242	1.261	1.282	1.303	1.358	1.430	1.481	1.553
1989/90	1.202	1.221	1.241	1.261	1.314	1.384	1.434	1.503
1990/91	1.153	1.171	1.191	1.210	1.261	1.328	1.376	1.442
1991/92	1.124	1.142	1.161	1.179	1.229	1.294	1.341	1.406
1992/93	1.084	1.101	1.120	1.138	1.186	1.249	1.294	1.356
1993/94	1.064	1.081	1.099	1.117	1.164	1.226	1.270	1.331

Year of Assessment in which Expenditure was Incurred	5th April 1997	5th April 1998	5th April 1999	5th April 2000	5th April 2001	31st Dec 2001	31st Dec 2002	31st Dec 2003 et seq.
			Multiplier for Disposal in Period Ended					
1994/95	1.046	1.063	1.081	1.098	1.144	1.205	1.248	1.309
1995/96	1.021	1.037	1.054	1.071	1.116	1.175	1.218	1.277
1996/97	-	1.016	1.033	1.050	1.094	1.152	1.194	1.251
1997/98	-	-	1.017	1.033	1.077	1.134	1.175	1.232
1998/99	-	-	-	1.016	1.059	1.115	1.156	1.212
1999/00	-	-	-	-	1.043	1.098	1.138	1.193
2000/01	-	-	-	-	-	1.053	1.091	1.144
2001	-	-	-	-	-	-	1.037	1.087
2002	-	-	-	-	-	-	-	1.049
2003 et seq.	-	-	-	-	-	-	-	1.000

Capital Acquisitions Tax

Benefits taken from 1st December 1999 onwards

RATES OF TAX

Threshold amount	Nil	
Balance	20%	(Up to 20 November 2008)
Balance	22%	(21 November to 7 April 2009)
Balance	25%	(From 8 April 2009 to 6 December 2011)
Balance	**30%**	**(From 7 December 2011 onwards)**

EXEMPTION THRESHOLDS FOR GIFTS OR INHERITANCES

Group Thresholds	**A**	**B**	**C**
	€	€	€
From 1 December 1999	380,921	38,092	19,046
From 1 January 2001	402,253	40,225	20,113
From 1 January 2002	422,148	42,215	21,108
From 1 January 2003	441,198	44,120	22,060

From 1 January 2004	456,438	45,644	22,822
From 1 January 2005	466,725	46,673	23,336
From 1 January 2006	478,155	47,815	23,908
From 1 January 2007	496,824	49,682	24,841
From 1 January 2008	521,208	52,121	26,060
From 1 January to 7 April 2009	542,544	54,254	27,127
From 8 April to 31 December 2009	434,000	43,400	21,700
From 1 January to 7 December 2010	414,799	41,481	20,740
From 8 December 2010 to 6 December 2011	332,084	33,208	16,604
From 7 December 2011 onwards	**250,000**	**33,500**	**16,750**

Capital Acquisitions Tax

TABLE A

1	2	3	4
Years of Age	Joint Factor	Value of an interest in a capital of €1 for a **male** life aged as in Column 1	Value of an interest in a capital of €1 for a **female** life aged as in Column 1
0	.99	.9519	.9624
1	.99	.9767	.9817
2	.99	.9767	.9819
3	.99	.9762	.9817
4	.99	.9753	.9811
5	.99	.9742	.9805
6	.99	.9730	.9797
7	.99	.9717	.9787
8	.99	.9703	.9777
9	.99	.9688	.9765
10	.99	.9671	.9753
11	.98	.9653	.9740
12	.98	.9634	.9726
13	.98	.9614	.9710
14	.98	.9592	.9693
15	.98	.9569	.9676

1	2	3	4
Years of Age	Joint Factor	Value of an interest in a capital of €1 for a **male** life aged as in Column 1	Value of an interest in a capital of €1 for a **female** life aged as in Column 1
16	.98	.9546	.9657
17	.98	.9522	.9638
18	.98	.9497	.9617
19	.98	.9471	.9596
20	.97	.9444	.9572
21	.97	.9416	.9547
22	.97	.9387	.9521
23	.97	.9356	.9493
24	.97	.9323	.9464
25	.97	.9288	.9432
26	.97	.9250	.9399
27	.97	.9209	.9364
28	.97	.9165	.9328
29	.97	.9119	.9289
30	.96	.9068	.9248
31	.96	.9015	.9205
32	.96	.8958	.9159
33	.96	.8899	.9111
34	.96	.8836	.9059
35	.96	.8770	.9005
36	.96	.8699	.8947
37	.96	.8626	.8886
38	.95	.8549	.8821
39	.95	.8469	.8753
40	.95	.8384	.8683
41	.95	.8296	.8610
42	.95	.8204	.8534
43	.95	.8107	.8454

1	2	3	4
Years of Age	Joint Factor	Value of an interest in a capital of €1 for a **male** life aged as in Column 1	Value of an interest in a capital of €1 for a **female** life aged as in Column 1
44	.94	.8005	.8370
45	.94	.7897	.8283
46	.94	.7783	.8192
47	.94	.7663	.8096
48	.93	.7541	.7997
49	.93	.7415	.7896
50	.92	.7287	.7791
51	.91	.7156	.7683
52	.90	.7024	.7572
53	.89	.6887	.7456
54	.89	.6745	.7335
55	.88	.6598	.7206
56	.88	.6445	.7069
57	.88	.6288	.6926
58	.87	.6129	.6778
59	.86	.5969	.6628
60	.86	.5809	.6475
61	.86	.5650	.6320
62	.86	.5492	.6162
63	.85	.5332	.6000
64	.85	.5171	.5830
65	.85	.5007	.5650
66	.85	.4841	.5462
67	.84	.4673	.5266
68	.84	.4506	.5070
69	.84	.4339	.4873
70	.83	.4173	.4679
71	.83	.4009	.4488

1	2	3	4
Years of Age	Joint Factor	Value of an interest in a capital of €1 for a **male** life aged as in Column 1	Value of an interest in a capital of €1 for a **female** life aged as in Column 1
72	.82	.3846	.4301
73	.82	.3683	.4114
74	.81	.3519	.3928
75	.80	.3352	.3743
76	.79	.3181	.3559
77	.78	.3009	.3377
78	.76	.2838	.3198
79	.74	.2671	.3023
80	.72	.2509	.2855
81	.71	.2353	.2693
82	.70	.2203	.2538
83	.69	.2057	.2387
84	.68	.1916	.2242
85	.67	.1783	.2104
86	.66	.1657	.1973
87	.65	.1537	.1849
88	.64	.1423	.1730
89	.62	.1315	.1616
90	.60	.1212	.1509
91	.58	.1116	.1407
92	.56	.1025	.1310
93	.54	.0939	.1218
94	.52	.0858	.1132
95	.50	.0781	.1050
96	.49	.0710	.0972
97	.48	.0642	.0898
98	.47	.0578	.0828
99	.45	.0517	.0762
100 or over	.43	.0458	.0698

Table B

(Column 2 shows the value of an interest in a capital of €1 for the number of years shown in column 1)

1	2	1	2
Number of years	Value	Number of years	Value
1	.0654	26	.8263
2	.1265	27	.8375
3	.1836	28	.8480
4	.2370	29	.8578
5	.2869	30	.8669
6	.3335	31	.8754
7	.3770	32	.8834
8	.4177	33	.8908
9	.4557	34	.8978
10	.4913	35	.9043
11	.5245	36	.9100
12	.5555	37	.9165
13	.5845	38	.9230
14	.6116	39	.9295
15	.6369	40	.9360
16	.6605	41	.9425
17	.6826	42	.9490
18	.7032	43	.9555
19	.7225	44	.9620
20	.7405	45	.9685
21	.7574	46	.9750
22	.7731	47	.9815
23	.7878	48	.9880
24	.8015	49	.9945
25	.8144	50 and over	1.000

Chartered Accountants Ireland *Code of Ethics*

Under the Chartered Accountants Ireland *Code of Ethics*, a Chartered Accountant shall comply with the following fundamental principles:

(a) **Integrity** – to be straightforward and honest in all professional and business relationships.

(b) **Objectivity** – to not allow bias, conflict of interest or undue influence of others to override professional or business judgements.

(c) **Professional Competence and Due Care** – to maintain professional knowledge and skill at the level required to ensure that a client or employer receives competent professional services based on current developments in practice, legislation and techniques and act diligently and in accordance with applicable technical and professional standards.

(d) **Confidentiality** – to respect the confidentiality of information acquired as a result of professional and business relationships and, therefore, not disclose any such information to third parties without proper and specific authority, unless there is a legal or professional right or duty to disclose, nor use the information for the personal advantage of the professional accountant or third parties.

(e) **Professional Behaviour** – to comply with relevant laws and regulations and avoid any action that discredits the profession.

As a Chartered Accountant, you will have to ensure that your dealings with the tax aspects of your professional life are in compliance with these fundamental principles.

You will not be asked to define or list the principles, but you must be able to identify where these ethical issues arise and how you would deal with them.

Examples of situations that could arise where these principles are challenged are outlined below:

Example 1

You are working in the Tax Department of ABC & Co and your manager is Jack Wilson. He comes over to your desk after his meeting with Peter Foley. He gives you all the papers that Peter has left with him. He asks you to draft Peter's tax return. You know who Peter is as you are now living in a house that your friend Ann leased from Peter. As you complete the return, you note that there is no information regarding rental income. What should you do?

Action

As a person with integrity, you should explain to your manager Jack that your friend Ann has leased property from Peter and that he has forgotten to send details of his rental income and expenses. As Peter sent the information to Jack, it is appropriate for Jack to contact Peter for details regarding rental income and related expenses.

Example 2

You are working in the Tax Department of the Irish subsidiary of a US owned multinational. You are preparing the corporation tax computation, including the R&D tax credit due. You have not received some information from your colleagues dealing with R&D and cannot finalise the claim for R&D tax credit until you receive this information. Your manager is under pressure and tells you to just file the claim on the basis that will maximise the claim. He says, "It is self-assessment, and the chance of this ever being audited is zero." What should you do?

Action

You should act in a professional and objective manner. This means that you cannot do as your manager wants. You should explain to him that you will contact the person in R&D again and finalise the claim as quickly as possible.

Example 3

Anna O Shea, Financial Controller of Great Client Ltd, rings you regarding a VAT issue. You have great respect for Anna and are delighted that she is ringing you directly instead of your manager. She says that it is a very straightforward query. However, as you listen to her, you realise that you are pretty sure of the answer but would need to check a point before answering. What should you do?

Action

Where you do not know the answer, it is professionally competent to explain that you need to check a point before you give an answer. If you like, you can explain which aspect you need to check. Your client will appreciate you acting professionally rather than giving incorrect information or advice.

Example 4

The phone rings, and it is Darren O'Brien, your best friend, who works for Just-do-it Ltd. After discussing the match you both watched on the television last night, Darren explains why he is ringing you. He has heard that Success Ltd, a client of your Tax Department, has made R&D tax credit claims. Therefore, you must have details regarding its R&D. Darren's relationship with his boss is not great at present, and he knows that if he could get certain data about Success Ltd, his relationship with his boss would improve. He explains that he does not want any financial information, just some small details regarding R&D. What should you do?

Action

You should not give him the information. No matter how good a friend he is, it is unethical to give confidential information about your client to him.

Example 5

It is the Friday morning before a bank holiday weekend, and you are due to travel from Dublin to west Cork, after work, for the weekend. Your manager has been on annual leave for the last week. He left you work to do for the week, including researching a tax issue for a client. He advised you that you were to have an answer to the issue, no matter how long it took. It actually took you a very short time and you have it all documented for him.

Your friend who is travelling with you asks if you could leave at 11am to beat the traffic and have a longer weekend. You have no annual leave left, so you cannot take leave. You know that if you leave, nobody will notice, but you have to complete a timesheet. Your friend reminds you that the research for the client could have taken a lot longer and that you could code the five hours to the client. What should you do?

Action

It would be unprofessional behaviour and would show a lack of integrity if you were to charge your client for those five hours.

Suggested Solutions to Review Questions

Chapter 1

Question 1.1

Inflated Gains

1. Maurice – Capital Gains Tax Computation 2012

		€	€
Sale proceeds			80,000
Deduct:	Allowable cost		
	House	20,000	
	Legal costs	600	
		20,600	
	Indexed @ 1.819	37,471	
	Legal costs on disposal	750	(38,221)
			41,779
Deduct:	Annual exemption		(1,270)
			40,509
CGT @ 30%			12,153

2. Vincent – Capital Gains Tax Computation 2012

	€	€
Sale proceeds		9,300
Deduct: Allowable cost	1,200	
Indexed @ 1.406		(1,687)
		7,613

Less: Annual exemption		(1,270)
Taxable gain		6,343
CGT @ 30%		1,903

3(a)   John

	€
Cost June 2001	7,600
Sale 31/12/2012	7,800
Actual profit	200

Capital Gains Tax Computation for 2012

		€
Sale proceeds		7,800
Cost June 2001	€7,600	
Indexed @ 1.087		(8,261)
"Loss"		(461)

No gain/no loss

Note: Indexation cannot create a loss where there is an actual monetary gain.

3(b)   Philip

	€
Cost July 1980	3,000
Sale proceeds December 2012	2,700
Actual loss - maximum allowable	(300)
Capital Gains Tax Computation 2012	
Sale proceeds	2,700
Cost: €3,000 indexed at 3.240	(9,720)
"Loss"	(7,020)
Restricted to maximum allowable loss	(300)

Note: Indexation cannot create an allowable loss greater than the actual monetary loss.

3(c)   Paul

	€
Cost June 1973	5,700
Sale proceeds December 2012	5,500
Actual loss	(200)

Capital Gains Tax Computation 2012

	€
Sale proceeds	5,500
April 1974 MV €5,800	
Indexed at 7.528	(43,662)

"Loss"	(38,162)
Restricted to maximum allowable loss	(200)

3(d)   **Oliver**

	€
Cost July 1980	15,000
Sale proceeds	18,000
Actual gain	3,000

Capital Gains Tax Computation 2012

Sale proceeds	18,000
Cost €15,000	
Indexed @ 3.240	(48,600)
"Loss"	(30,600)
Therefore, no gain/no loss.	

Note: Indexation cannot operate so as to turn an actual monetary gain into an allowable loss.

Question 1.2

Enhancement Examples

1.   **CGT Computation 2012**

	€
Sale proceeds	650,000
Deduct:	
Allowable costs	
Acquisition cost €260,000 − €10,000 = €250,000	
Indexed @ 1.356	(339,000)
Enhancement expenditure	
August 2001 – not capital expenditure	0
May 2004	(90,000)
Chargeable gain	221,000
Annual exemption	(1,270)
	219,730
CGT due @ 30%	65,919

2.   **CGT Computation 2012**

	€	€
Sale proceeds		400,000
Deduct:		
Allowable costs		
1. 6 April 1998 €85,000 × 1.212	103,020	
2. Expenditure August 2001		

€20,000 @ 1.087	21,740	
3. Expenditure February 2003		
€39,250 @ 1.0	39,250	(164,010)
"Gain"		235,990
Deduct annual exemption		(1,270)
		234,720
CGT @ 30%		70,416

Question 1.3

Joe Loss

2012 – nil assessment (net loss €5,800).
Relief for the €5,800 loss will be given as follows:

€

(1st)	2011	1,370	(€100 + Exemption €1,270)
(2nd)	2010	1,420	(€150 + Exemption €1,270)
(3rd)	2009	1,520	(€250 + Exemption €1,270)
	Restricted total relief	4,310	

Note: It should be noted that for each of the three years, no effective loss relief has been received for the first €1,270 of losses used, as that amount of the loss merely replaced the annual exemption. CGT paid for 2009, 2010 and 2011 will be refunded.

Question 1.4

Michael Gain

	€
Courtaulds Shares: proceeds	1,162
MV 6/11/74: €888 @ 7.528	(6,685)
Indexed loss	(5,523)
Monetary gain	274
=> No gain/No loss	
Box Shares: proceeds	1,662
Cost €1,732 × 2.678	(4,638)
Indexed loss	(2,976)
Restrict to monetary loss	(70)
Cox Shares: proceeds	16,000
Cost €1,693 × 1.331	(2,253)
Chargeable gain	13,747

Nox Shares: proceeds		1,305
Cost		(623)
Chargeable gain		682

		€
Summary	Chargeable gain	13,747
	Chargeable gain	682
	Allowable loss	(70)
		14,359
Annual exemption		(1,270)
		13,089
		@ 30% = €3,927 CGT due

Question 1.5

Morry Bund

The loss of €16,000 can be set against the chargeable gains for the previous three years of assessment on a last in, first out basis.

		€
2011	Chargeable gain	Nil
2010	Chargeable gain	7,000
Less:	Terminal loss	(7,000)
		Nil
2009	Chargeable gain	5,000
	Less: Terminal loss	(5,000)
		Nil

The balance of the terminal loss cannot be set against the chargeable gain for 2008 and is lost.

A refund of CGT arises as follows:

		€
2010		7,000
	less exemption:	(1,270)
		5,730 @ 25% = €1,432
2009		5,000
	less exemption:	(1,270)
		3,730 @ 25% = €932

Personal Representatives

No CGT liability arises on death. They take over his assets at market value at the date of death. The CGT arising on the sale of the cottage is:

	€
Sale proceeds	88,000
Less MV @ date of death	(82,000)
Gain	6,000
CGT @ 30% = €1,800	

They are not entitled to annual exemption or the benefit of Mr Bund's unused losses.

Mrs Bund

The transfer of the shares in a plc to a legatee is not treated as a disposal for CGT purposes. Mrs Bund therefore takes the asset at its market value at the date of death. The loss arising is:

	€
Sale proceeds	27,000
Allowable cost	(30,000)
	(3,000)

Question 1.6

Derek Cotter

				€	€
1	12-Jan-2012	Sold - market value			50,000
	31-Jan-2000	Value at date of inheritance		8,000	
		Indexed at	1.193		(9,544)
		Gain			40,456
2	05-Feb-2012	Sale of Florida home			320,000
	30-Oct-99	Cost		110,000	
		Indexed at	1.193		(131,230)
		Gain			188,770
3	05-May-2012	Sale of shares in plc			30,000
	30-Apr-2002	Cost price		50,000	
		Indexed	1.049		(52,450)
					(22,450)
		Limited to monetary loss (€50,000 − €30,000)			(20,000)
4	10-Dec-2012	Sale of house			2,000,000
	31-Dec-1992	Purchase price		300,000	
		Less cost used (see note)		(100,000)	
				200,000	
		Indexed at	1.356		(271,200)
		Gain			1,728,800
		Note			
		Cost attributable to 2001 disposal is:			

$$€300,000 \times \frac{€500,000}{€500,000 + €1,000,000} = €100,000$$

5	21-Dec-2012	Deemed sale price of chair			3,500
	3-Dec-2001	Cost		2,600	
		Indexed	1.087		(2,826)
					674

Summary
Tax payable on 15 December 2012

1	Sale of shares	40,456
2	Sale of holiday home	188,770
3	Sale of shares	(20,000)
		209,226
	Less exemption	(1,270)
	Taxable	207,956
	CGT 30%	62,387

Summary
Tax payable on 31 January 2013

1	Sale of shares	40,456
2	Sale of holiday home	188,770
3	Sale of shares	(20,000)
4	Sale of house	1,728,800
5	Sale of chair	674
		1,938,700
	Exemption	(1,270)
	Taxable	1,937,430
	CGT 30%	581,229

Total liability for year	581,229
Less paid 15 December 2012	(62,387)
Due 31 January 2013	518,842

Chapter 2

Question 2.1

(a)   Disposal of shares in French company.

Gain is taxable when remitted.

<u>Gain</u>

		€
Proceeds		65,000
	€	
Cost 1994/95		
$\dfrac{8,000}{16,000} \times €60,000 =$	30,000	
Indexation factor 1994/95	1.309	
Indexed cost		(39,270)
"Gain"		25,730

Proceeds remitted to Ireland = portion of gain taxable in 2012, i.e. €10,000.
Gain is deemed to be remitted first.

(b)   Sale of UK rental property

	€
Proceeds	200,000
Cost	(180,000)
Renovations	(30,000)
Loss	(10,000)

Note: No indexation as there is a monetary loss. UK property is taxed on a remittance basis from 20 November 2008 and losses are not allowable.

(c)   Sale of H plc shares

		€
Proceeds		24,000
	€	
Cost	8,025	
Indexation factor 1998/99	1.212	
Indexed cost		(9,726)
Gain		14,274

Jacques' Capital Gains Tax Liability 2012

	€
Gain on disposal of shares – amount remitted	10,000
Gain on disposal of H plc shares	14,274
Total	24,274
Annual exemption	(1,270)
Taxable gains	23,004
CGT @ 30%	6,901

Note: No relief is available for the loss incurred in 2011 as the loss arose on the disposal of an asset only liable on the remittance basis.

Chapter 3

Question 3.1

Louise

	Holding	**Cost**
July 2003	4,000	6,000
October 2003	2,000	–
	6,000	6,000

	€
Proceeds	15,000
Cost	

$$6,000 \times \frac{5,000}{6,000} = \qquad (5,000)$$

Gain		10,000
Less: Exemption		(1,270)
		8,730

$$€8,730 \times 30\% = €2,619 \text{ CGT due}$$

Note: No indexation as acquired after 1 January 2003.

Question 3.2

Lorraine McCarthy

	Holding	Cost	
Acquired 01/07/1972	6,000	1,320	(M.V 6/4/1974)
Rights issue 1/11/1983	12,000	4,080	
	18,000		

		€
Deemed proceeds		16,800
Less		

$1,320 \times \dfrac{10,000}{18,000}$ $= 733 \times 7.528 = 5,518$

$4,080 \times \dfrac{10,000}{18,000}$ $= 2,267 \times 2.003 = 4,541$ $\qquad$ (10,059)

Gain	6,741
Less exemption	(1,270)
	5,471

$$€5,471 \times 30\% = €1,641 \text{ CGT due}$$

Question 3.3

Martin Doyle

	Holding	Cost	
Acquired May 1967	4,000	3,000	(MV 6/4/1974)
Rights issue 6/1/1988	2,000	6,000	
	6,000		

Sale to Orla: No CGT due on inter-spouse transactions

	€
Sale to Gerry:	
Deemed proceeds	9,000
Less	

$3,000 \times \dfrac{900}{6,000}$ $\times 7.528 = 3,388$

$6,000 \times \dfrac{900}{6,000}$ $\times 1.583 = 1,425$ $\qquad$ (4,813)

Gain	4,187

Sale on open market

Less proceeds		43,200

$$3,000 \times \frac{3,600}{6,000} \times 7.528 = 13,550$$

$$6,000 \times \frac{3,600}{6,000} \times 1.583 = 5,699 \qquad (19,249)$$

Gain		23,951

Summary

Sale to Orla	-
Sale to Gerry	4,187
Sale on open market	23,951
	28,138
Less exemption	(1,270)

$$26,868 \times 30\% = \underline{€8,060} \text{ CGT due}$$

Chapter 4

Question 4.1

Philip Even – Computation of Gains/Losses for 2012

		€
1. Gift to Wife	Exempt	Nil

2. Gift to John

Market value (connected persons) at 1/9/2012	200,000
Deduct:	
CUV. €3,000 @ 2.253	(6,759)
Development premium €2,000 @ 1	(2,000)
Gain	191,241

3. Sale of Farm

Sale proceeds	260,000
Less: €32,000 Indexed @ 1.442	(46,144)
Gain	213,856

4. Sale of National Loan Stock

Exempt Government Security	Nil

5. Sale of Antique necklace

Exempt – non-wasting tangible movable property sold for less than €2,540	Nil

6. Sale of Painting

No loss relief available. Loss arose on the disposal
of tangible movable property for less than €2,540,
consideration deemed to be €2,540 and so no loss deemed
to arise.   <u>Nil</u>

7. Gift of Licensed Premises

Market value on disposal	875,000
Less: Allowable costs	
January 1983 – €50,000 indexed @ 2.253	(112,650)
June 1989 – €60,000 indexed @ 1.503	(90,180)
March 2006 – €50,000 indexed @ 1	<u>(50,000)</u>
Gain	<u>622,170</u>

8. Sale of Development land

Sale proceeds	18,000
Allowable cost	
(no indexation – acquired after 1/1/03)	<u>(10,000)</u>
Gain	8,000

9. Sale of Vase

Exempt as a disposal of non-wasting tangible
movable property for less than €2,540   <u>Nil</u>

Computation of CGT payable		Dev. Land
Rate of CGT	30%	30%
	€	€
2. Gift to John		191,241
3. Sale of farm	213,856	
7. Gift to mother	622,170	
8. Sale of development land	<u>–</u>	<u>8,000</u>
	836,026	199,241
Deduct:		
Unrelated to development land losses	<u>(6,000)</u>	
	<u>830,026</u>	830,026
Development land losses		<u>(1,500)</u>
		1,027,767
Development land losses may be set off against		
all gains		
Annual exemption		<u>(1,270)</u>
Taxable		<u>1,026,497</u>
CGT @ 30%		<u>307,949</u>

Question 4.2

Mrs O'Sullivan

(a) Chargeable Gain on Sale of Property

	€	€
Proceeds		1,585,000
Less: Selling costs		
Legal costs	12,500	
Agent's commissions	7,000	
		(19,500)
		1,565,500
Deemed cost of property €60,000 × 7.528	451,680	
Enhancement in 1994/95		
€162,000 × 1.309	212,058	(663,738)
Chargeable gain		901,762

(b) Tax on sale of Development Land

Proceeds		1,800,000
Deemed cost: current use value of property		
€12,500 × 7.528	94,100	
Deemed cost: development value of property		
(€25,000 − €12,500) = €12,500 × 1	12,500	(106,600)
Gain		1,693,400
CGT @ 30%		508,020

Question 4.3

Bill O'Rourke

Capital Gains Tax Computation 2012

	€	€
Proceeds		1,680,000
Costs of disposal		(18,000)
		1,662,000
Cost: 06/04/1986 €75,000 (all current use value)		
Indexed @ 1.637	122,775	
Incidental costs: €4,251		
(all attributable to current use)		
Indexed @ 1.637	6,959	(129,734)
Gross gain		1,532,266

Exempt portion of gain - private residence

	€
Current use value at date of disposal	800,000

Costs of disposal attributable to private residence	$\dfrac{€800,000}{€1,680,000} \times €18,000$	(8,571)
		791,429
Indexed cost of acquisition - as above		(129,734)
Exempt gain		661,695
Chargeable gain = gross gain − exempt gain		
€1,532,266 − €661,695 =		870,571

Alternative Calculation

	€
Excess of proceeds over current use value (Development premium):	
€1,680,000 − €800,000 =	880,000
Costs attributable to development premium	
€880,000/€1,680,000 × €18,000 =	(9,429)
Taxable gain	870,571

Question 4.4

Mr Smart

Shop premises

		€
Sales proceeds		695,000
Cost of disposal		(7,000)
		688,000
Value at 6/4/1974 as indexed €10,000 @ 7.528		(75,280)
Enhancement expenditure as indexed: €12,000 @ 1.406		(16,872)
		595,848
Personal exemption		(1,270)
Capital gain		594,578
CGT @ 30%		178,373

Holiday cottage

Sales proceeds (deemed to be market value)	(Note 2)	20,000
Cost		(25,000)
Loss	(Note 1)	(5,000)

Notes:

1. This loss can only be set against future gains made on transactions with his nephew as this is a sale to a connected person.
2. Also in this situation market value is substituted for the sale proceeds.

Question 4.5

Christine Martin

1.	Disposal of shop		€
	Proceeds		224,000
	Less:		
	Related costs		(3,100)
	Less:		
	Cost 63,000 × 1.406		(88,578)
	Chargeable gain		132,322

2.		Holding	Cost
		€	€
	March 1995	1,500	6,800
	July 1997	300	1,050
	January 1998	900	–
		2,700	
	Proceeds		9,000
	Less:		

$$€6,800 \times \frac{2,000}{2,700} \qquad = 5,037 \times 1.309 \qquad (6,593)$$

$$€1,050 \times \frac{2,000}{2,700} \qquad = 777 \times 1.232 \qquad (958)$$

	Chargeable gain		1,449

3.	Proceeds		2,600
	Cost		(1,900)
			700
	Potential CGT due 700 × 30% =		210
	Max. CGT: 2,600 − 2,540 × 50% =		30

Summary

	30%
1.	132,322
2.	1,449
	133,771
Annual exemption	(1,270)
	132,501
CGT @ 30%	39,750
Plus CGT at (3)	30
Total	39,780

Chapter 5

Question 5.1

(a) The transfer of a business to a company is treated as a disposal for CGT purposes. However, if the business is transferred as a going concern together with all the assets other than cash in exchange for shares in the new company, the gain may be rolled over against the cost of the shares issued.

Only partial rollover relief is available where the consideration is only partly satisfied by shares as in this case.

Chargeable Gains Arising

(i) Incorporation of Business

	Workings	€
Warehouse	1	78,640
Goodwill		130,000
Gain		208,640
Deferred	2	178,834
Chargeable in tax year 2012		29,806

(ii) Disposal of Vase

		€
Sale proceeds		88,000
Cost: MV 6 April 1974	10,000	
Indexation factor	7.528	
Indexed cost		75,280
Chargeable gain		12,720

(iii) Disposal of Shares

	€
Sales proceeds	5,000
Cost (no indexation as there is a monetary loss)	(10,000)
Loss	(5,000)

(iv) Capital Gains Tax:

Initial period to 30 November:

	€
Incorporation of business	29,806
Less: Loss relief – loss forward	(10,000)
Less: Annual exemption	(1,270)
	18,536
CGT @ 30%	5,561

Later period:

	€
Incorporation of business	29,806
Disposal of vase	12,720
	42,526

Less: Loss relief re shares	(5,000)
Less: Loss relief – loss forward	(10,000)
Less: Annual exemption	(1,270)
	26,256
CGT @ 30%	7,877
Less paid re initial period	5,561
CGT	2,316

(b)   The CGT of €5,561 is payable by 15 December 2012. The CGT of €2,316 is payable by 31 January 2013.

(c)   The base cost of shares in O' Dowd Ltd for a future disposal is:

	€
Cost of shares	630,000
Less: Deferred gain	178,834
	451,166

Workings

1.   *Chargeable Gains:*

	€	€
Warehouse		
Market value		400,000
Cost – May 1981	120,000	
Indexation factor	2,678	
Indexed cost		321,360
Chargeable gain		78,640
Goodwill		
Market value		130,000
Cost		Nil
Chargeable gain		130,000

Plant and Machinery

No capital loss can arise in respect of the plant and machinery as capital allowances will have been claimed on this expenditure.

Stocks and debtors are not chargeable assets.

2.   *Deferred gain:*

The amount deferred is restricted as follows:

$$\text{Maximum deferred} = \text{chargeable gains} \times \frac{\text{value of shares received}}{\text{value of total consideration}}$$

Value of Total Consideration:

	€
Warehouse	400,000
Plant and machinery	40,000
Goodwill	130,000

Stock	48,000
Debtors	117,000
	735,000
Consideration received : Loan	50,000
Creditors	55,000
Shares	630,000
	735,000

Maximum
Deferral: $208,640 \times \dfrac{630}{735}$ = 178,834

Chapter 6

Question 6.1

(a)

Disposal of shares in family company on 1 August 2012	€
Proceeds (market value)	800,000
MV 1/12/74 = €40,000	
indexed @ 7.528 =	(301,120)
	$498,880 \times 30\% = €149,664$

No CGT is payable on this gain - on the assumption that it is a "family company" as defined for the purposes of the relief, and assuming no restriction in the relief arises out of the underlying assets of the company.

(b)

	€
Sale of shares by Paul	900,000
Cost (deemed - market value)	(800,000)
	100,000
Annual exemption	(1,270)
	98,730
CGT @ 30% =	29,619

In addition Paul has to pay the tax relieved on the transfer of the shares to him – €25,000. This is calculated as follows:

The additional CGT payable by Paul is the CGT which would have been payable by his father if he had not qualified for full relief from CGT on a disposal to his son.

If his father had not qualified for this relief, he could have qualified for the relief available for a disposal of qualifying assets to **a person other than a "child"**.

If the proceeds had been less than €750,000, the father would have qualified for full relief so no additional CGT would have been payable by Paul on the subsequent sale. He would only have paid the €29,619. In this case, as the proceeds on the disposal by the father exceeded €750,000, his father would only have qualified for marginal relief. Marginal relief in this case would have restricted his father's liability to €25,000, i.e. €800,000 − €750,000 = €50,000 × 50% = €25,000, so this is the amount payable by Paul in addition to the €29,619. Total CGT payable by Paul for 2012 = €29,619 + €25,000 = €54,619.

Question 6.2

(a) **Capital Gains Tax**

Sean should qualify for retirement relief on the disposal of his shares in Tara Foods Limited as he meets the conditions as follows:

 − He has attained the age of 55 years
 − The shares are in Sean's trading "family" company and are held for at least 10 years
 − Sean has been a working director of the company for at least 10 years, during which period he has been a full time working director for at least five years.

However, full relief is not available to Sean as his shares derive some of their value from quoted investments which are not chargeable business assets.

The amount qualifying for retirement relief is determined by the formula;

Chargeable Business Assets
Total Chargeable Assets

$$\frac{650,000}{770,000} \quad \frac{(600,000 + 50,000)}{(600,000 + 50,000 + 120,000)}$$

(Stock and trade debtors are not chargeable assets).

The premises qualifies for retirement relief as it falls within the definition of "qualifying assets" for the purposes of the relief, i.e. a building which the individual has owned for a period of not less than 10 years ending with the disposal and which was used throughout that period for the purposes of the company's trade and is disposed of at the same time and to the same person as the shares in the family company.

(b) **Capital Gains Tax Computation**

	€	€
Deemed sale proceeds		800,000
Cost 1977/78	100	
Index factor	4.490	
Indexed cost		(449)
Gain		799,551
Exempt portion		
€799,551 × 650,000/770,000		(674,946)
Chargeable gain		124,605
CGT @ 30%		37,381

Premises

The gain on the premises is not taxable.
No annual exemption is due.

(c) The retirement relief claimed at (b) in respect of the shares will be clawed back if the shares in Tara Foods Limited are disposed of by Michael within six years of the date of transfer by Sean, and the retirement relief claimed at (b) in respect of the property will be clawed back if the property is sold by Michael within six years of the date of transfer by Sean. The relief granted to Sean will in effect be withdrawn.

(d) The relief is withdrawn not from Sean who had the benefit of the relief but by way of Michael being taxable on the gain, i.e. Michael will have to pay the difference between the CGT already paid and the amount which would have been payable by Sean if the retirement relief were not available.

Question 6.3

(a) Colin's CGT liability
Disposal of shares in Crawfords Sportswear Ltd

This disposal does not qualify for retirement relief as **Colin did not own the shares for at least 10 years**. The period of ownership of the trade prior to its transfer to the company is not taken into account, as Colin would not have qualified for relief on transfer of a business to a company. Relief on transfer of a business to a company would not have applied, as not all of the assets of the business were transferred to the company, i.e. the premises were not transferred.

The **premises let to the company does not qualify for retirement relief**, as it was not used for the purposes of the **company's business for 10 years.**

The cost of the shares for CGT purposes is their market value at 1 January 2005, i.e. the market value of the net assets taken over. Net assets transferred were:

	Market Value
	€
Fixtures and fittings	50,000
Goodwill	80,000
Stocks	120,000
Debtors	25,000
Creditors	(110,000)
Net assets transferred	165,000

Gain on disposal of shares:

	€
Market value	500,000
Market value January 2005	(165,000)
Gain	335,000

Gain on disposal of premises:

		€
Market value		250,000
Cost June 1980	20,000	
Indexation factor 1980/81	3.240	
Indexed cost		(64,800)
Gain		185,200

Gain on disposal of holiday cottage:

	€
Market value	120,000

	€	
Market value 10 October 1983	25,000	
Indexation factor 1983/84	2.003	
Indexed cost		(50,075)
Gain		69,925

Gain on disposal of brooch:

	€
Market value	3,000

	€
Market value 1 December 2003	(2,400)
Gain	600

Note: No indexation as acquired post 2002. Also marginal relief does not apply. (50% × (€3,000 − €2,540)) > 30% × €600.

Colin's CGT Liability 2011

	€
Gains:	
Shares	335,000
Premises	185,200
Holiday cottage	69,925
Brooch	600
	590,725
Annual exemption	(1,270)
	589,455
CGT @ 30%	176,836

Chapter 7

Question 7.1

(a) When a company redeems its own shares at a premium, in this case €590,000, the premium is, on first principles, liable to income tax under Schedule F.

However, if it can be shown that:

(i) the company is a trading or holding company;

(ii) both the company and the vendor are resident (and ordinarily resident in the case of an individual) in the State;

(iii) the buy back is not part of a scheme or arrangement the purpose of which is to enable the shareholder to participate in the profits of the company;

(iv) the share redemption benefits the trade of the company;

(v) the shares have been held for five years;

(vi) the shareholding is substantially reduced; and

(vii) the shareholder, post-redemption, is no longer connected with the company (shareholding less than 30%),

then the proceeds of €600,000 can be regarded as a capital receipt.

(b) Provided all tests are met, Alan's liability to CGT is as follows:

	€
Proceeds	600,000
Cost 10,000 × 1.442	(14,420)
Gain	585,580
Less annual exemption	(1,270)
Taxable	584,310
CGT @ 30%	€175,293

Alan may qualify for retirement relief, but we do not have sufficient information to establish whether he does.

(c) If Alan fails the tests, he will be liable to income tax under schedule F.

	€
Schedule F	590,000
@ 41%	241,900

The company will be obliged to deduct DWT of 20% from the payment, and Alan will be entitled to a credit for the DWT. Alan will also be liable to the USC and possibly PRSI.

Chapter 13

Question 13.1

John is the disponer as he instructs Mary to make the payment to Peter (the beneficiary).

Question 13.2

The date of the disposition is when the mother agrees to the future transfer. The beneficiary (daughter) does not become beneficially entitled in possession until she has her first child and this will be the date of the gift.

Question 13.3

Paddy gets a gift of €1,000,000 less consideration of €100,000 and Nora gets a gift of €100,000 both from Joyce.

Question 13.4

Memorandum

To	:
From	:
Date	:
Re	: *Capital Acquisitions Tax Queries*

I refer to the matters recently raised by you.

(a) Disposition

For Capital Acquisitions Tax (CAT) purposes, a gift or inheritance is deemed to be taken where a disposition is made by a person, the disponer, as a result of which another person, the donee, becomes beneficially entitled in possession, see (c), to any benefit otherwise than for full consideration.

"Disposition" is the method by which ownership of the benefit provided is transferred. A simple example of a disposition is where a person transfers a property to another person. The deed of transfer in this case is the disposition.

The term disposition is defined very widely in CATCA 2003 and includes the following:

(1) Any act by a person as a result of which the value of his estate is reduced, e.g. the transfer of property otherwise than for full consideration.

(2) Any trust, covenant, agreement or arrangement.

(3) An omission or failure to act by an individual, as a result of which the value of his estate is reduced.

Example:
This includes the passing of a resolution by a company which results directly or indirectly in one shareholder's property being increased in value at the expense of the property of any other shareholder, if that other shareholder could have prevented the passing of the resolution by voting against it.

(4) The payment of money.

(5) The allotment of shares in a company.

(6) The grant or creation of any benefit.

(7) The transfer of any property or benefit by will or on an intestacy.

(b) Date of the Disposition

The CAT Act defines the date of the disposition as:

(1) The date of death of the deceased in the case of a benefit taken by will or on an intestacy.

(2) The date of the death of the deceased in the case of benefits derived under the Succession Act 1965.

(3) The latest date when the disponer could have exercised the right or power which has been waived, where the disposition consisted of a failure or omission to exercise a right of power.

(4) In any other case, the date of the disposition is the date on which the act or, where more than one act is involved, the last act of the disponer was done by which he provided or bound himself to provide, the property comprised in the disposition.

(c) Beneficially entitled in possession

"Entitled in possession" is defined in CATCA 2003 as meaning, "having a present right to the enjoyment of property as opposed to having a future such right". CAT only arises where a person obtains the current enjoyment of a property as opposed to being entitled to enjoyment of the property at some time in the future.

A person has a "beneficial interest" in property if he is entitled to the benefits arising from a property without necessarily having legal ownership of the property.

For example X by deed appoints Y, his son, as trustee of a fund of investments the income from which is to be paid to X's wife, Mrs X, for the duration of her life. After Mrs X's death the fund is to be transferred into the ownership of X's son. Y is the legal owner of the investments. However, as the income from the investments is paid to Mrs X for her life, as soon as the deed is executed giving her the life interest, she is said to have a beneficial interest in the investments. Y also has a beneficial interest in the fund as he is entitled to the benefits from the fund in the future. Mrs X is said to be beneficially entitled in possession to the fund. However, her son Y, while having a beneficial interest in the fund, is not "entitled in possession" as he has a future interest rather than a current interest.

Signed:

Chapter 14

Question 14.1

Location of Assets

The CGT Act does not include rules for determining where property is situated. General law determines where property is located. The main rules are as follows:

(1) Land and buildings
Situated where they are physically located.

(2) Debts

(i) A simple contract debt is situated where the debtor resides.
(ii) A speciality debt, i.e. a debt payable under a sealed instrument, is situate where the instrument happens to be.
(iii) A judgement debt is situated where the judgement is recorded.

(3) Securities/shares
Situated where the share register is kept, if the securities/shares are registered. Bearer securities/shares are situated where the security/share certificate is physically located.

(4) Tangible property e.g. cars, furniture, moveable goods
Situated where they are physically located

(5) Cash or currency of any kind
Situated where they are physically located. Bank balances are located in the country where the bank branch is at which the account is kept.

Question 14.2

Gift and Inheritances Tax Queries During Year Ended 31/12/2012

(a) A gift or inheritance taken during the year ended 31/12/2012 will be a taxable gift or inheritance if:
(1) Regardless of whether the gift or inheritance consists of Irish or foreign property,

    (i)   The date of the disposition is on or after 1/12/1999 and the **disponer** is Irish resident or ordinarily resident in the State at the date of the disposition, or

    (ii)   The date of the disposition is on or after 1/12/1999 and the **donee/ successor** is Irish resident or ordinarily resident in the State at the date of the gift/ inheritance,

Provided that in the case of a non-Irish domiciled person, such a person will only be regarded as resident or ordinarily resident in the State on the relevant date if he has been resident in the State for the previous five tax years and is resident or ordinarily resident on the relevant date, i.e. date of the disposition for the disponer and the date of the gift/inheritance in the case of the beneficiary.

    (iii)   The date of the disposition is before 1/12/1999 and the disponer was domiciled in the State at the date of the disposition.

(2)   The gift or inheritance consists of Irish property (even though none of the rules under 1 above are satisfied).

(b)

(1)   As the disponer is Irish domiciled and Irish resident both the Irish and the UK property are taxable inheritances. Rule 1(i) above applies. (In any event as the donee is also Irish domiciled and resident at the date of the inheritance the inheritance would be a taxable inheritance even if the disponer had not been Irish domiciled and resident.)

(2)   The date of the disposition, i.e. the date of Gordon's death, is after 1/12/1999. The property inherited is not Irish property. As the successor, Dermot is Irish resident and domiciled at the date of the inheritance, the inheritance is a taxable inheritance. Rule 1(ii) above applies.

(3)   Neither the disponer nor the successor are Irish resident or ordinarily resident at the relevant dates. The property inherited is Irish property. The inheritance is a taxable inheritance. Rule 2 above applies.

(4)   The property inherited is not Irish property. The disponer is not resident or ordinarily resident in the State at the date of the disposition and the successor, Nevin, although Irish resident, is not Irish domiciled. Therefore, he is only taxable if he has been resident in the State for the preceding five tax years and resident or ordinarily resident on 16/9/2012. As he is, the inheritance is a taxable inheritance.

(5)   The disponer is Irish domiciled and resident in the State at the date of the disposition. This is, therefore, a taxable inheritance. Rule 1(i) above applies. It is irrelevant that one of the successors is not resident in the State. (In any event, as the entire property consists of Irish property, even if neither the disponer nor the successors were Irish resident at the relevant dates, the inheritance would be a taxable inheritance).

(6)   As the donee, Darren, is Irish domiciled and is ordinarily resident in the State, (he only ceased to be resident in Ireland in 2011 and, therefore, is still ordinarily resident), the gift is a taxable gift. Rule 1(ii) above applies.

(7)   The date of the disposition, i.e. the date of the deed under which the house was transferred initially to Maxine's niece and then to her son Stephen, is before

1/12/1999. Rule 1(iii) therefore applies. The gift is a taxable gift as the disponer was Irish domiciled at the date of the disposition.

(8)   As the disponer is Irish domiciled and Irish resident at the date of the disposition, the gift is a taxable gift. Rule 1(i) above applies. (In any event, as the donee is also Irish domiciled and Irish resident at the date of the gift so that, even if rule 1(i) was not satisfied, the gift would be a taxable gift by virtue of rule 1(ii)).

(9)   The disponer is Irish resident and ordinarily resident but not Irish domiciled. For Rule 1(i) to apply, however, Jean must also have been resident for the last five years and be resident/ordinarily resident, as she is foreign domiciled. Since Jean is so resident and ordinarily resident, the gift of both the Irish and the foreign shares is taxable. (Had Jean not triggered a liability, Amelie would not be taxable on the French shares as she has not been resident for the last five years. Clearly, she would be taxable on the Irish shares).

(10)   The date of the disposition, i.e. the date of Janet's death (Declan inherits the property by virtue of his mother's will), is before 1/12/1999. The property inherited is not Irish property. Rule 1(iii) above therefore applies. The disponer is Janet. As Janet was not domiciled in Ireland at the date of the disposition, i.e. 1989, the inheritance is not a taxable inheritance.

Question 14.3

1.   *Memorandum*

To :	
From :	
Date :	
Re :	*Capital Acquisitions Tax Queries*

I refer to the matters recently raised by you.

(a)   Taxable Gift

A gift of property situated in Ireland is a taxable gift. However, regardless of whether property comprised in a gift is Irish or foreign property, a gift will be a "taxable gift" if:

(1)   the date of the disposition by virtue of which the gift is taken is before 1/12/1999 and the disponer is domiciled in the State at the date of the disposition;

(2)   the date of the disposition by virtue of which the gift is taken is on or after 1/12/1999; and:

    (i)   the disponer is either resident or ordinarily resident in the State at the date of the disposition; or

    (ii)   the donee is either resident or ordinarily resident in the State at the date of the gift.

Provided that in the case of a non-Irish domiciled person, such a person will only be regarded as resident or ordinarily resident in the State on the relevant date if that date is on or after 1/12/2004 and if he has been resident in the State for the previous five tax years and is resident or ordinarily resident on the relevant date, i.e. date of the disposition for the disponer and the date of the gift/inheritance in the case of the beneficiary.

(b)   Taxable Inheritance

An inheritance of property situated in Ireland is a taxable inheritance. However, regardless of whether property comprised in an inheritance is Irish or foreign property, an inheritance will be a "taxable inheritance" if:

(1)   the date of the disposition by virtue of which the inheritance is taken is before 1/12/1999 and the disponer is domiciled in the State at the date of the disposition;

(2)   the date of the disposition by virtue of which the inheritance is taken is on or after 1/12/1999; and:

    (i)   the disponer is either resident or ordinarily resident in the State at the date of the disposition; or

    (ii)   the successor is either resident or ordinarily resident in the State at the date of the inheritance.

Provided that in the case of a non-Irish domiciled person, such a person will only be regarded as resident or ordinarily resident in the State on the relevant date if that date is on or after 1/12/2004 and if he has been resident in the State for the previous five tax years and is resident or ordinarily resident on the relevant date, i.e. date of the disposition for the disponer and the date of the gift/inheritance in the case of the beneficiary.

(c)   Domicile

The term domicile broadly refers to the country which an individual considers as his natural home.

An individual acquires a domicile of origin at his birth and this is normally that of his father. The domicile of origin is usually retained unless the individual takes steps to acquire a domicile of choice.

(d)   Date of the Disposition

CATCA 2003 Act defines the date of the disposition as:

(1)   The date of death of the deceased in the case of a benefit taken by will or an intestacy.

(2)   The date of the death of the deceased in the case of benefits derived under the Succession Act 1965.

(3)   The latest date when the disponer could have exercised the right or power which has been waived, where the disposition consisted of a failure or omission to exercise a right or power.

(4)   In any other case, the date of the disposition is the date on which the act or, where more than one act is involved, the last act of the disponer was done by which he provided or bound himself to provide, the property comprised in the disposition.

(e)   Date of the Gift

The date of the gift is the date of the happening of the event upon which the donee becomes beneficially entitled in possession to the benefit.

Signed:

Chapter 15

Question 15.1

MEMORANDUM

To :	
From :	
Date :	
Re :	*Capital Acquisitions Tax Agricultural Relief*

I refer to your recent query regarding the relief from CAT available on the transfer of land by a client to his son.

(a) Nature of the Relief

Where an individual qualifies for agricultural relief in respect of a gift of agricultural property, the value of the property is reduced by 90% for CAT purposes.

The taxable value of a gift is calculated by deducting from the market value of the property comprised in the gift any consideration given and any liabilities, costs and expenses payable out of the gift. Where an individual qualifies for agricultural relief in respect of a gift of property, the amount of any consideration given or liabilities, costs and expenses payable are also reduced by 90%.

For example a father gifts land valued at €1 million to his son. The land is subject to a mortgage of €20,000 which is taken over by the son. The son pays stamp duty of €10,000 on the transfer. If the gift qualifies for agricultural relief, the taxable value of the gift received will be as follows:

	€
Market value	1,000,000
Agricultural relief (90%)	(900,000)
Agricultural value	100,000
Stamp duty €10,000@10%	(1,000)
Mortgage €20,000@10%	(2,000)
Taxable value	97,000

(b) Agricultural Property

Agricultural relief applies to gifts or inheritances of "agricultural property". Agricultural property is:

Agricultural land, pasture and woodland in the EU including crops, trees, and underwood growing on such land and including such farm buildings, farm houses and mansion houses as are of a character appropriate to the property, and farm machinery, livestock and bloodstock thereon and entitlements under the EU Single Farm Payment Scheme.

(c) Definition of Farmer

In order for a gift to qualify for agricultural relief, the recipient of the gift must be a "farmer" after receiving the gift (i.e. the date of the gift) and on the "valuation date".

There is no requirement that the recipient be a farmer in the normal sense of the word or to be trading as a farmer. "Farmer" is defined by the legislation as:

– an individual in respect of whom not less than **80% of the market value of all property to which he is beneficially entitled in possession (taking the current gift or inheritance into account) is represented by the market value of agricultural property in the EU**. In this context, an individual is deemed to be beneficially entitled in possession to any assets which are the subject of a discretionary trust of which he is a settlor and an object, and also to any future interests in property to which the individual is currently entitled.

For the purpose of the 80% test, the gross value of assets are taken ignoring any liabilities or charges. There is one exception, i.e. borrowings used to purchase, repair or improve an off-farm principal private residence are deductible for the 80% test.

Continuing with the example at (a) above, if after the gift the son's only other asset consists of a house valued at €120,000 with a mortgage of €100,000 attaching to it and a car valued at €20,000, the son will qualify as a "farmer" as after taking the gift his assets will be made up as follows:

	€	%
Agricultural property	1,000,000	96
House (net of mortgage)	20,000	2
Car	20,000	2
Total assets	1,040,000	100

The farmer test does not have to be satisfied to the extent that the gift consists of trees or underwood.

(d) Withdrawal of the Relief

The agricultural relief will be withdrawn if, within six years after the date of gift or inheritance, the property is sold or compulsorily acquired and is not replaced with other agricultural property

– within a year in the case of a sale, or
– within six years in the case of a compulsory acquisition.

If part of the proceeds on the disposal of agricultural property are reinvested, then a similar fraction of the relief is clawed back.

There is no withdrawal of the relief to the extent that the property which qualified for agricultural relief consists of crops, trees or underwood.

If the agricultural property is development land and it is disposed of in the period commencing six years after the date of the gift or inheritance and ending 10 years after that date, then the CAT will be recomputed. Agricultural relief will only be given in respect of the current use value of the property, i.e. there will be no relief given in respect of the development value, and CAT is recalculated and payable accordingly.

Signed:

Question 15.2

Inheritances:

	Margaret	Liam	Eva
	€	€	€
Holiday home	180,000		
Stocks and shares	230,000		
Irish Government stock	101,500		
Shares in Fine Arts Ltd			950,000
Agricultural property		1,090,000	
Cash		50,000	
Mortgage		(120,000)	
Creditors		(15,000)	
Funeral expenses		(20,000)	
	511,500	985,000	

Inheritance Tax

Margaret:

	€
Taxable value of inheritance	511,500
CAT payable:	
Group threshold: €33,500 @ Nil	Nil
Balance €478,000 @ 30% =	
CAT payable	143,400

Liam:

	€	
Taxable value of inheritance	125,500	(W1)
Tax payable:		
Group threshold: €33,500 @ Nil	Nil	
Balance €92,000 @ 30% =	27,600	

Eva:

Market value of shares	950,000
Value attributed to investment property	(350,000)
Value excluding investment property	600,000
Business relief	(540,000)
	60,000
Value attributed to investment property	350,000
Taxable value	410,000
Group threshold @ Nil	(250,000)
Balance	160,000
CAT @ 30%	48,000

Workings

W1

	€	€
Market value of agricultural property		1,090,000
Less agricultural relief at 90%		(981,000)
		109,000
Less mortgage €120,000 × 10%		(12,000)
Less farm creditors €15,000 × 10%		(1,500)
Taxable value of agricultural property		95,500
Cash	50,000	
Funeral expenses	(20,000)	30,000
Taxable value of total property inherited by Liam		125,500

Clearly Liam qualifies as a "farmer"

Value of agricultural property $= €1,090,000$

Value of total property
$(1,090,000 + 30,000^* + 200,000 - 130,000)$ $= €1,190,000$

Agricultural property as percentage of total property $= 92\%$ (greater than the required 80%)

*As the funeral expenses will have been paid by the valuation date, the residue will be €50,000 − €20,000 = €30,000.

Question 15.3

Mr Murphy

XYZ Chartered Accountants
Main Street

4 June 2012

Mr Murphy
Director
Murphy Electrical Wholesalers Ltd
Church Street

Re: Proposed transfer of shares to Jake Murphy

Dear Mark

I refer to our recent telephone conversation in which you asked me to advise you on the tax consequences of the transfer of your entire shareholding in Murphy Electrical Wholesalers Ltd to your son Jake.

Background

My understanding is that you inherited all the shares in Murphy Electrical Wholesalers Ltd (MEWL) on the death of your brother in June 1995. At that time the shares were valued at €2 million. The shares are now valued at €3.5 million and you are considering transferring your entire shareholding to your son, Jake.

Taxation consequences of transfer of shares

Capital Gains Tax

The gift of shares will be treated as a sale by you of your shares at market value for CGT purposes. I have estimated that the CGT arising will be €283,800 (see **Appendix 1**).

Stamp Duty

Stamp duty of 1% of the value of the shares will be payable by Mark, i.e. €35,000.

Capital Acquisitions Tax

Assuming your son has not previously received any taxable gifts from you or your wife, CAT will be payable at the rate of 30% on the excess of the taxable value of the shares received from you over €250,000. The taxable value of a gift is normally calculated as the market value of the property which is the subject of a gift less any consideration given and any liabilities payable out of the gift. However, if the property which is gifted consists of business assets or shares in certain unquoted companies, the taxable value is further reduced by 90%. This relief is known as business relief. The conditions which must be satisfied if business relief is to apply to the transfer of shares to your son are outlined in Appendix 2.

Assuming the only cost payable by your son is stamp duty, if your son qualifies for business relief, the taxable value of the shares for CAT purposes will be €346,500, and his CAT liability will be nil, calculated as follows:

	€
Market value of shares	3,500,000
Less stamp duty @ 1%	(35,000)
	3,465,000
Business relief @90%	(3,118,500)
Taxable value	346,500
Less tax free amount	(250,000)
Taxable	96,500
CAT @ 30%	28,950
Less CGT credit (lower of €28,950 and €283,800)	(28,950)
CAT liability	Nil

If, however, business relief does not apply, your son's CAT liability will be as follows:

	€
Market value of shares	3,500,000
Less stamp duty @ 1%	(35,000)
	3,465,000
Tax free amount	(250,000)
Taxable	3,215,000
CAT @ 30%	964,500
Less CGT payable	(283,800)
CAT liability	680,700

As can be seen from these computations, your son's CAT liability may be reduced by the CGT payable by you on the transfer of the shares to him. This credit for CGT will only apply if your son does not dispose of the shares within two years after the date of the gift.

Conclusion

As outlined, if Jake qualifies for business relief, a substantial CAT liability can be avoided. Accordingly it is important before any decision is taken to transfer the shares to Jake that we should meet to go through these conditions and make sure that they are satisfied.

In making a decision to transfer the shares to Jake, you should also bear in mind that:

- if you were to wait until you are 55 years old to gift the shares to Jake, you could benefit from "retirement relief", provided the necessary conditions, e.g. being a full-time director for five years, can be satisfied; or
- if he were to inherit the shares from you rather than by receiving them as a gift, **there would be no CGT liability**, and Jake's CAT position would be unchanged.

Accordingly, bearing in mind the significant CGT cost associated with the transfer, you might decide ultimately to wait a few years to gift him the shares or, alternatively, leave him the shares in your will. We can however discuss this aspect further when we meet as there are rules to be satisfied before full retirement relief applies.

Yours sincerely

TAX DIRECTOR

Question 15.3 Appendix 1

Murphy Electrical Wholesalers Ltd

Capital Gains Tax Liability on Transfer of Shares by Mr Mark Murphy to Mr Jake Murphy

		€
Market value of shares		3,500,000
Market value in June 1995	2,000,000	
Inflation factor	1.277	
Indexed value of €2 million		(2,554,000)
Capital gain		946,000
CGT @ 30%		283,800

Note: Mark Murphy does not qualify for retirement relief as he did not work full-time in Murphy Electrical Wholesalers Ltd.

Question 15.3 Appendix 2

Murphy Electrical Wholesalers Ltd

Business Relief – Conditions to be Satisfied

In order for a gift of shares in an unquoted company to qualify for business relief for CAT purposes the following conditions must be satisfied:

(1) The recipient of the gift must, after receiving the gift of shares, either:

   (a) control more than 25% of the voting shares in the company;
   (b) together with his relatives, control the company; or
   (c) hold at least 10% of the issued share capital and have worked full time in the company for the five years prior to the gift or inheritance.

(2) The company's business must not consist wholly or mainly of:

   (a) dealing in currencies, securities, stocks or shares, land or buildings; or
   (b) making or holding investments.

   In determining whether a company's business consists wholly or mainly of one of (a) or (b) above, wholly or mainly can be taken as more than 50%. Each case is looked at separately but, broadly, it can be taken that if more than 50% of a company's assets and more than 50% of its income is derived from business activities other than (a) or (b) above the company will satisfy this test.

(3) The shares must have been owned by the person making the gift, or by him and his spouse, for at least five years prior to the gift.

(4) To the extent that the value of the shares is attributable to any non-trade assets owned by the company, that portion of the shares will not qualify for business relief. For example, a company valued at €5 million on an assets basis owns an investment property valued at €1 million. Only 4/5ths of the value of any shares in this company transferred by way of gift or inheritance will qualify for business relief.

(5) To the extent that the value of the shares is attributable to any business assets which were not being used wholly or mainly for the business for a continuous period of two years prior to the date of the gift, or if acquired less than two years ago for the period since acquisition, must also be left out of account. An asset is not regarded as being used wholly or mainly for the purpose of the trade where it was used wholly or mainly for the personal benefit of the owner of the shares or any of his relatives. This provision is aimed at significant assets which have an impact on the value of the shares, e.g. a private yacht or a large house provided to a director/shareholder. Assets such as the typical company car while used for the personal benefit of a director/shareholder would not normally impact upon the value of the shares in a company.

(6) The company need not be incorporated in Ireland. It can be incorporated anywhere.

Question 15.4

SANDRA

(a)   James

	€
Assets inherited:	
Investment property: €520,000 × 1/2	260,000
Shares €1 million × 20% (Note 1)	200,000
Business relief relating to shares (Note 2)	(135,000)
Share of residue (Note 3)	74,000
Taxable	399,000

Aggregate A		
Current benefit	399,000	
Gift from mother in 1999	167,000	
	566,000	
Group threshold: €250,000 @ nil	Nil	
€316,000 @ 30%	94,800	
Tax on Aggregate A		94,800
Aggregate B		
Gift from mother in 1999	167,000	

Tax on aggregate B = nil as €167,000 is less than the group threshold amount of €250,000.

Tax on Aggregate A – Tax on Aggregate B = Tax on inheritance

Tax on inheritance is therefore	94,800

(b) John

As the inheritance was taken from his wife, the benefits under the will are exempt from inheritance tax <u>and</u> are not taken into account (for aggregation purposes) in calculating CAT on later gifts or inheritances from other sources.

Notes:

(1) Tyrex Ltd is a private company which after the receipt of the shares by James is under the control of his relatives. Therefore, the value of the 20% shareholding in Tyrex Ltd inherited by James is valued as if it were part of a controlling holding, i.e. the value of a 20% shareholding is taken to be 20% of the market value of the company as a whole. No discount is given for the fact that a 20% interest is a minority interest.

(2) Business relief

		€
Total value of Tyrex Ltd		1,000,000
Value attributable to non-business assets:		
House	300,000	
Less mortgage	(50,000)	
		(250,000)
Value attributable to relevant business property (balance)		750,000

Accordingly, 75% of the value of the shares in Tyrex Ltd is attributable to relevant business property.

	€
Value of shares inherited by James	200,000
Value attributable to relevant business property (75%)	150,000
Business relief @ 90%	135,000

(3)   Residue

	€
Bank accounts	60,000
Policy	104,000
Expenses	(16,000)
	148,000
50% share to James	74,000

Chapter 16

Question 16.1

(a)   Michael

This is a taxable gift as the disponer, Michael is Irish domiciled and resident. The relevant group threshold is €250,000 – gift from parent to a child.

Total gifts/inheritances received from persons within same group threshold:

	€
Gift from father on 1/1/2012	40,000
Less small gift exemption	(3,000)
Jewellery inherited from mother	20,000
Total	57,000

As this is less than the group threshold of €250,000, no CAT is payable.

(b)   David

This is a taxable gift as the donee, Mary, is Irish resident and domiciled. The relevant group threshold is €33,500 – gift to a child of a brother or sister. The previous gift of shares taken by Mary from her uncle in December 1998 is not a taxable gift as it was a gift of foreign property taken before 1 December 1999 from a person who was not Irish domiciled. Accordingly the 1998 gift is ignored. A gift from a cousin is within the Group C €16,750 group threshold.

CAT payable in respect of the current gift is, therefore:

	€
Value of gift	50,000
Less small gift exemption	(3,000)
	47,000
Group threshold: €33,500	
CAT liability €13,500 @ 30%	4,050

(c)   Bridget

This is a taxable inheritance as the disponer, Bridget's uncle, was Irish domiciled and resident at the date of his death.

Gifts and inheritances previously received from persons within the same group threshold include the inheritances from an aunt in March 1994 and the inheritance from Bridget's grandmother in September 1989. The inheritance in 1989 is ignored as it was taken before 5 December 1991. The inheritance in 1994 of the house in the

US is not a taxable inheritance as the date of the disposition, i.e. the death, was before 1 December 1999, the property inherited was foreign property and the disponer was not domiciled in the State at the date of death. Accordingly the only taxable gift/inheritance taken into account in calculating the CAT on the current inheritance is the inheritance of Irish quoted shares.

CAT on Aggregate A:	€
UK property	120,000
Irish quoted shares	50,000
	170,000
Group threshold: €33,500 @ Nil	
Balance €136,500 @ 30% =	40,950
CAT on "Aggregate A"	40,950
CAT on Aggregate B:	
Irish quoted shares	50,000
Group threshold: €33,500 @ Nil	
Balance €16,500 @ 30% =	4,950
CAT on "Aggregate B"	4,950

CAT on Aggregate A − CAT on
Aggregate B = €40,950 − €4,950

CAT payable in respect of inheritance of UK property	€36,000

Question 16.2

Sarah

(a) Patrick

	€
Assets inherited:	
Government stock	14,000
Aggregate A	
Current benefit	14,000
Gift from mother in 2001	467,000
	481,000
Group threshold: €250,000 @ nil	Nil
€231,000 @ 30%	69,300
Tax on Aggregate A	69,300

Aggregate B

Gift from mother in 2001		467,000
Group threshold:	250,000 @ nil	Nil
	217,000 @ 30%	65,100
Tax on aggregate B =		65,100

Tax on Aggregate A – Tax on Aggregate B = Tax on inheritance

Tax on inheritance is therefore €69,300 – €65,100	4,200

(b)   Harry

The inheritance received by Harry is exempt because:

(i)   He was not domiciled or ordinarily resident at the date of the inheritance; and

(ii)   The inheritance comprised of Irish Government Securities, which qualify for exemption from Irish income tax when beneficially owned by persons who are not domiciled or ordinarily resident in the State; and,

(iii)   Sarah owned the securities at 24 February 2003; accordingly she was only required to have owned the securities for six years.

Chapter 17

Question 17.1

Mr O'Donovan

ABC & Co

Chartered Accountants

17 November 2012

Mr O'Donovan
3 New Street
Dublin

Re: Proposed Property Transfers

Dear Mr O'Donovan

You asked me to advise you on the taxation consequences of the proposed property transfers to your daughters on 1 December next.

Stamp Duty
Lorraine and Sheila will have the following stamp duty liabilities:
Lorraine: €350,000 × 1% = €3,500
Sheila: €250,000 × 1% = €2,500

Capital Gains Tax

You will be treated as disposing of both properties at market value for CGT purposes. Stamp duty and other legal fees incurred in connection with the properties are deductible in calculating the taxable gains. Accordingly, although the property to be transferred to Sheila has increased in value since you acquired it, taking account of your stamp duty and legal fee, overall a capital loss arises.

I have estimated, however, that a CGT liability of approximately €20,512 will arise on the deemed disposal of the property to Lorraine (see **Appendix 1**).

Capital Acquisitions Tax

Both your daughters will be treated as receiving a taxable gift from you equal to the market value of the property transferred to them. An individual may receive gifts or inheritances up to a total value of €250,000 from parents over his lifetime (since 5 December 1991) without giving rise to any CAT liability. Total gifts and inheritances in excess of €250,000 are subject to CAT at 30%.

I understand both Lorraine and Sheila have previously inherited assets valued at €150,000 and €215,000 respectively from their mother in 1999. (Sheila also previously received a gift of shares from an uncle, however, this is ignored). In addition, because Lorraine has been living rent free in an apartment owned by you for the last few years, she is treated as receiving a taxable gift from you each year equal to the market rent which would have been payable by her in respect of the apartment.

Taking account of the above, I have estimated that the transfer will give rise to a CAT liability of approximately €88,350 for Lorraine and €63,750 for Sheila, see **Appendix 2**. Your CGT liability of approximately €20,512 however relates to the disposal of the property to Lorraine and therefore may be offset against Lorraine's CAT liability reducing the CAT payable by Lorraine to approximately €67,838. However, if Lorraine disposes of the apartment within two years, the CGT credit will be clawed back.

Exemption from CAT for Residential Properties

There is an exemption from CAT for gifts or inheritances of residential property provided certain conditions are met. The main conditions to be satisfied are that:

(a)   the recipient of the property must have occupied the property as his or her only or main residence for a period of three years prior to the date of the gift or inheritance;

(b)   the recipient must continue to occupy the house as his or her only or main residence for a period of six years commencing on the date of the gift or inheritance; and

(c)   the recipient must not, at the date of the gift or inheritance, have an interest in any other house.

There are extra conditions to be satisfied in the case of gifts (not inheritances)

(i)   The dwelling house must be owned by the disponer for three years prior to the gift and, where the gifted house has replaced another property, each house must be owned by the disponer for the relevant part of the three-year period that it was occupied by the beneficiary.

(ii)   Any period during which the donee and the disponer occupied the dwelling house as their principal private residence will be disregarded for the purposes of (a) above, unless the disponer is compelled by reason of old age or infirmity to depend on the services of the donee during the three-year period of occupancy. This means, for example, that generally co-habiting couples or children living with their parents are excluded from this exemption in the case of gifts (not inheritances).

Lorraine has been occupying the apartment which you intend to transfer to her since 1 April 2010. If you delay the transfer of the apartment to her until 1 April 2013, no CAT will arise on the transfer of the property to her.

In the same way, you might consider allowing Sheila to live rent-free in the apartment for a three year period before transferring the property to her so that she too can avail of the CAT exemption.

As noted above, however, both your daughters will have to continue to live in the apartment for at least six years after the gift in order to continue to avoid a clawback of the relief given. The relief given is, however, not clawed back if they sell the apartment within the six-year period provided they reinvest the proceeds received in a replacement residence. I understand Lorraine is due to be seconded abroad for a six month period this year and this period will count as a period of occupation of the apartment for the purpose of the relief. If each of your daughters can avail of this exemption, the gift of the property will not be aggregated when calculating CAT due on any future gifts or inheritances from you. This is clearly beneficial.

If you have any queries on the above or wish to discuss any of the issues raised further please do not hesitate to give me a call.

Yours sincerely

Question 17.1 – Appendix 1

Capital Gains Tax Liability on Transfer of Properties

Transfer to Lorraine O'Donovan

		€
Market value of property		350,000
Cost in November 1999	220,000	
Legal fees and stamp duty	15,000	
Total cost	235,000	
Inflation factor	1.193	
Indexed cost of property		(280,355)
Capital gain		69,645
Annual exemption		(1,270)
Taxable gain		68,375
CGT @ 30%		20,512

Transfer to Sheila O'Donovan

	€
Market value of property	250,000

Cost in July 2010	240,000
Legal fees and stamp duty	28,000
Total cost	(268,000)
Capital loss	(18,000)

The loss arising on the property transferred to Sheila may not be offset against the gain arising on the transfer of the property to Lorraine as the loss arose on a **disposal to a connected person**.

Question 17.1 – Appendix 2

Capital Acquisitions Tax Liability on Transfer of Properties

Transfer to Lorraine O'Donovan

	€	€
<u>Cumulative gifts/inheritances received from parents:</u>		
Inheritance from mother		150,000
Gift of rent-free apartment from father:		
2010 €1,500 × 9 months	13,500	
2011 €1,500 × 12 months	18,000	
2012 € 1,500 × 11 months	16,500	48,000
Gift of property from father:		
Market value	350,000	
Less stamp duty	3,500	346,500
Total		544,500
Tax-free amount		(250,000)
Taxable		294,500
CAT @ 30%		88,350
Less CGT credit		(20,512)
CAT payable		67,838

Transfer to Sheila O'Donovan

	€	€
<u>Cumulative gifts/inheritances received from parents:</u>		
Inheritance from mother		215,000

Gift of property from father:

Market value	250,000	
Less stamp duty	(2,500)	247,500
Total		462,500
Tax-free amount		(250,000)
Taxable		212,500
CAT @ 30%		63,750

Question 17.2

Credit for CGT

(a) Janet's CGT liability 2012

<u>Shares in Fogarty Fabrics Ltd</u>

		€
Market value		950,000
Cost – market value March 1997	340,000	
Indexation factor	1.251	
Indexed cost		(425,340)
Gain		524,660

Exempt due to retirement relief

$$\text{Proportion} = \frac{\text{Chargeable business assets}}{\text{Chargeable assets}}$$

$$= \frac{€130,000 + €215,000 + €70,000}{€130,000 + €215,000 + €70,000 + €350,000} = 54.25\%$$

Exempt portion of gain €524,660 × 54.25%		(284,628)
Taxable gain		240,032

House

		€
Market value		250,000
	€	
Cost	40,000	
Indexation factor	1.503	
Indexed cost		(60,120)
Gain		189,880

Vase

	€	€
Market value		3,100

	€	
Cost – market value June 1980	150	
Indexation factor	3.240	
Indexed cost		(486)
Gain		2,614

Farmland

	€	€
Market value		1,500,000

	€	
Market value 6 April 1974	80,000	
Indexation factor	7.528	
Indexed cost		(602,240)
Gain		897,760

CGT liability for Janet 2012

	€
Shares	240,032
House	189,880
Farmland	897,760
Total	1,327,672
Losses forward	(10,000)
Taxable gain	1,317,672
CGT @ 30%	395,302
CGT on vase (marginal relief):	
(€3,100 – €2,540) × 50%	280
Janet's CGT liability 2011	395,582

Note: No annual exemption is available as retirement relief was claimed.

(b) CAT liabilities

Shares received by Adam

	€
Market value of shares	950,000
Value attributed to investment property	(350,000)
Value excluding investment property	600,000
Business relief	(540,000)

	60,000
Value attributed to investment property	350,000
Taxable value	410,000
Small gift exemption	(3,000)
	407,000
Previous gift from mother	100,000
	507,000
Group threshold @ Nil	(250,000)
Balance	257,000
CAT @ 30%	77,100
CGT attributable to gift of shares	

$$€395,302 \times \frac{€240,032}{€1,327,672} = €71,467$$

Less CGT credit	(71,467)
Adam's CAT liability	5,633

House

Received by Julie €250,000 × ½ =	125,000
Received by Nigel €250,000 × ½ =	125,000

Julie

Taxable value	125,000
Less small gift exemption	(3,000)
Taxable	122,000

Julie has not previously received any taxable gifts or inheritances and, as the taxable gift less annual exemption is less than the Group A threshold of €250,000, no CAT liability arises in respect of the gift to her.

Nigel	€
Market value of gift	125,000
Small gift exemption	(3,000)
	122,000
Group C threshold @ Nil	(16,750)
Balance	105,250
CAT @ 30%	31,575
CGT attributable to gift of ½ house	

$$€395,302 \times \frac{€189,880}{€1,327,672} = €56,535 \times ½ = \quad (28,268)$$

Nigel's CAT liability	3,307

Note: The previous gift from his aunt is ignored as the Group B €33,500 threshold applies.

Vase

	€
Market value of gift	3,100
Small gift exemption	(3,000)
Taxable	100
Previous inheritance	75,000
	75,100
Group threshold @ Nil	(33,500)
Balance	41,600
CAT @ 30%	12,480
CAT attributable to previous inheritance:	
Inheritance	75,000
Group threshold @ Nil	(33,500)
Balance	41,500
CAT @ 30%	12,450
CAT attributable to current gift €12,480 – €12,450	30
Less CGT payable by Janet (max)	(30)
Sally's CAT liability	nil

Farmland

	€
Market value	1,500,000
Agricultural relief (90%)	(1,350,000)
Taxable value	150,000
Less small gift exemption	(3,000)
Taxable	147,000

Kevin has not previously received any taxable gifts or inheritances and, as the taxable gift is less than the Group A threshold of €250,000, no CAT liability arises in respect of the gift to him.

Note: the credit for CGT will be clawed back on any beneficiary who disposes of the asset within two years of the date of the gift.

Question 17.3

Ronnie

(a)   CGT liability

Government Stock

Exempt from CGT

Disposal of business to Jake

Vans – no capital gain (loss relieved via capital allowance system)

Stocks, debtors– non chargeable asset

Goodwill

	€
Market value 16/7/2012	300,000
Cost January 2006	(55,000)
Gain	245,000

Disposals to Brendan

Vans – no capital gain (loss relieved via capital allowance system)

Office building

	€
Market value 16/7/2012	250,000
Cost January 2006	(80,000)
Gain	170,000

Cash – non chargeable asset

CGT liability:

Gains	€
Goodwill	245,000
Premises	170,000
Total	415,000
CGT €415,000 @ 30%	124,500

Note: Retirement relief does not apply as the business was only owned for six years.

(b)   CAT liability

Janet
No CAT liability arises as Ronnie had owned the securities at 24 February 2003 and Janet is not Irish domiciled or ordinarily resident.

Jake
Taxable value of gift

	€
Business	1,280,000
Less business relief @ 90%	(1,152,000)
Taxable value	128,000
Cash	20,000
Total taxable value	148,000
Inheritance from mother	450,000
Total gifts/inheritances within Group A threshold	598,000

Group A threshold taxed @ Nil	(250,000)
Balance taxable @ 30%	348,000
CAT @ 30%	104,400
CAT attributed to previous inheritance (Note 1)	(60,000)
CAT in respect of current gift	44,400
Credit for CGT (Note 2)	(9,000)
CAT payable	35,400

Notes:
(1) €450,000 − €250,000 = 200,000 × 30% = 60,000
(2) Credit for CGT

CGT on disposal of business = goodwill €245,000 @ 30% = €73,500
CAT attributable to goodwill
As the CGT relates only to the goodwill, the CGT can only be credited against CAT re goodwill, i.e. CAT re goodwill only is

$$\frac{€44,400 \times €30,000 \text{ (i.e. } 300,000 \times 10\%)}{€148,000} = €9,000$$

Credit limited to lower of CGT or CAT, i.e €9,000.
The credit for CGT will be clawed back if the van business is disposed of within two years.

Brendan

Taxable value of gift	€
Vans	40,000
Office building (Note 1)	250,000
Cash	50,000
Total taxable value	340,000
Inheritance from mother	450,000
Total gifts/inheritances	790,000
Group A threshold taxed @ Nil	(250,000)
Balance taxable @ 30%	540,000
CAT @ 30%	162,000
CAT attributed to previous inheritance (Note 2)	(60,000)
CAT in respect of current gift	102,000
Credit for CGT (Note 3)	(51,000)
CAT payable	51,000

Notes:
(1) Business relief does not apply to the gift of vans and office buildings as the relief only applies to gifts of business interests not business assets.

(2) €450,000 – €250,000 = 200,000 × 30% = 60,000

(3) Credit for CGT

CGT on disposal of building = €170,000 @ 30% = €51,000

CAT attributable to building = €102,000 × $\dfrac{€250,000}{€340,000}$ = €75,000

Credit limited to lower of CGT or CAT, i.e. €51,000.

The credit for CGT will be clawed back if the building is disposed of within two years.

Chapter 18

Question 18.1

Computation of Tax Payable

(a) Tom

This is a taxable gift as the donee, Tom's mother, is Irish domiciled and resident.

Value of the annuity:

In order to produce an annual income of €10,000, €200,000 of the 5% Government Bond would have to be purchased, i.e. €10,000/5%. At 92c per €1 of stock, €200,000 of this stock would cost €184,000. The value of a life interest in €184,000 received by a 59 year old woman is €121,955, i.e. €184,000 × .6628.

The relevant group threshold is €33,500, a gift from a lineal descendent. Tom's mother previously received an inheritance of €30,000, from her sister, also within the €33,500 group threshold.

CAT payable in respect of the current gift is therefore:

	€
CAT on Aggregate A:	
Value of gift	121,955
Less small gift exemption	(3,000)
	118,955
Inheritance from sister	30,000
	148,955
Group threshold: €33,500 @ Nil	
Balance €115,455 @ 30%	
CAT on "Aggregate A"	34,636
CAT on Aggregate B:	
Inheritance from sister 30,000	
Group threshold: €33,500	
CAT on "Aggregate B"	Nil
CAT on Aggregate A – CAT on	
Aggregate B = €34,636 - Nil	
CAT payable in respect of gift of annuity from Tom	34,636

(b)   Jason/Mark

UK Property

The inheritance of the UK property is a taxable inheritance. Although it is foreign property, it is taxable because, at the date of the disposition (i.e. Martha's death), the disponer, Martha, was Irish domiciled (the fact that she was UK resident is irrelevant as the date of the disposition was pre-1 December 1999).

The relevant group threshold is €33,500. Although the property passes to Mark on the death of his father, the disponer is Martha, his aunt. Jason has not previously received any taxable gifts or inheritances from a person within the €33,500 group threshold (an inheritance from a nephew belongs to the €16,750 group threshold).

CAT payable in respect of the UK property is accordingly:

Value of inheritance	300,000
Group threshold: €33,500 @ Nil	
Balance €266,500 @ 30%	
CAT liability	79,950

Cash and House

Both of these are taxable inheritances (as both the disponer and successor are Irish resident and, in any event, both consist of Irish property). Mark does not qualify for exemption in respect of the dwelling house as he had an interest in another dwelling house at the date of the inheritance.

The relevant group threshold is €250,000. As Mark has previously received a taxable inheritance from a person within this group threshold, i.e. his mother, his CAT liability on the current inheritance is as follows:

CAT payable in respect of the inheritance of cash and the house is, therefore:

	€
Cash	60,000
House	250,000
	310,000
Savings certificates from mother	190,000
	500,000
Group threshold: €250,000 @ Nil	
Balance €250,000 @ 30%	
CAT liability	75,000

As the previous inheritance received was less than the Group A threshold of €250,000, €75,000 is now payable in respect of the inheritance of the cash and shares.

Total CAT payable by Mark:

	€
CAT on UK property	79,950
CAT on Irish cash and house	75,000
Total CAT payable	€154,950

Question 18.2

Limited Interests

1. Martin

	€
Grocery business and premises	600,000
Business relief (90%) (assumed owned two years)	(540,000)
	60,000
House and contents	150,000
Bank accounts	15,000
Funeral costs	(8,000)
Incumbrance-free value	217,000
Discount factor for life interest	.8204
Taxable value of life interest €217,000 × .8204 =	178,027

2. Jack

Taxable value of Margaret's inheritance

	€

"Slice" of premises and business:

$$€600,000 \times \frac{€15,000}{€150,000} =$$ 60,000

Less business relief (90%)	(54,000)
	6,000
Discount factor for 10-year interest	.4913
Taxable value of 10-year interest €6,000 × .4913 =	2,948

Taxable value of John's inheritance

	€
Premises and business	600,000
Less Margaret's "slice"	(60,000)
	540,000
Business relief (90%)	(486,000)
	54,000
Residue	50,000
Costs €20,000 + €9,000	(29,000)
Taxable value	75,000

3. David

A taxable gift arises on the cessation of the payment of the annuity to Larry. David is taxable on the "slice" of the property returned to him.

The value of the "slice" is calculated by reference to the relative values at the date the payments cease, i.e. April 2012.

$$\text{Taxable value} = \text{Slice} = €375,000 \times \frac{€10,000}{€30,000} = €125,000$$

4. Alan

Taxable value of gift of covenant = capitalised value of the annuity × discount factor for life interest of 65 year old woman.

The capitalised value of the annuity is calculated by calculating the amount which would have to be invested in the most recently issued Government Bond, not redeemable within 10 years, in order to produce an annual income equal to the annuity. In order to produce an annual income of €10,000, €250,000 of a 4% Government Bond would have to be purchased, i.e. €10,000/4%. At 89c per €1 of stock, €250,000 of this stock would cost €222,500 = capitalised value of annuity.

Discount factor for life interest of 65 year old woman = .565

Taxable value of annuity = .565 × €222,500 = €125,712

5. Tom

Taxable value of Emer's inheritance

	€
"Slice" of farmland and farm assets:	
$€1,070,000 \times \dfrac{€15,000}{€50,000} =$	321,000
Discount factor for life interest	.8683
Taxable value of life interest €321,000 × .8683 =	278,724

Note: Emer is not entitled to agricultural relief in respect of her "slice" as she fails the farmer test, i.e. €321,000/€321,000 + €120,000 = 73%

Taxable value of Fintan's inheritance

	€
Market value of farmland and assets	1,070,000
Agricultural value – 10%	107,000
Less Emer's slice × 10%, i.e. €321,000 × 10%	(32,100)

Less proportion of costs:

$$€9,500 \times \frac{€1,070,000 - €321,000}{€1,145,000 - €321,000} = €8,635$$

Reduced for agricultural relief, i.e. €8,635 × 10%	(863)
	74,037
Stocks and shares	50,000
Cash	25,000
Remainder of costs €9,500 − €8,635 =	(865)
Taxable value of Fintan's inheritance	148,172

Question 18.3

Andrew McNeill

Gift 6th August 2012

	Total	25%
	€	€
300 acres	660,000	165,000
Farm buildings	28,200	7,050
Machinery	15,600	3,900
Livestock	24,400	6,100
Agricultural property		182,050
Cash in bank		126,000
Total assets		308,050

As agricultural property accounts for less than 80% of David's assets, he does not qualify as a farmer and so does not qualify for agricultural relief. However, business relief applies.

	€
Market value of property gifted	182,050
Less: business relief at 90%	(163,845)
	18,205
Small gift exemption	(3,000)
Taxable value	15,205

Group threshold amount of €250,000

No tax payable

Inheritance 25 November 2012:

	€
Farm land	1,080,000
Buildings	33,600
Machinery	19,300
Livestock	31,700
Total agricultural property	1,164,600
Agricultural property inherited 75%	873,450
Own agricultural property	
(25% previously received from father)	291,150
Agricultural property purchased	150,000
Total agricultural property	1,314,600
Other assets – investments	95,000
Total assets	1,409,600

As David's agricultural property accounts for in excess of 80% of the value of his total assets (i.e. 93.3%), he qualifies as a farmer and so qualifies for agricultural relief.

Inheritance Tax computation:

		€
Agricultural property – 10% × €873,450		87,345
Less: Costs × 10% × €25,000 × $\frac{€873,450}{€968,450}$ (Note 1) =		(2,255)
Taxable value of property	€	85,090
Investments	95,000	
Less: Costs × €25,000 × $\frac{€95,000}{€968,450}$	(2,452)	
Less: annuity (Note 2)	(59,375)	
Taxable value of investments		33,173
		118,263

Group threshold = €332,084

The total benefits received by David from persons belonging to this group threshold amounts to €133,468, i.e. €15,205 + €118,263 = €133,468. No CAT is payable on the inheritance from his father.

Notes:

	€
(1) Agricultural property	873,450
Other property	95,000
Total inheritance	968,450

(2) Deduction for annuity payable out of income from investments.

Total value of investments	€95,000

Appropriate part inherited by Rachel:

$$€95,000 \times \frac{€5,000}{€8,000} = \qquad €59,375$$

Note: do not apply table factor!

Question 18.4

SHANE

CAT Liabilities

<u>John</u>

Inheritance from father – CAT payable

	€
Shares in Murray Developments	1,500,000
Investment properties	850,000
Part of investment property attributable to Sarah (see below)	(133,333)
Mortgages charged on properties	(225,000)
Residue (Note 1)	92,000
Taxable value of inheritance	2,083,667
Previous gift with same group threshold (Note 2)	100,000
Cumulative gifts/inheritances within Group A threshold	2,183,667
Group threshold taxed @ Nil	(250,000)
Balance taxable	1,933,667
CAT payable @ 30% (Note 3)	580,100

Notes:
(1) Residue:

	€
Cash	146,000
Shares	50,000
Funeral expenses	(3,500)
Legal expenses	(8,500)
	184,000
50% each	92,000

(2)

Previous gift of property:

	€
Gross value	300,000
Less mortgage	(200,000)
Total	100,000

(3) Previous gift is less than Group A threshold, so no CAT attributed to this gift.

<u>Sarah</u>

The inheritance received by Sarah is the "appropriate part" of the entire investment property on which the annuity payable to her is charged, i.e.:

$$\text{Entire property} \times \frac{\text{Gross annual value of annuity}}{\text{Gross annual value of property}} =$$

$$€400,000 \times \frac{€10,000}{€30,000} = 133,333$$

CAT:

	€
	€
Value of inheritance	133,333
Factor for life interest for 63 year old	.6
Taxable value	80,000
Relevant Group threshold @ Nil	(33,500)
Balance taxable	46,500
CAT payable @ 30%	13,950

<u>Emily</u>

<u>CAT liability</u>

	€
House (Note 1)	950,000
Residue	92,000
Taxable value of inheritance	1,042,000
Previous inheritance with same group threshold	200,000
Cumulative gifts/inheritances within Group A threshold	1,242,000
Group threshold taxed @ Nil	(250,000)
Balance taxable	992,000
CAT @ 30%	297,600
CAT attributed to previous gift (Note 2)	Nil
CAT payable	297,600

Notes:

(1) Emily does not qualify for exemption in respect of the house as she had an interest in another dwelling house at the date of the inheritance.

(2) Previous gift was less than Group A threshold, so no CAT is attributed to this gift.

Qualifying insurance proceeds (section 72 policy)

Total CAT payable:

	€
CAT – John	580,100
CAT – Sarah	13,950
CAT – Emily	297,600
Total	891,650
Proceeds from policy	900,000
Excess subject to CAT	8,350

Excess falls into the residue and is split evenly between John and Emily.

	Total	John	Emily
	€	€	€
Excess	8,350	4,175	4,175
CAT @ 30%	2,504	1,252	1,252

Proceeds of policy are used to pay €891,650 above. Balance of €2,504 payable separately.

Question 18.5

Peter

(a) CGT liability

No CGT liability arises on the transfer to Stephen as the conditions necessary for Peter to qualify for retirement relief are satisfied.

(b) CAT liability

(1) Is Stephen entitled to agricultural relief?

Farmer test

	Agricultural Property	Other Property	Total
	€'000	€'000	€'000
Farmland gifted	5,000		5,000
House (less mortgage)		250	250
Car		20	20
Farmlands in Antrim	500		500
Site inherited from mother		450	450
Total	5,500	720	6,220

5,500/6,220 = 88.42% Therefore Stephen is a farmer and is entitled to agricultural relief.

(2) Taxable value of gift

	€
Agricultural value of property €5m × 10%	500,000
Less stamp duty and legal fees €165,000 × 10%	(16,500)
Less mortgage on land €350,000 × 10%	(35,000)
Less annuity payable *€540,000 × 10%	(54,000)
Taxable value	394,500

*Calculation of value of annuity

The capitalised value of the annuity is calculated by calculating the amount which would have to be invested in the most recently issued Government Bond, not redeemable within 10 years, in order to produce an annual income equal to the annuity. In order to produce an annual income of €30,000, €600,000 of 5% Government Bond would have to be purchased, i.e. €30,000/5%. At 90c per €1 of stock, €600,000 of this stock would cost €540,000.

(1) CAT payable

Relevant Group threshold is A €250,000. Previous gifts/inheritances received from persons within this group include the site inherited from Stephen's mother. (The farmland inherited from Stephen's uncle is Group B).

Aggregate A

	€
Current benefit	394,500
Small gift exemption	(3,000)
	391,500
Inheritance from mother	45,000
Cumulative gifts/inheritances within Group A threshold	436,500
Group threshold taxed @ Nil	(250,000)
Balance taxable	186,500
CAT @ 30% on Aggregate A	55,950

Aggregate B

Inheritance from mother	45,000
CAT on Aggregate B	nil

Tax on current benefit = tax on Aggregate A – tax on Aggregate B, i.e.:

CAT payable on transfer for Stephen = €55,950

Chapter 19

Question 19.1

Special Relationships – Group Threshold Amounts

1.	Group A	€250,000
2.	Group B	€33,500
3.	Group B €33,500. Group A €250,000 does not apply as uncle did not control company.	
4.	Group A– favourite nephew/niece	€250,000
5.	Group C	€16,750

6.	Group B – although father is deceased, grandson is not a minor, so Group A does not apply.	€33,500
7.	Group C	€16,750
8.	Group B	€33,500
9.	Group C	€16,750
10.	Group A favourite nephew/niece	€250,000
11.	Exempt	
12.	Group A – "child" includes stepchild	€250,000
13.	Group B	€33,500
14.	Group B – not favourite nephew/niece as did not work for previous five years	€33,500
15.	Group B	€33,500
16.	Group B	€33,500
17.	Group C	€16,750
18.	Group B – "child" includes adopted child	€33,500
19.	Group C not a child of a brother or sister	€16,750
20.	Group B	€33,500

Question 19.2

Jerome

Capital Acquisitions Tax Liabilities

Declan

Declan qualifies for business relief in respect of the shares inherited from Jerome, as he satisfies the necessary share ownership requirements after receiving the inheritance. (The company is also a trading company and Jerome had owned the shares for at least two years prior to the date of the inheritance.)

The relevant group threshold is Group A €250,000 as Declan qualifies as a "favourite nephew", i.e. the inheritance is of shares in a private company controlled by the disponer, Jerome, for a period of at least five years prior to the date of the inheritance, and Declan has worked on a full time basis for the company for the last five years.

	€
Market value of shares	350,000
Less business relief (90%)	(315,000)
Revised taxable value	35,000

As the revised taxable value of the inheritance is less than the relevant group threshold and Declan had not previously received any taxable gifts or inheritances, no CAT is payable.

Jonathan

Jonathan does not qualify for business relief in respect of the property owned by his father and let to Wiggies Wholesalers as he only got the property and did not get any shares. In order for the property to qualify for business relief the property and the disponer's interest in the company would have had to be given to the same beneficiary.

CAT liability

	€
Property	500,000
Residue (Note a)	29,250
Taxable value of inheritance	529,250
Group A threshold taxed @ Nil	(250,000)
Balance taxable	279,250
CAT payable @ 30%	83,775

Note (a): Residue: €65,000 − €2,500 − €4,000 = €58,500 × 50% = €29,250.

Previous gift from aunt is ignored as it belongs to the Group B €33,500 threshold.

Louise

The house is exempt from CAT, as Louise has lived in the house for at least three years prior to the date of the inheritance and owns no other dwelling house.

CAT liability

	€
Life insurance proceeds	350,000
Residue	29,250
Taxable value of inheritance	379,250
Previous inheritance with same group threshold (Note 1)	179,500
Cumulative gifts/inheritances within Group A threshold	558,750
Group threshold taxed @ Nil	(250,000)
Balance taxable	308,750
CAT @ 30%	92,625
CAT attributable to previous gift (Note 2)	Nil
CAT payable	92,625

Note:
(1) €179,500. The €250,000 Group A threshold applies to this inheritance as Louise's husband was dead at the time of the inheritance to her from her father-in-law.
(2) As the previous inheritance is less than the group threshold, no CAT attributed to this inheritance.

Chapter 20

Question 20.1

Administration

MEMORANDUM

To :	
From :	
Date :	
Re :	*Capital Acquisitions Tax Queries*

I refer to the matters recently raised by you.

(a)   Accountable Persons

The person accountable for payment of the tax is the donee or successor as the case may be.

(b)   Delivery of Returns

A person who is accountable for CAT is obliged to deliver a return where the aggregate taxable value of all taxable benefits taken by a donee or successor which have the same group threshold exceeds 80% of the group threshold amount.

If the valuation date arises in the period from 1 January to 31 August, the pay and file deadline is 31 October in that year; if the valuation date arises in the period from 1 September to 31 December, the pay and file deadline is 31 October in the following year. If the return is filed using ROS, the filing date is extended: for 2012, it is 15 November 2012.

Even if the 80% threshold has not been exceeded, a person must deliver a return if required to do so by notice in writing from the Revenue Commissioners. They must comply within the time set out in the notice.

The disponer must deliver a return if requested by notice in writing from the Revenue Commissioners. They must comply within the time set out in the notice.

(c)   Return Details

    (i)   The return must show:

        a)   every applicable gift/inheritance;

        b)   all property comprised in such gift/inheritance;

        c)   an estimate of the market value of the property; and

        d)   such particulars as may be relevant to the assessment of tax in respect of such gift.

    (ii)   Also, the taxpayer must make on the return, an assessment of such amount of tax, as to the best of his knowledge, information and belief, ought to be charged and paid.

    (iii)   Finally, he must pay any tax which he calculates is due.

(d)   Defective Return

Where an accountable person, who has made a return becomes aware, at any time, that the return is defective in a material respect, by reason of anything contained or omitted from it, he shall, without being asked by the Revenue Commissioners:

(i)   deliver to them an additional return;

(ii)   make an amended assessment; and

(iii) pay the outstanding tax.

The above action is required within three months of becoming aware of the defect in the original return.

(e)   Undervaluation of Property

A surcharge ranging from 10% to 30% will be levied where the market value of property is underestimated in returns for CAT purposes. The legislation contains a table setting out the percentage surcharge to be levied depending on the extent to which the property was undervalued.

The surcharge applies to the total amount of tax ultimately attributable to the property. In addition, interest penalties will apply to the tax underpaid as well as to the surcharge.

Signed:

Question 20.2

Robert

Split of estate

		Total	Sheila(2/3)	Ruth(1/6)	Angela(1/6)
		€	€	€	€
House		600,000	400,000	100,000	100,000
Mortgage thereon		(60,000)	(40,000)	(10,000)	(10,000)
		540,000	360,000	90,000	90,000
Newsagents		900,000	600,000	150,000	150,000
Government Stock		66,000	44,000	11,000	11,000
Holiday home		150,000	100,000	25,000	25,000
Cash	45,000				
Income tax liabilities	(15,000)				
Legal expenses	(6,000)				
Funeral expenses	(3,000)				
Net cash		21,000	14,000	3,500	3,500

Ruth and Angela also received the insurance proceeds of €200,000.

(a) CAT

Sheila

Sheila has no liability to CAT as she was the spouse of Robert. The fact that they had been separated for 10 years is irrelevant. They are still legally married.

Ruth
CAT liability

	€	€
Newsagents	150,000	
Business relief @ 90%	(135,000)	15,000
Life insurance €200,000 × 50%		100,000
House less mortgage (Note)		90,000
Government Stock		11,000
Holiday home		25,000
Net cash		3,500
Taxable value of inheritance		244,500
Group A threshold taxed @ Nil		(250,000)
CAT payable		Nil

Notes

House does not qualify for exemption from CAT as Ruth had an interest in another dwelling house at the date of the inheritance, i.e. the holiday home in Kerry.

Ruth has not previously received any taxable gifts or inheritances and the current benefit is below the threshold so no CAT is payable in respect of the current inheritance.

Angela

CAT liability

	€	€
Newsagents	150,000	
Business relief @ 90%	(135,000)	15,000
Life insurance €200,000 × 50%		100,000
House less mortgage (Note)		90,000
Government Stock		11,000
Holiday home		25,000
Net cash		3,500
Taxable value of inheritance		244,500
Group A threshold taxed @ Nil		(250,000)
CAT payable		Nil

Notes: House does not qualify for exemption from CAT as Angela had an interest in another dwelling house at the date of the inheritance, i.e. the holiday home in Kerry.

As Angela has not previously received any taxable gifts or inheritances and the current benefit is below the threshold so no CAT is payable in respect of the current inheritance.

(b) Payment of tax

If interest charges are to be avoided, CAT must be paid by 31 October 2013.

Chapter 21

Question 21.1

Lemmon Limited

	12 months ended 31/12/2012		2 months ended 28/02/2013	
	€		€	
Case I (time-apportioned)	264,000	[12/14]	44,000	[2/14]
Case III (actual)	3000		2,000	
Total income	**267,000**		**46,000**	
Chargeable gain	4,687	[Note 1]		
Total profits	271,687		46,000	

Corporation tax:

€	€	€	€	€	€
264,000 × 12.50%	33,000	44,000 × 12.50%	5,500
4,687 × 12.50%	586		
3,000 × 25%	750	2,000 × 25%	500
	34,336		6,000

Note 1   Chargeable gain adjusted for CT:

$$\frac{1,953}{0.125} \times 0.30 = €4,687$$

Rentco   A.P. ended 31/12/2012

Case V	€50,000
CT at 25%	€12,500

Distributors Limited   A.P. eight months to 28 February 2013

Case I	€20,000
CT at 12.5%	€2,500

Payment of CT liabilties and filing returns

Lemmon Limited

A.P. 31/12/2012:

The preliminary tax is payable by 23 November 2012 – must be 90% of the CT liability for **current** A.P.

The balance is payable at the same time as the company is due to file CT return (23 September 2013). What if not paid or underpaid? Interest is charged at 0.0219% per day or part of day.

A.P. 28/02/2013:

This accounting period is only two months, so 90% must be paid by 23 January 2013 and the balance is paid when return is filed (23 November 2013)

Rentco Limited A.P. 31/12/2012

90% by 23 November 2012

Balance to be paid when return is due to be filed, i.e. 23 September 2013

Distributors Limited   eight months ended 28 February 2013

90% of the current liability is due by 23 January 2013.

Remainder is to be paid when return is due to be filed, i.e. 23 November 2013.

Chapter 22

Question 22.1

The corporation tax computation would be as follows:

Telstar Ltd Corporation Tax Computation for 12 Month Accounting Period Ended 31 December 2011

		€	€
Profit before tax per accounts			116,000
Add:	Depreciation	15,149	
	Motor leasing (1)	240	
	Entertainment (2)	1,050	
	Finance lease charges (3)	1,300	
	Legal fees (4)	2,400	20,139
			136,139
Less:			
	Grant for extension of premises (5)	10,000	
	Employment grant (6)	1,000	
	Patent royalty (7)	1,600	
	Dividends from Irish quoted shares (8)	1,300	
	Profit on sale of van (9)	1,000	
	Profit on sale of shares (10)	2,000	
	Bank deposit interest (11)	600	
	Finance lease payments (3)	9,400	
	Capital allowances	7,272	(34,172)
Case I Schedule D			101,967
Case III Schedule D – bank interest (gross)			600
Case IV Schedule D – royalty (gross $= \dfrac{1,600}{80} \times 100$)			2,000

Total income			104,567
Chargeable gain (12)			3,418
Total profits			107,985
Corporation tax:			
Case I:	€101,967 @ 12.5% =	€12,746	
Chargeable gain:	€3,418 @ 12.5% =	€427	
Case III and IV:	€2,600 @ 25% =	€650	13,823
Less: income tax suffered on royalty 2,000 × 20% =			(400)
Corporation tax payable			13,423

As this is a small company, i.e. corporation tax payable in 2011 was less than €200,000, if interest charges are to be avoided, preliminary tax of €80,000 (100% of preceding period) or 90% of this period (i.e. 90% × €13,423 = €12,081) must be paid on/before 23 November 2012 and the balance of €1,342 must be paid on/before 23 September 2013.

Notes:

1. There is no motor expenses restriction. The lease payments are in respect of a category B vehicle leased when its retail price was €25,000. Therefore, the amount disallowed is $€6,000 \times \dfrac{€25,000 - €24,000}{€25,000} = €240$

2. Entertainment costs disallowed:

	€
Christmas gifts for suppliers	150
Entertainment costs incurred by MD	350
General customer entertainment	550
	1,050

   Costs incurred for benefit of staff, i.e. Christmas party and prizes, are deductible.
3. Finance lease charges (i.e. interest) disallowed and gross payments made deducted.
4. Legal fees are of a capital nature and fall to be disallowed.
5. Grant for extension of premises is a capital receipt and not liable to corporation tax.
6. Employment grant is not taxable.
7. Patent royalty:
   This is not taxable under Case I. The gross amount is taxable under Case IV of Schedule D. However, the income tax suffered can be set off against the corporation tax chargeable. As only the net amount (i.e. the amount after deduction of standard rate income tax) has been credited in the Income Statement, then this is the correct amount to deduct.
8. Dividends from Irish quoted shares. Dividends received from other Irish companies are not liable to corporation tax.
9. Profit on sale of van is a capital profit and not a trading receipt and so is not taxable under Case I. (See Note 12)

10. Profit on sale of shares is a capital profit and not a trading receipt and so is not taxable under Case I. (See Note 12)
11. Bank deposit interest.
    This is taxable under Case III as it was not subject to DIRT.
12. Chargeable gain.
    (a) *Sale of van*
    Although a loss arose on the sale of the van, this is not an allowable loss. Relief for this loss will be given through capital allowances.
    (b) *Sale of shares*

	€	€
Proceeds		6,000
Cost	4,000	
Indexation factor 2000/2001	1.144	
Indexed cost		(4,576)
Gain		1,424
Chargeable gain €1,424 × 30/12.5 =		3,418

Question 22.2

Zaco Ltd Corporation Tax Computation Year Ended 30 September 2012

		€	€
Profit per Accounts			379,900
Add:	Repairs	5,200	
	Professional fees	300	
	Political donations	750	
	Entertainment	600	
	Depreciation	13,000	19,850
			399,750
Less:	Dividends	3,600	
	Profit on sale of investments	5,200	
	Interest on tax overpaid	1,200	
	Profit on sale of fixtures and fitings	4,300	(14,300)
			385,450
Less:	Capital allowances		(9,846)
Case I Schedule D			375,604
Case III UK dividends			600
Total Income			376,204
Add:	Chargeable gains		Nil
			376,204

Corporation Tax:

Case I: €375,604 @ 12.5% = €46,950

		€	€
Case III:	€600 @ 12.5% =	€75	
Corporation tax liability			47,025

Notes:

(1) Chargeable Gains

		€	€
Sale of investments			
(a) Sale of National Loan Stock			Exempt
(b) Quoted investment company shares			
	Cost of shares	1,000	
	Indexation factor 1.232		
		1,232	
	Proceeds	5,548	4,316
(c) Sale of plant			
	Cost	8,000	
	Proceeds	11,100	
	Gain		3,100
Total gains			7,416
Less capital loss forward			(10,000)
Capital loss forward to 2013			(2,584)

Question 22.3

Alpha Limited Corporation Tax Computation Year Ended 31 December 2012

			€	€
Case 1	Profit per accounts			424,605
	Add	Rent and rates	1,000	
		Repairs	15,000	
		Insurance	350	
		Loss on sale of investments	600	
		Legal expenses	2,000	
		Depreciation	13,260	
		Subscriptions (Note 1)	1,835	
		Other interest - not trade (Note 4)	7,000	
		Motor expenses (Note 2)	845	
		Sundry (Note 3)	2,201	
		Entertainment	1,191	
		Finance lease charges	1,700	46,982
				471,587
	Less	Irish dividends	4,500	
		Interest on National Loan Stock	2,500	
		Gain on sale of Irish shares	1,000	
		Amortisation of IDA grant	240	

	Interest on tax overpaid	475	
	Rents received	6,000	
	Deposit interest	1,500	
	Finance lease payments	12,200	(28,415)
			443,172
Capital allowances			(26,006)
Case I for period			417,166
Less loss forward			(20,000)
CASE I			397,166
CASE III	Interest on National Loan Stock		2,500
	Deposit interest		1,500
CASE V	Gross rents	6,000	
	Less rent and rates paid	1,000	
	Insurance	350 (1,350)	4,650

CHARGEABLE GAINS (Note 5) 185 × 30%/12.5%   444

Profits for year	406,260
Less charge (protected interest)	(7,000)
Profits liable to CT	399,260

Corporation tax (Note 6)	€
€397,166 × 12.5% =	49,646
€444 × 12.5% =	55
€1,650 × 25% =	412
	50,113

Notes to Solution:

Note 1:

Subscriptions	€
Football club	20
Political	1,815
	1,835

Note 2: Motor expenses
Leasing charges

$$€21,126 \times \frac{€150,000 - €144,000^*}{€150,000} = €845$$

*€24,000 × 6

Note 3:

Sundry	€
Interest on late payment of VAT	1,630
Parking fines	30
Gifts to customers	541
	2,201

Note 4: Protected Interest

As there is a common director, there is relief as a non-trade charge – see **Chapter 23**.

Note 5:

	€	€
Gain on Irish quoted shares		1,000
Less:		
Loss forward	215	
Loss on UK shares	600	(815)
Gain		185

(There is no indexation as the shares were purchased in 2007. The loss on the UK shares is €600, i.e. the actual monetary loss.)

Note 6: Non-trade charges are offset against total profits. The taxpayer can choose which source of income/gain against which to offset the non-trade charge. It is most tax efficient to offset the €7,000 against income taxable at 25% (€2,500 + €1,500 + €4,650 − €7,000) = €1,650 – see **Chapter 23**.

Chapter 23

Question 23.1

Nifty Investments Limited
Accounts Year Ended 31 March 2012

			€
Profit per Accounts			90,000
Add:			
Depreciation		10,000	
Interest		9,000*	
Patent royalties		8,000*	27,000
			117,000
Less:			
Loan interest		6,000*	
Bank interest		1,000*	
			(7,000)
			110,000
Less: Case I charge	(Note 2)		(10,000)
Case I			100,000
Case III			1,000
Case IV	(Note 1)		6,000
Income			107,000

Chargeable gain	(Note 3)	26,400
Profits		133,400
Less: non-trade charge	(Note 4)	(9,000)
Profits liable to tax		124,400
Corporation tax due on profits (Note 5)		15,550
Add: Income tax withheld by Nifty		2,000
Less: Income tax deducted from receipts		(1,200)
Total tax liability		16,350

*Add back or deduct the amount in the income statements.

Note 1:

	Net received	Tax deducted	Taxable Case IV
Loan interest	4,800	1,200	6,000

Note 2:

	Net paid	Tax withheld	Deductible as a charge
Patent royalties	8,000	2,000	10,000

Note 3: As the tax rate for year ended 31 March 2012 is 12.5% and the CGT rate is 30%, these are the rates at which you gross up the gain. €11,000 × 30/12.5 = €26,400.

Note 4: As the interest is paid to an Irish bank, there is no requirement to withhold income tax. As the interest qualifies as a non-trade charge, it is deductible against total profits. When calculating corporation tax, it will be offset against any profits taxable at 25% firstly, as that would save most tax.

Note 5: Corporation tax liability on €124,400

	€
€98,000 × 12.5% =	12,250
€26,400 × 12.5% =	3,300
Corporation tax	15,550

The non-trade charge of €9,000 is offset firstly against the €7,000 liable at 25%. The balance of €2,000 is offset against income taxable at 12.5%, i.e.:
€100,000 – €2,000 = €98,000

Chapter 24

Question 24.1

Enya Limited

31/3/2009		€	€
Case I			60,000
Case III			10,000
Case V	2009	5,000	
	re 2010	(4,000)	1,000
	Taxable income		71,000
Corporation tax: €60,000 × 12.5% =			7,500
€11,000 × 25% =			2,750
Corporation tax payable			10,250
31/3/2010			
Case I			70,000
Less: trading loss from 2011			(70,000)
Case I			–
Case III			5,000
Case V			–
Income			5,000
Corporation tax: €5,000 × 25% =			1,250
Less: Relief on a value basis (loss memo)			(1,250)
Corporation tax payable			Nil
31/3/2011			
Case I			–
Case III			10,000
Case V			6,000
Taxable income			16,000
Corporation tax: €16,000 × 25% =			4,000
Less: Relief on a value basis (loss memo)			(4,000)
Corporation tax payable			Nil
31/3/2012			
Case I		10,000	
Less: loss		(10,000)	–
Case III			3,500
Case V			8,000
Taxable income			11,500

Corporation tax: €11,500 × 25% =	2,875

Loss Memo

Relevant trading loss for y/e 31/3/2011	130,000
Utilised by way of	
- section 396A(3) against y/e 31/3/2010	(70,000)
Utilised by way of	
- section 396B(3) against y/e 31/3/2011	
€32,000 × 12.5% = €4,000	(32,000)
Utilised by way of	
- section 396B(3) against y/e 31/3/2010	
€10,000 × 12.5% = €1,250	(10,000)
Utilised by way of section 396(1) forward	(10,000)
Loss forward to 2013	8,000

Question 24.2

Hells Bells Ltd

Year ended 31 March 2012

	€	€
Case I		167,000
Section 396A(3) loss back (Note 1)		(125,250)
		41,750
Case III		10,000
Case V	4,000	
Less loss	(3,000) (Note 2)	1,000
Total income		52,750
Chargeable gain		–
Total profit		52,750
Tax		
€11,000 @ 25%		2,750
€41,750 @ 12.5%		5,218
Tax payable		7,968
Less: Relief on a value basis (Note 4)		(3,094)
Corporation tax payable		4,874

Nine months ended 31 December 2012

Case I	–
Case III	20,000
Case V	–

Total income	20,000
Chargeable gains (*Note 3*)	–
Taxable profits	20,000
Tax	
€20,000 @ 25%	5,000
Less relief on a value basis (loss memo)	(5,000)
Tax payable	Nil

Note 1:

Loss available for carry back	€190,000
Trading profit of corresponding period	
€167,000 × 9/12 =	€125,250
Offset total	€125,250

Note 2: A Case V loss can be carried back to a previous accounting period of the same length.

A loss for nine months can be carried back against income for nine months, i.e.:

€4,000 × 9/12ths = €3,000.

Note 3:

Gain	10,000
Less: capital loss forward	(19,000)
Capital loss forward	(9,000)

Note 4: The maximum tax that can be saved is 9/12ths of the corporation tax, i.e. €7,968 × 9/12ths = €5,976. However, the losses still available are only €24,750. Therefore, the value of the losses is €24,750 × 12.5% = €3,094. This is the maximum reduction in corporation tax.

Loss Memo	€
Relevant trading loss for p/e 31/12/2012	190,000
Utilised by way of	
- section 396A(3) against y/e 31/3/2012 (i)	(125,250)
Utilised by way of	
- section 396B(3) against p/e 31/12/2012 (ii)	
€40,000 × 12.5% = €5,000	(40,000)
Utilised by way of	
- section 396B(3) against y/e 31/3/2012 (iii)	
€24,750 × 12.5% = €3,094	(24,750)
Loss forward to 2013	Nil

(i) to (iii) shows sequence of claims.

Question 24.3

Monk Ltd

Year ended 31 December 2012

	€
Case I	–
Case III	30,000
Case V	<u>20,000</u>
Total income	50,000
Chargeable gain	<u>26,000</u>
Taxable profits	76,000
Tax	
€50,000 @ 25%	12,500
€26,000 @ 12.5%	<u>3,250</u>
	15,750
Less: Relief on a value basis (loss memo)	<u>(10,000)</u>
Tax payable	<u>5,750</u>

The gain on development land cannot be sheltered as it is liable to CGT payable
€100,000 × 25% = €25,000

Year ended 31 December 2011

	€
Case I (€360,000 – €20,000)	340,000
Less: Case I loss forward section 396(1)	<u>(20,000)</u>
Case I	320,000
Less: section 396A(3)	<u>(320,000)</u>
Case I	–
Case III	5,000
Case V	<u>15,000</u>
Total income	20,000
Chargeable gain	<u>12,000</u>
Taxable profits	32,000
Tax	
€20,000 @ 25%	5,000
€12,000 @ 12.5%	<u>1,500</u>
Tax payable	<u>6,500</u>

Loss Memo

Relevant trading loss for y/e 31/12/2012	
€310,000 + €90,000	€400,000
Utilised by way of	
- section 396A(3) against y/e 31/12/2011	(€320,000)

Utilised by way of	€
- section 396B(3) against y/e 31/12/2012	
€80,000 × 12.5% = €10,000	(80,000)
Loss forward to 2013	Nil

Must claim under section 396A(3) first as is required by law and then on a value basis in the current period.

Question 24.4

Monaghan Limited – Year ended 30 June

	2010	2011	2012
	€	€	€
Assessable Case I profit	180,000	Nil	140,000
Section 396(1) loss relief	(20,000)		(140,000)
Section 396A loss relief	(160,000)	____	
Case I	Nil	Nil	Nil
Case III – Interest on Government Stocks	5,000	30,000	10,000
Case V – Rental income	10,500	20,000	20,000
Capital gains – as adjusted	10,200	40,000	50,000
Total profits	25,700	90,000	80,000
Less non-trade charges	–	–	(50,000)
Taxable profits	25,700	90,000	30,000
Corporation tax @ 12.5% (Note 1)	1,275	5,000	3,750
Corporation tax @ 25%	3,875	12,500	
Corporation tax	5,150	17,500	3,750
Section 243B relief (Note 2)	(1,250)	(1,250)	(750)
Section 396B(3) relief (Note 3)	(3,900)	(16,250)	
Corporation tax liability	Nil	Nil	6,750

Note 1: Non-trade charges paid in y/e 30/6/2012 are offset against income liable at 25% first.

Note 2:
Excess trade charges in y/e 30/6/2010 and 30/6/2011 = €10,000.
Relief on a value basis in y/e 30/6/2010: €10,000 × 12.5% = €1,250
Relief on a value basis in y/e 30/6/2011: €10,000 × 12.5% = €1,250
Excess trade charges y/e 30/6/2012: €6,000 × 12.5% = €750. Relief for €4,000 charges paid in July 2012 will be given in y/e 30/6/2013.

Note 3: Losses for y/e 30/6/2011 available to carry forward and offset against profits arising in the year ended 30/6/2012 and subsequent years.

		€
Case I adjusted loss before capital allowances		450,000
Capital allowances		80,000
Total loss		530,000
Utilised by way of section 396A relief y/e 30/6/2010		(160,000)
Utilised by way of section 396B relief:		
y/e 30/6/2011 €130,000 @ 12.5% = €16,250		(130,000)
y/e 30/6/2010 €31,200 @ 12.5% = €3,900		(31,200)
Losses available to carry forward	to y/e 30/6/2012	208,800
Utilised against y/e 30/6/2012		(140,000)
Losses available to carry forward	to y/e 30/6/2013	68,800

Chapter 25

Question 25.1

Corporation Tax Computation Period Ended 31.12.2012 – Z Ltd

	€
Case I	Nil
Case III income	20,000
Total profits	20,000
Corporation tax at 25%	5,000
Less: loss relief on a value basis	(5,000)
Corporation tax	Nil

Corporation Tax Computation Period Ended 31.12.2012 – B Ltd

		€
Case 1	Adjusted trading profit	180,000
	Deduct: Case I losses forward	(16,000)
	Deduct: Group relief surrendered by Z Ltd	(56,000)
		108,000
Case III	Interest	4,000
Case V	Rents	20,000
Profit liable to corporation tax:		132,000

Corporation tax

108,000 × 12.5% = 13,500

24,000 × 25% = 6,000   19,500

Loss memo

	€
Loss	96,000
Used on a value basis in Z Ltd €40,000 × 12.5% = 5,000	(40,000)
Claim section 420A balance of loss	(56,000)
Loss available	Nil

Note

It should be noted that Z Ltd could have opted not to claim section 396B relief and instead surrender losses of €96,000 to B Ltd.

Question 25.2

A Ltd – Corporation Tax Computation Period To 31/3/2012

	€
Case I profits	Nil
Case III income	1,000
Case V income	20,000
Liable to corporation tax	21,000
Corporation tax at 25%	5,250
Less: loss relief on a value basis	(5,250)
Corporation tax payable	Nil

B Ltd – Corporation Tax Computation Period To 31/3/2012

	€
Case I	56,000
Less group loss surrendered by A Ltd.	(48,000)
	8,000
Case III	2,000
Case V	25,000
Liable to corporation tax	35,000
Corporation tax	
8,000 @ 12.5% =	1,000
27,000 @ 25% =	6,750
Corporation tax payable	7,750

C Ltd – Corporation Tax Computation Period to 31/3/2012

	€
Case I	48,000
Less: Case I loss forward	(26,000)
	22,000
Case III	3,000
Case V	2,000
Liable to corporation tax	27,000

Corporation tax:

22,000 @ 12.5% =	2,750
5,000 @ 25%=	1,250
Corporation tax payable	4,000

Loss memo

Loss	90,000
Used on a value basis in A Ltd	
42,000 × 12.5% = 5,250	(42,000)
Claim section 420A balance of loss to B Ltd	(48,000)
Loss available	Nil

Alternatively, part of the loss could have been surrendered to C Ltd to reduce its Case I income to nil.

The loss forward of €4,000 in A Ltd is carried forward to be used against trading income of the same trade in A Ltd.

Question 25.3

(a)

Queen Group

	Note	Queen Ltd	Pawn Ltd	Rook Ltd
		€	€	€
Profit/(loss) per accounts		202,313	(2,030)	(80,586)
Disallow:				
– depreciation		12,000	10,000	16,000
– entertainment		1,350	1,200	1,650
– interest	(1)	400	10,720	–
		216,063	19,890	(62,936)
Less: grant release		(3,000)	–	–
		213,063	19,890	(62,936)
Capital allowances		(7,375)	(3,000)	(5,627)
Case I loss forward		–	(80,000)	–
		205,688	(63,110)	(68,563)
Group relief re trading losses	(2)	(68,563)	–	68,563
Case I		137,125	–	–
Case III deposit interest		23,846	–	–
		160,971	–	–

Corporation tax payable	
PAWN Ltd	Nil
ROOK Ltd	Nil
QUEEN Ltd	

Profit for period   160,971

€137,125 @ 12.5% = €17,141

€23,846 @ 25% = €5,961

Corporation tax   23,102

(b)   **Losses Forward**

PAWN Ltd   63,110

ROOK Ltd   Nil

QUEEN Ltd   Nil

Notes:

(1) The interest paid by Pawn Ltd is not allowed as 'a charge on income', as there is no common director. The amount charged in arriving at the profit is disallowed, as it is not a trading expense.

(2) The trading loss of Rook Ltd can be offset against the trading income of Queen Ltd. Pawn Ltd has no income for this period, as it is covered by losses forward and these cannot be grouped.

(c) Payment of tax

As QUEEN Ltd is a small company (its prior period CT was less than €200,000), preliminary tax is the lower of €55,000 × 100% or €23,102 × 90%, i.e. €20,792. The preliminary tax of €20,792 is due on/before 23 November 2012. The balance of €2,310 is due on/before 23 September 2013, at the same time as the tax return.

(d) Payment of the Dividend

100% of the shares in QUEEN Ltd are held by a company resident in an EU Member State. As this company owns >5% of the shares in QUEEN Ltd it qualifies as a "parent" company. Dividends may be paid to a parent company without deduction of DWT.

Chapter 27

Question 27.1

Lance Investments Ltd

(a) DWT payable

	Gross Dividend	DWT	Notes
	€	€	
Mr C (resident in the State)	60,000	12,000	(1)
Mr A (resident in UK)	40,000	Nil	(2)
Mr R (resident in US)	20,000	Nil	(2)
UK Investments Ltd (resident in UK)	140,000	Nil	(3)
Spanol Investments Ltd (resident in Spain)	160,000	Nil	(3)
Thailand Investments Ltd (resident in Thailand)	20,000	4,000	(4)

Local Investments Ltd
(resident in the State)   60,000   Nil   (5)

                                       500,000   16,000

Notes

(1) Irish resident individual not exempt from DWT.
(2) Resident in EU/treaty country, exempt from DWT.
(3) Owns at least 5% of Irish company, resident in EU country and shareholders test satisfied so exempt from DWT.
(4) Resident in and controlled by residents of a non-treaty country. Therefore, the dividend is liable to DWT.
(5) Irish resident company so exempt from DWT.

The total DWT payable by Lance Investments Ltd is €16,000.

(b) The DWT must be paid before 14 December 2012.
(c) The following shareholders must make a declaration to Lance Investments Ltd confirming that they are a non-resident person who is beneficially entitled to the dividend and attaching the following certificates before a dividend may be paid to them without deduction of DWT:

    (1) Mr A and Mr R must provide certificates from the tax authorities in their respective countries confirming they are resident for tax purposes in the UK, or US, as appropriate.

    (2) Local Investments Ltd must make a declaration to Lance Investments Ltd to the effect that the company, being the company beneficially entitled to the dividend, is a company resident in the State. The declaration is valid for five years.

Neither UK Investments Ltd nor Spanol Investments Ltd are required to make any declaration to Lance Investments Ltd in order to be exempt from DWT as both qualify as "parent" companies, i.e. they each are resident in the EU and each own at least 5% of Lance Investments Ltd.

Chapter 28

Question 28.1

1. (a) TCA 1997 provides that the company must account for tax as if the loan were a net annual payment after deduction of tax. For example, if the loan amounted to €8,000 in the accounts to 31 December 2012, than the calculation would be:

                                      €
Grossed up loan   10,000
Income tax at 20%   (2,000)
Loan   8,000

A return of these figures must be made to the Inspector of Taxes on the return of income for the year ended 31 December 2012. The tax due of €2,000 is collected as part of the corporation tax for that year and, therefore, assuming the company is a "small" company, unless preliminary tax is based on 100% of the previous year, €1,800 (90%) is payable on/before 23 November 2012 and the balance of €200 is payable on/before 23 September 2013 in order to avoid interest.

If and when the loan is repaid, the company may claim a refund of the sum of €2,000.

Exemption from this tax charge is, however, available where:

- the business of the company is, or includes, the lending of money, and the loan is made in the ordinary course of that business;
- a debt is incurred for the supply of goods or services in the ordinary course of the business of the close company, unless the credit given exceeds six months or is longer than the period normally given to the company's customers; or
- the borrower satisfies the following conditions:
  - total loans to borrower or spouse or civil partner do not exceed €19,050; and
  - the borrower works full-time for the close company or any of its associated companies; and
  - the borrower and/or his associates is not the beneficial owner of, or able to control more than 5%, of the ordinary shares of the company or an associated company.

(b) **Corporation Tax liability**

Year ended 31/12/2012

	€
€500,000 @ 12.5% =	62,500
€33,000 @ 25% =	8,250
Corporation tax liability	70,750

Surcharge:

	€
Case III and Case V	33,000
Less: corporation tax @ 25%	(8,250)
	24,750
Less: 7.5%	(1,856)
	22,894
Less dividends paid within 18 months	(9,300)
	13,594

€13,594 × 20% = €2,719 surcharge due

Question 28.2

(a) **Corporation Tax Computation for y/e 31/12/2012**

	€	€
Net profit per accounts		32,900
Add: Depreciation	15,000	

Sundry (Note 1)	800	15,800
		48,700
Less: interest on		
Government Securities	8,500	
Capital grants	1,500	(10,000)
		38,700
Less: Capital allowances		(4,000)
Case I Income:		34,700
Case III Income:		
Interest on Government Securities		8,500
Total income		43,200
Corporation tax		
€34,700 @ 12.5% =	€4,337	
€8,500 @ 25% =	€2,125	
Corporation tax payable		6,462

(b)   Surcharge:

	€
Case III	8,500
Less: Tax at 25%	(2,125)
	6,375
Less: 7.5% relief	(478)
	5,897
Less: Distribution	(800)
	5,097
Surcharge @ 20%	1,019

(c)   Specific Items:

Note 1: The expense payment is treated as a "distribution" and added back in the Case I computation.

Close Ltd will be required to deduct DWT @ 20% from the payment of €800 to Y, who will be assessed to income tax and USC as follows (assume Y's marginal income tax rate of tax is 41% and USC is 7%).

Additional income tax payable	€
Schedule F: €800 @ 41%	328
Less: DWT €800 @ 20%	(160)
	168
Add: USC @ 7%	56
	224

Question 28.3

(a) **Corporation Tax computation for y/e 31/12/2012**

		€	€
Net profit per accounts			1,870,000
Add: Entertainment	W1	11,900	
Finance lease interest		2,000	
Depreciation		100,000	
Loss on sale of plant		20,000	
Architects fees		15,000	148,900
Less: Finance lease payments		15,000	
Profit on sale of building		1,480,000	
Rents		200,000	(1,695,000)
			323,900
Capital allowances			(50,000)
Case I			273,900
Case I losses forward			(210,000)
			63,900
Case V	W2		181,000
Income			244,900
Chargeable gain	W3		Nil
Total profits			244,900
Corporation tax			
€63,900 @ 12.5% = €7,987			
€181,000 @ 25% = €45,250			53,237
Income tax on loan 550,000 × 20/80			137,500
			190,737

(b) **CGT liability (see Note 3)**   331,680

(c) **Surcharge computation**

	€
Case V income	181,000
Less: CT @ 25%	(45,250)
	135,750
Less 7.5% relief	10,181
	125,569
Surcharge due @ 20% =	25,114

Workings

1. Entertainment disallowed

	€
Entertaining customers	6,000

Entertaining suppliers	5,000
Christmas gifts for suppliers	900
	11,900

2.   Case V income

	€
Portion of premium subject to	
Corporation tax: €50,000 $\times \dfrac{(51-20)}{50} =$	31,000
Rental income (€200,000 − €50,000)	150,000
Case V income	181,000

3.   Chargeable gain

Sale of plant

No allowable loss arises on the sale of the plant as full relief is given for the loss via capital allowances.

Sale of building

	€
Proceeds from building	1,500,000
Legal fees	(18,000)
	1,482,000
Cost May 1974: 50,000	
Indexation: 7.528	(376,400)
Gain	1,105,600
CGT @ 30%	331,680

As the building constitutes "development land", CGT is payable rather than corporation tax.
CGT liability: €1,105,600 @ 30% = €331,680.

Question 28.4

Servisco Ltd
Year Ended 31 December 2012
Corporation Tax Computation

	€
Case II professional income	430,000
Less loss forward	(9,000)
Less loss carried back (Note 1)	(10,000)
	411,000
Case III interest on Government Stocks	50,000
Case V rents	100,000
	561,000
Chargeable gains €54,000 $\times$ 30/12.5	129,600
	690,600

Corporation tax

€540,600 @ 12.5% = €67,575

€150,000 @ 25% = €37,500   105,075

Note 1: Loss carried back of €10,000 is offset against trading income taxed @ 12.5%. Surcharge computation

1. 'Trading income' of the company is:

		€
Case II	Professional income (Note 2)	430,000
Case III	Interest on Government Stocks	50,000
Case V	Rents	100,000
		580,000

Note 2: Income of the current period, i.e. ignore loss forward and loss back. Trading income is income less estate and investment income, i.e. €580,000 − €50,000 − €100,000 = €430,000.

2. "Distributable trading income"

	€
Trading income	430,000
CT @ 12.5%	53,750
Distributable trading income	376,250

3. "Distributable estate and investment income"

	€
Case III	50,000
Case V	100,000
	150,000
FII	7,500
	157,500
Less: CT @ 25% (but not on FII)	(37,500)
	120,000
Less trading deduction (7.5%)	(9,000)
	111,000

4. Surcharge computation

			€
(a)	50% distributable trading income €376,250 @ 50%	=	188,125
(b)	Distributable estate and investment income (DEII)	=	111,000
			299,125
	Dividend paid		(70,000)
	Liable to surcharge		229,125

	€
DEII	111,000
Dividends	(70,000)
Liable @ 20%	41,000

Balance €229,125 – €41,000 = €188,125 liable @ 15%

Surcharge

	€
€41,000 @ 20% =	8,200
€188,125 @ 15% =	28,219
229,125	36,419

Question 28.5

Machinery Ltd
Corporation Tax computation for year ended 31 December 2012

	€	€
Net profit from trading		627,000
Add: Depreciation	59,790	
Loan interest treated as a distribution		
	2,171 (Note)	61,961
		688,961
Less: Capital allowances		(10,700)
Case I		678,261
Case III bank interest		10,000
Case V rents		50,000
		738,261
Corporation tax		
€678,261 @ 12.5% = €84,783		
€60,000 @ 25% = €15,000		99,783
Add income tax (Note)		648
Total due		100,431

Surcharge Computation	€
Estate and investment income €10,000 + €50,000	60,000
Less: CT @ 25%	15,000
	45,000
Less: 7.5% × €45,000 =	(3,375)
	41,625
Less: distributions made	(2,171)

Excess		39,454
Surcharge @ 20%	=	7,891

Note: Interest limit
Lower of:
(a) 13% × €20,000 = €2,600
(b) 13% × €34,000 = €4,420
Therefore, interest limit €2,600
Loans from directors (and/or associates) with material interest

	€
	€
V. Duffy	4,000
Mrs V. Duffy	5,000
G. Duffy	5,000
S. Duffy	5,000
D. O'Connell	5,000
L.T. Smith	10,000
	34,000

Interest on above loans €4,771
Distribution: €4,771 − €2,600 = €2,171 DWT @ 20% (€434) must be deducted from this.

Income tax deducted from:	€
■ Interest of €2,600 × 20%	520
■ Interest on other loan	
(€5,410 – €4,771) × 20%	128
	648

Question 28.6

Calculation of Distributable Estate and Investment Income
1. Income of the company for the accounting period

	€	€
Case II	100,000	
Less charges (section 243A)	60,000	40,000
Case III income		100,000
Income		140,000

2. Estate and investment income for the accounting period

	€
Case III income	100,000
Less a portion of trade charges:	
€60,000 × $\dfrac{€100,000}{€200,000}$	(30,000)

	70,000
Less non-trade charges	(50,000)
	20,000
Less tax @ 25%	(5,000)
Distributable E and I income	15,000
Less 7.5%	(1,125)
Distributable E and I income	13,875

Calculation of distributable trading income

Trading income is	€
Income	140,000
Less E and I income (before non-trade charges)	(70,000)
Trading income	70,000
Less CT €70,000 @ 12.5%	(8,750)
Distributable trading income	61,250

Calculation of Surcharge

	€
Distributable E and I income	13,875
50% of distributable trading income	30,625
	44,500
Dividend paid	(30,000)
Surcharge on	14,500
All taxable at 15%, as DEII is less than	
dividend paid – €14,500 @ 15%	
Surcharge	2,175

Chapter 29

Question 29.1

Equities Limited

Case III

			€
	National Loan Interest		35,100
Less	Management Expenses:	€	
	Accounting fees	1,000	
	Secretarial fees	12,000	
	Auditor's remuneration	6,000	
	Directors' remuneration		
	10% × 175,100 =	17,510	
	Stockbroker's charges	3,000	(39,510)
Excess			(4,410)

The company can carry forward the excess of €4,410 to offset against profits of future accounting periods.

Chapter 30

Question 30.1

Overseas Limited

	€
1. Corporation Tax:	
Case I	
Branch trading profits	600,000
Case III	
Branch interest income	20,000
	620,000
Chargeable gains	
Gain on branch assets €32,000 × 30/12.5	76,800
	696,800
Corporation Tax:	
€676,800 @ 12.5% = €84,600	
€20,000 @ 25% = €5,000	89,600
2. Capital Gains Tax:	
Sale of land	
€50,000 @ 30%	15,000
3. Income Tax:	
Dividend from Irish quoted company	8,000
Plus Dividend Withholding Tax	2,000
Gross dividend	10,000
Income Tax @ 20%	2,000
Less Dividend Withholding Tax	(2,000)
Net liability	Nil

Chapter 31

Question 31.1

Foreign Income Ltd
Accounts Year ended 31 December 2012
Corporation Tax Computation

	Workings	€
Case I		700,000
Case III	1	274,342

Income		974,342
Corporation tax		
€700,000 @ 12.5% = €87,500		
€180,000 @ 12.5% = €22,500		
€94,342 @ 25% = €23,585		133,585
Less: Foreign tax	2	(12,500)
Corporation tax		121,085

Workings
1. **Case III**
   - ■ Dividend from UK Subsidiary Ltd €87,500
     - Credit for underlying tax
     - $\dfrac{€87,500}{1-0.125*} - €87,500 = €12,500$
     - Dividend regrossed to €87,500 + €12,500   €100,000

   *Irish effective rate of 12.5% is lower than UK effective rate of 26%. **Dividend regrossed at lower Irish rate.**

   - ■ Dividend from UK Company Ltd. Foreign Income Ltd is a portfolio investor. No credit, but taxed at 12.5%   €80,000
   - ■ Dividend from Monaco Ltd
     - No foreign tax credit is given as there is no treaty, etc. and less than 5% ownership
     - Taxable at 25% (no treaty, etc.) dividend received in Ireland was   €94,342

   Case III   €274,342

2. **Creditable Taxes**

   Foreign
   UK tax re UK Subsidiary Ltd €100,000 × 12.5%   12,500

Payment of dividend
Foreign Income Ltd will be required to deduct DWT @ 20% (€10,800) from the dividend of €54,000 paid on 1 February 2012. The DWT must be paid to Revenue before 14 March 2012.

Question 31.2

Templemore Limited

Corporation tax computation for the year ended 31 December 2012

	€	€
Case I		50,000*
Case III		
Interest from UK (1)	10,000**	
Dividend from UK subsidiary (2)	42,857*	
Dividend from UK company (3)	20,000*	
Peruvian dividend (4)	7,000**	79,857
		129,857

Corporation tax €112,857* @ 12.5% =	€14,107		
€17,000** @ 25% =	4,250		18,357
Less Credit relief			
UK dividend from subsidiary: €42,857 @ 12.5%			(5,357)
Peruvian dividend €7,000 @ 15%			(1,050)
Corporation tax due			11,950

Workings
1. Interest income is usually taxed where recipient is resident so any UK tax deducted can be recovered in full from UK Revenue Authorities.
2. UK effective rate is 20%

    As the Irish rate is lower, gross up net dividend at 12.5%, i.e:
    $$\frac{37,500}{100 - 12.5} \times 100 = 42,857$$

    As it is a trading company in the UK, the dividend is taxable at 12.5%.
3. As it is a portfolio investment in the UK, the dividend is taxable at 12.5%.
4. As Templemore owns at least 5% of share capital, credit relief is available. The Peruvian effective rate is 15%. As this is less than the Irish effective rate, gross up net dividend at 15%, i.e.:
    $$\frac{5,950}{100 - 15} \times 100 = 7,000$$

    The dividend is taxable at 25% as Ireland does not have a tax treaty, etc. with Peru.

Question 31.3

Touchdown Limited
CT Computation for the year ended 31 December 2012

		€	€
Case III			
National loan interest			41,400
UK dividend			<u>10,000</u>
			51,400

Less	Management Expenses		
	Directors' salaries 10% × €52,640 =	5,264	
	Accounting and secretarial	3,750	
	Charitable contribution	800	
	Stockbrokers' fees	<u>250</u>	<u>(10,064)</u>
			41,336

Less:	Charges paid		
	Bank interest (Note 1)		<u>(0)</u>
			41,336

Corporation Tax	€10,000 @ 12.5%	= 1,250	
	€31,336 @ 25%	= <u>7,834</u>	9,084

Note 1

Does not qualify as a charge, as it does not own more than 5% of the UK company.

WELCOME TO MEETINGS NOT STARTING WITHOUT YOU

Chartered Accountants work at the highest levels in Irish business. In fact six out of ten Irish Chartered Accountants work at Finance Director level or above.

Discover our flexible training options:
CharteredCareers.ie

Chartered Accountants Ireland